Minstrel Magic

George Mitchell - A Lovely Man

The Story of the George Mitchell Choirs

Eleanor Pritchard

Saron Publishers

Published by Saron Publishing in 2017
Copyright © 2017 Eleanor Pritchard

Every effort has been made to trace the copyright holders of the photos used. Thanks to the BBC, Alamy, the Press Association and the Robert Luff Estate for permission to use photos. Any information about any other copyright holders will be gratefully received and will be redressed in any future editions
Thanks to Macmillan for permission to quote extensively from *The Bandsman's Daughter* by Irene Thomas

All rights reserved

No part of this publication may be reproduced, stored in a retrieval system, or transmitted, in any form or by any means, without the prior permission in writing of the publisher, nor be otherwise circulated in any form of binding or cover other than that in which it is published and without a similar condition including this condition being imposed on the subsequent purchaser

ISBN-13: 978-0-9956495-4-5

Saron Publishing
Pwllmeyrick House
Mamhilad
Mon
NP4 8RG

saronpublishers.co.uk

Follow us on Facebook or Twitter

DEDICATION

To Michael

CONTENTS

Acknowledgments
Foreword
Prologue
Chapter 1   Page 15
Chapter 2   Page 26
Chapter 3   Page 36
Chapter 4   Page 48
Chapter 5   Page 57
Chapter 6   Page 72
Chapter 7   Page 87
Chapter 8   Page 100
Chapter 9   Page 111
Chapter 10   Page 124
Chapter 11   Page 133
Chapter 12   Page 147
Chapter 13   Page 158
Chapter 14   Page 177
Chapter 15   Page 196
Chapter 16   Page 211
Chapter 17   Page 217
Chapter 18   Page 241
Chapter 19   Page 254
Chapter 20   Page 265
Chapter 21   Page 173
Chapter 22   Page 282
Chapter 23   Page 290
Chapter 24   Page 300
Chapter 25   Page 315
Chapter 26   Page 325
Chapter 27   Page 334
Chapter 28   Page 344
Chapter 29   Page 365
Chapter 30   Page 380
Chapter 31   Page 385

Chapter 32	Page 393
Chapter 33	Page 404
Chapter 34	Page 412
Chapter 35	Page 426
Chapter 36	Page 435
Afterword	Page 448

ACKNOWLEDGMENTS

There are so many people to thank. Everyone has welcomed me into the Mitchell family with warmth. I hope their joy and love for the days they spent with George comes across - he must have been a very special man.

Firstly George's widow Dot Marshall who, with her second husband John, has been endlessly supportive over innumerable coffees and lunches. She has given me unprecedented access to her archives. Thanks to the ex-singers, dancers and technical people who played a part in George's story - they are too many to name, but special thanks go to Keith Leggett, Glyn Dawson, Peter Pennington, Peter Clare, Peter Kingston, Richard Archer, Maggie Savage, Ann Mann, Daphne Bell, Jeff Hudson and Harry Currie. Also to Pat Heigham, Douggie Squires, Charles Chilton, Don Maclean and John Henshall. I'm grateful to the sole remaining Musketeer John Boulter for the time he has taken in phone calls and face to face chats to provide me with inside information. Thanks to all those involved in the Minstrel reunions - John and Dana Asher, and Angie Astell in particular - for making me feel so welcome. Thanks too to Maryetta, Mary and Maggi for lovely memories of afternoons over tea and photos.

I had huge help from Jeff Walden at BBC Archives, and also from Patricia Convery at the Arts Centre Melbourne, who opened their archives on a day to suit me, despite normally being closed.

Special thanks to John Want who created the wonderful cover in memory of his father Les, one of the show's principals.

I could never have survived the many ups and downs of this book without the support of my fabulous family. Thanks to my daughters, sons-in-law and beautiful, funny, weird and wonderful granddaughters. Without my husband, I would have been a nervous wreck long before now - my love as always.

Final and very special thanks must go to Head Minstrel Roy Winbow. Without his help, encouragement, daily texts, emails and red wine, this book would certainly never have been finished. He is a true friend.

SOME NOTES

All money conversions in this book use thisismoney.co.uk, though this is a notoriously difficult area in which to be accurate. They are included merely as a guide.

The observant reader may notice that some people interviewed for this book are quoted in the past tense and some in the present. This is deliberate and indicates whether the person is still with us or not.

Please be aware that some terms, now seen as outdated or even offensive, occur in contemporary quotes used in this book.

FOREWORD

'George Mitchell won a bet the other day but lost his argument. We had met in Piccadilly Circus. Just then Jack Benny walked by. "Amazing place, London," said George, cigarette in hand as usual. "Nobody ever recognises anybody. I bet you the price of a drink that nobody recognises Jack Benny." We followed Jack the length of Regent Street to Oxford Circus. George won his bet. "There you are," said George triumphantly. "This is the safest place in the world to hide yourself." Just then a woman approached him. "Excuse me troubling you, Mr Mitchell, but please could I have your autograph?" *Sunday Chronicle 1951*

This is the story of the man behind one of the greatest success stories in post-war entertainment. His choirs broke world records throughout the 1950s and 1960s on stage, screen and records. In 1961 the *Black and White Minstrel Show* was hailed as the greatest light entertainment programme in the world, sweeping the board at the first Golden Rose of Montreux Festival and giving the BBC the accolade as producers of the world's best light entertainment show. Twenty years later, the BBC was doing its best to pretend the show had never existed, airbrushing it from history. Just what had gone wrong?

But like the music, it refuses to die...

Minstrel Magic

PROLOGUE

The large room in the Shropshire country club buzzes with talk and laughter as people greet friends they haven't seen for years. Black and white balloons float above round tables set for lunch. Former Black and White Minstrels and Toppers crowd round display boards filled with photos, theatre playbills and record sleeves. Minstrel CDs play constantly in the background. Noise levels rise until someone spies a figure in a wheelchair approaching.

'Hush, he's coming. Remember, he knows nothing about this.' The word spreads rapidly, and the noise dies away, leaving the buzz of expectation still vibrating around the room. Everyone turns to watch as the glass doors at the far end of the room open, and a man in a smart grey suit is wheeled in by his wife. *When The Saints Go Marching In* blares from the speakers and immediately the entire room joins in.

In shock, the man in the wheelchair does a double-take, as he realises he knows all the people assembled. He stares around before joining in the singing himself. Laughter and applause break out, and the man buries his head in his hands, quite overcome. Turning to his wife, he asks, 'Did you know about this?'

'George, this is your day,' says organiser ventriloquist Neville King. 'We want you to make the best of it, mate. We want to thank you for the best years of our lives.'

So just who was this man who inspired such loyalty that, twenty years after the last televised *Black and White Minstrel Show*, cast and crew had travelled from as far away as New Zealand to attend his 80th birthday? The story starts in Falkirk, Scotland, in 1917...

Minstrel Magic

CHAPTER 1

Squalling and crying, the baby who was to change the face of light entertainment in Britain forty years later was born on February 27, 1917, into a country enduring one of the worst winters of the twentieth century. It was also a country at war, though no one could have foreseen the impact on this baby of a future world war.

His mother Barbara named him George, and together they joined his grandfather's household in the little village of Carronshore, today part of the Falkirk district in Scotland. In 1917 it housed about a thousand people, all dependent on the dominant Carron Iron Works or the Carron coal mines, which supplied the fuel for the foundries. The Carron Company had been founded in 1759 and ten years later was described as 'the greatest of the kind in Europe....above 1200 men are employed.' It was still the largest foundry in Britain, now involved in producing munitions for the British Army. This was a close-knit community. Everyone knew everyone else, bound together in a way that only mining and iron works areas can be, constantly living with a sense of shared danger. Sons followed fathers down the mines or into the foundries, and no one strayed far from home.

George's grandfather John Laing was a prominent member of the community and a legend in his own right, still remembered as forming Falkirk's first choral union. He was driven by music, but no one gave a thought to a career in music in the late nineteenth century, so he worked for seventy two years as a check weighman at the ironworks, reserving choral singing for what little leisure time remained after he came home from work. As precentor of Carron's United Presbyterian Church, he conducted Sunday singing, then during the week, he'd hurry home from work to wash and change, before burnishing his silver conductor's baton. This precious item had been presented to him in 1891 by the Carronshore Musical Association, an association he'd founded in the 1870s. Then he'd leave to rehearse one or other of his choirs. At one time, he ran three amateur choirs, many of whose singers were miners from the Carron Company mines, as were his audiences. Years later George was asked why his grandfather chose choral music, instead of orchestral or bagpipes. George dryly responded, 'My grandfather was a true Scot. Singing is the cheapest way to make music.'

Not only did John work for the Carron Company but their house was owned by the company, as were all the homes in the area. Rid Row – or Red Row as it was known because Carron painted every door and window red – consisted of two dozen houses, built right opposite the blast furnace which lit the houses up all night long. George recalled a local story: 'One of the local lads saw his neighbour repainting his door green, and he said, "What are you doing, Jock?" "I'm painting the door." "That's no paint, paint's red."' As George said, 'Terrible joke.'

The house on Rid Row, always full of song, was also full of people, always teeming with friends and relatives. John himself came from a relatively small family, having only four brothers and sisters, but he and his wife Jeanie had twelve children, and his brothers and sisters produced large families to rival John's. His brother George had ten children, and brother Alexander managed eleven! Many inherited Grandpa John's flair for music. Two played the bagpipes and accompanied the family choir. 'That's why they say Scotland the Brave. If you can sing with those things playing, you'll sing with anything,' recalled George wryly. George's mother Barbara was the seventh of John's brood and a soloist at the United Presbyterian Church for nearly twenty years. And it was in this church choir that Barbara met Robert Mitchell who also came from a large family, having ten brothers and sisters. Music dominated his life as well, as he sang with the Gellatly's Male Voice Choir. They were married on September 11, 1915, when Barbara was thirty and Robert twenty-five. When George was born, Sergeant Robert Mitchell was 'somewhere in Mesopotamia'.

Robert had a mixed war. With the Scottish Horse, he played a prominent part in organising his unit's variety shows, prefiguring the similar achievements of his son in another world war. George remembered, 'My father was taken prisoner in Italy, and there he was kept for two years. Severely injured by a load of shrapnel, he was forced to march to Germany's Langensalza prison camp where he got Red Cross parcels with tea bags and other goodies but no cigarettes. With his usual luck, his prison guard had distant relatives in Edinburgh – he spoke pretty good English and told Dad he'd love a cup of English tea. Dad dried used bags on a rafter to get a decent second cup and offered the guard three tea bags for a pack of cigarettes.'

Although he was decorated by the Italians, Robert always said he was classified as a deserter because he should have gone to Dunkeld in Scotland for demob. When the troop train arrived in Edinburgh, they were told to line up for the lavatory and then return to the train. But Robert stepped into the bar of the Caledonian Hotel, had a few whiskies and strolled up Princes Street to the Waverly Hotel, had a few more and knew he could catch a bus home from there. So he was never demobilised. 'A bit later on, this tall guy comes into the house, the war's been over about a year; I was told this was my father,' recalled George. 'I went up to Dunkeld where the Scottish Horse were, and his name wasn't there. It wouldn't have worried him much.' According to Dot, George's widow, 'He hated his father at first' but Robert soon became idolised by his little son.

The Mitchell family continued to live with John and Jeanie after Robert's return, filling the house even more, and giving George a baby sister Jean in 1920. George remembered the Laing cottage fondly: 'There were two huge rooms and a little kitchen. The beds were double deckers, with curtains across so there were two whopping great beds three feet from the ground and then, about six feet from the ground there were another two great beds on top of them, with curtains around them too. So it was quite a climb up to the top bunk. In some cases, it was tough for the smaller children because where there was a crush, the big one went down the centre, and the two others were put down the other end, so their faces were up against the feet of the one in the middle. Fortunately, I was so small that my grandfather kept me in his room. As I grew older, I fully expected to get into one of those beds but I didn't.'

The beds weren't the only cause for merriment: 'There was a little hut in the field opposite, 200 yards away up a steep slope. It smelt a bit, now that was the loo which served three other houses too. At night it was hard to find for a wee toddler. I remember absolutely bursting late one night and crept out trying not to wake anyone. I ran across the fields with what little moonlight there was, only to return to the house yelling my head off and crying my eyes out. I screamed that I'd tried to go to the toilet, but somebody had left a wheelbarrow in there, and I couldn't pull it out. Grandpa got his boots on and said, "Come on, lad." He went off at great speed and came back laughing and said, "That's old Tum in there, and he's got a wooden leg, and it sticks straight out when he sits on the loo seat." Oh dear, so much for the wheelbarrow.'

John spent most evenings away from the house, either at the district council or with his choirs, but when he got home, he always insisted on waking George. George's earliest recollection is of 'my grandfather waking me several nights a week, always after choir practice, and his first remark was, "You're not sleeping, are you, son?" I'd open my eyes, and he'd say, "There you are, son, there's the pandrops." He always stuck a little bag of sweets under my pillow whenever he got in.' He'd sing baby George nursery rhymes, and sometimes more ribald songs never meant for infant ears: 'They say I whistled before I could talk. *Squire Chodomleigh* was the first song I learnt. Whether I mispronounced a word or there was a saucy word in it, I can't remember, but it was always good for a laugh from the grown-ups.'

Sunday was the day for Church music. The entire family, now numbering fifteen, marched to church three times every Sunday: 'The bell started ringing at 10.45, but if you waited for its summons, you were too late, for by then, every seat was filled! Before we left, dolled up in our Sunday best, Grandpa issued each child with a clean neatly folded handkerchief, three peppermint sweets [pandrops] and a coin for the collection – a penny for the older children and a halfpenny for those of us under five. He led the way with my grandmother, followed by the youngest children leading back to the eldest in strict order of seniority. As we crossed the fields, there was a singing rehearsal. When we reached a certain clump of bramble bushes, Grandpa would reach into his pocket for his tuning fork, strike it on the heel of one of his boots and say, "Remember now, this is your note." After church, he'd hoist me onto his shoulders, holding onto my legs and I'd hang onto his head, and he'd march me up Aidenhead's Brae, quite a climb, because the Salvation Army played there on Sunday mornings and we never missed that.' When they got home, his grandmother whipped George's suit off, replacing it with his dungarees, then an hour or so later, put his suit back on him, and everyone would set off back to church.

John soon took George's musical education a stage further: 'Once I started walking, he dragged me to choir rehearsals, three or four a week, carrying me on his shoulders along the railway track to the rehearsal hall. They went on quite late, but he always made sure I slept in the following morning. He took me anywhere

where music could be heard, even to the Salvation Army on the street corner.'

At some stage during these early years, John was doing a Spot the Ball competition and let young George mark where he thought the ball was. As a result, John won a solid gold hunter on a heavy gold chain which he wore for the rest of his life. George well remembered his grandfather's words: 'George, you'll fall down a drain many times and always come up with a gold chain around your neck.'

George had a special place in John's heart: 'I think he must have been psychic. Otherwise, why would he have left me all his music treasures – his ebony and silver baton, his music, his metronome? Also a writing desk with his name on it and a Bible. With dozens of grandchildren in the family, he could have chosen any one of us. None of the others had anything. He said to me, "You're going to be a musician, my son, you wait till you grow up." My mother thought the baton would bring me success, although Grandfather would probably turn in his grave if he could hear the sort of numbers it conducts now.' Although later features mention George never went on stage without this baton, it was far too precious to risk. His widow Dot says, 'He'd lose batons, break them, sit on them, snap them, so he would never risk this precious memento from his grandfather.'

But Robert had itchy feet, and Carronshore wasn't the place for him. They moved first to Leeds and then to London, where Robert quickly established himself as a sales executive for a heating engineering firm, Sankeys, but 'had about five firms selling all sorts of strange things. I think he got the first coloured baths that came over from Germany and special wooden fireplaces designed. He had his fingers in about sixteen pies, and he used to write articles for magazines.'

Although George was sad to leave his beloved grandfather, music was to stay in George's life. Although both Robert and Barbara loved singing and were very fond of opera, Robert couldn't take anything too heavy. He was a Mozart fan. When George was 11, Robert decided to introduce him to opera. Despite having doubts - Wagner is pretty heavy going for a schoolboy - he chose a performance of *Siegfried*, conducted by Sir John Barbirolli. It became the turning point in George's life.

As the curtain rose, Robert started to say, 'How do you...?' George was leaning forward anxiously in his seat. 'Shhh,' he reprimanded his father without turning his head. And that's how he remained until the curtain came down for the interval. 'Like to stretch your legs?' asked Robert. 'No, I'll stay,' said George. 'We might miss something.'

Siegfried bowled George over: 'I'd never had such an experience. I couldn't sleep for the themes that ran in my head all night. Next morning I went straight to the public library and borrowed the score.' The very first record he bought with his own pocket money was a recording of *Gotterdammerung*. However, the following week, he bought Artie Shaw's *Concerto for Clarinet*: 'I realised there should be no such thing as highbrow or lowbrow music. It's all music, some good, some bad. What I don't go for is the musical appreciation that sets up as the arbiter of taste for everyone else, that says this or that is the only good music, and everything else is rubbish. Half the trouble with a lot of classical enthusiasts is that they forget that symphonies and operas were often written to make money. Verdi in his popular operas didn't really need an orchestra – just a great big guitar. He made his pile, then started to write what he really wanted to when he was seventy.'

His parents found him a piano teacher and soon George was having two lessons every week, including theory and harmony. Within three months, he was writing simple orchestrations. But he was theory-happy: 'I was a rotten pupil. I couldn't be bothered with scales and practising footling little pieces. It was the music itself that enchanted me. I just wanted to know about music. I studied scores and heard them in my head as piano music. I wanted to know what this music business was all about – how anyone set about producing such marvellous sound.' His parents became tired of suggesting he practise and being told, 'I can't be bothered – I want to go out to play.' After nine months, George refused to have any more lessons: 'I'd learned enough to play the piano to satisfy myself, and I've improved with the years!'

Even though music was once again his passion, he began to revel in school life. Attending Southgate County Grammar School, he proved to be a bright boy, particularly good at maths, music and perhaps surprisingly sports. Although it might be hard to imagine him as an athlete, it was here that he excelled, playing halfback for the football team, and excellent cricket and tennis, which he loved. He was good too because, in summer 1945, he was part of the RAPC team which played at Wimbledon. With the war in Europe over, Wimbledon Lawn Tennis Club staged a series of matches between Allied servicemen. George played on Court 2 in the finals against HGN Lee, who had been a member of Britain's winning 1933 Davis Cup team with Fred Perry and Bunny Austin, though perhaps inevitably he lost.

Robert encouraged George at school but thought history and Shakespeare were rubbish: 'Dad reckoned *Henry V Part 11* was actually *Part Eleven* as he said that was what it felt like. He read loads of history books – he said they were a load of rubbish as they were always written by the winners – so he reckoned most history was propaganda, only accepted by people who couldn't think for themselves.' George's academic prowess was such that he was presented with the School Prize, a complete leather-bound works of Shakespeare (which, given his views on Shakespeare, probably didn't please Robert particularly!). George won this prize two years running, leading Robert to say, 'Well, someone had to.' George thought that being sent to a top notch school (at considerable cost) might have had something to do with it!

The headmaster, a Mr Everard, loved Gilbert and Sullivan operettas and so the school staged one every year. George volunteered every time – 'I was very keen' – but sadly he always found himself at the back of the stage. 'I couldn't sing so they'd shove me as far back on stage as possible, with instructions not to sing too loudly. They said although I could read music, I couldn't pronounce it. As I was fairly tall, I was always the policeman at the back or the sentry standing behind the rest with a spear, or a very tall Japanese servant in *The Mikado*. Everyone made sure I didn't get within ten yards of a kimono.'

Even though George was to lead a very crowded life, he never forgot his early days. In July 1952, he revisited his old school, where he adjudicated at the House Musical Festival, raising much laughter when he wryly commented that one house's entry in the musical trio section did not have their instruments tuned correctly. The School's magazine recorded, 'Mr Mitchell's criticisms were concise and to the point. (He) told us how pleased he had been to attend the Competition but said he would like to be invited next year as a guest and not in the unenviable capacity of adjudicator so that he may enjoy the entertainments the more.' The following day the school was delighted to learn that 'George had presented the school with £20 (£2,000) for a cup to be competed for by the various House choirs and for some similar encouragement of choral music in the School.' Ex-pupil David Cooper recalls an old school friend telling him that George caused a minor sensation amongst the non-musical boys by parking his pink Cadillac outside the school. Sadly there's no record of George ever owning a Cadillac, let alone a pink one.

But George's health was worrying his parents. His eyes were never strong but more worrying still was something that had the doctors baffled. One day, sent to the corner shop for eggs, he collapsed half way home, breaking all the eggs. Despite protesting he couldn't remember what had happened, he got a clip around the ear from a very annoyed Barbara. When it happened again, a few weeks later, they took him to a doctor, but no one could find the answer. It wasn't until he went into the Army in 1940, that an alert medical officer diagnosed Menière's Disease, a disorder of the inner ear which causes bouts of severe dizziness and sickness. This dogged him throughout his life, causing particular problems on stage, as one later choir member Frank Davies remembers: 'George had tremendous courage. He would continue conducting even as his face grew darker and darker as he suffered the onset of an epileptic fit, which he would slowly bring under his control. What he went through to achieve that, only he really knew, though he once chose to discuss it with me at great length. The cliché, the show must go on, was abundantly apparent in George's brave attitude, on many more than one occasion.' Daphne Bell, later such an important part of the Mitchell organisation, recalls him having 'dizzy turns, always a worry as to whether he'd remain on his feet'. And Maryetta Midgley remembers being with George 'in a corridor, he clutched a hook and held his head. He never made it a thing.' Though it wasn't epilepsy, the impact on George's life was potentially as severe. George's widow Dot recalls, 'Once in the early Sixties, he fell onto a Tube line, missing the live wire by inches.' But by force of will, he fought to carry on a normal life.

Robert's wanderlust never left him, and although the family never moved from London, Robert and Barbara spent most summers and some winters touring Europe: 'I had wonderful trips, Cannes, Nice, Menton, Rome, Verona, Pisa and Naples – fantastic.' Even Britain held its attractions and Robert would often whisk them away at a moment's notice: 'It was, "Where are we going today, Barbara? Let's go down to the Old Ship at Brighton for lunch." And that's what they'd do. My parents were gipsies, off somewhere all the time, and I loved it.'

Despite this carefree attitude, the family was financially secure, so much so that they employed a housekeeper: 'As the years went on, we had a lovely Irish housekeeper Mary Sullivan, great soul, who's been with the family ever since and is absolutely wonderful.'

Having money meant Robert could indulge in his passion for cars, a passion George shared all his life. At a time when few people sported a car, Robert always had the latest motor. George remembered one in particular: 'It was a Trojan, something like an Army tank going across the Dales.' These cars were stretched to their limits during their European holidays.

Despite Robert taking the family away on an extended European holiday six weeks before George sat for his matriculation at 16, George still managed to do well in his exams, gaining a Distinction in Maths. He had no idea what he wanted to do next. Still passionate about music, he never considered it as a job possibility: 'Music was my hobby, my interest in life, but I never gave it a thought as a career.' Robert had a good friend John Douglas, a dour Scott who stood no nonsense. Not an obvious friend for the fun-loving Robert, John headed up a large City firm of accountants, Sawyers in Budge Row, and agreed to give George a job. £500 (£31,000) secured his articles, a sum George thought 'ridiculous'. Robert put half down, and George agreed to pay the rest by instalments from his wages. 'I'll make an accountant of him all right,' John Douglas told his father.

George's first task involved a leather-bound volume approximately four inches deep. Inside were a thousand flimsy pages each inscribed with columns of £ s d. 'I want you to check the addition,' said Douglas, which George managed within his first day and proudly handed the volume back to his boss. 'That's fine. I've got another thirty-nine like that,' said Douglas. 'You can start on them tomorrow.' Stacked in two columns, the volumes almost reached the ceiling, enough to put off any but the most determined student. However, George was certainly that. But matters weren't quite what they seemed. Far from being a test of the fledgling accountant's mathematical ability, George discovered that the thousands of columns were a test of character. He was being tested for conceit rather than calculation. 'We use adding machines,' he was eventually told. 'The boss just wanted to see if you'd stick it.'

It was a steep learning curve, but George loved it – the order, the precision, the clarity of the figures. Soon he was being sent out to audit the books of big organisations all over London. But the testing continued. After five days with the makers of a well-known food product, he returned with his final audit complete. 'Back already?' said John Douglas. 'Did ye know that's usually a two-week job?' 'Well, there you are, sir,' said George 'And there's no mistake. You can see the figures tally all right.' He stood back and waited. Surely even old Douglas could not withhold a brief word of praise for such speed and efficiency? But the face of the Scot remained sphinx-like. He looked up and over his heavy-rimmed specs. 'Oh, they tally, do they?' he repeated. 'And have ye never heard, young man, of compensating errors? I want you to go back tomorrow and check all your figures again.' George certainly later approved of these methods. 'Everything I did had to be checked and double-checked. I was not wild with enthusiasm for this method of teaching, but it has been invaluable to me. It made me terribly careful and accurate. I suppose it turned me into a perfectionist.'

Sawyers carried out work all over the country, and George was soon spending most of his time away from London. The first time he was asked to audit a company outside the capital, he didn't realise the implications: 'They were a big firm, Fray Bentos who made Oxo cubes. I thought it would be good fun but didn't realise what auditing a company of this size really meant. Then I understood I'd be away for fifty weeks. I thought this was a bit crazy, but it sounded good. I was on a gravy train for a year, and it was all marvellous, 'cos I never took my salary, such as it was because I still had to pay for my articles, I just left the money there. The rest of the time, my expenses were all paid, plus I had 17/= a day (£55) for sundry expenses. Fray Bentos had a depot in virtually every main town in the UK, so I've been in every good hotel in Britain, such as the Adelphi in Liverpool, the Black Boy in Nottingham, the Gresham in Dublin, the Caledonian in Edinburgh. It was terrific, quite a trip, and got me well in with the old boy [John Douglas].' George spent his evenings cramming from textbooks and ledgers, and soon passed the intermediate examination of the Institute of Chartered Accountants.

But music was still uppermost in George's mind. He took every opportunity to visit the Albert Hall, Queen's Hall, Covent Garden, Sadler's Wells; anywhere that concerts and opera, especially Wagner, were being performed: 'I watched Henry Wood, Beecham, Adrian Boult and Toscanini every night for a week for a shilling behind the tymps doing a complete Beethoven cycle. I also saw Lauritz Melchior in *Otello*. Little did I realise I would talk to Sir Adrian years later in the coffee queue at Aeolian Hall or that John Barbirolli would be conducting at EMI Abbey Road studios adjacent to me.' And he carried on building up his record collection: 'Wagner continued to be my hero until I discovered Schumann. Now Wagner is my second favourite composer.' Saturday nights he played with a dance band but still treated it as nothing more than a hobby. 'I played piano in a dance band for fun but was never interested in light music. It sounds crazy now, but I had no intention of doing it professionally.'

But childhood issues with his eyes surfaced again: 'Long nights at the books, late evenings with a band...it began playing the deuce with my eyes.' Much of his childhood reading far into the night by the light of a shaded lamp had started the damage. As an apprentice accountant, he further strained his eyesight by the day-after-day scrutiny of accounts books. At first, there was just strain and headaches, but Robert feared his son was going blind. After one accountancy exam, the trouble became so serious that Robert took George to a specialist whose verdict was grave: 'Your son's eyes are very bad. I'll prescribe new glasses, but they'll probably do him only six months.'

CHAPTER 2

In 1933, during the strangely-timed European holiday just before his Matriculation exams, George became friendly with a young German lad. George and Fritz, also aged 16, shared a passion for tennis and spent much of the holidays playing. But Fritz was also a mountain rescuer and one day, took George up the highest mountain in the area, an odd pastime considering George's Menière's. This was George's first experience of climbing, and this was proper mountain climbing! George had never been more scared in his life. They took a day and a half, most of which Fritz and his mates spent hauling George up on ropes. When they reached the top, George nearly lost consciousness, but at least he could say he got there. He and Fritz often spent summers together for the rest of the decade and in September 1938 found themselves somewhere on the German borders, just in time to witness the annexation of the Sudetenland. Fritz, George and the local kids thought it great fun, posing for pictures on a tank, throwing rose petals at the Germans, along with the locals who were delighted because they expected the Germans to bring money and prosperity.

But war was soon declared on Germany, and Fritz and George were not to meet again. However, Fritz's father happened to be a German general and soon the 'men in suits' arrived at Robert's home to talk to George; something similar was happening to Fritz. George never knew how they learned about their friendship, but the authorities were eventually satisfied that George posed no risk. Although George survived the war, Fritz wasn't so lucky.

But George had other things on his mind. He had met and fallen in love with Irene who worked in the typing department at Sawyers, who, so said George, 'was the only person in the whole place who didn't seem very old. Everyone else must have been in their forties and fifties.' They had a small wedding at Leatherhead on June 1, 1940, after which George borrowed Robert's car and the newlyweds honeymooned in Torquay, trying to forget the outside world, now once again at war.

Minstrel Magic

Keen to join the war fever, George tried to volunteer as soon as war was declared: 'Of course, Father insisted it had to be the Argyle and Sutherlands or the Black Watch. But to my dismay, my dreadful eyesight meant I was rejected, which was comical because later they took you if you were half-blind. In those days they'd say something about, "You'd never get the gas mask on", so I was thrown out of everything. The only thing left to do was to sit and wait.' Eventually ordered to report to the Pay Corps HQ at Finsbury Park, he enlisted on September 2, 1940, and was sent to the Bank of England offices in the City. As he said, 'it's almost like being in Civvy Street!' But being based in the City of London in 1940 was far from safe as the Pay Corps staff had to stay on duty during the Blitz. George was fire-watching on the Bank of England's roof on December 29/30, 1940 when the Germans dropped thousands of incendiary bombs on the City. Everything around St Paul's, including Sawyers, his old office, was burned and a greater area destroyed than that lost in the Great Fire of London in 1666: 'It was quite a sight from the top of the Bank of England. It was even worse next morning when I had to march a unit to see if anything could be done. It was impossible, they were falling in holes, tripping over hoses, oh what a mess. Loads of business people were leaving tube stations and walking close to parts of buildings not totally destroyed and laughing their heads off seeing our antics. Oh, what a lovely war!' During the Blitz Robert and Barbara were bombed out and found temporary accommodation in Tolworth, near Surbiton, Surrey. Irene went with them, and George joined whenever he had leave.

George's department handled pay ledgers for regiments all over the globe and with vast numbers of men being transferred, moved to a hospital or posted missing, the accountancy system nearly collapsed. George dealt with queries from all over the world, work which he found easy, but he became increasingly frustrated with one particular form, dealing with used equipment and payment: 'There was a lot of fiddling going on with this form. Nothing was tied down too closely, so identity theft was rife. But I couldn't get anyone to agree it needed redesigning.' It took the by-now Corporal Mitchell quite a fight to implement an amended form. But the Army quickly realised just how foolproof the new system was, and George received a special War Office commendation which he saw as one of his biggest achievements – 'I'll always be proud of that.'

Minstrel Magic

But George wasn't going to let a war come between him and music. He found an old piano which he started playing to relax in his off-duty hours. Once he started thumping out tunes on the piano, (hardly expertly given his mere nine months of tuition!), people quickly gathered around and sang or danced: 'I started banging out the first notes, and everyone sang away like mad in spite of the awful canteen piano. I then jotted down a few pieces such as *Trepak* and the *Hawaiian War Chant* and wrote some very corny tunes, easy to sing.' Gradually more and more grouped around the piano, singing along with the music and George soon realised that there were quite a lot of good voices there. One of his regular fans, an ATS girl called Dot Mackenzie, had a wonderful soprano voice and George quickly decided that they could all have a lot of fun if he developed a choir as background to Dot. He was overwhelmed with applications and chose about 16 men and girls to join them. However, he soon realised that average voices improved immeasurably if, instead of singing solo, they sang in groups. After that, he made the choir the act's main part with solo parts as contrast.

The choir quickly became really popular, and George was overwhelmed with even more applications to join. He had to turn down most of these as sixteen was always George's preferred number for his choir. Eight men, eight women, two in each voice range, which allowed him to write the four-part close harmony he loved and which gave the distinctive Mitchell sound that became his hallmark for years to come.

But he got no support from the Army. The Battalion already had a dance band, so officials saw no need for another musical diversion. The dance band had a grand piano and was allowed practice time during the day, but the Army made George and his singers rehearse in the basement and in coffee breaks and evenings, making do with an old upright piano, ill-tuned and lacking several notes. The grand piano used by the dance band was considered too good for the upstart choir to use. Despite this, requests for appearances by the choir flooded in, but the Army was determined not to make this easy either. Every appearance had to be approved by their commanding officer, Col Murrell, who grudgingly agreed only as long as he was credited. Often permission was just as swiftly withdrawn. George was told very firmly that 'appearances by the Choir can only be made at Service functions and in the cause of charity, and applications must be forwarded in the usual way when it is desired to give a performance. It will be clearly understood that no appearances will be made at any time upon the commercial stage. Furthermore, no time during office hours may be granted for rehearsals, and if it is your wish to rehearse after office hours, personnel stationed at Marylebone must proceed in their own time.' This infuriated George: 'I remember my frantic, frequent and unsuccessful attempts to get some rehearsal time – and how ridiculously annoyed I was because the Battalion Orchestra got a double lunch break to rehearse and never lost any members on overseas draft. Looking back, I think that perhaps it was the result of the band's system of never playing at a unit dance without payment, whereas we were pleased to give our services *gratis*.'

The difficulties just urged George and the singers on more: 'I remember the tremendous incentive given to us by the sarcasm and criticism of a few members of the Battalion revue cast and orchestra at our early performances. Having nasty natures, a few of us vowed to make them eat their words.' And eat them they did. As George later wrote, 'Special comment must be made regarding the phenomenal number of rehearsals attended by choir members after their normal working hours, and the loyalty shown by those who always turned up for a show in spite of leave, sickness or any personal arrangements which may have been made; the detailed work of rehearsals, funds and the endless odd jobs which have been cheerfully undertaken by Stella Wood from the choir's first appearance to date; the orchestrations on which Tom Gillison devoted his après time; the general help and advice given at all times by Neb Wolters.'

Soon they were appearing nightly at the Royal Artillery Theatre Woolwich with the Battalion Road Show, as well as performing in one-off concerts all over London where they frequently topped the bill. The Swing Choir, as it was now called, mainly sang music written by George which ensured their voices were shown to the best possible advantage but they also performed jazzed-up versions of pieces such as *A Persian Market* and *In a Monastery Garden*. The regular repertoire soon included songs such as *All Just the Same, Scots Missed, Dimitrov, Sentimental Journey, Bye Bye, Riding on a Rainbow, Tzena, Tzena, Louisiana Hayride, El Campanchero, Sabre Dance, Wally Dunn, Sing, My Heart, In the Shade of the Old Apple Tree, There's a New World, Jacob's*

Minstrel Magic

Ladder, Tipperary Samba, Old MacDonald, Bless This House and *Glass Mountain*.

George's childhood realisation that music shouldn't be compartmentalised came to the fore: 'We'd sing anything from folk to pop, Wagner to Schumann. The Latin-American medley, later in the *Black and White Minstrel Show*, we did in those army days.' In later years, once fame had hit, he went on record as saying, 'I don't go mad on most pop tunes. I don't use more because they're not very good. Far too many offer no more than the basic beat of jungle drums, which is all very well for dancing. Moreover, their musicians don't know how to finish. I love moderns such as Stravinsky, Sibelius, Prokofiev and Shostakovich and can listen to Basie and Ellington until the cows come home. But I can't stand "middle music". I guess I must be too Scotch [sic] to spend money on records to hear a couple of times, then throw away. I prefer music that you can live with and explore. I don't listen much to pop or musical comedy music. The evergreens are something quite different. Any of my colleagues will tell you how enthusiastic I get about the Minstrel songs. Any music that has lasted so long and still sounds so good MUST be good – and I go for music that's good.' George's ideal was to see symphony concerts and operas drawing the same sort of crowds as the Beatles and similar pop groups: 'This happens on the Continent. I try to get to the opera in Verona, to the festivals at Munich and Vienna – but sometimes I just cannot get near the box office, the concerts are so fully booked. Promenade concerts get similar support over here in Britain. The kids sit there packed almost to suffocation with hardly a cough all through the concert – it's marvellous. But nobody cares, nobody publicises the fact. But when another crowd of youngsters scream at some new beat group, then it's all over the front page.'

George himself often accompanied the choir on the piano, though gradually he confined his role to conducting, sometimes from the front or often from the wings. The music was infectious, and George soon found he needed to choreograph routines to enhance the visual interest of the choir: 'There was no standing still with that choir. I moved the singers around, then we tried a few dance routines.' He discovered a real talent for this and would know exactly what he wanted and how to get it but was always willing to listen to others' ideas. George next introduced comedians and impressionists, so they could now offer a ready-made self-contained entertainment package to camps and garrisons throughout London: 'We became an act. The boys and girls loved it, it was all a lark. They kept moving all the time they were singing, just like today. We figured it would be harder for the audience to hit us if they started to throw things. But we had a captive audience, and we were a great success.' Future stars Jon Pertwee and David Jacobs compèred the show. Still forced to wear uniform all the time, the choir needed to be resourceful, and many a stitching session resulted in added bows and buttons, frills and flowers, with everyone pitching in to make the whole show a joint venture, mirrored later by the family feel to George's shows.

The show at the Garrison Theatre, Woolwich in November 1944, where they shared the bill with professional cellist Val Kennedy, seemed like any other. The audience couldn't get enough of George and the choir, but they gave Val a hard time. Stung by the unfairness and unable to restrain himself, the kindly George strode onto the stage and appealed to the audience to give him a chance. An impressed Val didn't forget this small act of kindness and praised the choir far and wide. When he met George Melachrino, the hugely talented musician, now conducting the British Band of the Allied Expeditionary Forces, the choir was all Val talked about. Melachrino told BBC producer Ronnie Waldman, who had produced the Kentucky Minstrels with Harry S Pepper before the war. News of the choir's popularity had already reached Ronnie and, always on the lookout for new talent to keep both home and service listeners entertained, he quickly agreed to audition them. George asked permission to attend this audition from his commanding officer, Col Murrell, who said casually, 'I don't see why not, Mitchell, as long as it's done in off-duty hours,' and with that comment, began one of the greatest stories of post-war entertainment history.

Nerves were high on January 24, 1945, audition day. Why George chose the *Hawaiian War Chant* with its twisting words is anyone's guess, though it was a choir favourite, but the risk worked. Ronnie immediately offered George a spot on *Variety Bandbox*, the BBC's top weekend radio show, broadcast live to a regular listening audience of fourteen million from the Queensberry All-Services Club where thousands of forces personnel tasted bright lights and fun.

Minstrel Magic

Sunday, February 11 was extremely nerve-racking for everyone and none more so than George. His scrapbook recalled, 'I remember my knees knocking furiously. I thought they would never stop, but when I worked it out afterwards, the nervousness had lasted for only fourteen bars of music.' He played the piano, with Tom Gillison on accordion and George Causby on drums. Later, he recalled he 'assumed the role of the great conductor, much to the amusement of the choir'. The crowd gave them a thunderous ovation. Press reviews the next day loved them, and by Tuesday, fan mail was flooding into the BBC. A typical letter came from HMS *Myng's* crew, saying, 'The female soloist was terrific, and many of us listened anxiously for her name to be announced. We wondered if we could get in touch with, write to, obtain a photograph of, or anything to do with this grand ATS girl with the wonderful voice. Any time it would be possible to hear this choir and soloist, many eager ears would be listening in.'

The BBC listened. *Stage Door Canteen*, another elite wartime radio show, quickly snapped them up. The members of the *Stage Door Canteen* entertainments committee read like a *Who's Who* of entertainment – Arthur Askey, Jack Buchanan, Cicely Courtneidge, Noel Coward, Bebe Daniels, John Gielgud, Robert Helpmann, Jack Hulbert, Vivien Leigh, Beatrice Lillie, Vic Oliver – all names George was destined to work with in the years ahead. Already he and the choir were mixing in top-flight circles. Soon they were appearing regularly on *Stage Door Canteen* and *Variety Bandbox*. A telegram would arrive, such as the one 'asking if the Swing Choir could broadcast *Variety Bandbox* on 27 May, rehearsal 2.30, record 6-7pm'. George kept the contract for this show which reads, 'Fee 1 = 15 guineas (£630), repeat overseas = £3.18.9 (£161), Home Service = 5 guineas (£215), other repeats = 10 guineas (£430). Signed by Captain Hutchings for the services of Sgt George Mitchell and his Swing Choir.' The Army was still controlling the choir's movements, and all such fees quickly disappeared into Army coffers.

Stage shows continued all over London and the S East of England. Often below them on the bill were stars such as Cyril Fletcher and Violet Carson, who later found fame as Ena Sharples in *Coronation Street* but who was a notable pianist in the 1940s. Soon, they were topping the bill above names such as Wilson, Keppel and Betty, and Florence Desmond, both very high-flying famous variety acts, as well as Max Bygraves, Peter Cavanagh, Don Arden, Alfred Marks and Vic Oliver.

Matters developed so fast that George spent much of the early part of 1945 living on his nerves. His *I Remember* list for 1945 included, 'I remember the words of *All Just the Same* shaking like a leaf in Irene Coe's hand as she deputised for Dot Mackenzie at a few minutes' notice and sang a very difficult solo part.' But worse was to come: 'On March 16, we made the greatest faux pas of 1945. The choir came in on the wrong beat of our signature tune and "the band played on". Both sides stuck it out to the bitter end – and it certainly was bitter – leaving me at the piano in a state of collapse. The audience actually APPLAUDED, and from then on I knew that to have even a small reputation was worth much gold and I was convinced the limitations of discordant swing music on the ear of the general public had not been reached so far.' His greatest worry that year, he recalled, was that 'the first performance of *Manuelo* had to be a broadcast – it was written in a hurry and was under-rehearsed – some of the gang were actually reading the words from scraps of paper. Our lucky star must have been doing its stuff because the tremendous enthusiasm of the Queensberry audience at the end of the number produced the largest lump I have ever had in my throat.'

George's nerves kicked in again when the choir appeared at the vast Earl's Court arena later in 1945: 'I was to conduct Geraldo's orchestra. It seemed an awful cheek for a sergeant to wave the baton for Geraldo's orchestra.' Although his parents planned to attend, they hesitated when it started to rain. Once they decided to go, they had no time to change, so they drove to Earls Court in their gardening clothes, intending to slip into the back, but the hall was packed. They were thinking of driving home again when George appeared and they found themselves ushered to front row VIP seats. The proudest pair in the hall were Robert and Barbara, seated between a general and a naval captain – and Robert still in his gardening clothes!

Nerves or not, George was making an impression. The BBC was planning a new programme, featuring young people. George wrote, 'I was asked to attend a script conference. After carefully making sure they really meant me, I joined forces with Cecil Madden, Stephen Williams, Cedric Stokes, Peter Cavanagh, Sandy Sandford, Jack and Eddy Eden, Robin Richmond, Diana Decker and Dick Dudley. A new show, to run for several weeks, was discussed. (I was allowed to speak frequently). Eventually, it was decided that the choir would open and close the programme each week and also sing any number of my own choice during each programme.' Keen to placate the Army, producer Cecil Madden wrote to George's commanding officer, saying they would record the programme on Sundays to reduce the time the choir would be needed during working hours. Early test recordings were remade over and over until the BBC was happy with the show, called *Knocking at Your Door*, but George panicked even more when he was offered a second spot: 'Little did they know the difficulties we were having in producing enough new material without adding to the burden.' But typically George said 'Yes' and worried later.

By the year's end, recordings of the choir's broadcasts had been heard as far away as Hollywood, Hawaii, North Russia, Darwin, Sweden, Iceland and British Guiana as well as by ships at sea. His *I Remember* list gives small snapshots of that magical year 1945:

•The glorious effect in our signature tune when the AEF orchestra improved on the trumpet breaks and their terrific brass section let rip.

•How worried we were when Miki (Barbara Boyle) collapsed after a broadcast.

•The number of times I sat until the early hours writing out parts, wondering if it was worth all the bother. The next morning I always decided it was.

•How sweet the twins (Olive and Jose Prime) looked in their tango scene.

•Joan's great solo on her first broadcast, as cool as ice – followed by Emyr, clowning at the mike, getting laughs from his audience and coming away after a short solo with sweat pouring down his face.

•How queer I felt when two Marines headed a queue for the first autographs I'd ever given.

•Dot [Mackenzie] singing *Besame Mucho* better than I had ever heard anyone singing it.

•Tom, sitting in the freezing cold basement at Classic House, scribbling out band parts in his usual race against time.

•Vi didn't look very well during one of the broadcasts – I found out later that she had fractured her elbow earlier that day.

•When little Arthur, announced as a soloist for a joke, had to sing one word in the middle of a number. He missed it, and I nearly fell off the piano stool laughing at his expression as he ripped up his 'notes' and marched off stage in a temper.

- The classic phrase uttered by Fred Holmes when I got a little hot under the collar at a rehearsal – 'Don't worry about him, he only plays the piano.'
- Miki and Frank clowning the solo parts of *All Just the Same* for the first time.

To George and the choir members, life seemed good.

CHAPTER 3

By mid-1945, peace had arrived, and gradually choir members were demobbed, returning to their pre-war jobs. But new members swelled the ranks such as a young returned Prisoner of War named Alan Cooper who was posted to the RAPC at Finsbury Circus. As he recalls, 'I was introduced into the Singers, and we used to rehearse in Classic House in Old Street. I had been a singer before my call-up, am/dram, Gilbert and Sullivan, my office concert party, and was thrilled with the music and singing.' Alan was to remain with George until the 1970s, becoming a stalwart not only as a singer but as George's right-hand man in the growing George Mitchell enterprise.

The Swing Choir's final appearance in uniform was *Stars in Battledress Cavalcade* at the Albert Hall on June 2, 1946. This hugely promoted show, the peak of wartime entertainment, saw them sharing the bill with Janet Brown, Peter Cavanagh, Nat Gonella, Arthur Haynes, Ken Morris, Charlie Chester, Freddie Frinton, Walter Midgley and Terry Thomas, all top show business names.

George was demobbed in June 1946 and wryly recalled, 'On the day I was demobbed, Colonel Morrell asked me if I would like to buy that upright piano we had used to practice with – I thought that pretty funny.' Once again a civilian, George quickly got a job in the Wages Department with Surbiton Town Council, beating off the opposition. George noted laconically there were 'six hopeful candidates. Got the job,' which he started in early September.

And that seemed to be that, or so all later features written about the choir stated. Even George reinforced this 'recollection' in later programmes. But it simply wasn't what happened. True, they weren't making enough money to keep them, but George fully intended to keep the choir going as a sideline, much as his grandfather had done in the evenings back in Carronshore. Those who lived close enough continued to rehearse several evenings a week, and George even advertised for 'Semi-pros. Those interested should write to George Mitchell.' It was at this time that Daphne

Bell joined the set-up – she, like Alan Cooper, was to become a lynch-pin of the choir. As she recalled, 'a friend of a friend introduced me to George and he asked me to join. I had no intention of turning professional. My voice had been trained, and I could read music, but I wanted to be a dancer. But I did join the choir, and we turned professional. My mother was very against it, but I stuck out and went.'

He had many meetings with BBC producers Ronnie Waldman, George Melachrino and Cecil Madden, all of whom had used him during the war. He also met Blanche Littler, who, with her brothers Emile and Prince, was one of the most powerful figures in British theatre, with an almost total monopoly on musicals and pantomime. They performed in a few stage shows and appeared in *Stage Door Canteen* and a show for Army Radio, and recorded eight songs. Cecil Madden even recommended them to BBC television producers. George somehow managed to buy the choir members new outfits as they could no longer perform in uniform, though this proved difficult in post-war London.

And most telling of all, he signed to agent and impresario Robert Luff. Bob, as he was known, had been booking star acts for years, after starting in publicity and journalism, followed by three years producing commercial radio programmes in Europe up to 1939. During the war, he saw active service in India and Burma, while his entertainment interests were run by his business partner Beryl Evetts, a famous dancer, responsible for booking many big bands, including the Squadronnaires. The well-known agency numbered many famous names amongst its clients, including Beryl Reid, Semprini, Kenneth Horne and Richard Murdoch, and presented numerous stage shows and, in conjunction with the Empress Hall Management, many ice shows including *White Horse Inn*.

George recalled the fateful meeting in 1945: 'A chap in the Gordon Highlanders came up to me, he ran an agency in London and said if I turned professional, would I let him handle me? Of course, I had no intention of turning professional, so I said, "If ever I do turn professional, you've got it." ' Now Bob reappeared in George's life and on August 11, 1946, George signed a sole agency agreement with Robert Luff Enterprises. According to Michael Lock, Bob Luff's accountant for years, it was a marriage of convenience: 'They weren't close and didn't socialise, but both saw the commercial potential.' They couldn't have been more different in temperament, George driven by perfection in performance, Bob by the financial potential. 'The quarrels between George and Bob were always about money,' recalls later Head Minstrel Roy Winbow. 'Silly things like the actual amount people were paid for rehearsals. There were always issues with George paying us - if you were classed as a George Mitchell Singer, he paid you, but he always held onto cheques as long as possible. But he and Bob respected each other.'

Life in Britain was still grim in 1946, if not more so than during the war. Everywhere was drab and broken, rationing still dominated lives and continued to do so until 1954, and no one could foresee what the future held. Everybody was exhausted and hungry for escapist entertainment. Cinemas were booming, filled to capacity night after night. Even with a smaller population than today, people made ten times as many visits to the cinema as they do now. But theatres were suffering badly. Nothing new was being produced, and many stars were still overseas, entertaining the troops, so theatres often played to empty houses.

But radio was in every front room. Most people listened to it at every meal, with four out of five eating their evening meal while enjoying whatever light entertainment the BBC put out. The BBC felt it had a similar morale-boosting job to do in these early post-war years, one they fulfilled by producing night after night of star-studded entertainment. Programme makers fell over themselves to produce more and more quality shows with multi-talented stars, and listening figures were huge. Many of the programmes developed in the war ran continuously for decades. Although on the face of it, the Light and the Home Service were very different from each other, with the Home being more serious in nature, in reality programmes were very interchangeable. Programmes which started life on one were usually repeated not only later the same week on the same frequency but were often re-run on the other Service. Shows were almost interchangeable, with the same narrow band of famous names appearing over and over in shows often only differentiated by their titles. A bartering system existed with for instance Charlie Chester's show having Ted Ray as a guest; a few weeks later, Charlie Chester would turn up as a guest on Ted Ray's own programme.

Despite now having an agent, George found choir dates few and far between. Many, like George, who had provided night after night of morale-boosting radio entertainment during the war found themselves no longer quite so much in demand, as stars involved in *ENSA* returned to the home front. After a *Stage Door Canteen* appearance in mid-October, there were few shows in 1946 or early 1947. They appeared in *Variety Matinée* which also starred the Beverley Sisters, Bill Kerr, Max Bygraves and Vera Lynn, quite a star turnout for an early afternoon slot! An equally star-studded *Variety Bandbox* was broadcast in late April. Alongside the singers were Frankie Howerd, Petula Clark, Bill Kerr, Peter Cavanagh, Max Wall, Tony Hancock and Edmundo Ros. Such a plethora of talent on one bill is almost unbelievable when viewed by 21st century standards.

Initially, it seemed the choir had little to show for their endless rehearsing. But Bob wasn't about to let the choir get stale. With radio dates few and far between, in Spring 1947 he organised a small tour at weekends and Bank Holidays, which travelled to Watford, Margate, Hove and Eastbourne. Variously called *Radio Party* and *Melody Cruise*, the choir, billed as 'George Mitchell and his BBC Swing Choir, a modern, rhythmic, vocal and instrumental ensemble', was the only constant on the bill. With a nice touch of irony, the choir shared the stage with the Squadronnaires at the *RAF Band Show* in May, where they stepped into the breach at very short notice indeed. The Squadronnaires had of course been given plenty of time to practice and perform during the war. Now they were on the same bill as the 'upstart' choir who had been refused such luxury treatment. Playing with the Squadronnaires was trombonist George Chisholm, who later featured heavily in the *Black and White Minstrel Show*. The *Musical Express* was impressed: 'This new outfit is something to be watched. They have what is needed in our business. Over twenty voices, well drilled and perfectly in tune, singing swingy arrangements, is something worth hearing. I'll bet they're a top-liner in a few weeks.' And they were.

Fate stepped in, in the first of several 'right place, right time' events in the choir's career. Renowned radio producer Charles Chilton wanted a black choir for a new series *Cabin in the Cotton*. Already a top radio producer, Charles gained major international recognition as writer/producer of the acclaimed *Journey Into Space*, and later as writer and producer of *Oh, What a Lovely War* with Joan Littlewood. Now in 1947, he wanted to produce a series of musical shows about Negro spirituals, set around the *Uncle Remus* stories. The programme was ground-breaking, the first of a crop of programmes made specifically for radio, as opposed to being merely adaptations of music hall and variety. He had already cast the great Trinidadian bearded baritone Edric Connor in the title role, Benny Lee as Brer Rabbit and the fourteen-year-old Petula Clark as the little girl. All were already well-known, Pet having captivated audiences since 1942. All Charles needed was a choir. He knew exactly what sound he wanted but despite increasingly desperate searching, no choir came close to providing Charles with the sound he needed. The BBC's choral groups were too formal: 'They were useless and didn't sound right. Then I remembered hearing the Swing Choir and decided to use them.'

George could hardly believe his ears when a phone call came out of the blue one evening from Charles – he later called Charles 'possibly the best radio producer and writer ever'. All later features dramatised this pivotal moment, relating how George explained to Charles, 'I haven't a singer left. It was just a wartime caper, and now we're back in our jobs, the thing's finished.' The idea was endlessly repeated that George 'phoned Daphne Bell, the ex-ATS telephonist who'd found out in the Pay Corps that she could sing. She recalled the address of Alan Cooper, and Alan could get in touch with Frank – and remember the twins? So it went on. At the end of the week, George could say, "Sixteen of the old gang are willing to have a go." ' This tale was reinforced by George himself at a Foyle's lunch in 1982 when he was the speaker.

But of course, this wasn't true. The choir was ready to go, still rehearsing several times a week, and had just finished their mini-tour. And of course, Bob was working, albeit relatively unsuccessfully, behind the scenes to find work for the choir. However, it made a wonderful story, and the Mitchell organisation proved time and again that it was brilliant at spotting good publicity stories.

Even so, what Charles was offering – a much more demanding weekly slot – was very different from their usual work. It meant learning new songs very quickly and moving away from their tried and trusted repertoire. And every choir member now had a regular job and family life. They were insurance clerks, sales reps, garage mechanics, shop assistants and cashiers. Knowing he couldn't commit unless they were behind him, George broke the news to the choir and was delighted to discover that behind him they were.

George could tell Charles Chilton he'd found his choir, a deal they celebrated with a party at a Victoria pub.

Charles wanted George to write a signature tune and also arrange four or five Negro spirituals for each programme. George recalled, 'I'd never done anything like that before and hadn't the faintest idea, so I bought lots of books.' But the BBC still thought of the choir as amateur and refused to pay George for the arrangements, wanting them done by BBC orchestrators, despite Charles Chilton's wishes. So George did the arrangements for free so that he could control the choir's sound. They rehearsed for weeks, in one another's homes, sometimes far past midnight. But this put enormous strain on everybody, especially George. Everyone was working during the day, and now rehearsing late into the night. Few of them could read music and George had to spend hours teaching them the new songs they needed to learn every week. Some, such as Daphne Bell and Alan Cooper, had musical backgrounds but the rest were in deep water and needed to learn fast. When one left because of the strain, Alan's mother said, 'What about Les, the young chap upstairs? I hear him singing every morning.' So into the breach, without even an audition, stepped 19-year-old Les Rawlings, another one who was to stay with George for decades.

Charles recalls, 'It was useful working with the same people. You got to know them and how they worked. The first time I heard the choir was on the day of the broadcast, but I had faith in George, I liked him.' He wasn't the only one. 'He was a lovely man, very professional and easy to work with,' remembers Pet Clark. George remembered her too, 'She was trying to play the organ the first time I saw her, but her feet couldn't reach the pedals.'

But George quickly regretted accepting Charles' invitation: 'This was the first show where I didn't select my own numbers. Now I was expected to sing what I was told to. I was scared. It was beyond me.' He cut his sleep down to five hours a night, and everyone worried about the amount of weight he lost.

Two nights before *Cabin in the Cotton* was due to start, he panicked. 'I can't do it,' he told Charles. 'We haven't the time, the choir's not as it should be.' He found it hard to cope and decided to pull out. Charles remembers this critical moment vividly: 'George wanted to stop, but I took him to a Bond Street café and persuaded him to stay with the show.' George later said, 'It was on *Cabin in the Cotton* I learned the only inspiration is hard work. I was thrown in at the deep end. That's how I learned to swim.'

The first broadcast was on Sunday, August 3. That Sunday remained burned into George's memory. Out of the thousands of broadcasts he made over the years, this first *Cabin in the Cotton* was the only one that actually terrified him. But he needn't have worried; it was a howling success from the start. By Tuesday the BBC was flooded with enthusiastic mail, and press comment was equally keen. The show ran for fourteen weeks, ending on November 2, during which time the choir created the first of many records by broadcasting over fifty spiritual and plantation songs, all arranged by George: 'I loved it all. Early on, we did *Jacob's Ladder* and all the swinging songs.'

When it was announced that the show was ending, listeners and press hit the roof. The Musical Express led the way: 'My spies tell me [it] is coming off, and no one seems to know why. I understand the listening figures have gone up every week and though I don't set much store by such things, it proves the programme is popular. Then why is it coming off? Your guess is as good as mine.' It was to return, now called *Way Down South*, in April 1949.

Life now turned upside down for George and the singers. The choir was an instant hit, and every producer wanted them. George, ever-willing to please and terrified it wouldn't last, said 'yes' to everything and the choir of sixteen quickly found themselves inundated with work. There was even talk of a Canadian tour. George said, 'It just took off, we were turning down as much as we were doing. My wrists were going from writing so much.' So he gave up composing and stuck to arranging songs such as *Sweet and Low, Golden Slumbers, Cucaracha, Our Village, Mexican Hat Dance, Nymphs and Shepherds, Cherry Ripe* and *Greensleeves*.

Soon, much to everyone's amazement, not least his own, George and the singers became vital cogs in most programmes, as backing singers, crooning the signature and closing tunes, or even with their own spots. They were regulars in many of the BBC's weekly programmes such as *Variety Bandbox, Easter Parade* and Gracie Fields' *Special Jubilee Show*. In mid-March 1948, yet another Charles Chilton series *When Soft Voices Die*, billed as 'songs of many lands', began broadcasting which reunited the choir, now consisting of twenty-four voices, with Edric Connor. The first half was dedicated to songs from *Cabin in the Cotton*. In the second half, they sang songs from the forthcoming film *It's a Wonderful*

Day as well as songs from a future programme called *This Is Disney* which went out in March. They also joined Edric on stage with *Edric Connor and the George Mitchell Choir* at London's Criterion Theatre, with Ted Heath's band at the London Palladium, and in *Variety Concert Hall*, broadcast from RAF Creden Hill, Hereford. At Christmas, they recalled Walt Disney in *With a Smile and a Song* for the Home Service. From January until April 1948, the choir had only sixteen evenings off, roughly one evening a week on top of still working full-time. George had even less spare time as he spent most of those sixteen evenings meeting people like Charles Chilton, Bob Luff and Jack Hulbert, all the time discussing yet more work.

However, with this success came a brand-new problem for George and he quickly faced an agonising choice. Could he continue doing all this work and ensure it was up to his high standards? Perhaps Irene got tired of a virtually non-existent husband. She and George now had two young children and were still living with George's parents. Everyone including George was also working full time to support families. The radio and stage work was now at least bringing in money for everyone and not disappearing into Army coffers, but the BBC didn't pay that well. And who knew how long it would continue? For all George knew, his choir might be a five-minute wonder.

But everyone was exhausted. Something had to go, either the choir or their jobs. George was in a dilemma. He turned to his father, Robert, for advice who immediately realised that George, despite the opposing options he was suggesting, had already decided to go with the choir. Knowing the time to gamble was while George was young, Robert immediately offered to support the choir for eight weeks. George said, 'I decided to burn my boats and have a go.' But he was still worried about the responsibility he carried for the choir. What if the singers left their jobs and followed him into show business, only to find it was a flash in the pan? With his father's promise behind him, he put the question to the choir. They too were uncertain. Eventually, some chose to stay with their full-time jobs, not trusting to the uncertainty of show business, others weren't so dedicated to singing that they wanted to do it full-time. But enough chose to follow George. Even so, he took it slowly, moving some to full-time singing immediately, with others, including new recruits, following over the next few months.

Minstrel Magic

By December 1948 the entire choir was professional and full-time. George himself left work at Surbiton on April 8, 1948. His diary laconically records, 'Left Surbiton Boro' Council (Wages Dept)'. The George Mitchell Choir was born.

Everyone breathed huge sighs of relief as it quickly became obvious that George had made the right decision. More and more work piled up. Producers – Charles Chilton, Glyn Jones, William Lyons – always tried to book the choir for their new programmes as they knew they could rely on George. Soon hardly a musical programme was broadcast that didn't include the singers in one guise or another. The rapidly growing body of fans could easily listen to the choir four or five times in one evening on programmes such as *Variety Bandbox*, *Melody Time* with Geraldo and his Orchestra, plus repeats of *Waterlogged Spa* and *ITMA*. And three months after George left work to run the choir full-time, the BBC gave them the ultimate accolade – their own show. *The George Mitchell Choir* went out on the Home Service in the coveted Friday evening 8.15pm slot. The *Sunday Empire News* said, 'Today the George Mitchell Choir becomes a No 1 BBC feature.'

The invitation to join the BBC's flagship programme *ITMA* was even more astounding to George. *ITMA* had been a national institution since its inception in 1939, making stars of people like Hattie Jacques, Deryck Guyler, Maurice Denham and Jack Train, apart from its main star Tommy Handley. When Tommy wanted a special number for one edition, George wrote the arrangement within three hours. Sadly Tommy died unexpectedly on January 9, 1949. George and the choir went to the service at Golders Green crematorium, which five thousand people attended with thousands more lining the six-mile route. The BBC decided the show couldn't continue without Tommy, though the replacement show also included the singers.

Because all these shows were repeated several times each – *ITMA*, for instance, was broadcast on the Home Service on Thursdays, repeated on the Home on Saturdays and further repeated on the Light on Sundays – the choir seemed constantly on the air. George said, 'Things were bursting at the seams.' A doorman at the BBC is reported to have said, 'Busy! He's in everything except the news! But you wait – someday they'll set that to music so that it can have a Mitchell choir.'

But George quickly faced yet another dilemma. He had always selected choir members for their singing voices alone. During the war, their performances were sufficiently infrequent to allow them to practise for hours to get it right, and George's piano-thumping taught those who couldn't sight read. But work was now coming in so fast, George needed singers who were musically trained, and sight reading became the most important requirement. George reported, 'Every week I get about sixty applications for auditions. Most are quite useless because they can't read music. For this job, they must be quick sight-readers – sometimes we only have half an hour with a new number before we sing it on air.' Dot Mitchell recalls, 'They often did two or three sessions a day, going from one to another. They'd look at the music on the bus or tube, and then straight into recording; didn't have time to mess about.' This wasn't easy for George: 'I realised some of my best friends would have to go as they didn't read music, and our rehearsal time was very limited.' But it wasn't all bad news. Dot explains, 'Looks didn't matter for radio, but there was a lot of PR stuff and stage work, where looks did count. They had to be able to move as well. Most ex-Army members were now in their thirties, and you needed younger ones for summer shows. So he kept the older ones for PR and radio, and things like cabaret at the Lord Mayor's banquets. But some were by now too old for this exhausting work, and so George extremely reluctantly had to let them go.'

George became renowned for producing excellent work very quickly, even writing music where needed, which led to so much work pouring in that soon he needed even more singers, and he quickly gained a reputation for producing a choir of almost any size at the drop of a hat. The problem was he never quite knew how much work there would be. One week he might need thirty singers, the next only ten. George's solution was to develop an inner permanently-employed core of sixteen singers, all of whom were superb sight readers, and kept these as far as possible for radio as this work was fast moving with often little rehearsal. He then employed a varying number of singers on a self-employed basis for specific shows which peaked at Christmas and in the summer. Many of these singers, like Frank Davies, worked at other jobs in the day and sang for George on radio and stage at night but so much work poured in that the self-employed singers could more or less count on as much work as they wanted.

But so much work occasionally meant things went wrong. It was during yet another new series *Songs of the Years* in July 1948 that George experienced the choir's worst moment. He knew the show was under-rehearsed and was worried about when they were on. The laid-back producer told him they would be called five minutes beforehand, so most singers went to their dressing rooms, as did George, where he listened to the show going out live. To his horror, he heard their music start but no choir! Luckily choir member Terry Willett was standing in the wings, and she started off solo. The rest of the choir walked on stage and joined in, trying to look unconcerned. To the listeners, it was just a novel introduction of a Mitchell Choir arrangement.

Dashing around the country occasionally produced nightmares. Years later, George recalled one concert in Birmingham in particular: 'I suppose the most terrifying nightmare is not being able to appear. Touch wood this has never happened, but I had a near miss. We were at Elstree Studios for a Rosalind Russell picture. That evening we were due in Birmingham. Most of the choir were already there, but because a particularly large crowd was needed for the film, some were at Elstree with me. I had checked trains, and we had plenty of time to reach Birmingham. Or so I thought. We left the studio to find fog had descended like a blanket. The train crawled and crawled, and we reached Euston to see our next train disappearing into the darkness. One of the chaps got into the guard's van. The rest didn't make it. By the time the next train got us to Birmingham, the show was half over. It must have been bewildering for the audience. The scene was a comedy one, with the boys sitting on the girls' knees but half the girls had empty laps. Then suddenly each girl had a man. Since then I've never booked an engagement in London and one in the provinces on the same day. With five thousand TV and radio shows, and heaven knows how many stage shows, I suppose being late for only one wasn't a bad record.'

The ever-supportive *Melody Maker* was incredulous: 'What is wrong with Birmingham? I doubt whether the hall was one-third full. As it was, however, the audience had its money's worth, with honours going to the Mitchell group. Their singing was exhilarating and forceful, not to say versatile. For the life of me, I cannot understand why their fan following (which must be quite large) was not here to welcome them.'

By the end of the 1940s, it looked like the singers were at the top of the tree and could go no further. Their meteoric rise to the top had astounded everyone. The *Scottish Daily Mail* reported, 'Radio's busiest set of singers achieve a new vocal marathon this week by broadcasting in five home shows and one away. Last night they sang twice – first as the Singing Silhouettes in *Stand Easy* and then under their own name in Geraldo's *One Night Stand*. Tomorrow they begin as the *Waterlogged Spa* Glee Party and then switch from Light to Third by singing under their own name in *Third Division*. If *ITMA* were still on the air, they would be singing on Thursday as the Kerbside Choristers. Instead, they bob up again on Friday as the Hi-Gangsters. On Saturday they round off the week by singing in Geraldo's *Dancing Through*.'

In the first six months of the amazing 1949, they broadcast a mind-boggling 189 times in 181 days – the year's total was 266 broadcasts, on top of their 104 stage appearances. Take just one fortnight. On Tuesday, May 10, they were in *Hit Parade*; the next day *The Days of '49*, *Waterlogged Spa* and *Way Down South*. On Thursday *Waterlogged Spa* was repeated; on Friday it was the turn of *Hi Gang* and *Melody Lane*. Saturday saw *Dancing Through* and *Footlight Favourites*, with *Hi Gang* being repeated on Sunday. On Sunday they did a concert where the *Richmond Herald* said, 'You would think to fulfil fourteen engagements in one week would be enough for any choir, but for this choir, it is by no means impossible. They went one better on Sunday when they gave their fifteenth concert of the week to the old people at Kingsmead.' On Monday they appeared in *Sweet Corn*, repeated on Tuesday, along with an appearance in *Hit Parade*. *Waterlogged Spa*, repeated on Thursday, and *Way Down South* were broadcast on Wednesday. Friday saw them in *Hi Gang* and *Melody Lane*, with *Dancing Through* going out on Saturday. The repeat of *Hi Gang* closed a frantically busy but typical two weeks.

In December 1948 alone, they made thirty-six broadcasts, and in the last third of the year, 119 radio appearances in 122 days. George could relax and congratulate himself on making the right decision to turn professional, though with typical modesty, he found it hard to believe and played down the enormous success: 'Within about six months, we were there. It was the biggest fluke in show business. Just happened to be in the right place at the right time, I suppose. The secret of my success? Just luck, I've just had lucky breaks all the time.'

CHAPTER 4

But not everybody was happy. One possibly jealous colleague wrote, 'If Mr Mitchell really wants to scale the peaks, let me, as an ex-choirmaster, offer a word of advice. Take your singers into purdah for a month, Mr Mitchell, and train them to the limit. Instil in them some of the sensitivity of the Glasgow Orpheus Choir, the attack and brilliance of the Liverpool Choral Society, the musicianship of the BBC Singers and you're home. You'll emerge – provided your training has been severe enough – with a body of singers that should make Mr Fred Waring's Pennsylvanians sit up.' George's reactions to this suggestions are not recorded anywhere! Another spat, 'The George Mitchell Choir should always be kept out of camera shot.'

But producers took no notice of such envy. As the *Evening Standard* reported, 'George Mitchell's choir is now by way of being a light industry. Mitchell has sections working in TV, gramophones recordings, commercial radio, films, and he also runs a successful stage act. During the first six months of 1949, there were only eight days when the choir wasn't booked on the air or in gramophone studios.'

Already hugely popular in this country, their international ratings were boosted when they came third in a Favourite European Musicians Poll staged by the American Forces Network in Germany. Even more amazing to the choir were some special visitors to a couple of recordings. Daphne Bell recalls, 'One day, in the front row at a *Hi-Gang* recording were two young girls – they were HRH Princesses Elizabeth and Margaret.' This was the start of many future links with royalty. But this was not always helpful to the singers. A few years later, Princess Margaret visited Lime Grove Studios to watch *Tin Pan Alley*. This used ingenious staging, usually involving lots of hearty singing and dancing for the choir. For instance, *Lizzie Borden* was written as a square dance; between each verse the chorus of jurors, citizens and neighbours got up to dance, yelling, '*You cain't chop y'r Momma up in Massachusetts.*' One singer recalled, 'We stood in two tidy

Minstrel Magic

lines while the small blue-eyed figure passed by with attendant satellites, on her way to the control room to watch the show. We really knocked ourselves out – we loved the number anyway – and when it was over, we leant against the scenery, panting and sweating, waiting for a clearance. Instead, the floor manager said the princess had enjoyed it so much that she would like to see it again. Flattering but exhausting, especially in our ill-fitting button-boots.' The princess recognised one of the singers, Leslie Baker, from an appearance at Windsor Castle, and asked if she could join the group. She did – as second soprano. Baker's verdict on her singing: 'She was very good too.'

Despite the amount of radio work, George still loved the buzz of live stage work. In the summer of 1949, accompanied by the Tommy Wolfe Quartet, George and the choir set off most Sundays in a hired bus to give a series of concerts at South Coast resorts. Daphne Bell remembers, 'We weren't allowed to move in Sunday shows, so they were billed as concerts.' Dot Mitchell recalls, 'The kids lugged around the scenery and costumes – there were no roadies. The scenery went between the bus seats, with baskets of costumes in the back. Some lads were very good carpenters and made the scenery too. George devised the staging, he always had good ideas for the choreography, lighting and makeup. The critics were always impressed with the staging of the shows.' At Hastings, 'Their previous visit was such an outstanding success this early return visit was arranged,' so said local press, before adding, 'It was highly diverting. First, there was a full house, attracted by a choir which has won thousands of adherents. This choir never failed to justify its reputation for rhythmic vitality and command of the finest tonal nuances. Teamwork is exemplary, and their power of expression applied in a thoroughly musical way.' 'Unavailable' to the BBC as they were 'on holiday', the group spent one August week in Southport, appearing twice nightly in *Holiday Programme*, from where George reported, 'weather shocking but good for business', and a second week in Bournemouth.

But the autumn's major departure was their first proper variety tour. Opening in Dudley in mid-October, George's core singers headed the bill in a show which travelled the length and breadth of England. Press comments called them 'excellent in their well-chosen programme'. Not content with entire weeks in every venue, George arranged Sunday concerts as well. Once again, press coverage was extremely enthusiastic, particularly in Swansea. The

South Wales Post called them 'a model of timing and slickness – an object lesson in presentation'. The *Llanelli Mercury* almost ran out of words: 'What can one write? To attempt to gild the lily would be futile – it is the tops. Beautifully sensitive, absolute control', whereas the *South Wales Evening Post* reported 'repeated calls for more but time limitations prevented any response. George Mitchell paid the Swansea audience a great compliment by saying, "We would like to sing to you all night – who wouldn't to an audience like this?"'

And it didn't end there. Film producers quickly snapped them up to add to their soundtracks, such as the new British musical *It's a Wonderful Day*. Now, even though they had only been professional for a few months, they had already achieved that rare caption of success – 'of stage, screen and radio'. Films followed thick and fast. Shortly, they featured in J Arthur Rank's *County* cartoons and in two famous Gainsborough films, *Here Come the Huggetts* and *Vote for Huggett*. These films teamed them up with Petula Clark again and meant they worked with star names such as Jack Warner, Kathleen Harrison and Diana Dors. Ever keen to expand the choir's ventures and always willing to try anything new, George agreed to them appearing at the Gaumont State Cinema, Kilburn in a new venture for Sunday night cinema – films were shown until 7.30, followed by a concert at 7.45. Even more daringly, they spent the summer season in *Rose Marie on Ice* at the Haringey Arena, London. It was the largest ice spectacle ever staged there, with a cast of two hundred which initially gave the conductor great difficulties synchronising the choir's voices with the skaters' movements. Ironically in the light of later Minstrel controversy, the skaters were, of course, miming to Mitchell voices, yet no one saw this as cheating in any sense whatsoever.

The recording company Decca used them extensively, initially as backing singers to stars such as Vera Lynn, though often reviewers preferred the choir to the famous singer they were supporting. Soon they were recording under their own name. *March Hare*, for the soundtrack of the film of the same name, received great critical acclaim and became George's first hit record. After its release, George received a bizarre call from a BBC producer telling him to listen to the soundtrack of the *March Hare*. 'There's an American vocal group on it,' he was informed, 'from which you can pick up some pretty good tips.' That BBC producer's face must have been deep red when he learned it was actually one of George's groups.

And they were expanding into America, albeit with yet another name. The Daily Mail reported, 'Under the name of the Unitones, they recorded *The Birthday Waltz/While We're Young* for Decca – a lilting new British song, a worthy follow-up to their *St Bernard Waltz* record, now sweeping across the US.'

By now, the BBC knew that George would say 'yes' to anything he was asked to do so the choir was the obvious choice for two radio experiments this year. On Easter Monday they, together with stars Geraldo and Anne Shelton, took part in *Hello Paris,* a joint BBC/French Broadcasting Service programme, broadcast simultaneously in both countries. Later in the year, George agreed to the choir appearing in *UK to USA*, recorded in front of 2000 GIs at Burtonwood American Forces Camp, Warrington. The show was beamed to the BBC's New York office where it broadcast coast to coast just before Christmas. Also on the bill were Vera Lynn and the Squadronnaires. This show certainly involved a very long day for George and the choir as they travelled up on the 8.35am train and came back on the midnight train, even though they were offered hotel rooms. There was too much work to allow them to be out of London any longer than absolutely necessary.

Much to his surprise, George found himself also in demand. His fame as an arranger led to a surprising phone call in late June 1950, from Noel Coward who was worried about his new musical *Ace of Clubs*, due to open in London in twelve days' time after disappointing provincial try-outs. At his wits' end, Noel asked George to rearrange the vocal items. It was a tough job in a very short space of time. George recalled, 'It was a real disaster – good songs destroyed by the cast and a third rate orchestral score.' George cut out the poor actors and 'got my old pal Phil Green to sort out the orchestral parts, and Noel was very happy. My last memory is of Phil Green (still in his carpet slippers) starting to leave the pit, when the show's star Robert Helpmann came prancing down the stage and said, "Mr Green, haven't you forgotten something?" Phil growled, "NO." "What about the *Queen*?" Helpmann asked. Phil told him the orchestra could play that in their sleep, he'd already had enough queens to deal with for the rest of his life and he was off to the nearest pub to get drunk. Great days for my childish sense of humour.'

George's success was ruffling feathers at the BBC. The next few years were peppered with arguments between the BBC and George and Bob, which showed just how different George and Bob were from each other. George's aim was all about getting the sound right, whereas Bob was driven by money. George hated confrontation, but Bob never seemed happy unless he was trying to get one over on the BBC. He fought them over fees and expenses, he fought them on the *George Mitchell Glee Club*, he fought them until they agreed to change how George was paid, then fought them to change the system back when it became clear the new system didn't work to his or George's advantage. He had an amazing ability to muddy the waters around every issue and nearly always succeeded in bewildering the BBC to such an extent that they not only backed down but ended up convinced it was all their fault. George meanwhile concentrated on the music and let his agent get on with it.

George's chief competitor was the in-house Revue Chorus which the BBC was disbanding, much to the Revue Chorus' distress. George was getting an average of £94 (£3,000) per week from the BBC - less than the Revue Chorus - and providing far more voices. The BBC discussed putting George under some sort of contract as he was 'supremely good at his job', but as usual at the BBC, talking was as far as it went. The only change was that Michael Standing, the BBC's Head of Variety, suggested to George that he should ask higher fees and there the matter rested, at least for a few months.

It reared its head again, once George's choir got bigger. The singers now numbered about a hundred, and the BBC feared listeners would get fed up hearing the name. But George found an ingenious solution – give them a wide variety of names, such as the Top Hatters, the George Mitchell Singers, the George Mitchell Choir, the Mitchell Maids, the Mitchell Men, the Glee Club, the Quintet, the Octet, the George Mitchell Singing Ensemble.

But producers became fed up with not getting what they perceived as the George Mitchell Singers and George himself at recordings. In vain George argued that all his singers were equally talented and so it shouldn't matter who turned up – there were no such things as a No 1 and a No 2 choir – and if he couldn't be present at a recording, then his assistants were equally capable. Producers complained that they never knew from week to week how many singers they were getting and that there was no consistency, though they never complained about their quality. The BBC was furious, telling George to send the number of singers they were paying for. But George wouldn't accept this. He was

Minstrel Magic

determined that the music would always receive the sound it deserved, even if he lost out financially by providing a bigger choir than he was paid for. Yes, he retorted, sometimes he sent fewer voices than he was contracted to do, but more often he sent extra voices, depending on the particular music. In *Variety Playhouse*, for example, one week might need eight girl singers, the next week twenty-four mixed voices for something operatic, so he felt the BBC were doing well out of it, as he received the same money, whether he produced the contracted number of singers or more.

At first, the BBC accepted this but asked Bob to tell them if 'substitutes' were used. Neither Bob nor George was happy with the amount of work this involved but agreed for the sake of peace. But soon more producers were complaining about expecting the 'original choir' but being palmed off with the 'Second XI'. They also weren't happy that George occasionally used an assistant instead of attending broadcasts himself. Bob felt any assistant should be paid as if George were there in person. This was one of the few battles the BBC won as they eventually decided they would pay reduced fees for programmes supervised by an assistant.

Bob now turned his attention to overtime rates. Several programmes, such as *Songs From the Shows*, needed a lot of extra rehearsal. George, happy to provide this time at his own cost to achieve the sound he wanted, clashed with Bob who was keen the singers should be paid overtime by the BBC at the same rates as the musicians, although none of George's singers was a member of Equity or the Musicians' Union. The BBC strongly disputed this, once again getting their own way, and things calmed down for a while until a programme called *All Star Bill*. George expected a lot from his singers in this programme, which involved extra rehearsal time. George had recently increased his rates, and the BBC was also worried by rumours that the Musicians' Union was trying to persuade the choir to join which would have meant further increases. All of this put the programme over budget. The BBC's answer was to reduce the choir to one day's rehearsal, singing less complicated songs to compensate. George wasn't at all happy with this lessening of the choir's output, and Bob was less than happy with the reduced income. However, in typical fashion, Bob successfully argued that he had cancelled Sunday concerts to provide the original amount of rehearsal time, so the BBC was forced to pay the higher amount after all.

Minstrel Magic

The BBC's Variety Booking Manager, Pat Newman, who generally sided with George, felt that George didn't fight hard enough for extra rehearsals if he felt they were needed. He frequently correctly accused George of offering to do extra rehearsals out of good will which didn't help the situation. He wrote to Bob saying, 'It does not assist us if Mitchell goes around saying it won't cost producers anything', and asked Bob to insist that George be business-like. Pat's advice was that if George did insist on extra rehearsals, and producers, with one eye on costs, still refused, then George should produce under-rehearsed work with which the producer would have to be happy. One can only imagine George's horror at this suggestion.

The most serious row, also involving *All Star Bill*, blew up over a stage show called *Moulin Rouge* and rumbled on for eighteen months. In mid-1952, the inner core set off on a nationwide tour as part of *Moulin Rouge*, a variety show in which they appeared in four segments, including one devoted entirely to them. Reviews as a whole were mixed, but the choir was always well-received, being called 'charmingly normal young people, totally devoid of the exotic in hair styles, makeup and costume .... a single responsive instrument that fills the stage with fresh and rousing melody'.

All was going well until one September weekend when the show was in Edinburgh. This was the first Sunday when both *All Star Bill* and *Star Show* were to be recorded - in London. George arranged for other Mitchell Singers to be used for both shows, but, because of the earlier issues around personnel, the BBC soon disabused George of this solution. Producer Dennis Main Wilson blamed Bob for not reading the contract properly, though the BBC admitted its part in the confusion. The outcome was that George, after the second house on Saturday in Edinburgh, brought himself and the core singers south from Edinburgh, recorded both shows and returned to the next week's venue by coach, swiftly asking the BBC to reimburse his costs. Dennis Main Wilson, feeling partly responsible, promised George he would suggest the BBC helped. George and the choir continued this punishing schedule week after week, but by December, the BBC still hadn't agreed to reimburse George. Pat Newman, appalled to learn George was carrying such costs, told Bob he didn't want him accepting any BBC bookings for the choir until he had told them the full liability, including whether the Corporation was getting the full Number One Choir, the Number Two Choir, and assistant or George himself!

Minstrel Magic

By January 1953, it had got completely out of hand. Memos flew back and fore at the BBC as the matter dragged on, with Dennis Main Wilson being blamed for letting George and Bob think the BBC would help. The BBC also objected to Dennis' 'friendly little chats' with George about the issues. There were strong feelings within the Corporation that they shouldn't pay anything, arguing George had to move his choir from one theatre to the next in any case. They also refused to pay George's First Class sleeper fare from Edinburgh, and would at best only contemplate reimbursing a Third Class seat. It escalated when Bob, having got wind of this thinking, put in a greatly increased claim, as the same situation and costs had been repeated every weekend since mid-September. Matters got even worse when the BBC refused to pay George his appearance fee for both shows as he could obviously only be at one recording. However, the BBC was forced to relent on this issue as *Star Show's* producer was happy to work with George's assistant and allow George to attend the recording of *All Star Bill*, as George could be in the *Star Show* studio within five minutes if necessary.

By Spring 1953, the BBC was ready to compromise as they acknowledged someone should have realised that travelling costs were mounting. However, they now argued over whether to pay the full amount or half of it. They also asked Bob to deduct the costs of moving the choir from one venue to another. Bob replied that George didn't pay those anyway as they were covered by the *Moulin Rouge* management. But trouble occurred there too as *Moulin Rouge's* management now refused to cover the costs because the singers were no longer moving with the main company. By April, Newman was 'losing the will to live' and had even taken the file home to try to sort out the chronology and apportion blame - he failed completely! In May, the Head of Programme Contracts said the situation was 'partly due to the temperament of George Mitchell himself who is a nice person to deal with and anxious to meet our requirements but somewhat impractical over details and extremely difficult to pin down to a discussion'. The BBC eventually agreed to pay the whole amount, leaving Bob victorious once again.

But *Moulin Rouge* provided Bob with yet another fight and yet another victory over the BBC. In August 1952 *Radio Times* concluded the programme details of *All Star Bill* with the words 'The *George Mitchell Glee Club* are appearing in *Moulin Rouge* at the Empire Theatre Sheffield.' This was the first time this sort of recognition had happened, but it triggered yet another battle. The BBC wasn't happy with the acknowledgement, doubting that the same personnel were involved in both shows, despite the still-running battle over expenses, and asked Bob for a breakdown of personnel in the two shows. Bob used his usual delaying tactics, in the hope the BBC would forget about it. Months later, Pat Newman wrote, on a copy of a letter to George, 'Ignored as usual. I'll get as tough as I can with their slapdash methods.' Eighteen months later, Pat was still trying to get the names he wanted, to see if they corresponded with the *Moulin Rouge* singers. A pencilled BBC note on a December 1953 letter says 'the BBC must resist giving credits as long as possible'. In early 1954, Newman felt they were on rickety ground, repeatedly losing this sort of battle, which he now felt was no longer worth fighting.

And the issue of fees still wouldn't go away. George was paying his core singers less than Equity rates, arguing that they were paid a weekly salary and so not entitled to the higher Equity hourly rate or the fees for repeats. Both the BBC and Equity disapproved of this, though George rightly felt the singers preferred it this way, many staying with him because of the guaranteed weekly money. But the BBC was also booking the choir less often, and so George's finances were beginning to look rocky. Both Equity and the Musicians Union were still trying to get George to sign with them, but he continued to resist. Matters became acrimonious until eventually a compromise was agreed. The singers would now join Equity, but George didn't have to pay them the exact fees and repeats as long as he made sure they received extra if payments came to more than their weekly contracted amounts. But even this complex compromise didn't solve the problems.

Within weeks Bob asked the BBC to return to the old scale of sliding fees for extra rehearsals, and also asked them to pay more than the minimum. The BBC refused, but their position was weakened by the fact that extra rehearsals had already been booked for *Star Bill* despite the BBC agreeing to keep a strict eye on rehearsal times. Producers were reminded that Mitchell singers were only to be paid for rehearsals the producers requested, not ones that George felt were necessary. The BBC also increased George's personal fee, but Bob remained unhappy, pointing out that George had to pay him commission, but he had so little to play with that Bob was only charging him 5% commission, instead of the usual 10%.

CHAPTER 5

Arguments like these with the BBC show just how important it was to George that the sound his singers created was as perfect as possible. It didn't matter to him how many rehearsals he wasn't paid for, or how many more singers he needed to provide, as long as what the audience heard was the best it could possibly be. One word appeared over and over in press reviews - 'Perfect'. Though this generally referred to the singers' performances, it applied equally well to George himself.

He was never seen less than immaculately dressed. He would come to rehearsals in Savile Row suits, buying two or three at a time. Shorts and open neck shirts were kept for his back garden. Even on holiday in Fiji, he was pictured wearing long white trousers, a white open-necked long-sleeved shirt, and white shoes. Another favourite was a dogtooth check black and white jacket. As singer Mike Rogers recollects, 'He would turn up at rehearsals looking like a tailor's dummy. Always in smart made to measure suits, usually Prince of Wales checks, cream poplin shirts and a smart tie, together with highly polished brogue shoes. In the winter months, all this would be accompanied by a cashmere camel hair coat - an extremely smart man. All this to sit at the piano and take us through our paces.' Sound engineer Pat Heigham remembers, 'He never sat down on the second day (in the studios) because he didn't want to crease his trousers.' Producer Charles Chilton later wrote that 'thirty years as the most successful choirmaster of the century has made little difference to the outward appearance of George Mitchell. He wears the same style clothes, smokes the same brand of cigarettes, and remains the same weight as he always did. The only visible signs of his phenomenal success are the large and powerful cars he drives. Apart from these his material demands from life are modesty itself.'

A chain smoker all his life, George was rarely without a cigarette in his hand. Sound engineer Mike Cotton remembers, 'George would invariably come into the sound control room to see how the

[Minstrel] show was shaping up. We'd offer him a cigarette, probably a Players Weight, one step up from a Woodbine, knowing he'd say, "Have one of these" and produce his State Express 555s which he left on the sound desk, and we'd spend the afternoon smoking and talking.' But not everyone was happy with this. Clem Vickery, a later speciality Minstrel act, recalls that principal Glyn Dawson went to see George one day. George Inns was also there and complained about the smoke possibly damaging Glyn's voice, which upset George.

His search for perfection started with auditions. Often he auditioned well over 1200 singers to find the sixteen or so that he was happy to add to a production. For the successful auditionees, it must have been like winning the *X Factor*. But the real work started once a singer was accepted. Rehearsals were hard work. Certainly, Dot recalls that George showed no mercy to singers then: 'He'd say "I wrote a 'G'. Didn't I write a 'G'? What did I hear?" ' George was aware of the choir's reactions: 'The boys have set phrases to suit most situations including the rehearsal "death look" which I apparently bestow freely for bad intonation or carelessly placed consonants.' Dot remembers, 'If the choir went too far, he'd break the baton and throw it down, and it would go dead quiet. We realised he was disappointed with us, so this made us feel worse. He'd walk out and listen to the recording. We'd feel so small, we didn't want to let anyone down. He'd raise his voice but never shouted.' Later Minstrel principal Jeff Hudson recalls, 'He'd say to singers, "I'm not a singer, but I'd like to suggest you can maybe improve on this." ' Tenor Ted Darling remembers rehearsals: 'I never really saw him panic. He was very laid back. The only time he'd get angry was with his glasses. He'd play piano for rehearsals and had problems with his glasses on more than one occasion.' Howard Neil recalls, 'George was first and foremost a musician and a Ladies man. He was easy to work with, being so quiet. He was also a good conductor even when we were miming!'

Despite Howard's comments, the girls came out of it worse than the boys. Charles Chilton recalls, 'George worked the choir hard, often reducing the women to tears. But he was a great perfectionist, and the choir admired him.' Maryetta Midgley remembered, 'He got exasperated with us for chatting. I never saw him being unfair, but while the boys could do no wrong, the girls were a bit silly in his eyes. He'd bang the keyboard, "Can I have peace? We have to get this done." He'd blow up, get a reaction.

Minstrel Magic

When Margaret Savage was pregnant, she was being sick, and George said, "Come on, we're waiting for you." This was hard, but he was probably right. He was fully professional, conscious of time. It was amazing how we produced such quality with such little rehearsal time.' Carl Ewer remembers George often reduced the girls to tears, though Ann Mann, singer and later producer, recalls, 'He never reduced me to tears. I had the producer mentality, I was tough. It was only because he was a perfectionist and professional. The rate we worked, an incredible turnaround, you had to get it first time or at worst second. I still miss him.' George certainly couldn't have been happy the day Dai Francis took twenty seven takes to get a song right. John Boulter recalls George hitting his forehead saying, 'This must be a world record!!'

And it wasn't just the sound that required perfection. Press reviews of early stage shows frequently comment that 'George Mitchell kept his singers perfectly in time and that is difficult when they are moving around the stage to dance movements or changing partners'. Television shows were subjected to the same attention to detail: 'Infinite care appears to have been taken with the grouping of choir and soloists, and the timing of each number, so that a satisfying effect of precision, pace and ultimately perfection was achieved.'

Such passion for perfection meant George was rarely pleased. He took an almost masochistic delight in this striving: 'If something is adrift, I criticise and subsequently alter it. I also keep videotapes of the television shows and play the worst bits to annoy myself. I will never lower my standards. If I ever think my work is not done to the best of my capacities, I will stop and never write another note.' Each performance would be followed by George explaining to the singers what they could have done better. After the first *Glee Club* show, he recalled, 'It's a stock joke (but taken seriously) with the choir that I'm never satisfied. When each show ends, I'm usually full of gloom, anxious to tell the kids how terrible it was! I am a perfectionist. So immediately the studio lights were doused and the cameras switched off, I began tearing a strip off the singers as usual, "doing my act", as the kids call it, showing them where we'd have to do it better next time, or else. At that moment, somebody handed me a telegram. I tore open the envelope and read, "Good luck for tonight. You'll need it. (Signed) us." I looked around at the Glee Club, all trying desperately not to smile, despite the wigging I'd been giving them. That telegram was a wonderful gesture of loyalty. And beautifully timed. A pity it wasn't on TV!'

Singer Mike Rogers remembers, 'He never said, "Well done" or "Yes, that was great", so we never knew if he was pleased with our efforts. But a few years ago he sent me a repeat cheque and a little note to thank me for all my hard work – that meant so much to me. I'm sure he always appreciated our input, but shyness perhaps held him back.' But Carl Ewer remembers one public acknowledgement: 'When we had to sing a song in German once, everyone had trouble remembering the words, but I'd done German and found it all right. Afterwards, George said, "I knew I could count on Carl to remember the German." It made me realise he did appreciate me after all.'

Later Minstrel production manager Sandy Macfarlane recalls, 'George was never really happy with any show - there was always something that he would pick on (the nature, I suppose, of a perfectionist). At the end of the opening show of my first [Minstrel] season, I said to him, "Everything all right?" "Well," he said, "There were a couple of things here and there." The next year I said, "How was it this year, George?" "Well, you see, the band did this, and there's something else...." He always managed to find something to niggle about. In my third year, in Scarborough, I warned everybody the show was to go through without a single fault – or else!! And so it did. I went to George at the end and said, "How was that then, George?" He paused a moment then said, "Err!!....Errrr!! .....Errrrr!!!.. Ah yes, there were some jingles missing from two finale tambourines. Get a new set!!!" I looked at him quizzically, and then he added, "Well, I have to complain about something, don't I??!" A new set of tambourines was duly ordered - Luffy nearly fell off his wallet, and George and I retired swiftly to the bar.' Carl Ewer, however, recalls that perfection wasn't always achieved: 'One of George's best expressions was, "It'll be all right with the picture." He'd use this when perhaps the sound wasn't quite as good as it would have been for radio when all you hear is the sound, but on TV you had the picture as well so if the sound wasn't quite up to radio standards, George would use this expression.'

This passion for perfection extended to the slightest detail. Singer Maggi Lawler recalled, 'He was passionate about the look of everything. It all had to match. I turned blonde once, and he went mad; I had to go back to my natural black very quickly.' Carl Ewer also fell foul of the Mitchell eye for detail: 'I grew a moustache, and George said it looked like a dirty mark on the screen, so I shaved it off.' Alan Hollidge remembered, 'It always amazed me he could hear me come in a fraction of a second behind the other basses – but he taught me a great deal about choral singing.'

A huge part of the later success of the Minstrels was down to this search for perfection. The precision and uniformity obviously satisfied some deep subliminal yearning in audiences for order, even if that order was not apparent. George spent much of the dress rehearsals in the control room, checking that everyone who came into camera shot knew the words they were miming to. If they didn't, the shot was changed. The movements had to be very precise too - arms could be moved so far and no further, for instance. Even the Toppers' hair came under intense scrutiny. Half were blonde and half brunette and the dance sequences were arranged so that these alternated in the line-up. Heaven help everyone if a Topper fell ill and the symmetry was disrupted. A much later letter to the *Radio Times* said how delighted the writer had been to realise that the semaphore in the programme actually spelt out MINSTRELS, a tribute to the depths the search for perfection went.

Of course, the pre-recorded sound that was used for the major Mitchell shows gave George complete control over a programme. It must have been a huge weight off his mind once the sound was safely - and perfectly - recorded. But perfectionists are never happy and usually end up with mannerisms to control their fate. Harry Currie remembers 'a very ordinary human being who was in the right place at the right time, but he had his insecurities and his faults'. Others remembered he would 'tug at his ear when concentrating, stub the end of his cigarette with his thumb, bang his forehead with the palm of his hand when worried, rub his signet ring on his jacket to bring him luck before an important premiere.'

But equally the perfection guaranteed by pre-recorded sound and the subsequent miming, both on television and on stage, proved to be the undoing for some people such as the *Evening Chronicle* reviewer who wrote, 'It is almost too perfect to mean much. Everyone is almost too precise and accurate to appear human - and this lack of atmosphere is not helped by the obviously reinforced singing on tape.' The *Oldham Evening Chronicle* agreed that 'everything seems automatic enough to be a film, and one wonders where the talent lies to warrant such approval when a team mimes to music. Is it in the original singing, or the perfect synchronisation, or the efficient movement?' Towards the end of the Minstrels' career on stage, one first-night reviewer wrote 'shows that get into the *Guinness Book of Records* and last twenty glorious years must still torment their innovators when all the garlands have been hung. The show opened to offer in sound and vision a perfect image once more of its immaculate colour-telly profile - marvellous costume, polished and imaginative décor, easy movement, pleasant voices. All received with acclamation and in many ways deservedly so. That strange alchemy produced by nostalgia and martial precision had worked yet again. So why the torment? [George underlined these four words and added question marks!] By refusing to take any risks with a safe formula, the impresarios have handed over the initiative to the paying customers. And as the show moves into its third decade, can the Minstrels be sure they are appealing to as large and wide an audience as during the first ten years or even the second? [at this point, George wrote 'YES!!'] What can you do with perfection when the audience begins to get restless, or when it becomes harder to find the artistes who can and want to produce it?'

A very complex and private man, George hated the limelight, though the early years with the choir didn't seem so problematic as he often appeared on stage with the singers. The BBC even managed to get him in front of cameras and mikes occasionally with frequent appearances in programmes such as *In Town Tonight* and *These Radio Times* in the late 1940s and early 1950s.

They achieved a real coup in 1962 when he became the castaway on *Desert Island Discs*. It needed quite a few retakes as time after time, perfectionist George wasn't happy with his responses and asked to do it again but throughout, he came over as very diffident and genuine. Asked if he'd be any good on a desert island, he said, 'I don't think I could stand up to it at all. I like to have hordes of people around me, I usually have. I would undoubtedly be terrible. I doubt I could build a shelter. I'm pretty useless when it comes to things like that. I'd have to bank on being rescued.' He chose his records on the basis of those he could stand to hear over and over again, though he admitted the decision had been very difficult as he had about two thousand albums to choose from.

Minstrel Magic

His first record was from Ravel's *Daphne and Chloe Suite No 2*, which George said was beautifully scored. His second choice was Richard Strauss' *Don Juan*, conducted by Toscanini, which took him back to pre-war concerts at the Queen's Hall, which he'd attended night after night. Other choices included Chopin's *Scherzo in C Sharp Minor*, which George laughed that he'd decided was impossible to play, Schumann's *Wanderlied*, *Fugue in G Minor* by Bach and the closing scene from *Die Gotterdammerung* by his favourite composer, Wagner, though the BBC accidentally played *Siegfried's Rhine Journey* by mistake. The selection was completed by two of his own records, firstly *Wimoweh* with John Boulter from the *Around The World In Song* album, and secondly *Side by Side* by the Minstrels, which he felt typified the Minstrel show: 'They really let fly on this, and they really enjoyed doing this, and it's pretty obvious, I think, when you hear it, you'll agree with me.' The track he chose as his favourite was Wagner, his luxury was a 'great heap of manuscript paper and a few pencils' and his book the score of *The Ring*, 'if anyone could carry it'. During the show, he said he'd like to have the world's best choir. Lots of listeners wrote in saying he already had it!

This Is Your Life wasn't to be so lucky. In 1982 George was quite happy to appear, together with wife Dot and a troupe of current Minstrels, in the *This Is Your Life* tribute to Stan Stennett. But woe betide the production company that tried to get George onto his own *This Is Your Life*. They tried twice. Wife Irene blocked the first one, and when daughter Alison told her father about the second attempt, he rang the programme makers up and threatened legal action. One later feature commented that George's reticence was legendary: 'He even managed to dodge appearing on *This Is Your Life* twice!! "After dining with various famous stars, I realised that forty or fifty pairs of eyes were watching every movement, hoping that my guest would scratch his or her nose, dribble the soup or do a tap dance on the table. For this reason, I never employed a personal publicity agent, managed to escape *This Is Your Life,* avoided interviews and guest spots."'

Singer Howard Neil remembers, 'I always thought he was quite shy around us singers and dancers. Give him a set of session singers in a recording studio, and he was in his element.' He hated appearing in front of the cameras even more: 'When I'm conducting the choir, I'm fine, I'm completely relaxed. But when I have to go in front of those cameras to make the announcements,

Minstrel Magic

I'm terribly nervous. Don't ask me why. I've only been doing it for thirty years! I'm no good as a star. I just have not got what it takes to appear before the cameras and be a personality. I feel I have nothing to offer TV either in voice or looks. If I felt more frequent appearances would be of value to my choirs, I would make them like a shot. I'm not a particularly glamorous character, and besides, I don't think people care a tinker's cuss who runs the choir as long as the voices sound right.'

But George Inns was determined to get him on camera, if only during the Minstrels' conducted sequence where he soon became known as 'the most famous back in television'. But even this proved difficult. Singer Mike Rogers remembers the agonies George went through: 'The part he most hated was the finale when he conducted the Minstrels with his back to the camera but then had to face Camera 1 and take a bow. George Inns really had to work hard to get him to agree to this form of recognition.' A later director tried what he thought would be the simplest of all movements for a musician. Principal Roger Green remembers, 'Once, the director asked George to walk to his position on stage in tempo to the song's musical introduction while clicking his fingers at the same time. George was one of the most talented musicians of his time but could he co-ordinate his finger-clicking with walking in tempo to the music? The answer was a definite No! After several attempts, the director conceded defeat and George took up his usual position in front of the choir before the cameras rolled.' Nevertheless, he occasionally got brave enough to appear as a stooge to comedian Don Maclean, who spent years compèring the show: 'He didn't like the TV camera, and was incredibly modest.' Oddly Don went on to say, 'I used to do gags about him – he liked it if he was made fun of.' Odd for such a shy man to enjoy being joked about.

Typical of a shy person, George found it difficult to express gratitude face to face. Head cameraman on the Minstrel shows, Eddie Stewart, remembers well, 'He was a very shy man, a very honourable man, but always very friendly, chatting to all of us and the sound boys. He recognised all the boys on the crew. At the end of one series, just before we went on air, I looked in my viewfinder and couldn't see anything at all. Then I realised there was something in the camera. I put my hand in and pulled out a great wad of fivers, plus a note, "Ed, give this to your crew." He did this every year to sound and camera crews. He wouldn't give it face to face because he was afraid of being embarrassed.'

George also treated his singers at the end of a series. Mike Rogers recalls, 'On these social occasions, he was always the first to buy the drinks, but then was quickly on his way so one never really got the opportunity to speak at length.' However, George was well known for only ever carrying a £5 or £10 note and at one such party, Ted Darling recollects, 'He said, "Could you lend me £10? I'd like to buy everyone a drink." He never paid me back.'

Stars who occasionally worked with George also recognised this shyness. Max Bygraves said, 'George was so shy, embarrassingly so, but a nice solid friend, nonetheless. He quietly suggested I should sing more – something I hadn't figured on in those days. I took his advice, and today I owe several million record sales to his advice.'

Though George always tried to get out of other people's parties, he enjoyed being in control of his own. Mary Moss recalls, 'The office was the venue for the occasional party - although George was essentially a shy man, he enjoyed giving a party for his core singers at Christmas.' Maggi Lawler was also present at these parties: 'He adored red wine and produced the most magnificent red wines, but none of us could appreciate them. We'd club together and buy him cigars.' But his favourite drink was good whisky. Dot again: 'He loved single malts – Glenmorangie, Glenfiddich, Glenlivit – but wouldn't touch Irish or American whiskies.' Keith Leggett remembers whisky in the office: 'Every Friday before we left work, we gathered in the main office for a drink. George always had his beloved Scottish best whisky and Daphne and I would have a decent drop of sherry. George always asked me to have a Scotch, and I always refused. One day I said, "OK, George, I'll have one with a drop of coke." The Beatles had made this popular. "You bloody won't," said George, "You're not spoiling my decent Scotch with coke." So I never did get my drop of whisky with George.' Reg Bracken, a friend in later life, recalls, 'One of the last times I saw George was when Linda [Reg's daughter] and her husband drove me to Albrighton and wasn't I glad to have a chauffeur. As always George poured a very good measure of whisky.'

This loyalty and admiration extended beyond the choir. Ted Darling states that 'the band loved working for him too. The orchestra gradually increased over the years, from one trumpet and one trombone to three of each, or a full brass section. George loved that. He had a great respect for the band. If you respect someone's talent, you get it back. They all loved working for George. Musicians are a tough bunch – they'd say in other places that they enjoyed working for him. There was no hassle, no shouting.' Choreographer Douggie Squires too was full of admiration: 'George Mitchell and George Inns were a great team to work with and those Mitchell days are treasured ones. George was always there with his cool demeanour - the elegant pencil thin moustache and his sense of humour. When I had my own dance and song groups later, the Young Generation and Second Generation, I realised how much I had learnt from the Mitchell Organisation and the gang - about working as a team and his ability to choose the right people to make a good mix vocally as well as personality wise.'

George had a great talent for making and retaining friends. Even those who worked for him viewed it as a great time in their lives. Principal John Boulter called George 'lovely', a sentiment echoed by many others. Keith Leggett, who worked more closely than most with George, reports, 'Working with George was wonderful – a lovely man and a fantastic boss. Daphne (Bell), George and I were a real team, and I had so much respect for him as a person and an employer.' Daphne agrees: 'George was charismatic, great fun with a good sense of humour.' Unsurprisingly George and Daphne remained lifelong friends. She recalls, 'He was a good friend and got on well with my husband, Tom. George was asked who he'd like to be on a desert island with. He said "Tom", because he was capable enough to get them off the island. George wasn't practical. What an amazing and wonderful time we had. It wasn't work, it was a very enjoyable life. I look upon all old friends as family.' Singer and producer Ann Mann and her husband, famous pianist Brooks Aehron whom she met through the Minstrels, remained friends with George for years, often going to his house for dinner: 'George was a knowledgeable, clever, likeable, sociable, funny man who gave people an enormous amount of pleasure and created brilliant shows. We had wonderful arguments about Andrew Lloyd Webber. George thought he copied everything and could quote passages in Schumann which Lloyd Webber had copied. We disagreed gracefully.' Later singers such as Roy Winbow saw a similar man: 'George was quiet, not an extrovert; he never had an ego that needed constant feeding, not like the rest of us vagabonds and gipsies. Occasionally we'd see bits that showed you he was extremely talented, intelligent, witty and a bit of a nut like the rest of us.'

Some friendships went on long after the choir had disbanded. Principal Margaret Savage recalls, 'To me, George was just great to work for. Over the years my family increased, and all the time I would have to tell my lovely boss, 'Eh George I don't think I will be able to do all of the next series". George would reply, "Oh naw Haggis no another yin! Well, hen, when you're ready, gee us a call," he'd say. He was very understanding. George and Dot were very kind and invited us (and now four children!) over to their fabulous house in Kissimmee in Florida, picking us up at the airport and treating us like royalty. The children had the best time ever with Disney visits all arranged, they couldn't have spoilt us more. The next time we went was at Christmas, and on New Year's Eve, they had a party for all their friends. We had a great Hogmanay party. I tell you the Glenfiddich was flowing that night and between Dot and myself, the Highland fling and the Gay Gordons were given fair belting. We won't forget those holidays or their kindness. I like to think of George as a good friend, he is missed very much. He gave me many opportunities to express myself in song, grow in confidence, make so many friends, and have the best job anyone could have for all those years from 1962 – 1978. I consider myself very very lucky to have had a job which I was paid for and enjoyed so very much.'

George would do everything he could to support his friends. Much later in 1979, he was glad to lend his support to a new project of Minstrel producer Ernest Maxin's. On May 14, a week of sold-out previews opened at the Royalty Theatre in London for *Barnardo*, which had been written and directed by Ernest. Princess Margaret, as well as George and Dot, attended the Royal Gala Charity performance on May 21, with all the proceeds going to Barnardo's, as well as a percentage of all tickets sold throughout the run. George's singers featured in the show and also on an EP of four songs issued from the show, but sadly Barnardo's was not to get rich from the profits. After dire reviews - the *Financial Times* called it 'a naïve, sentimental, uncomplicated tale with the characters asked to do no more than speak simple dialogue and sing a song if necessary' - the show closed after forty-three performances. Dot recalls, 'There wasn't enough backing. George never thought it would get off the ground - he didn't put any

Minstrel Magic

money into it, he wasn't a backer - but he did it for friendship. He did the best he could, but it was just not on.'

His wit stayed in many people's memories. 'He is a typical Celt,' according to Irene Thomas, 'one moment thumping his forehead in despair and a few minutes later reducing us all to helpless laughter. The quality I found most endearing was his wit. Not a mere sense of humour but real wit, spontaneous, wry and lugubrious, capable of deflating pomposity and yet kindly enough not to hurt sensitive people. To three tenors, none of whom would admit to singing a wrong note, he'd say, "Whoever it is, nudge him - he'll be sitting next to all three of you!" Very often we had to rehearse in small rooms full of upturned tables and piles of chairs, with no piano. On those occasions, we relied on Phyllis Whitaker. Phyl had perfect pitch and could hum any note asked for with complete accuracy. A typical Mitchell exchange in an upstairs rehearsal room would be:

George: "Oh hell, no piano...give us an A, somebody."

Dai Francis: "Fa...there y'are, George. I know it's right, I brought it all the way up from the piano downstairs."

George (not to be outdone): "Somebody must have trodden on it on the way up, then." '

This humour didn't disappear. Sandy Macfarlane, later production manager, recalls, 'One Sunday morning, while listening to the Desmond Carrington show on Radio 2, after he'd played a Minstrel Medley, he said, "That was, of course, the Black and White Minstrels conducted as always by the 'late' George Mitchell." I thought this quite funny and told Bob Luff, who thought it hilarious and immediately phoned George. "Did you know you've done so little work recently for the BBC that they think you're dead!!" To which George said, "It doesn't say much for my agent either!!" Silence from Luffy and, as they say, "Curtains".'

But George did enjoy some of the trappings of fame, attending dinners such as the one at the Grocers' Hall in 1961 to celebrate the 25th anniversary of the BBC and also attending dinners at the Mansion House. As he later explained, 'It was a great honour to be Lord Mayor of London for a year, and he was expected to provide the famous with a dinner for which the centuries-old gold plate was everywhere. I was amazed to find I had to join a small table for the ARTS! I had a real nightmare with Rudolf Nureyev, the gay ballet dancer, who spoke no English and Yehudi Menuhin who thought I reeked of the popular music I'd arranged. I spoke to the old boy who arranged this event every year, and at the next dinner, I got Sir Bernard Lovell of Jodrell Bank – a space investigator into the stars. A real charmer, as was the poet (can't remember his name) and the owner of our biggest bookstores Foyles.' Years later, Christina Foyle invited George to speak at one of the famous Foyles' literary lunches. Probably much to his own surprise, he accepted and gave a well-received speech recounting the growth of the choir, even though some of it repeated the fallacies about its beginnings which by now had become accepted fact.

Where George and agent Bob Luff really differed was where money was concerned. Rumours abound of huge rifts between them, mainly over money. Whereas George would run what he saw as necessary extra rehearsals for which he wouldn't get paid, even though he would have to pay the singers, Bob even rationed the water in the showers in Scarborough when he owned the Futurist Theatre. Often in the early years, money was tight. BBC rates were low, and even after the singers joined Equity, matters didn't improve much. George's singers were never well-paid, but this was largely Bob's doing. Dot recalls, 'George always wanted to pay over the odds, but he had nothing to do with the actual salaries, except for the principals. The BBC paid the television show cast, and Bob paid them for the stage shows but George fought time and time again with Bob for his principals to get good rates.' By the late 1950s, one unnamed newspaper reported, 'His singers, he claims, are the highest paid of their kind. Rarely do they earn less than £18 weekly (£275); often they earn £40 (£600).' The Daily Herald asked George if the choir brought in the more mundane pound notes: 'He replied, "I've a turnover of £100,000 a year (£1.5m)."'

In the early days, George operated a two-tier system; the permanently salaried inner core had fixed incomes no matter how much work they did, whereas the other singers were paid on a 'job' basis and paid their own self-employed stamp. At some stage, George decided he had to make his salaried group also self-employed. This meant they had to pay the higher NI rate which, says Frank Davies, 'didn't go down well but they were now free to choose other work which of course they couldn't as they hadn't built up any contacts'. Maryetta Midgley remembers the day it all changed, and typically she stood up for herself: 'Daphne said George was changing things and gave out the cards. Everyone was floored, thinking they'd been given the push. I didn't get mine. Six months later, I was given a crumpled card without stamps, so I told them to put stamps on it. Daphne said George wouldn't do that. I got nasty, and George paid in the end. After that, we all paid our own stamps.'

Nobody stayed for the money. Everyone agreed the pay wasn't the best, but working in such an organisation was compensation enough for most singers. If they didn't like it, they didn't stay. People wanted to join because it offered regular guaranteed work and most Minstrels saw being part of the show as the highlight of their career. It certainly opened doors to other career moves as producers knew hiring ex-Mitchell Singers meant they were getting well-trained talented professionals. His regular singers were paid regardless of illness, which was highly unusual in show business. From the totals that were paid per show in the mid-1950s, George seems to have retained anything from £15 (£260) to £27 (£470) for himself, with Bob taking somewhere between 4% and 5%. The amount singers received varied enormously between radio and television. Television fees for BBC appearances stayed static at around 13 guineas (£435) per singer, whereas radio paid more in the region of £2/12/6 (£47) at the start of one year, rising to about £5/15/0 (£100) by December.

However, low pay became a regular bone of contention, even though there were other reasons for staying with George. Maggi Lawlor reported that, in 1953, 'the pay was very poor – I received £11 a week (£191) in Blackpool and couldn't live on it.' Not much had altered by 1961 when Kay Matthews said, 'the pay was appalling. The girls were paid less than the boys, even though we did the first and second parts of the shows and the boys only did the second half.' In the hot summer of 1976 Head Minstrel Roy Winbow recalls, 'I had a huge argument with Bob Luff when I asked for another £5 (£50) per week for the singers. Some were existing on baked beans.' Bob told Roy it was none of his business, to which Roy retorted, "Yes, it is if they can't perform properly." They were falling like flies because of the heat and lack of nourishment.'

Harry Currie, who had major problems with George throughout his time in the Mitchell Organisation, recalls problems with salaries when the Minstrels were at the Victoria Palace: 'Bob and George were pretty cagey about salaries. Tony, Dai and John were unhappy about what they were getting for the Victoria Palace –

much less than any other leads in a West End musical - so they decided to try getting what they considered fair payment for what promised to be a hit show. They were foiled. Knowing the weakest link was John with four or five kids, they talked to him first, playing on his need to care for his family, and got him to settle for far less. Then they called Tony and Dai in and said, "We can't give you more than John, it wouldn't be fair," so they were all foiled.' In fairness to George, John doesn't recall this at all. Dot Mitchell recalls, 'They weren't paid star wages because they were not stars – the stars were everyone together and the show.'

CHAPTER 6

Perfectly arranged music, wonderful singers but the Mitchell empire's greatest strength was the incredible loyalty George himself inspired. The *Weekly Sporting Review* said, 'This man is unique. Come backstage, and you'll see what I mean. The kids in the choir worship him. If he's sick, they work ten times harder. "We're a family party," said George, "a working outfit. It's team spirit which speeded our success. The choir learn a ballad in a sixth of the time they should have for it. Anything short of impossible, the choir will do." As another newspaper reported, 'The discipline among his choirs off stage is relaxed and friendly. He achieves order without force. He maintains control of his colony of singing birds by commanding their respect and regard.'

It all started with choosing the right people, not just those who could produce the Mitchell sound but those who were capable of fitting in with the Mitchell family; if they didn't, they were soon out of a job. Minstrel Howard Neil recalled, 'George had a real gift for choosing the right people to employ.' Principal John Boulter agrees: 'George had an eye for people. Everybody he found was marvellous.' Principal Ted Darling admires George's talent for getting the best out of singers: 'George could put his finger on what suited them best. He knew Margaret Savage was a fun person. She could play a drunk or serious stuff. He just knew what would work. Tony Mercer - he recognised he sounded like Crosby. George didn't ask him to do anything other than sing, he just stood there. George couldn't have chosen three more contrasting principals, he hit the nail on the head. It was right from the word go. You have to admire that.'

What kept them there was the family feel to the choir. George said, 'Nobody has a contract – I don't want to keep people if they don't want to stay. We're more like a club, we're all close friends, but we're highly professional.' Of course, there were contracts for seasonal work - George couldn't risk losing one of a quartet or sextet in a seaside summer show half way through a season - but even if they did go, he could replace them easily and very quickly.

Irene Thomas remembered, 'The Mitchells were like a family unit, all types and ages and temperaments. We made up an organisation which had its own way of working, its own catch-phrases (anything slightly inaccurate or out of tune would be "Near enough for jazz" or "Very adjacent") and its own jokes.'

The choir was effectively one big happy family, particularly in the early days when it was so much smaller. Then they spent nearly the entire time together, travelling to and from recordings or in the rickety old bus taking them to concerts. Even when this broke down occasionally, as it did once on their way to a Sunday concert in Margate, everyone carried what they could and hitched lifts to the concert.

The family dynamic was enhanced by the amount of fun everyone managed to have, however unlikely the setting. George recalled, 'One tenor kept snakes as pets. Occasionally he brought one to rehearsals or into the dressing rooms and drove everyone crazy. But one night at the Palladium, the gang got their own back. The boys were lined up ready to go on stage for a four-minute production number. With perfect timing a brick was passed, hand to hand, from the back of the line. It reached the snake charmer as he was stepping onto the stage – too late for him to get rid of it. All through the complicated singing and dancing routines, which included a hand-clapping number, he held the brick in front of a packed audience and tried to pretend it wasn't there. no one in the audience seemed to notice that when the hand-clapping started, the tenor was making no noise. He was still wondering how to dispose of a nine-inch brick in the middle of a giant floodlit London stage.'

The touring Glee Club also had its share of practical jokers. Soprano Mae Craig had a weakness for jukeboxes. Everywhere they went, she tracked one down, and before the coffees were served, the more sensitive choristers were plugging their ears with their fingers. Then one day Mae arrived at a café and found the juke-box bearing an 'out of order' sign. It was the same when they moved on to yet another town. In fact, Mae found it impossible to locate a working jukebox. She didn't realise one of her companions was making sure he reached every café first with an *Out of Order* placard.

Not all jokes went down well as singer Frank Davies recalls: 'Our bass/baritone solos were sung by Alan Young, also our touring manager and known to us by his real name Sid. His final solo was Mussorgsky's *Song of the Flea*, and the final words are "With quick dispatch", and of course the flea is, as the Goons would say, deaded. I spotted a flit gun which the Stage Manager used for unwelcome insects that might interfere with the show. I asked if I could borrow it to use when Sid sang these final words. The Stage Manager cottoned on to the funny side and said not only could I use the flit gun, but he would order the spotlight to pick me and the gun up precisely as the gun's spray hit the imaginary flea and deaded it. It worked perfectly and got a huge laugh and enormous applause for Sid's rendition. A far greater response than he'd ever received before. But he was furious with me. Of course, it never was repeated, and he never again received that kind of applause. George loved it since he always enjoyed a bit of fun.'

At one concert in the Rhondda, one joke happened so fast it's doubtful if the audience noticed. George recalled, 'When we finally started five minutes late, several choir members were distinctly merry. Occasionally high spirits get the better of discretion. The forty singers stood in tens on rostra. Halfway through the second half, I was whacking away in front when the ten lads on the back rostrum started what we call a 'shuffle'. The end men just shuffle slightly towards the middle. The chaps next to them get a nudge and move inwards too. Gradually, slowly but surely, the men moved in towards the middle. Suddenly there was a dull thud – and only nine blokes were left. The centre chap had been squeezed out. It was done so quickly that, although I was facing them, I didn't notice him fall. He'd popped out of the line like a cork from a bottle. I never discovered whether anyone else had seen the tenor do a disappearing act.' Choir captains rarely clamped down on such practical jokery, seeing it as a contribution towards the 'let's-enjoy-life-while-we're-singing' atmosphere which pervaded all of George's groups.

Nicknames added to the fun. Principal Ted Darling recalls one works dinner and concert in Holland: 'There was a printed programme for it, with funny references to everyone. Mine was "Dancing and Screaming Lord Ted and his Mozart Chamber Four Comrades (a short break may be called at any time during Lord Ted's performances)". This was because Douggie Squires had kept changing the routines and I objected and asked him to stick to one routine.' Other singers had funny references too. Bob Hunter's was 'Big Ed Hunter – you can bring Pearl, she's a darn nice girl', and soprano Maryetta's was 'Naughty Maryetta, Walter, Walter, let me sing contralto', [a reference to Maryetta's famous father]. Maryetta had been called 'Right again' when she first joined. She recalls, 'Sometimes I'd come in, and it sounded wrong, but it always turned out I was right. For instance, I'd come in after 15 bars rest which was what was written, but it should have been written with 16 bars rest.' Glyn Dawson was widely called 'Landed', one of his pet words. Guests weren't exempt either. A later Minstrel show featured 16-year-old Michele Summers, making her show business debut. The team dubbed her 'One-take Charlie' as she only needed twenty minutes to record her two Deanna Durbin songs.

The stars they worked with also got caught up in the singers' high jinks, enjoying working with such a nice bunch of people. As well-known singer Bruce Trent, appearing in *Variety Playhouse* early in 1954, said, 'Anything I could say to praise their work would only be repeating what has already been said. But I would like to mention the other sort of support they gave me. Not vocal. Moral. I've been with them dozens of times on the air, and as soon as you walk into the studio and hear their "Hello's" and "Hiya's" and see their friendly smiles, you feel at ease and think, well, someone's on my side anyway.' On tour at one point, American pop sensation Guy Mitchell conducted the choir, using a bowler hat and an umbrella. But they got their own back. The *New Musical Express* reported, 'Guy Mitchell proved his eminence as a trouper by ad-libbing the second chorus of *Chickaboom* and then blaming his absent-mindedness on the George Mitchell Singers whom, he claimed, were "making faces at me". ' The *West Lancashire Evening Gazette* reported, '(Blackpool's) North Pier singer Frankie Vaughan was put out of his stride at a *Blackpool Night* rehearsal this week. The George Mitchell Singers, waiting to rehearse themselves, gave him the full swoon and scream treatment. And Frankie could hardly sing for laughing.'

The singers had their favourites. Irene Thomas recollected, 'We almost fought to be allowed to take part [in Harry Secombe's shows], our affection overcoming the knowledge that Harry is almost impossible to work with because his fellow artistes are in a state of near-hysteria all the time, such is his inexhaustible fund of goonery.' The singers also liked working with Ruby Murray. Irene Thomas remembered a series of programmes with her with the dancers under the direction of George Carden, 'much respected for a very good reason. He was the most severe disciplinarian I've ever encountered, and his dancers were superb as a result. He was an excellent choreographer where singers were concerned too. He realised that singers have words and notes to remember, must see the conductor somehow all the time, and must not be out of breath just before they are due to sing sixty four bars fortissimo.' But it wasn't always fun. Irene Thomas recalled one Dave King broadcast: 'Dave King was remembered for the weird situations we found ourselves in…why on earth was I, at one point, hiding under a shop counter with two huge malodorous Old English sheepdogs?'

The choir loved George and working for him. Most agree he genuinely cared for his singers as well as the work they produced and often went beyond what he needed to do, to support them. Keith Leggett, with George for years as a singer before moving into the office, recalls, 'He was very loyal to his singers who were always very proud to be one of his singers.' Similarly Ted Darling says, 'Everybody got a great buzz out of working with George. He did no ranting and raving, never raised his voice to anyone.' Irene Thomas summed it up: 'I really loved working for him. I don't think luck had much to do with George's success, it was due to a combination of outstanding talent and sheer hard work, allied to a charming and persuasive manner that kept us working for him when we could probably have made more money elsewhere. Working for most choirmasters after working for George was like drinking Coke after vintage champagne.' Maryetta Midgley strongly agrees: 'I loved him to bits, I would have crossed fire and water for him. Everybody wanted to be loyal to him.'

Much of this loyalty was inspired by George going that extra mile. Glyn Dawson recalls, 'I found George very good. When recording as a soloist, he'd give encouragement, as did Daphne. He was genuine, a caring man, a business man but friendly. He and Daphne Bell thanked me personally after several touring show performances.' Mary Moss remembers, 'Whatever you did, you always felt looked after, safe.' Maryetta feels the same: 'He was a gentleman with a capital G. Everybody he worked with was a perfect gentleman or lady; there were no dark horses, everyone was lovely. He sent me to Max Factor in Bond Street to learn how to do makeup.' Soloist Delia Wicks recalls an occasion which also shows the lengths choir members would go to for George: 'One morning we were recording at Lansdowne but woke to deep snow. I walked to the studios, and when I got there I was so afraid I was late, but only George and a few musicians were there. He said, "Don't worry, you look in a state. Go and get a stiff Scotch."'

Years later in 1972, George made repeated efforts to trace former members of his choir, to split a royalty cheque with them for a 1949 show which had recently been repeated. And the support went further than the singers. Ventriloquist Ken Wood who joined the second Australian Minstrel tour in 1968 as a speciality act remembered a particular kindness: 'I stumbled out of the lights after my first spot and there was George who said, "You gave us a lift just when we needed it." And of course, the Minstrels never needed a lift.'

George's help sometimes came too late, as it did for Minstrel Michael Rowlett who recalls, 'I turned up to film an (unauthorised) Colgate ad in Kensington and was promptly whisked off to Bognor! The assistant cameraman left the film too near the water, and it was swept off to sea, and by 4pm we eventually got started. PANIC! I've got to be at the theatre by 5.45 – no chance. Phone call to agent – agent phones theatre – Michael at dentist. Dirty deed done! The following evening I arrived at the theatre to be summoned to Ossie's [Whitaker] office where he brandished an anonymous note saying, 'Michael not at dentist but shooting a commercial.' Instant dismissal!!' However, in a move which shows his caring nature, George phoned Michael the next morning, asking, 'Why didn't you phone me? I would have squared it.'

Parents trusted their daughters to George. A later Television Topper remembers, 'I was asked to choose between the touring (Minstrel) company or the London company. I was still at convent school and had to get permission from the nuns and my mother, and she said "Yes" to London.' Mitchell Maid Helen Stewart remembers joining: 'I'll always have wonderful memories of my time with [the Minstrels], in particular, company manager Sandy McFarlane who was my protector. I was away from home for the first time at the tender age of 18!! And he ensured that I was safe.'

George worked the singers hard but looked after them well. In later years when the Minstrels were safely established in the Victoria Palace, physiotherapist Alf Tasker was permanently based in a room under the stage, treating stresses and strains. 'I get someone to treat nearly every night,' he said. 'It's a fast show, and a girl can twist a knee or even crack a rib by turning sharply. I think in my time I must have given about 40,000 treatments and only had to send a dozen to hospital because I couldn't cope.' Maryetta Midgley was taken ill while they were working in Amsterdam: 'I remember being unwell half way through the series, and George arranged for me to go to hospital in the UK.' And her story of George's generosity: 'He used to help people financially. Moira Butt hurt her head and couldn't do a TV show. I stood in, and he paid both of us.' But he was still the boss. Maryetta remembers she had just started working for him, when, in one show, 'Mary Brown and I each sat on a boy's lap, sang two lines, then went off set and changed. This was live TV, but I couldn't work out what I was meant to do next. Then to my horror, I saw Mary and the two boys. I was petrified. I got through the rest of the show and went to the dressing room where one of the girls said, "George wants to see you." When he asked me what had happened, I just burst into tears. He didn't know what to do with tears, so he just said, "That's all right. I just thought you might have been knocked on the head by the boom," and shuffled off.'

By 1951 George was working an eighteen-hour day, and something had to give. In his case, it was family life. Still asleep when the children - Alison and Robert - went to school in the morning, he was out at work when they arrived home in the evening. Often he'd not get home till 2am, long after the children - and probably Irene - were in bed. Son Robert recalls, 'I never met him till I was about 11 - I used to go to school in the morning, and he'd still be in bed. I'd come back at night, and he'd be out at work, and I'd go to bed, and he'd come home.' Weekends were equally full of work. Holidays became precious but very rare. But despite working all hours, there was still too much work, so George was forced to delegate. He hated this because it meant losing complete control, the worst thing for such a perfectionist. Some rehearsals were handed over to people like Fred Tomlinson, one of his singers, though George always tried to be present at recordings. Irene Thomas recollects, 'Fred was our wild boy, our own brilliant eccentric, one of whose tricks for calling everyone to order at the start of rehearsal was to pound out the opening bars of *Belshazzar's Feast, fortissimo* on the piano, bawling "In Babylon..." in a deafening baritone.' George and Fred became extremely good friends, to the extent that George was Fred's best man in 1956.

Another one whom George trusted to help - this time with musical arrangements - was Tommy Sampson who started working with George about 1954. As a member of the Salvation Army, Tommy played cornet in the Cambridge Heath Salvation Army band and in 1946 had formed and played trumpet in what was called 'one of Britain's most exciting 20-piece orchestras'. However, the Salvation Army was very unhappy with his move to George's organisation and, for the 'sin' of working with George, Tommy was drummed out of the Army. He said, 'I pray to be re-admitted, and I still want to go back' but the Salvation Army didn't see much hope of that. 'We have no objection,' said Colonel Rance, 'to our bandsmen appearing on TV if they play the classics, but jazz and what is called pop music are too much associated with the seamier side of life to have our official sanction.' Moving on to a notable career as a jazz musician, Tommy was not to be reconciled with the Army until 1993.

Office work was mounting too. He never had a huge office staff, working from home before hiring Dinely's Studios from two spinster sisters he knew, and then an office in Marylebone High Street. George stayed at Dinely's Studios until he was semi-retired and with his eyesight going, he didn't want to drive into London; after he let it go, he worked from a large studio on the top floor of his home, Wansbeck, in New Malden. His office staff rarely exceeded himself, Daphne, Alan Cooper and an occasional singer such as Mary Moss who helped out between singing engagements. A feature mentioned, 'You might expect to find him in a lush office behind a battery of telephones and a box of cigars. But that's not so. It's necessary to chase him around rehearsals to pin him down to an interview, for he is a shirt-sleeved employer. "How many hours a day do I work? Just about every hour there is," George confessed, "I honestly can't remember [all the stage shows] offhand. When four or five of my provincial groups are in nearby towns, I hop into the car and spend two or three days out of London having a look at them." Nor did paying two hundred singers seem to cause him worries. He estimated his payroll at around £3,000 (£96,000), though he added cautiously that their costumes "cost a bob or two as well." ' The feature concluded: 'Slim, bespectacled, friendly George Mitchell still looks more like an affable City man than a celebrity of show business. But when it comes to blending other people's voices into a harmonious sound,

Minstrel Magic

he has the magic touch. And for magical talents in the entertainment world, the financial reward is high.'

Another area which threatened to take over George's life, and leave him no time for anything else, was the need to hold almost constant auditions to ensure that he had access to enough singers who met his high standards. This task was immense. Auditions were held twelve or fifteen times a year, peaking around the need to find singers for long summer and Christmas seasons, but most applicants were rejected. Irene Thomas remembers that George would often despair: 'We always knew when George had spent the mornings at auditions; he'd sit over a cup of tea and shake his head glumly threatening to grow long ears with flaps like a spaniel's to let down whenever he hears the opening bars of *Adele's Laughing Song* from *Die Fledermaus*. Once is nice; three or four times in a morning is tedious.' Dot remembers George was always very kind to people he turned down, saying, 'That was a good performance, but it's not quite what I'm looking for. Go away and work on such and such and who knows?' Successful singers usually started off in stage shows alongside experienced members and could work their way through the various layers into the inner group if they were good enough.

Occasionally George would hear of someone good and go and see them for himself. Glyn Dawson remembers that George asked him to 'come with me to see the *Vic Oliver Show* at the Little Theatre. He wanted to see one of the personnel in the show and took me as company.' When he was looking for a new principal in 1962 to take the first Minstrel tour out to Australia, someone recommended Jeff Hudson who well remembers his first meeting with George: 'He came out to Jersey where I was a band leader, singing in cabaret, and asked if I'd be interested. Later, I went to Dinely's to audition for Daphne where George played piano. He gave me sight reading parts in bass clef. This was a problem for me - I can read treble clef, but bass clef is more difficult. Kindly George said, "I'm not much of a pianist so don't worry." '

But help with the auditions was right at hand. Daphne Bell who had joined the choir in 1946 had quickly become George's right-hand woman. He came to rely on her completely, saying, 'I take her word about those she chooses – and that's another load off my back.' Although she never stopped singing with the choir, she also ran George's office and organised every last detail of the choir so was in a perfect position to take over the major burden of auditioning for new choir members. She recalls, 'I auditioned for all the shows – summer, pantos, broadcasts – recording them and still performing in them. Once the Black and Whites started, I auditioned for them too all over the country. In Southampton, I auditioned Pam Rhodes successfully. Heather Harper sang with us, as did Irene Thomas, who went on to win *Brain of Britain* in 1961. Cliff Mitchelmore's daughter joined us too. The requirements were rigorous. Men needed a minimum height of 5'9" and a maximum age of 30 with an ability to move well. Girls had to be between 5'5" and 5'7", aged 17-25, with attractive looks and figures. Males had to be of a certain height, visually good. They had to be able to move well enough too.'

George's overriding requirement, apart from a good voice, was the ability to sing clearly. George was constantly surprised by how many singers failed to articulate properly and complained, 'If I can't hear the words, neither will the audience.' Singer Irene Thomas recalled, 'During the Carl Foreman film *The Victors* we were singing *Deck the Hall with Boughs of Holly* when Carl charged out of his cubicle. "What the hell goes on? It sounds as though you're singing *Troll the ancient Yuletide carol*. What is it supposed to be?" "*Troll the ancient Yuletide carol*," we chorused gleefully. To do him justice, all he said was, "Oh my Gard," and disappeared again.' Occasionally this clarity caused problems, such as the time in June 1954 when they sang a Russian folk song *Our Village* in *Star Bill*. The communist *Daily Worker* went to town: 'Perhaps the BBC reckons it can fool most of the listeners most of the time, but it must also realise that some alert ones will always catch it out. The Glee Club gave a rendering of *Our Village*. I didn't hear it myself, but you'd be surprised at the number of listeners who let me know about it. I gather the BBC has heard too. The listeners who knew the English translation of this collective farmers' song knew that a certain line runs, "It's the finest village in our Soviet land." What they heard from the BBC was, "It's the finest village in our native land." Possibly the Glee Club, among whose admirers I count myself, didn't know about this petty piece of faking. However, the BBC should know that it wasn't missed.'

Competition was fierce, and only the most determined managed to succeed. Betty Harrison was adamant she wasn't going to take no for an answer. In July 1950, she wrote fifty letters asking for an audition. George recalled, 'Then she telephoned at all times of the day and night, singing, trying to convince me to take her on. I asked her to wait a few weeks, but instead, she hopped on a train and walked in. She was so keen I hardly bothered to hear her. Now she's in my regular choir.' Irene Thomas auditioned in 1954 for George at the BBC Maida Vale Studios and remembered singing *The Old House*, then a couple of scales. I also did a sight-reading test, and then the sort of test where you pick the middle or lower note out of a chord to see if you could sustain a harmony part in choral music, then a short unaccompanied passage to see how capable you were of keeping in tune unaided. "Right," said George. "Are you free next Sunday? We need an alto voice for the broadcast at the Camberwell Palace."'

Such speed in using successful singers was normal, as Maryetta Midgley found in the late 1950s. She was the daughter of world-famous tenor Walter Midgley, with whom George was very friendly. Walter had auditioned singers for George at the end of the war. Maryetta recalls, 'George always made out he didn't know one voice from another and so used people who did.' Walter was a Royal Opera House principal tenor and off on tour when Maryetta, only 16, saw the audition advert: 'I was at Trinity College on a scholarship, but I didn't want to stay there. However, my father didn't want me even to audition until I was 21. So I started nursing. I'd only been there three weeks when I saw George was looking for a top soprano for the Harry Belafonte series. Robert de Cormier [Belafonte's musical arranger] was used to writing for a black choir with a high soprano, and George didn't have one. When I got to Dinely's Studios, the queue was all the way down from the 2nd floor and along the road. I had my nurse's uniform on so I went to the front and said I had to be back on duty in two hours, so Daphne let me go in early. Phyllis Whitaker was also there – she played the piano. I sang *We'll Gather Lilacs*. A man's voice came from around the corner, where George's feet were sticking out. "What note is that?" he asked. "Top C." Phyllis confirmed I was right. He gave me *Something about a Soldier* and asked me to sing the second line. I didn't know the song at all and sang it too slowly but right. Then I went back to work. George thought I was green as a stick and too young at 16, but Daphne persuaded him. He rang my mother that evening: "How would you feel if I gave your daughter a job?" My mother said, "You'd be mad, and her father doesn't want her to do this." "I can persuade him. Can she be at Shepherd's Bush Theatre tomorrow?" My mother and I were stunned – we just sat with cups of tea and shook, but I was at Shepherd's Bush next day. Father came home on Thursday, saying, "I've rung George, told him he's mad, but I wouldn't let you do this for anyone but him. He'll look after you." I went straight into live TV on Saturday – it was the scariest thing ever.'

Not everyone intended to audition. Jan Bolitho was waiting to audition for another programme when Phyllis Whitaker saw him and said, 'We'll see you next.' He got the job! Kurt Gänzl accompanied a friend, but as George's regular pianist wasn't there, Kurt ended up playing for everyone, all of whom were awful. Kurt said, 'I can do better than that,' and he did, getting the job.

One new Minstrel who joined the Blackpool show was rather unusual. Most new Minstrels were reasonably experienced in stage or music work, but Russell Stone was only eighteen, abandoning his A levels to join. He had no singing experience and didn't even take any music to his audition. 'I was in the Upper VIth,' he remembers, 'and working towards being an engineer when in February I realised I didn't want to do this. A teacher said, "So what can you do?" "Sing." So he suggested I look at the *Stage*. At my first audition, I landed the job with the show, then had to wait fourteen weeks to join at Blackpool. The first week I watched the show from the back of the stalls, [to learn the routines], then you go in number by number. The first one I did, the lights immediately blinded me but everyone helped me, and I was guided by the hands of a succession of Minstrels and Toppers.' Keith Leggett, back as Head Minstrel after returning from Australia, remembers Russell: 'He was such a country bumpkin when he joined but boy, did he develop - he had real talent. He was the very first person I knew that took drugs - it wasn't the thing that Minstrels did.'

George wasn't the only person to have trouble with moving to music. 'Some couldn't even walk and swing the opposite arm properly,' says Dot. 'You knew you didn't have a hope of getting anywhere with them.' In later years, principal Roger Green found the singing audition easy; he had different views about the dancing: 'I was astonished when I turned up for the audition, to find a queue of at least two hundred would-be Minstrels, stretched round the block. After queueing for an eternity, I got to sing for the great man himself. At the end, George announced he'd like me to join the Minstrels for a Paignton summer season. However, my joy was short-lived when he sent me to West Kensington, where the cast was rehearsing the TV show, so choreographer Roy Gunson could assess my dance ability. This put the fear of God into me because a dancer I was not. I remember the feeling of fear and trepidation as he took me through some complicated dance steps (well, I thought they were!) while cast members scrutinised my every move. Fortunately, it was worth it because two weeks later I was informed I had indeed passed.'

Female dancers were just as difficult to find. Ballet mistress Denise Shaune often auditioned as many as eight hundred dancers to find eight who 'completely came up to what we wanted'. She only took two minutes to decide about a girl: 'Some girls' legs are too short, some too long. We need girls with average leg lengths because the costumes are uniform. We like to get the girls when they are 17 because they can be moulded into a team much more easily and they tend to work harder.'

Probably the most famous audition was that of Glyn Dawson, later principal with the touring Minstrels: 'A friend of mine suggested I audition. I had to report to Dinely's Studios where I waited with about twenty other men. Eventually, I was called in. I saw a lady pianist half way down, and three people sitting behind a table at the far end. These were Alfred and George Black, who were theatre producers, and Joan Davis, a producer and choreographer. The pianist was lovely Phyllis Whitaker. I gave her a copy of *Questa Quella*, an Italian operatic number. After the song, Mrs Davis asked, "Can you sing in English?" I said, "Yes, my dear," went to the piano, where Phyllis suggested *Because*. Then I was sent to see the choreographer. He told me probably I'd be doing the best of the summer shows at Blackpool with Jewel and Warriss. After another wait, I was told to see George. I knocked, and there was George Mitchell himself. He and I stood face to face and eye to eye as we were both a very similar build. He said, "Well, Glyn, I've been advised you have a very nice tenor voice." I thanked him, then he said, "Can you move?" I was stunned for a second or two, then replied, "Well, no, I've only been married a few years, and I've got a very young daughter." George took his glasses off and did a complete roundabout turn. He put his glasses back on and said, "I don't mean move away from home." I was getting perplexed, so he asked me if I'd seen a theatre show. I replied, "Yes, when I was 8, I saw my cousin in a pantomime." George took his glasses off, turned round again and said, "Can you dance?" I said with a big smile. "Yes, I can tango, foxtrot, waltz or any kind of dancing." We both then had a good laugh. Ever since, each time we met, we said, "Can you dance?"'

True to the Mitchell tradition, George managed to gather good publicity from auditions. One spring, he sent Daphne Bell and Keith Leggett to run a series of auditions in five provincial cities. Newcastle was chosen for the first auditions, with Glasgow next. Two days later the team were in Manchester, with Cardiff and then Birmingham ending the tour. Keith said, 'We decided to take the auditions to the provinces instead of getting the entertainers to come down to London, and we've been very impressed with the talent so far.' In Newcastle, two reporters auditioned comically for the show. Daphne Bell, in on the joke, dealt suitably with them, saying to one, 'You were great, but your sister with the beard let you down. You were also lousy singers and too old. And too fat. And too short. Your dancing reminds me of a couple of carthorses cavorting through a meadow. And the beard would have to go as there are no bearded Minstrels. But you're fine at waving the hats.' In Cardiff, newspaers icked up on Jamaican Frederick Nation's audition. He said, 'I know the show has been criticised for its attitude to black people, but that doesn't bother me. As far as I'm concerned it's just an excellent and professional production.' Daphne told the local press, 'Yes, of course we certainly consider coloured people for parts in the show, but we have no coloured Minstrels at the moment.'

As always happens, George's success attracted the occasional oddball as people would do anything to be associated with his success. A newspaper interview with an unnamed man relates he 'was offered an audition with the hit show (the Minstrels)' while he was in the West Country. On his way to London, he grabbed a flask of coffee from a service station. But he'd added salt instead of sugar which affected his throat, so he said, and despite drinking lots of water, he couldn't sing and so missed his chance. George wrote, 'Rubbish!' and 'Oh yeah?' beside this. One potential choir member, nightclub singer Reginald Davidge, told West London magistrates how he had been battling to make headway in show business since leaving prison and pleaded for another chance so that he could keep an audition date with 'a famous choir'. The magistrate thought Reginald a fraud and sent him to prison for stealing a pork pie. Years later, one even managed to get onto a radio programme called *Memories of the Minstrels,* narrated by John Boulter. A supposed army colleague of George's inaccurately recalls, 'George was an officer in the RAPC Leicester, and while there, he formed a choir, and that's how the Rapcats (RAPC and ATS) came into being. I lost sight till after the war when he blossomed out with the Black and White Minstrels.'

CHAPTER 7

George was stunned when at the end of 1949, the BBC gave his singers their own radio series, *Since It Is Evening*, 'an aperitif of melody, featuring the George Mitchell Choir'. The newspapers didn't miss the sheer unexpectedness of this accolade. The *Sunday Empire News* marvelled, 'What a long way you can travel in six months – if you happen to be George Mitchell. George has realised the ambition of all broadcasters - a BBC series of his own. Nice going for a choir that turned professional only six months ago.'

This series of six shows led almost immediately into the very first *George Mitchell Glee Club* which was broadcast on the Light Programme on December 30, the eve of the decade that changed everything. Featuring the Mitchell Maids and Men in 'a musical get-together for the family', it was produced by 25-year-old Dennis Main Wilson, who later produced *The Goon Show, Hancock's Half Hour, Citizen Smith* and *Till Death Us Do Part*. George recollected, 'He was a funny little man with some grandiose ideas and gave me a real fright, but he made me famous. He came up with fantastic ideas for lots of comedy in the sequences. Dennis made sure every show ended in a blaze of glory. Everybody was roaring for more.'

Preparations for this series took so much time that George had to reduce other work. He spent all his time arranging songs such as *Old MacDonald, There's a New World, Ding Dong Bell, The Mule Train, Wanting You, Dry Bones, Tales from the Vienna Woods, Old Dan Tucker* and *Long Long Ago*. He agreed with Dennis that the show needed a proper 'club' feel, so they planned to involve the audience in items where they sang the melody while the Glee Club provided the harmony, such as *I Want to be Happy, The Echo Told Me a Lie* and *Lily of Laguna*. At the end of the programme, the singers were to go into the aisles and join hands with the audience as everyone sang *Auld Land Syne*. The choir were given new uniforms, the sixteen girls wearing smart blue tailored boleros, with maroon collars, and full blue skirts, the twenty-four men blue shirts under double-breasted maroon dinner jackets, with maroon silk facings.

The *Radio Times* launched the series with a major feature: 'The new shows will do much towards breaking away still further from the original appellation "swing choir" and show the versatility of the singers. From what we hear, you can expect George Mitchell's special arrangements of everything from the latest popular tunes to traditional ballads, from Strauss to bebop and from musical comedy to operetta, as well as choralised excerpts from Dvorak's *New World Symphony* and Debussy's *Clair de Lune*.' The proposed use of *Clair de Lune* caused consternation within the BBC, where they worried that George was taking 'extreme liberties with classic and contemporary works of the more serious music'. Dennis retorted, 'George has kept Debussy's harmonic construction and has transferred the original piano score into the medium of the human voice.' However, his pleas fell on deaf ears, and the choir was banned from singing this wordless version of *Clair de Lune*.

Reaction to the first show - from the Brangwyn Hall, Swansea, as 'it was desired to start the series off from the Land of Song' - was so good that the BBC developed the show into a high-budget sixteen-week series and in an innovative move, recorded it on location around Britain. The choir travelled hundreds of miles, performing in places as far afield as Swansea, Northampton and the Isle of Wight. In a popular move, Leslie Mitchell was added as Master of Ceremonies. This was the start of a long friendship, as Dot Mitchell recalls: 'Leslie and George were very close, like brothers. Everyone thought they looked alike. They were often mistaken for each other.' A further innovation was to involve local choirs which guaranteed large audiences - 'This got bags of publicity and all the free seats full.'

Reviews were very enthusiastic: 'It's a club up our street all right. No membership cards, no general meetings, no officials and Bravo, no subs! If you listen and like it, then you're 'in' the Glee Club. Recently a little old lady hobbled around backstage after a Glee Club get-together and sorted out George's boss Dennis Main Wilson, to thank him for the show. Her superlatives were sincere: "What a choir," she said, "and they all look so ordinary." '

Despite its coveted slot, Dennis fought hard to change the Glee Club's time and day, reminding the BBC that the programme was expensive and 'it's a great pity its listening figures should inevitably be lowered by the opposition of *Twenty Questions* on the Home'. But Dennis needn't have worried. The Glee Club proved so popular that George was overjoyed to discover that 'we knocked *Twenty Questions* out of the ratings, and Kenneth Adam [BBC's Head of Publicity] was furious. But there it is, the all singing Mitchells, superb quality, very popular.' The show became so popular it soon went out internationally via the Overseas Service.

But panic was setting in behind the scenes. The BBC was breaking new ground with this series which was exceedingly complicated to balance. Everyone was worried that the sound would suffer if a different regional Outside Broadcasting team handled each show. JH Davidson, the BBC's Assistant Head of Variety Music, was adamant that 'the only way to make this programme up to the technical standard required (and justify the large amount of money being spent on it) would be to have the same OB team of two engineers, plus a regional OB engineer'. Dennis was furious when this suggestion was vetoed and tried in vain to get the decision reversed.

But he was to be proved right when after one recording, he was forced to send the BBC yet another memo, saying, 'The overall reproduction of the *Glee Club* last night was so bad that I am giving a full list of comments.' Complaints ranged from an 'appalling' drop in the level of the signature theme to difficulties with the cuts needed to avoid overrunning. Audience reaction was stopped almost before it started, which in turn caused problems for the continuity announcer and killed the show's climax. Leslie Mitchell's links within the show were also broadcast at too fast a speed, making his voice sound far too high. George also complained bitterly, sending an official letter of protest. The BBC was quickly forced to reverse its decision, and future shows went perfectly.

The sound problems were exacerbated by the venues chosen for the shows. One singer reported, 'We sang in all sorts of odd places from castles to canteens. The poor engineers were extraordinarily ingenious at improvisation. But the end results were not always what we had expected. In one village hall, there was no suitable little room to use as an echo-chamber – essential if the sound is to be mellow. The hall keeper said the only place he could think of was the Ladies. So the engineers pinned a notice "do not enter" on the door and moved in. And right in the middle of *Rose Marie*, the soprano hit her top notes to the accompaniment of rushing waters.'

But eagle eyes at the BBC became deeply concerned with the cost of this series. No one had told the Finance Section that the budget had been increased, so they complained endlessly about overspends. Dennis Main Wilson was furious: 'It is most disconcerting to feel, when one is working night and day seven days a week on this extremely complicated venture, that the powers that be seem to doubt the efficiency and/or capability of the producer.'

Dennis' final idea for the series shocked both George and the BBC. Full of eccentric ideas, Dennis proposed taking the singers to sea on board the PS *Royal Eagle* down the Thames to Southend, recording a *Glee Club* as they went. But everyone quickly got caught up in the excitement of such an innovative idea and the BBC duly stumped up the extra budget. Dennis wanted the atmosphere of good fun and high spirits of the two thousand trippers on board to be enjoyed by the seven million Club listeners, as the usual *Glee Club* format was recreated on the ship.

The technical problems were immense. A BBC mobile transmitter had to be set up on board to send signals to a special receiving station constructed on Southend Pier, then on to Broadcasting House by land line. Extra electricity supplies were also needed, not least for Harold Smart, leading the Glee Club Sextet, who set the BBC OB engineers the tricky problem of producing the right kind of electricity supply for his Hammond organ. Both the ship's owners and crew, led by Captain Traynier, were as helpful as possible, allowing the BBC engineers to run mike cables everywhere and to alter the position of loudspeakers on board. Bob and Mac, two BBC engineers, worked into the early hours to ensure everything would be working in time. As the *Radio Times* put it, 'This should be no more difficult than producing a couple of P & O liners out of a hat!'

The show made major news. The two thousand tickets became prizes in competitions in all the major papers. In a huge accolade, the *Radio Times* not only carried a two-page feature but also featured the show on its cover – the first of many covers George and his choirs achieved. Newspapers, television and cinema newsreels covered the London departure and the arrival in Southend, with many newspapers placing reporters on board.

Bob and Mac may have got things working by 8.30am on the morning, but they weren't to stay that way. Dennis tempted fate by saying, 'The arrangements are so much under control that nothing can foreseeably happen to upset them, not even the weather. We've squared the weather clerk, and in any event, there is seldom rough weather in the Estuary in the summer months.' But the weather wasn't to oblige.

Royal Eagle cast off from Tower Pier at 8.30am, passing under Tower Bridge. Trouble started almost immediately. George remembered, 'There was a strong wind on the Thames, and the musicians were going mad trying to stop their music blowing away. The boat was ransacked for paper clips, clothes pegs, anything, that would hold it on the stand. To no avail. The music from the orchestra stands just floated down the Thames, and it was a total disaster.' During one stormy patch, 'Mr Smart and his music were suddenly pitched right across the deck, and he found himself playing on the starboard side instead of the port.'

But soon the weather improved to something approaching proper summer temperatures and the day quickly became blazing hot. And here lay the heart of the problems. The only place there was room for the choir was in the observation lounge whose glass windows exacerbated the heat. The first sign of trouble came during a trial run which showed that, with the singers standing in line, the sound balance was faulty, so a raised dais was quickly built for the tenors and basses. But that produced further problems – the taller ones couldn't stand erect without bumping their heads on the ceiling. So they had to spend the day with their necks bent at an angle of 40 degrees! It became so hot that frequent calls were made on the ice in the fridge. George recollected, 'Every time the refrigerator doors opened, the organ just groaned and dropped a fifth.' Obviously, Bob and Mac, the BBC engineers, hadn't yet quite got it right.

Everyone was very dispirited by the time the ship reached Southend at 11.30. After the weeks of planning, it seemed nothing was going right. They steamed out into the North Sea, before turning round and returning to Southend. Over lunch, the two Mitchells, George and Leslie, finalised the script, in readiness for the actual recording, planned to start as the ship approached Southend Pier on its return journey. Leslie Mitchell was to jump overboard – landing, it was hoped, on the pier head – where he would join the thousands of Southend residents and holiday-making Club members thronging the pier to greet the steamer-cum-Club house. He would then introduce the sixty voices of Freda Parry's Ladies Singers, after which he was to leap back aboard the *Royal Eagle* to enable the captain to keep to his time schedule because by now, hundreds of returning trippers from Southend had re-embarked on the ship, determined to go on enjoying themselves. The captain would cast off, and to the strains of a farewell chorus from thousands of Club members on the pier head, the *Glee Club* would continue on board, with the singers joined by all the passengers.

After the earlier trials of the day, things started to run according to plan. George remembered arriving back at Southend: 'We were weary and fed up. Only the sight of the crowds who lined the pier gave us heart. We arrived to a colossal reception, to be greeted by the mayor and their quite famous ladies' choir.' The recordings happened, Leslie Mitchell didn't end up in the sea, and the ship set off on its journey back to Tower Pier, to the strains of the Freda Parry Choir singing *Now Is The Hour*. What no one knew was that behind it all lay a note of tragedy, for twenty-four hours beforehand, Freda Parry's husband had died. She thoughtfully kept the news from everybody, including her choir, so that nothing would impair their singing. The trippers settled down and, together with the choir, sang their favourite tunes for three hours until, as the *Royal Eagle* gently nosed her way to Tower Pier, everyone sang the choir's signature tune *Open Up Dem Pearly Gates*, as Tower Bridge's centre sections rose in salute. It then slowly closed, bringing another *Glee Club* meeting to an end.

George realised the moment he walked into the studio the next morning that something was wrong. He recalled, 'I listened to the recording and thought I was hearing an old-fashioned gramophone that kept running down and had to be constantly rewound.' Investigations quickly discovered what had gone wrong. Every time the fridge door had been opened to remove ice cubes to cool down the choir, it wasn't only Harold Smart's organ that dropped in tone. The power to the recording equipment was also reduced. As the revs dropped, so the choir's voices dropped a couple of tones and then rose again. The recording had to be scrapped. The choir hastily rushed into the studio to record the whole programme again. Seagulls and chugging engine noises were added by Sound Effects, and the show was a great success when it was transmitted. Despite the near-disaster, George remembered Dennis wasn't deterred: 'He (later) went one step too far when he wanted to put us aboard the new French plane, the Caravelle, and record the show over France. He didn't get away with that one.'

Dennis was to take the choir bravely on the river once again in Coronation week in 1953. Presumably, the near-disaster on the PS *Royal Eagle* had been forgotten, though this time Dennis kept the boat firmly in the river. This last show in the Julie Andrews' *Pleasure Boat* series, renamed *The Show Boat* for this broadcast, took over the Woolwich Ferry which needed a special licence to go up river away from her normal working route across the river. With an audience on board, she sailed to Greenwich, where 3700 spectators on the pier promenade, surrounded by candy floss awnings and a full naval 'dressed' ship, were given a ninety-minute show from the open-air upper deck.

Despite its huge success, the *Glee Club* series was never recommissioned on radio. Dennis Main Wilson tried hard to persuade the BBC to give them another series, telling the BBC, 'George has recast quite a few singers, plus they've benefited from five months' hard work with Moss Empires. Their attack is more virile, their tone truer to pitch.' The likely reason is the cost of the series, particularly the *Royal Eagle* programme. Bob told a concerned BBC that George had lost money on the series which forced the BBC to discuss whether to increase fees for any new series or not recommission it. Bob, wily as ever, battled with the BBC, promising all sorts if only the Corporation would give them another series but this was one battle Bob wasn't to win for several years.

Disappointed that the show hadn't been recommissioned, George quickly capitalised on the *Glee Club's* success by getting Bob to arrange a major tour of Moss Empire's provincial theatres which was orchestrator Alan Bristow's first venture with George. Jeremiahs said the public would never go to see a choir, and George himself had misgivings, even though they had already done a few one-off concerts and the occasional week in variety. However, this time the choir occupied almost the entire second half, with a variety of other artistes filling the first half, among them acrobats, comics and dancers, who changed weekly. Featuring choir members Micky Salisbury and Griff Griffith (who went on to become the very successful duo Miki and Griff), they sang melodies such as *Can Can Polka, Dry Bones, Faery Song, Old McDonald, Quicksilver, Teddy Bears' Picnic, El Cumbanchero, Take the Sun, Song of the Wild Goose, Bake a Cake, Show Boat Selection, Bewitched, Louisiana Hayride, Sabre Dance, Oh, You Sweet One, Bless This House* and *a Plantation Medley*. Many other singers, apart from Miki and Griff, went on to become famous in their own right. Ruth Madoc, Heather Harper, Irene Thomas, Pam Rhodes and Bill Lloyd Webber (Andrew Lloyd Webber's grandfather) all started their professional lives in the choir. Other early singers were children of people very well-respected in the wider musical world, such as the daughters of veteran singers Margaret Eaves, Mavis Bennett and Walter Midgley.

The tour was hugely successful, receiving tremendous acclaim from national and local press, as people relished the chance to see the singers onstage. Bob's publicity machine sprang into action, as George auditioned several local choirs, in case another *Glee Club* series happened. This brilliant publicity tactic produced inches of advance press publicity and filled two shows a night for the entire week. But rehearsals never stopped, even on tour, and as ever, the choir worked fast. After arriving in Bradford, they rehearsed a new song for three hours, before adding it to the show that evening.

Among other venues, the show ventured to Bath where the *Bath & Wiltshire Chronicle* announced, 'As far as the girls are concerned, this is undoubtedly the most glamorous vocal act in the country. They were an outstanding success. The audience were very reluctant to let them go, despite the fact they had already overrun their permitted time. Of interest may be a description to assist your mental picture next time you hear them on air. The eleven women wear black two-piece costumes, white shirts and black bow ties, beige silk stockings, high-heeled black shoes with white butterfly bows. The twelve men wear white linen jackets, black trousers, white shirts and black bow ties. Each member has a red carnation buttonhole. George Mitchell wears tails. He is unassuming and unaffected.'

During the tour, they also fitted in some one-off concerts, including one in Aberystwyth, West Wales, which was very nearly disastrous. It was snowing when the choir set out, and the snow thickened until the bus was creeping along the mountain roads at a bare 10mph. Wales that night resembled Antarctica, and no one ventured out. The choir was lost. Then a lone man appeared with an all-white sheep-dog dawdling miserably by his side. 'How far to Aberystwyth?' the driver shouted. The man shook the snow from his head. 'You'll never make it, boy bach,' he said. 'Not on a night like this. Where is it you are coming from?' They told him London, and he shook his head again and said, 'I would be for turning back to London if I were you. You'll never make Aberystwyth.' They low-geared on for 100 yards, and round the next bend, the signpost stood. And through the snow, they could read, 'Aberystwyth - 2 miles.' Arthur Lewis, one of the choir's Welshmen, never lived it down. If anything stupid happened after that, he had to suffer the comment, 'Daft as that Aberystwyth shepherd'.

What certainly wasn't daft was an invitation in the autumn of 1950 to appear in the *Royal Command Performance,* as the *Royal Variety Show* was then called. On the day of the show, George received scores of good-will telegrams, many from major stars such as Jack Hylton, Henry Hall, Lew and Leslie Grade, the Crazy Gang and Dennis Main Wilson. Despite the inevitable nerves, everything at the London Palladium went smoothly. George conducted the forty choir members as they closed the first half, backing stars Gracie Fields and Allan Jones in *Song of the Mountains,* the theme from *The Glass Mountain.* Melody Maker reported, 'Although his guiding influence has paved the way for another triumph, George bestows the credit on his "boys and girls": "They're the ones to congratulate," he points out. "They've worked really hard, and it's a great thrill for them to feel they've made the grade." ' The BBC tried very hard to broadcast the show but was firmly refused as theatre owners feared music halls everywhere would be empty as a result. They even refused the BBC permission to broadcast recorded extracts the following Sunday which showed how old school show business people viewed the still infant BBC. It was to be 1958 before the BBC was allowed to broadcast the whole show on the Light Programme.

George did well over a dozen *Royal Variety Performances* over the years, including two with the Black and White Minstrels. They were back the following year, 1951, held in a nice twist at London's Victoria Palace, the theatre which became home to the George Mitchell Minstrels for over ten years. Sadly George wasn't there to conduct them this year. He was in bed with flu and a temperature of 104, so the Glee Club had to manage without him. A friend of George's taped the whole show and played it back at George's bedside. George was in good company as King George VI was also too ill to attend (sadly dying the following February). The King didn't want to miss one of his favourite nights of the year, so the first part of the show was relayed to Buckingham Palace by landline and commentated on by Bryan Johnston. The Queen brought Princess Margaret and two of the King's nurses, giving them the best seats, next to her. After the stern refusal last year, theatre managements now allowed the BBC to broadcast the second part of this year's show, although the BBC didn't break the news until earlier that evening, to avoid influencing cinema and theatre attendance.

Now firmly established on radio and stage, George and his singers were beginning to break into television. Television in the 1950s was a completely different medium from nowadays. BBC TV had started up again in 1946 when it was reintroduced to a small circle of 25,000 middle-class households around London. Televisions were very expensive - about £100 (£2,300) - and few households could afford them, a mere 4% in 1950, though by the end of the 1950s, 72% of households had access to both BBC and the new commercial channel ITV. It was 1960 before the vast majority of the country could receive it. But in 1950, there was little to watch anyway. These were the days of only one channel, BBC, and even that was only available from 3pm onwards on weekdays and 5pm on Sundays, with a two-hour gap after *Children's Hour* to put the children to bed. After this, there were only two further hours of programmes, before everything shut down after the *Epilogue* at 10pm.

The BBC had no idea what to do with this new medium. Controversy raged within the Corporation, with many seeing it as a trivial diversion from the serious business of radio. Radio was the national medium, TV the province of the minority, very much the poor relation. Programming was consequently uninspired, particularly as the big managements blocked their stars from appearing on television. There was little light entertainment, drama was usually shown straight from the theatre, with a specially adapted play broadcast once a week. Nobody was writing stuff specifically for television, and programmes were a rehash of what had been shown for the few years before the war. Many shows were reminiscent of radio programmes just put in front of cameras, others were in essence theatre shows. The Corporation relied heavily on relaying stage shows from London and during the summer from the huge number of theatres serving the many and increasingly thriving seaside resorts. In any case, the picture was bad and outside broadcasts, where television had obvious advantages over radio, produced headaches. Even switching it on was a palaver. Lights had to be switched off, furniture moved around, all the time waiting for the set to warm up. Remote controls were a thing of the future, so you had to get up to adjust the sound, and even more annoyingly when the picture started slipping and the horizontal or vertical knobs at the back of the set had to be fiddled with. Nevertheless, those who possessed a set nearly always switched it on but preferred plays to music.

The fledgling television channel started to look with interest at George's versatile set of singers. In 1949 they gave them their own show called *Along the Gypsy Trail*, in which they became the Romany Singers, and in 1950 they appeared in *Carissima*, the biggest musical ever seen on television, with a cast of fifty. These programmes quickly showed that television producers, mostly moved from radio to television with no specialist training, had no idea how to use the singers. Often they'd be static, more often not in vision at all. Sometimes programmes only involved the singers in the opening. Maryetta Midgley remembers going 'to Shepherds Bush on a Green Line bus from home in Worcester Park, rehearsed, dressed, sang the show (only the opening number), left the building, back on the bus and was home in time to see the closing credits. We wore white satin shoes with three inch heels. Our feet were numb by the end because the shoes were dyed to match the frocks and had become half a size smaller. But we smiled throughout. It proves how much fun we must have been having. We were given blue satin dresses which were dead straight, with built up shoulders and no sleeves. You had to have good legs. We wore little flyaway skirts which came round the front on a belt with a little bow. There was built in support. When the lights came on, Mary Brown looked down and said, "Oh my God, we look as if we're wearing light bulbs."' Designers obviously still had a lot to learn.

One later attempt still couldn't get it right. The *Stage* was very unimpressed with a fifteen-minute programme called *Semprini*: 'Musical quarter hours are difficult. There's not enough time to have more than one performer and fifteen minutes can sometimes be too long to watch one performer constantly. To some extent,

Minstrel Magic

producer Ned Sherrin got over this problem by including the singers. Unfortunately, he swopped one immobile object, the piano, for immobile singers who stood around looking pretty and sickeningly sentimental. [You] realised how deadly dull the Mitchell Singers are. One thing the producer should have spotted was one singer clad in grey socks. With evening dress? Really!'

Gradually as the decade continued, the BBC got more confident in creating shows for TV, though several singers recall one debacle. *The Yana Show* starred Yana, a smoky-voiced ballad singer who was a rising star. The singers liked this show, as one of them recalled: 'It's a chance for us to wear elegant black lace dresses (really black lace leotards with overskirts) and huge 'diamond' collars and earrings.' However, the critics panned it. The *Liverpool Echo* thought, 'There were signs that some last-minute efforts had been made to put new life into the show. But it's still not right. Here's the remedy. Cut to half an hour. Bring in a compère and leave Yana to her singing. Keep Peter Jones for the funny bits, the Mark Stuart boys and girls for dance numbers and the George Mitchell Singers for background. And scrap the rest.' The *Sunderland Echo* agreed: 'When will the television boys realise that one cannot stage a spectacular show on a small television screen?' The BBC's audience research panels agreed. Anxious backroom discussions resulted in a complete revamp, the only survivors being George's singers, singer Ronnie Carroll and Yana herself. The new show was received much more kindly, though viewers still disliked Yana herself but considered the Television Toppers and the Mitchell Singers an asset to any show.

Gradually the number of programmes involving the George Mitchell Singers tipped over in favour of TV as it replaced radio as people's main form of entertainment. The friendly nature of the singers helped as TV began to find its feet. Obliging George was always happy, for no extra money, to let the singers do what the producers wanted. Irene Thomas remembered this time as happy: 'We began to be in great demand as singers-actors-extras in television variety shows, generally built around a star singer or comedian, and we saved the producer money by "dressing the set" in street or café scenes. These shows were broadcast from Lime Grove Studios, or the Shepherd's Bush Empire, or the Old King's Theatre Hammersmith. If it was for ITV, it might be made at the Wood Green Empire or the Hackney Empire. We loved both those theatres. There was a really fine pub next to the Wood Green

Empire and a famous "marble-hall" fish-and-chip emporium next to the Hackney Empire.'

This, plus George's helpfulness and reputation for producing a choir consisting of anything from one to twenty-six singers almost instantly, ensured the George Mitchell Singers remained in the highest demand. *Variety Parade's* producer William Lyon-Shaw reported, 'The ever-ready George Mitchell Singers are into their stride. I say "ever-ready" because, throughout this series, they have been asked to do many things outside their field – playing parts, dancing, assisting acts, voices off – and it's a delight to find that they're always ready to help, and attack each show with a zest and vigour which makes them outstanding as a vocal group.'

Douggie Squires was brought in to choreograph the choir. He recalls, 'If they were working with a comedian like Charlie Drake or Dave King they would be enlisted to appear in comedy sketches. George was ever co-operative and helpful no matter what the show or the star. I was thrilled to have a go, terrified but thrilled. It was an invaluable experience, and I loved it. It taught me a lot about utilising non-dancers in musical numbers and making them look good. The singers were not trained dancers, but whatever you threw at them they enthusiastically had a go. I had great times choreographing them whether backing Vera Lynn, Lulu or Frankie Vaughan.'

CHAPTER 8

By now, the singers were part of the national consciousness, the Take That or Spice Girls of their day. In the days before Twitter and Facebook, both George and Bob had a huge talent for manufacturing publicity out of virtually nothing. People were interested in absolutely anything to do with the singers and their lives.

When Miki and Griff married in 1950, the whole choir saw them off on honeymoon by singing to them on board the train at Paddington before they left for Torquay where further publicity was generated by their arrival. Both events were extensively covered by the national and local press, at a time when the country was yearning for some bright news. In later years, George used a freelance PR guy who travelled everywhere by bike - he even made this into a feature! Every opportunity for publicity was utilised. When a show visited a town, a connection between one of the singers and the area would always be discovered - either he or she came from the area or was searching for a lost relative or trying to find a lost service comrade from the war. Weddings and engagements were obvious sources of publicity, but there were less obvious publicity hooks - one couple had married and were travelling slowly north in a caravan to join a summer show for George, another group were learning Italian or practising on a unicycle.

When *Music for the Millions*, on tour in Bournemouth, fell foul of a Musicians' Union strike, George - or his publicity machine - quickly turned this to advantage, with the choir giving surprised holidaymakers several free concerts in the open air. Even illness was turned to advantage. Just before *Top of the Town* was due to start broadcasting in November 1953, seeming disaster struck. George provided singers for this show - one critic said, 'When have we ever heard a Dennis Main Wilson production without this team?' - and built the group around bass-baritone Tony Mercer, newly appearing with the choir. Just days before the show was due to begin, Tony went down with appendicitis. Anticipating he wouldn't recover for the first programme, Dennis chose to bill Tony as the 'mystery voice'. Happily, he was fit in time, but the secret remained. The 'voice' made an immediate resounding impact on listeners, and letters and phone calls poured in week after week. Press speculation was rife, bringing the show much welcome publicity. He was eventually unmasked via a studio identification parade, with many critics saying the BBC had a new star on their hands.

George became something of a personality himself in the 1950s. He was often asked to judge competitions in newspapers, featuring decisions such as 'the best-balanced programme of acts' or 'the best programme for a community singing contest'. Maybe unsurprisingly, the choir or the music they sang always featured highly in the winners' lists! For one such competition, the judging panel, including George, decided on *Cockles and Mussels, Daisy Bell, Auld Land Syne, Abide With Me, Love's Old Sweet Song, There is a Tavern in the Town, Down at the Old Bull and Bush, Lily of Laguna, Land of Hope and Glory, Nelly Dean, The Old Folks at Home* and *My Bonnie*, all songs which were to feature heavily in the Mitchell repertoire for years to come. Some prizes were quite bizarre. In 1955 George judged a *Daily Herald* competition, for which the first prize was a village store and post office. Comics, cartoons and other programmes frequently mentioned them. Individual Mitchell singers were also beginning to gain publicity. In *Vera Lynn Sings*, many viewers demanded to know the identity of the Mitchell Singer 'with the lovely smile'. Such requests became so frequent that Vera Lynn introduced him in one programme - it was tenor John Boulter. Lovely Maggi Lawler, one of the inner core, was featured in *Illustrated Chronicle* who wrote, 'Margaret Lawler has one of the most beautiful mezzo-soprano voices of all the girls who sing with the Mitchell Singers. After seeing this picture, viewers may well decide that her voice is not the least of her assets. What a pity we do not see her as well as hear her.'

In the Minstrel years, everything was turned into even more hype. The Victoria Palace show celebrated the 100,000th visitor, then the 500,000th, then the millionth. They had annual anniversaries, and parties every time they broke another record. Quite often, newspapers were allowed to try the show for themselves. The *Daily Mirror* sent reporter Eric Wainwright to join the cast for the conducted segment of one show: 'I was end

Minstrel Magic

man at the back. "Maybe nobody will notice you - I hope," said Head Minstrel Arthur Lewis. I had rehearsed all afternoon. A slow walk to time while banging the tambourine. "Come in on the word 'row'," explained Arthur. "Right foot down, bang and you're away. Step, bang, step, bang. Just keep it up, and you can't go wrong." I was soon ahead of the rest of the chorus. Panting a bit, I stopped to let the others catch up...*Michael, row the boat ashore, Hal-le-lu-jah*...now my feet were speeding up, and when we set out on the final uproarious chorus, I was away at a gallop, tambourine madly waving. "Nobody'll know you," John Boulter had said, "This is one show where we're all anonymous." A comforting thought as I stamped and banged, out of time before a packed house. It's a hard life being a Minstrel. On Dad Lewis' advice, I have hung up my tambourine.'

Similarly a few years later, another new member of the company only lasted one show! Reporter Joanna of the *Weekly News* was invited to join the show as a challenge. She joined in the *White Christmas* part of the Irving Berlin sequence at the end of the first half. Firstly she was dressed by Sheila Delaney, the ballet mistress, in a beautiful pale grey and silver coat and trousers, edged with fur. Partnered by Minstrel Roger Green, they rehearsed successfully, then Roger took her for tea. After that, Mary Oakley helped her with her makeup and took her back to the wings. At this point, trouble struck: 'A terrible thought hit me. How would I pick out Roger with his makeup on? I looked wildly round, but they all looked alike. Then I heard *White Christmas*. Gosh, I'll be on any second now. My heart was thumping like a big bass drum. Then to my great relief, he was beside me. In answer to a squeeze from Roger's hand, I stepped from the wings onto the stage. I could hear the singing, so I joined in, then - horror - out of the corner of my eye I saw all the other girls were silent. "Mistake number one," I thought, dreading what I might do next. Roger guided me round to face the audience. The Minstrels were now reaching the end of their song and raising their right hand. Was I to do the same? When I saw the other girls try to raise their hands, I followed suit. Now - two beats and step back on my right foot, I remembered. Back I went in perfect time. I was still shaking as the curtain dropped. "You were great," said Roger. I asked Roger what I had done wrong. I felt I must have made dozens of mistakes. "Oh no, you were singing as we went on, but you realised and stopped." "Is that all?" "Well, you shouldn't have raised your hand the first time," Mary chipped in, "but at least you kept it up so that it looked like everyone else was wrong." Just shows how friendly and welcoming the cast were.'

The casts never missed an opportunity either. In 1972 principal Glyn Dawson, and speciality acts Neville King and Norman Collier, were on a publicity visit when they witnessed an accident which ended up with milk bottles falling off a lorry. They immediately grabbed brooms and got to work sweeping up the glass and milk, and directing the traffic, much to the amusement of passers-by. Neville and Norman provided more fun in Bristol when they and Les Want were near the theatre one evening. Les recalled: 'Neville started talking down a drain, and throwing his voice back as if someone was trapped. A crowd gathered round, we said, "Keep talking to the man down there, we'll go and get the police, and the fire brigade." Then we left them there.'

In Bristol in 1976 Les provided a wonderful photo opportunity when he found four black lambs, on the farm where he was staying, minutes after they were born. He knew that if they stayed outside, exposed to the freezing conditions, they would probably die, so he bundled them up and took them back to the farmhouse. He said, 'They just looked like four pieces of rag lying on the ground. They were wringing wet and freezing in the sleet. They have been nursed through to survival.' He named them *Luff* and *Beryl* (after Bob Luff and his business partner Beryl Evetts) and *Mitchell* and *Daphne* (after George and Daphne Bell). The farm's owners said they might keep the lambs for breeding, given their narrow escape. Needless to say, the Luff Organisation put on a press conference and took the lambs to the theatre for press photos, where they had another narrow escape! Roy Hudd took one look at them and quipped, 'Aren't they beautiful? Anyone got a few potatoes and some peas?'

But soon George was getting worried. The early months of 1952 were very quiet, with barely any radio work on offer. He began to fear the bubble had burst. The death of George VI made everything worse as everywhere went quiet for some time. On the day he died, February 6, radio closed down after midday and again after the 6pm news, apart from news bulletins and memorial services. Cinemas and theatres closed too. The BBC cancelled many programmes altogether and altered its entire schedule for a week before the funeral, though most people saw this as overkill.

Minstrel Magic

But George had worked too hard to let the choir die away, and manufactured work by organising yet more Sunday concerts in places like Swansea, Cardiff and Luton, before starting a tour. Conducted by George Mitchell and billed as 'the personal appearance of one of radio's most sensational attractions', the choir took over most of this show, helped by Memory Man Leslie Welch, and featuring Joyce Sard and her clavioline. This was a sort of 'an electronic device, little bigger than a filing cabinet, with keyboard and speaker. It is so attached to an ordinary piano that a pianist can play both instruments simultaneously - the piano with the left hand and the clavioline with the right. Some twenty or thirty different instruments - from an organ to a banjo - can be simulated.' With soloists Eve Culley, James Charlton, Mae Craig and Alan Young, they sang *Riding on a Rainbow, Liberty Belle, Sabre Dance, Show Boat selection, Glass Mountain, A Guy is a Guy, Latin American – Bahia, Brazil, Mambo Jambo, Wedding Samba, La Golandrina, Mexican Hat Dance – Plantation Selection – Country Style, Louisiana Hayride, Old Dan Tucker, Chicken Song, Skip to my Lou – Minstrel selection – Shortening Bread, Peter on the Sea, Swing Low, David and Goliath, Polly Wolly Doodle, Dixie, Camptown Races, The Old Banjo – Bless This House, Hit Parade Medley, The Way You Look Tonight* and *Londonderry Air*. All standard fare for a Mitchell Singer.

But the tour seemed doomed from the start. It turned into 'as near to disaster as I've ever been', reinforcing George's fear that it was all over. After the opening show in Newcastle, the choir and George left the city by coach as usual, but they hadn't gone very far when the driver developed a painful carbuncle and couldn't drive for more than an hour, so they were delayed while a replacement was found. After this inauspicious start, the show moved around Scotland, mostly doing two shows a night. But audiences stayed at home. The two Aberdeen shows weren't well attended but the next night in Edinburgh nearly broke George's heart. He later recalled, 'No one knows what happened, but the vast hall was barely half full. It was a shattering experience, but I think we gave the best performance of our career. It was a sort of "We'll show 'em" attitude. We've been back again several times and had to turn people away. Yet here I was, a Scot in Edinburgh and only half a house...'

George was, however, heartened by the warm welcome they received from the Land of Song where the trip to Cardiff produced a memorable evening for two young Newport boys. Thirteen-year-old Terry Hoggett and his pal, 12-year-old Peter Stanley, wanted to hear the choir at the Capitol in Cardiff but had no money, so decided to hitch the twelve miles from Newport to Cardiff. Somewhere along the road, a large private bus offered them a lift. After the bus started off again, their fellow passengers, all of whom had surprisingly good voices, began to sing. Not to be outdone, young Terry added a beautiful soprano voice to the chorus. The man sitting in front of Terry turned and listened attentively. 'That's a nice soprano you've got. Are you interested in singing?' he asked. 'Yes sir,' said Terry, 'That's where we're going tonight, to see George Mitchell at the Capitol.' The man smiled and said, 'You can look at him now, I'm George Mitchell, and these are my singers.' George turned to singer Alan Cooper. 'We've got a new recruit. I think we'll put him on tonight. Now that you've had a rehearsal, how would you like to sing with the Mitchell Choir?' Young Terry was stunned into silence. 'Does your chum sing as well?' George asked. 'No,' said Terry, 'but he does play the piano.' Later that evening, Terry (still in his shirt sleeves) and Peter at the grand piano, were given a solo spot half way through the show, in *Land of My Fathers*, where the boys, backed by the choir, held the capacity audience spellbound.

The Rhondda Music Festival devoted an entire evening to the choir, which proved so popular that the organisers needed extra marquees and seating. The audience came from miles around, and the atmosphere became electric. Choir member Arthur Lewis was local, and up and down the Rhondda, his former pals heard that Arthur was returning with the famous Glee Club. Delighted their old friend had made good, they hired several buses and filled local pubs before the show. Pint after pint was lined up on the bar, all for Arthur. Over in the vast marquee, compère Glyn Jones announced, 'It's especially satisfying to introduce two Welshmen from this outstanding choir - your own Andy Day and Arthur Lewis.' But only Andy stepped forward. Arthur was still involved with his various pints! George won the eternal respect of Arthur that night by understanding what happens when a Welshman goes back to the Valleys after years away.

Fortunately for George, the quiet early months of 1952 had been the lull before the storm, and the singers were soon experiencing a period of intense activity unrivalled by anything they'd managed before.

One particular series which pleased George immensely was the return of *Glory Road*. His greatest desire always was to have a gospel choir onstage with his choir, though it was never to be. But the late 1940s and '50s gave him the chance to work with many black artists and use the music he loved. As well as working with Edric Connor in *Cabin in the Cotton* and *Way Down South*, the choir also worked in *Minstrel Boy*, with Ike Hatch, the famous black Kentucky Minstrels singer, and *Walk Together Chillun*, again produced by Charles Chilton who, like George, had a deep interest in American music. All these shows were steering George in the direction of his later greatest triumph, *The Black and White Minstrel Show*.

Walk Together Chillun, a 45-minute programme of black folklore and music, had already introduced George to the great American blues singer Josh White, who became a good friend. A blues singer from Greenville, Mississippi, ranked as America's third most popular male folk artiste behind Pete Seeger and Bob Dylan, Josh was one of the first openly politicised black artistes, a friend of radicals like Leadbelly and Pete Seeger. Despite his career in America being largely destroyed by the continuing McCarthy era, his star had continued to rise in Britain. Audiences loved the series, with the press enjoying it too. Typical is a *Christian World* review: 'It was one of those things which make it a privilege to own a wireless receiver. The Negro people at their best bring an enormous warmth and humanity to my heart. Nobody else can sing their Spirituals quite as they do themselves.' In his scrapbook, George has written large question marks alongside this cutting; did the reviewer think the choir were themselves black or was he was saying they weren't as good as they might have been? Audience response had been so great that the BBC asked Charles for six more programmes, renamed *Glory Road*. Because Josh was returning to the United States, these recordings were rushed into one week, which gave George little time to arrange the songs. Despite much midnight oil being burned, they only managed to record four programmes; the BBC dubbed some of Josh's recordings from earlier programmes into the last two. These shows left people clamouring for yet more, and their wishes were soon fulfilled.

Minstrel Magic

In April 1952, George was delighted to be able to record a third series of *Glory Road*. This new series of six programmes included Josh's young 12-year-old daughter Beverley. Charles had wondered if there was enough material left for a further six shows but 'then Josh took out his guitar and started to play. As he played, George wrote down, probably for the first time in manuscript form, many of the characteristically Negro melodies and harmonies'. Over the rest of the 1950s and 1960s, they collaborated several more times, recording programmes which covered the songs of slavery and the evolution of folk music, as well as a series in which Josh recalled his childhood Christmases. Singer Irene Thomas remembered these series as 'one of our most fascinating jobs. He was an amiable man with only one fault as far as we were concerned; he would only start recording in the evenings, and so the end of each session was very late.' Once, everyone was waiting at the Albert Hall for Josh to arrive. George eventually sent a taxi round all his usual haunts and found him jamming in Ronnie Scott's Jazz Club.

Although George's hope was to bring Josh's songs like *Free and Equal Blues* to mass audiences, he was also instrumental in introducing Josh to a less prejudiced way of life. George remembered, 'Josh had terrible trouble with his sight, and I drove him to the eye hospital. When we got there, he wouldn't get out of the car, he was shaking like a leaf. Then he said, "They'll never let me in there." When I asked him why, he said, "Because I'm black." I had to get the doorman to persuade him. When they welcomed him in and treated him decently, he couldn't believe it.'

Britain was still, by and large, a welcoming country for foreigners. Winning the war had added to the feeling of innate superiority which Imperial Britain had enjoyed for decades. At the same time, Britain was tied to being against racialism because the country saw itself as the complete opposite of racist Nazi Germany. Even though there was only a tiny minority of non-white Britons and most people had never seen any, people viewed themselves as non-racist, a uniquely tolerant and welcoming haven for refugees from poverty and persecution. They had been used to immigration for centuries, such as the large Irish migration to the mainland from the late C18th, which peaked in the mid C19th after the potato famine. Of course the Irish were never seen as an issue by the government as Ireland was initially part of the UK, with its rights preserved both after independence in 1922 and after Ireland left the Commonwealth in 1947. Large numbers of Jews had arrived from the late C19th onwards, though there was growing demand to control this immigration, contrary to the treatment of Irish immigration. Blacks had been present in the UK for centuries before the *Empire Windrush* docked in 1948. They'd come in as sailors and stayed, establishing small communities in ports such as Liverpool, Cardiff, London and Bristol, though they and Indian seamen suffered when slumps hit British trade. Entertainers had always been welcomed, though they remained limited to exotic roles – Minstrels were acceptable, a black Hamlet was not. When Samuel Coleridge-Taylor, the hugely influential composer, born in London to a white mother and an African father, died aged 37 in 1912, thousands of people attended his funeral in Croydon.

Most people were shocked by the segregation in America's Deep South and the introduction of apartheid in South Africa from 1948 onwards and treated it with deep contempt. Caribbean servicemen had raced to defend the mother country during the war, but the most impact was made by the arrival of black US servicemen. They were widely welcomed and lionised. There was uproar when the American authorities tried to implement a race bar in cafés, hotels and dance halls, including a major march in Manchester in support of black GIs, and the Americans were forced to retreat. White GIs who tried to apply the US colour bar were mocked and challenged.

After the war, most blacks and other immigrants went home - to the US or to the Caribbean – but jobs were plentiful, and no one objected to those who stayed. There was a critical labour shortage, and the government went to great lengths to encourage eastern Europeans to move here, even paying for their relocation. For many in colonial countries, Britain was viewed as the mother country and so the natural place to move to, particularly after the US closed its borders. Many had seen Britain at first hand during the war and realised that not all Britons were rich and educated, and so felt more able to move here. It was no longer an unknown. And it was easier too, as transport ship movements made travel easier and cheaper. The UK Government strongly supported the rights of all to emigrate to the mother country and so decided not to restrict immigration. The British Nationality Act of 1948 gave UK citizenship, with the right to enter, settle and work, to eight hundred million Commonwealth citizens and their families worldwide. This was logistically impossible of course, but the propaganda of empire made much of a family of races under the British flag. They thought it was a safe Act to pass as surely no one would want to move to the UK where it was cold, uncomfortable and crowded.

On June 21, 1948, the *Empire Windrush* landed at Tilbury from Jamaica. This wasn't the first ship to bring returning immigrants; the previous January the SS *Ormonde* brought 108 displaced Polish migrants workers from camps in India. No one had taken any notice, but of course, they weren't so visible. *Windrush* had 492 black men on board, so many that Jamaica was worried because of the brain and muscle drain. The ship was bringing back several hundred West Indian RAF servicemen who'd been home on leave. There were empty berths, so the Ministry of Transport allowed the shipping company to sell them. The places, costing £28.10.0 (£1,000) a berth, were only advertised two weeks beforehand, so most of those who bought berths came from better-off families. Even so, there was a huge queue for places. Sam King responded to the advert in his local paper and was successful after his family sold three cows to buy him a ticket.

Nobody thought to tell the Ministry of Labour that these immigrants were coming, and they only found out a few days before the ship was due to arrive. The Civil Service was dismayed and crippled by the anxiety of having an influx of uncontrolled people, after years of controlling everyone's movements and every last morsel of food. Initially, they tried to encourage them to return to the West Indies. Flight Lieutenant Smythe, an RAF officer for the Minister of the Colonies, was on board *Windrush* and was told to put out a leaflet encouraging them to go back. No one thought they would last one winter. But this didn't work. It was grey and raining when the immigrants arrived, but Sam felt it was a good omen when, a few hours later, the sun came out. Once they were here, the government wanted to do its best for them, and they were very well received locally by a curious, rather than hostile, press. Although there were few jobs in the area, all found work very quickly.

Yet racialism existed but was unacknowledged. There was an invisible colour bar, particularly in relation to rooms and jobs. Boarding houses and hotels frequently had notices saying 'no dogs, no blacks, no Irish'. But most people were unconcerned unless an immigrant moved in next door or started socialising with a white girl. Only a trickle of West Indians came after *Windrush*, and there were no real problems until the post-war reconstruction boom ran out of steam and unemployment jumped in the late 1950s. Resentment rose and the blacks, much more visible than eastern Europeans, were an easier target for those who objected to the presence of foreigners. But this was fuelled by a fear of change, rather than an inherent problem with colour, as people feared the loss of their jobs and housing. A massive shortage of housing caused social conflicts. Council houses were given to residents, so later migrants were thrown onto the private housing market and forced to settle in unsavoury areas of cities, thus becoming identified with the reputation of such areas, such as Notting Hill, then a massive slum. Trouble was being stored up for later.

CHAPTER 9

George was now moving in really exalted circles. In October 1952, the phone rang one day at George's Surrey home, and the voice at the other end said, 'Gene Kelly here. I've been listening to your choir in *All Star Bill,* and I'd like you for my film *Invitation to the Dance.*' George, stunned at what he was hearing, had the presence of mind to say, 'Delighted – what do you want me to do?' Gene explained, 'I've got several sequences in which we tell the story of different songs – Cole Porter's *Just One of those Things* for instance - and I want the vocal effect to fit the dance routines I've worked out. You're the only English outfit that can give me what I want.' When George and the choir visited Elstree Studios for a test recording, they found they were also wanted for an old-fashioned barbershop quartet sequence, special arrangements of *The Whiffenpoof Song* and that famous hit *I Feel a Song Coming On.* British musicians, both orchestral and choral, had a huge reputation for working fast and accurately and, strange as it may seem, American film companies found it better and financially worthwhile to record the music for their films in Britain. It would then be flown back to the States and incorporated in the film reels.

George and Gene experimented to achieve the effects Gene wanted, in the end using twelve voices 'plus Eric Whitley' – the first mention of Eric who featured ten years later in the first Australian *Black and White Minstrel* tour. At this stage, the film was to be all dancing and singing, with no dialogue, a very daring experiment, and one that Gene Kelly had had great difficulty in persuading MGM to make at all. Gene managed everything - choreography, music and the actual dancing, as well as directing the film. Maybe Gene attempted too much himself - the film previews were received so badly that a horrified MGM shelved it until eventually releasing it in New York in 1956, then more widely on the art-house circuit in March 1957. Time has however been kinder, with this film now regarded as a masterpiece. Sadly the songs recorded by the choir had disappeared by the time of its 1957 release.

Other huge films also involved the choir. In 1955 they recorded at Shepperton for the eagerly-awaited Ivor Novello film *King's Rhapsody*, which was sadly to disappoint at the box office. Directed by Herbert Wilcox, it starred Anna Neagle and Errol Flynn and premiered at Leicester Square in London. So anticipated was it that the fledgling Independent Television covered the event in a programme which followed Anna Neagle and Herbert Wilcox as they travelled to Leicester Square, after which famous people associated with Ivor Novello were introduced to viewers, an orchestra played selections from the score and the choir sang excerpts.

George's singers also appeared in the Marilyn Monroe hit *Gentlemen Prefer Blondes,* as well as the Jane Russell sequel *Gentlemen Marry Brunettes*, one sequence of which included the Ted Heath Band plus the choir. George also jumped at the chance to record eight songs for the forthcoming American musical *Where's Charley?*, made at Elstree with Broadway dancing star Ray Bolger, the Scarecrow from *The Wizard of Oz*. When the latest Disney film, *Alice in Wonderland*, was released, the BBC eagerly marked the occasion with *Adventures in Wonderland*, using Mitchell Maids, as well as a tribute to the film, which also used the singers. Walt Disney himself was in this programme which marked the first time George met Walt Disney, with whom he was to become good friends. One evening when the choir was rehearsing at the Aeolian Hall, Eve Blanchard remembers, 'George had made a beautiful arrangement of *Alice in Wonderland*. Walt Disney walked in and thought the arrangement was wonderful; we had to sing it again for him. He said he'd have used it in the film if he'd known of it.'

Another American great, keen to meet the choir, was Bob Hope, as recalled by one singer: 'The epitome of the professional approach was made plain to us one evening when we had made a short television film. Told to stay on stage, we sat about chatting in our white lace dresses with our "diamond" collars until we noticed the doors at the back of the stalls opening and a platoon of men coming down the centre aisle. They looked like the board of directors of a merchant bank, all wearing dark overcoats and black Homburg hats. The "chairman" of the board was unmistakable; no one else had that hockey stick nose. "George," said the producer, "I'd like you to meet Bob Hope. Bob, this is George Mitchell." "Glad to know you, George. How do you spell your name, one 'l' or two? Make a note of it." He never forgot names and was unfailingly polite.' George and Bob were also to become good friends.

Joseph Lilley of Paramount, who was a famous musical director and composer, with many awards to his name, was another who retained a link with George over the years. The two worked on several musicals in the late 1950s, including the Oscar-nominated *Li'l Abner* and *Alias Jesse James* with Bob Hope. After one collaboration, Joseph wrote to George via Lew Grade: 'A hasty note to thank you and Mr Luff for enabling me to enjoy the services of the George Mitchell Choir. The choir, beautifully trained, was excellent, and my only regret is that George and I couldn't get together socially afterwards. We both tried, but our respective business schedules seemed to be playing Fox and Hounds!!! George is a real nice guy and contains within himself the happy combination of a great musical talent and a practical business man. Please give him my respect and good wishes. Thank you again for your kindness to me.'

Still ever-present on radio and increasingly on TV, his singers also dominated theatreland in the 1950s. This decade was the heyday of seaside entertainment as families began to recover from the poverty and greyness of the post-war years. Although the first package holiday had arrived on the scene in 1950, the days of the Spanish Costas were yet to come, with less than 10% of people going abroad. Small wonder when package holidays were expensive. The first package tour included airfare, two weeks under canvas, all meals and wine in Corsica and cost £32.10 (£740). Do-it-yourself foreign holidays were even more expensive. The scheduled airfare to Nice, for example, cost £70 (£1,600). So Britain was still a stay-at-home nation, with most people looking forward to their one or two weeks by the sea. No wonder that seaside resorts such as Blackpool, Morecambe and Eastbourne flourished. The big resorts had dozens of theatres, where the old music hall traditions were still kept alive. To capture the widest possible audiences, theatres usually ran three or four different programmes twice nightly over a two-week period, changing midweek each week but using the same company. This enabled a family, in a resort for two weeks, to see four different shows during their holiday.

Minstrel Magic

Mitchell singers played a tremendous part in providing this entertainment. George's singers first did a summer show in 1953 in Bournemouth, and soon nearly all resorts had Mitchell singers in at least one theatre, while the top places like Blackpool and Eastbourne often had four or five groups at different theatres. By the heyday in 1958, they were in thirteen different summer shows in resorts from Bournemouth to Morecambe, Southsea to Edinburgh, with singers at four different theatres in Blackpool alone. Pantos followed much the same path. After a relatively low-key start in 1950 with just two pantos - one at the London Palladium and one in Wembley - by 1958 they were breaking all records, appearing in twelve pantos, ranging from two in Liverpool and two in Newcastle, to the London Palladium, via Coventry, Manchester, Blackpool, Aberdeen, Edinburgh, Glasgow and Sheffield. As ever, the singers stepped into whatever extra parts were required of them in these shows. Outlaws, villagers, fairies, villains, pirates, they threw themselves with gusto into the variety of work. And gradually what became a tradition grew up. Known for his helpfulness, George was more than happy for his singers to understudy the leads in both pantos and summer seasons. And often they were called upon to take over the role at very short notice.

The tradition seems to have started in 1957 when, in true Mitchell fashion, one of the group in *Puss in Boots* in Coventry, Margaret Davies, took over from the principal boy when the star succumbed to 'flu. The same year, Mitchell singer George MacPherson took over as the comic lead in *Mother Goose* in Glasgow, when an injured Duncan Macrae pulled out. Strengthening the tradition, Hermione Clarke took over the twin roles of Witch and Fairy Godmother in Newcastle's *Cinderella* when the actress playing those parts had to step into the principal boy role. 1958 turned out to be a bumper year for understudies. At the Glasgow Alhambra, George MacPherson understudied male lead David Hughes this time, once again having to step into the breach, and Dawn Haynes understudied principal girl Sheila Paton. George was getting a taste for taking over leading roles when, the following year, he went on for David again when he succumbed to 'flu. In Edinburgh in 1958, Derek Page deputised for puppeteer Alistair M'Harg who was out with laryngitis for much of January. Maybe it was something to do with the Scottish weather, but in the other Glasgow pantomime, soprano Pauline Greta took over from its star Vanessa Lee on Christmas Eve for several performances, after only two rehearsals. This fairy tale event was well covered in the newspapers. One Glasgow paper said, 'At literally a minute's notice, 26-year-old Pauline Greta rendered with verve and sweetness the solos and duets which Miss Lee sings. Though she was familiar with the arias, Miss Greta was worried about her ability to put over the dialogue...at the close of the matinée, Miss Greta was given a special round of applause for her lively performance in filling the breach.' The *Scottish Daily Mail* reported Pauline said, 'I can't believe it's true. I still haven't had time to phone my parents. What touched me more than anything was the huge bunch of flowers the rest of the boys and girls in the chorus had sent to me before the matinée was over.'

Not all replacements came from resident Mitchells. In 1961 *A Wish For Jamie* opened in Glasgow, where Glyn Dawson had understudied Kenneth McKellar the previous year in the same show at the same theatre. But at Christmas 1961, Glyn was in London. He recalls, 'I was rehearsing a Minstrel television show when I was asked by George to go to Glasgow, to understudy Kenneth McKellar again.' After driving north in his trusty van, Glyn remembers, 'The manager called me in the second house interval and told me to get on all Kenneth's clobber and start the second half, as Ken had a sore throat. I wasn't worried as I knew the main songs. However, only the other three boys in our dressing room knew Ken had gone home! Ha! Ha! The company was on stage, waiting for the music to start and the curtain to rise. When this happened, I marched down through the centre of the entire company and started singing. The band didn't know about the change, not even the conductor! When the leading lady marched through the company, she was dazed! I was on for some ten days and quite enjoyed it.' He did well financially, as not only did George give him a £20 (£430) bonus, but so did Kenneth McKellar!

This pantomime phenomenon spilt over into summer shows in 1959 when in Glasgow, 'Eve Boswell has been having a little voice trouble. Not enough to prevent her doing her usual delightful solo spot but the production numbers in which she also takes part threatened to increase the strain. So Joan Knighton, one of the Mitchell Singers, was asked this week to study everything Eve did during these numbers. Then she was called in to take Eve's place while the star watched the show from the stalls, hurrying backstage to be in time for her own spot. "I was nervous at first, but not now," said Joan.'

Once his singers were safely established in their summer shows, George occasionally found time to take a break himself, as other work reduced in the summer. Such holidays always centred around cars. Like his father, cars played a major role in George's life, so much so that he kept a book listing the cars he'd owned, all adorned with the number plate GM16, commemorating his favourite number of singers. He started driving in 1934 and said, 'I'm daft about cars and always will be.' After the war, when motoring had been so restricted, he proudly noted in his diary on June 15, 1948, 'bought Talbot car'. The following day, he records, doubly underlined, 'Rehearsal Dinely by car'. The two gallons of petrol he put in the car cost him 4/3 (£4.84). There were barely two million cars on the roads at this time, and it was very much a middle-class luxury.

By 1974 he had had about forty, including six Jaguars, three Rolls, a Bentley, two Rovers, two Fords, two MGs, two Facel Vegas, a Wolseley and a Peugeot 204. 'I like Jaguar cars,' he reported. 'I buy about one a year because I like to keep up with the latest models.' According to Dot, his favourite was the Vega, which Sir Francis Chichester borrowed when he returned from his around the world trip when the Queen knighted him. Several people remember this very special car. Ted Darling, for instance: 'A wonderful sports car. I also remember him having a deep blue Bentley with whitewall tyres, finally a Rolls convertible - very impressive in Scarborough.' Cameraman Eddie Stewart also remembers this car: 'He owned a French Facel Vega which was a luxury car. I remember walking up to the front entrance to the BBC one day and seeing it parked there. George told us all about it with great glee.'

In late 1959, the M1 opened, and it was inevitable that George, with his fascination with cars, took the first chance he could to drive this new type of road. Motorways had no speed limits then, and cameraman Eddie Stewart remembers, 'The first time he drove down the M1, he rejoiced telling us he did it in a phenomenal time, just over the hour. He must have gone like the wind. He also got animated talking about the road trip he took on the Road to the Isles, from Fort William to Mallaig in the Scottish Highlands, every September.' This first stretch of motorway was

Minstrel Magic

72 miles in length so by modern standards, he wasn't going fast, but in 1959, that sort of speed was unheard of.

He loved driving on the Continent as well, much as his parents had done. One newspaper feature said, 'Judging by the array of badges over the front bumper he must have toured most of the Continent. France, Italy, Switzerland - "I've not tackled Spain yet," he told me.' And this was indeed how the Mitchell clan spent their rare holidays, following the tradition started by Robert when George was young. In 1953 George took two weeks off in August, saying 'I thought I'd take this opportunity as my singers only have eight broadcasts while I'm away.' Though pre-war they'd crossed the Channel by ferry, Robert and the extended family had been among the first to fly themselves and their cars by Silver City to Europe when this service had opened in July 1948. Named after the Australian Broken Hill silver mine, Silver City flew the first passengers and cars in a converted Lancaster bomber from Lympne to Le Touquet. The service was a resounding success, and Silver City relocated to Lydd where the first new post-war UK airport was built in six months. The Duke of Edinburgh opened it on April 5, 1956, and unknown to most people, exported two cars to Le Touquet. It cost £25 (£435) per car and £4 (£70) per passenger; George and his family, always keen to enjoy new experiences, were among the half a million passengers who flew with Silver City between 1953 and 1957. The *Evening Advertiser* reported, 'Where most motorists seek the easiest roads, George deliberately looks for the most difficult, and can claim to have negotiated some of the worst roads in Europe.

A trip in 1953 tested his skill to the utmost. Two Mitchell cars were flown to France - Robert and Barbara went too - and the whole family set off through the steep Swiss mountain passes. George was negotiating the winding highway set into the mountainside outside St Gothard, when a boulder came down right in front of the car, shredding a front tyre and smashing the pipeline to the hydraulic brakes. Suddenly the car had no brakes! He and Robert tried to patch the pipeline with adhesive tape, but it was no use. Somehow George had to drive off that mountain and down into the nearest town, relying only on the handbrake and the nearside wheel scraping the kerb to slow them down. He said, 'Believe me, it was hair-raising! I love fast driving, and my wife says this was the only time she has known me drive slowly on a Continental road!'

Minstrel Magic

This didn't deter him and the following year, he managed another holiday. 'Apart from last year I haven't had a holiday since 1938,' he said. 'My wife has been on at me for years to let up a little and take a good holiday. This year we plan to take three weeks, on a road tour of Austria, Switzerland, Italy and the South of France. If TV and radio dates permit, we hope to visit some of the colourful festivals taking place on the Continent.'

But most of the time, there was far too much work to allow luxuries like holidays. George had shown there was major money in this work, and his choirs were so phenomenally busy there was room for at least another outfit. Certainly, George was by now having to turn away work. Charles Chilton recalls, 'It became difficult to get the Mitchell choir, so I tried others, but they were no good. Then Charles Young formed a choir for me, and it was the only one that was any use. I would have used George Mitchell if available, but they weren't. When Charles' choir turned up, half of them would be George Mitchell Singers in any case.'

George was perfectly happy with groups setting up almost in opposition, even if they came from within his own ranks. After all, 'I think,' said George, 'that we must have cornered 90% of the market in our field.' For those who kept George informed about what they were doing, and even asked for his help, the support was there. One of the earliest were The Coronets in 1954. The three men and two girls were all ex-George Mitchell Singers, all going to 'a good school', as the *Daily Mail* reported: 'That training shows in everything they do.' Some years later, Bill Shepherd, leader of the Coronets, recalled George as 'one of the finest people I ever worked with. Even when I left to form the Coronets, using former members of his choir, we were on the very best of terms. In fact, George advised me all the way.' Another member of the Coronets was Mike Sammes, who, after singing with George and the Coronets, formed what was really the only serious opposition to George - the Mike Sammes Singers. However, although this choir and the Cliff Adams Singers became household names, none reached the heights the Mitchells had - and were to reach even higher. This pre-eminence was all about the perfectionist that was George.

Often Mitchell groups in touring or summer shows formed trios or quartets while remaining working for George, none of which seemed to cause any problems with George. George sent the

Mitchellaires, two men and two girls, led by later Minstrel principal Tony Mercer, to Bournemouth for a summer season. The Mitchellaires grew increasingly popular as the season progressed. By early September, the group had become so popular that it went to a full-size act, doing five numbers to open the programme and three after the interval, though this was obviously under the Mitchell banner. But later in September, the quartet branched out by doing Thursday night concerts in places such as Bath and Cheltenham, on their own initiative.

The singers accompanying American singing sensation Guy Mitchell got on so well with one another that they formed their own singing group. The group, called the Lucky Stars, impressed Guy so much that he let them perform on stage during one show, before bringing them to the notice of the *New Musical Express*. Producer Ernest Maxin used them in *Showcase*, after which they were booked for the summer season at Bournemouth. When Guy returned to Britain the following year, he said, 'I'm eager to hear my favourite English singers again like Dickie Valentine and Joan Regan. Then too there are the Lucky Stars, I take particular interest in their career. I'm very proud of how quickly their careers have taken fire.'

Pot Luck at the Winter Gardens Blackpool in the late 1950s used a Mitchell Trio; the three men, Derek Franklin (who was married to comedienne Beryl Reid), George Taylor and Jack MacKecknie, were all from Birmingham and already well known to Blackpool Sunday concert audiences. They then made a record advertising a Birmingham brewery which might well have caused some domestic disharmony as Beryl Reid often publicised a rival Birmingham brewery. While the Minstrel show was at Glasgow, soloist Freddy Williams, together with guitarist Barry Westcott and double bass player Ernie Dorset, formed the Freddy Williams Trio. George fully backed them, allowing the trio to play the clubs after the show's second houses. Topper Jennie Jaconello was also allowed to audition for the part, which she won, of the Telephone Girl in a GPO advert in 1967. The advert won first prize at the International Advertising Film Festival and again provided excellent free publicity for the show.

During their Auckland stay, the Minstrel company on their second tour Down Under branched out into extra-curricular activities, which, given the scale, George must have known about and obviously approved. They developed a cabaret performance which became a huge success. This they frequently performed at what Minstrel Don Hirst called 'the most lavishly equipped ballroom I have yet seen [in Auckland Town Hall]'. The show opened and closed with the girls presenting ballets based on *Cabaret* and *Hello Dolly*, the company performed a variety of items, and then their folk group sang. One such performance was at the Air New Zealand Ball, for which they were paid $300 (£3000), enough for a bus to take them to the famous Rotorua mud pools, during their week's stay in Hamilton.

George must have known too about outside work done by the touring Minstrel shows. As Roy Winbow, Head Minstrel of the touring show in Paignton, remembers, 'we did an ad for Cadbury's Chocolate Fingers, which I choreographed at George's request. Les Want and Les Rawlings were in front of the line-up which consisted of myself and one other Minstrel, plus four girls. We filmed in the theatre, with us in Minstrel makeup and basic Minstrel costume.' They also filmed as extras in a Dick Emery series that was filming in Torquay. They were to repeat this extra-curriculum activity two years later in Blackpool, again for Dick Emery, and became extras in the 1977 Ken Russell film *Valentino* starring Rudolf Nureyev.

What George did disapprove of was not being kept informed - again, he needed to be in control. He didn't like being kept in the dark or having surprises sprung on him. He wasn't nearly so supportive of two ventures that Harry Currie, who was a principal Minstrel in the first Australian tour in 1962, tried to get past him. Harry Currie remembers, 'I met some people from Robinson's; they were already using the golly on the jar with sound and visual commercials. I asked them if they'd be interested in Tony Mercer doing a version of the jingle, and they were ecstatic about it - imagine Tony in his costume and blacked up, and that mellow voice singing *Look for the Golly, the Golly on the Jar*. Tony would have made a lot of money, and the cross-promotion would have been good for everyone. I told Tony about the idea, he took it to George, and George said, "Under no circumstances". Tony said it wasn't George's idea so he wouldn't go for it.' However, Dot recalls, 'George vetoed it because of copyright issues.'

Undeterred, Harry risked George's wrath again when the first Australian Minstrel tour reached New Zealand in 1963. New Zealand's HMV Records asked the soloists to make an album. Harry knew 'what would happen if we asked George – a resounding NO! He didn't want anyone doing anything not connected with the Minstrels. So we made the LP without asking, following the old precept it's easier to ask for forgiveness than permission.' He should have known better after the Robinson's run in. Jeff Hudson, also a principal with the show, recollects that Harry's was the business head behind the record, and that he had in fact instigated it, a memory supported by the fact that Harry was the album's producer. Called *Three Voices Go Places*, the album sleeve notes gave full credit to the show. Jeff recollects that the cover photo –the three soloists wearing Minstrel blazers, though nobody blacked up – was taken at Wellington Airport with a sign saying 'London 13,000 miles'. Inevitably George heard about it. Jeff remembers, 'Someone said, "We've heard from London, this album should never have been made." ' Harry recollects, 'The Victoria Palace guys told us George wasn't amused, though he didn't write and tell us so.' Trying to lessen any repercussions, Jeff reports, 'We registered with the Patent Office that we alone were on the record and that it was nothing to do with the George Mitchell Singers.'

George obviously had no problem with singers making their own records, however, as all three London Minstrel principals made LPs under their own name in later years, well supported by George. In 1965 John's first solo album *John Boulter Sings* was released to critical acclaim. Sales leapt up, radio plugged it, and reviewers raved about it – 'a truly magnificent record'. He went on to make at least three more albums at this stage of his career. He said, 'Having to wear black makeup all the time can become a bore. I've often wanted to get out of it for a change. It leaves no room for expression or personality. The name is known, the voice is known, but not the face. I have even been mistaken for a stagehand when I walk out of the theatre.' He believed the disguise was restricting his fame and earning power, but although he said he'd like to be recognised in his own right, he had no intention of leaving the show. By now, or perhaps because of the album's success, John was earning enough to buy a second car and a boat which slept six. Tony followed suit in 1969, issuing a solo album which by April had sold 70,000 copies. Dai completed the trio when he recorded an album later this year.

George could hardly believe it when Dennis Main Wilson reminded him one day that Feb 13, 1955, meant he'd been broadcasting for 10 years. Just where had the time gone? From that first *Variety Bandbox* at the Queensberry All-Services Club, the choir had now appeared in thousands of broadcasts and stage shows and been associated with all the top stars of the day. George kept mementoes of all the artistes with whom he had appeared, a roll of almost every famous name in the world of entertainment; one of his most treasured possessions was his first fan letter from a group of Servicemen and women. To mark this anniversary, he drew up a list of the stars he and the choir had appeared with. Apart from regulars such as Guy Mitchell, Geraldo, Vic Oliver and Ben and Bebe Lyon, the list included international stars such as Marlene Dietrich, Gracie Fields, Jane Russell, ice skater Sonja Henje, Howard Keel, Maurice Chevalier, Gene Autry, Johnny Ray, Danny Kaye, songwriter Sammy Cahn, Gene Kelly and Harry Belafonte.

The previous October, Dennis had pointed out to the BBC that George had recently achieved his 1000th broadcast and suggested they should air a one-hour documentary, either then or more appropriately during this February weekend. The Corporation was enthusiastic about the idea, allowing Dennis to plan a documentary tracing the rise of the choir. According to *Melody Maker*, 'It should be quite a gay programme for the choir has been associated with pretty well every light musical programme on the air.' But this of course was the problem. According to *Melody Maker*, 'He had the bright idea of celebrating George Mitchell's ten years on the air with a special programme. That was fine - until he started getting down to detail. Then he found George has packed a great deal into those ten years. Somehow into an hour's programme, Dennis has to bring you Danny Kaye, several *Command Performances, ITMA*, Pet Clark, Gracie Fields, Julie Andrews, and a host of musical milestones.'

Dennis also wanted to include as many as possible of the people who had been involved with the choir. Although many of the original choir were still with George, one person had disappeared completely. Dot Mackenzie, the original soloist, was far too important to leave out of any tribute programme but no one knew where she was. On February 12, the *Daily Mirror* ran a headline, 'Do You Know where Dot is?' The story went on, 'The BBC might do worse than send out one of their rare SOS messages - to find a singer. She's not exactly missing, but the BBC - and George Mitchell – don't know where she is. For after ten years on the air the story of the George Mitchell Choir is being put together for broadcasting. And all is complete - except for singer Dot Mackenzie.' Two days later, the same paper announced success! 'The voice the BBC was searching for was heard again at the weekend - when Dot Mackenzie rang Broadcasting House. When she rang, she spoke to Dennis Main Wilson who's producing the anniversary programme. Last night he said, "We're delighted. She'll be able to take part in the programme after all. It's the one link we wanted to complete the story." ' So Dennis was able to complete the programme, celebrating the choir with which he had so often worked. Years later, the BBC also celebrated George's thirty years in the business, when on May 29, 1974, Radio 4 broadcast a programme called *Celebrations*.

CHAPTER 10

BBC TV was about to get a shock. On September 22 1955, Independent Television was launched in the London area, though it was the end of 1959 before it reached all areas. Even then, not everyone could receive it as television sets had to be converted. The idea of a second channel - a commercial one - had been around for a while but nobody seriously thought it would be any sort of challenge to the BBC. The National TV Council was quickly formed to oppose the whole idea, with most of the intelligentsia joining it. Everyone feared that a commercial network would quickly become like the American networks, which were seen as 'vulgar', with little difference between programmes and adverts. One idea, which hit the ITV proposal even more, was that the BBC should be granted a second channel. The Government wavered for months over removing the monopoly. Both press and Parliament hotly debated the proposals. Eventually, the Television Act of 1954, which allowed the BBC's monopoly to be broken, was written to ensure that there was a clear distinction between programmes and adverts. Nevertheless, ITV was for years seen as the light-hearted frivolous counterpart to the BBC's supposedly more cultural contributions.

In the early years of ITV's existence, artistes generally had to choose which of the two channels to appear on. Performers such as Vera Lynn who signed to ITV were seen as 'defecting' and were generally never welcomed back to the BBC. However, George managed somehow to straddle both organisations, with about a third of his work being done for ITV in its early years. And ITV paid much better than the BBC. The new channel quickly signed the choir for several new series - *Confidentially*, a 'light-hearted half hour', *The Vera Lynn Show*, two new Bob Hope shows and the top-calibre series *Saturday Show Time*. The biggest ITV show launched that autumn was *Sunday Night at the London Palladium* for which George provided singers. Unwary enough to be sitting in the stalls in rehearsals, some singers were made to act as contestants. Both Maggi Lawler and Carl Ewer recall standing in the wings, positioned around the microphone, and puffing on cigarettes between lines. Maggi also remembered wearing glittering showgirl costumes for the final curtain calls, which caused problems if the singers weren't prepared. Irene Thomas recalled, 'The final revolve sometimes started with a sudden jerk, so it was prudent to position yourself to hold onto one of the big glittering letters.'

In response to the ITV threat, BBC TV launched several big new autumn shows, and fans had even more choice about where to see or hear the choir. *Forces Requests*, for instance, used the choir as The Northerners, where one edition became memorable when Mitchell singer Michael John couldn't find his trousers. The producer quickly made Michael sing in his underpants, with the cameras angled so that only his top half was seen. On Friday evenings, viewers could hardly turn on their televisions without falling over the choir - *Forces' Requests* on BBC at 7.30, followed by *Puzzle Corner* at 9, with *Confidentially* on ITV at the same time. Sundays evenings were also typically busy for the choir. On BBC Television, the singers appeared in *Night of a Thousand Shows*, while *Sunday Night at the London Palladium* went out on ITV later.

And so the 1950s progressed. Programmes piled up on programmes. George was inundated with work. In 1956, in a typical example, the choir appeared in one hundred and seventy-eight television programmes, one hundred and fourteen radio shows and sixteen Sunday concerts, a total of three hundred and eight appearances during the year, without mentioning stage shows. Daphne Bell recalls, 'We'd do two or three recordings on the same day, one say in the Paris Cinema and one round the corner in Piccadilly.' Presenter Jack Payne said, 'I must compliment George Mitchell on the high quality of his choirs. I wonder how many times his name appears in radio and television programmes? I understand he supplies more vocal groups for stage, radio and television than anyone else in the country. Without a doubt, it's Mitchell's attention to detail which has made him so successful. He takes infinite pains to get perfection, and he knows the business of music-making inside out.'

But several newspapers found them rather too ever-present on television screens: 'There will also be the George Mitchell Singers who, like the poor, always seem to be with us. Mr Mitchell's singers appear week after week in all kinds of programmes to which they add nothing that cannot be spared. If they were kept in reserve for high days and holidays, we might learn to admire them. As it is, we have to put up far too often with the choir's maunderings' They weren't the ones to feel this way. The *Stage* agreed that 'Saturday evening's *Variety Parade* provided the week's dullest hour on television......movement and voices in the distance came from the Peter Glover Dancers and the George Mitchell Singers, but neither group did anything to distinguish its work from all the songs and dances that have ever been.' The *Manchester Evening News* suggested, tongue in cheek, that 'the BBC would save them (the choir) a lot of travelling time if it built them service flats in one of the studios.' About the same time, the *Glasgow Evening Times* said, 'Cyril Fletcher in *It's Follies but It's Fun* – I was glad to hear the Peter Knight Singers as a change from the George Mitchell group.' Perhaps the choir was, after all, becoming a little too ever-present?

That didn't stop established stars constantly booking them. One such was American star Guy Mitchell who specifically asked for the choir for three consecutive tours of Britain. Another was Dave King for whom George provided a group of singers for his show at the London Palladium. For Maggi Lawlor, this was her first engagement with George: 'I joined aged 20, having been auditioned by Daphne Bell and got a call a few days later which I wasn't expecting so soon, to join the group at the London Palladium with Tony Mercer and Frank Davies and one other girl. She and I had to wear such horrid dresses. We were singing *Scotland the Brave* and held goblets in our hands. I was shaking so much with nerves that mine nearly slopped over. After the show had ended, Dave King asked for the same two girls to support him at Blackpool for a long season. I was horrified at having to leave London, but George promised to find someone to replace me as soon as possible. I'd ring up every week, but the answer was always "we're still looking". I just wanted to be back in London because that's where all the interesting work was - on radio and TV.'

By 1956 even George had lost track of his choirs. As one reporter recorded, 'How many choirs has George Mitchell, the King of Choirs? He answers, "Eleven - I think. Wait a moment, let me count 'em up. I've only three in West End shows at the moment, then there are three working for TV and radio, and five in the provinces. Yes, I should say there must be about eleven." He is sure, however, that he employs more than two hundred singers, men and women in equal numbers. "Last year there was between £2,000 (£50,000) and £3,000 (£75,000) going out every week in salaries," he says. "It'll be more this year, but I haven't found out exactly how much more – I daren't." And then the quiet-spoken head of this vast empire says this, "But we're only just beginning. There's a tremendous future." He hurries from one group to the other, in Scotland one night, London the next. Sometimes his radio and TV choirs will have three shows to share in one day but he has trusted lieutenants he leaves in charge. On the more important dates, George himself conducts.' By the end of the decade, annual income for the organisation totalled well over £100,000 (£2m), with the best-paid singers taking home £60 (£1,000) apiece per week. George himself was reported to be earning about £35,000 a year (£800,000).

Some singers, of course, preferred the regularity of a long theatre run, while others thrived on the immediacy of work and the variety of music that the inner group covered. As Irene Thomas was later to recall, 'Most radio was live then, and TV too, which meant that programmes had to be exactly the right length – no cutting or editing, and in the case of television, even when the show could be pre-recorded, if anything went wrong the whole programme had to be done again.' This was equally true of the pre-recorded radio shows, so the ability to work fast and well was of paramount importance to George's reputation. One possibly unseen problem with the organisation's size and flexibility was the difficulty of keeping in touch with choir members. Many had no phones; indeed, Carl Ewer remembers going out daily to use a call box at the end of his road to phone Daphne to check if any work was available. Carl who loved working for George, recalls another problem he and his fiancée faced: 'We cancelled our wedding three times because we couldn't get George to confirm a date when I wouldn't be needed. You were always afraid of missing a show or a series. If you weren't there for the costume fittings, then you wouldn't get the series. When we did get married, I did actually miss a series.'

Of course, this level of work occasionally produced unexpected problems. Irene Thomas recalled one particular time: 'The only real snag was that the words and music of the songs we did in vision had to be learned in a very few days and sometimes refused to stay in our heads. One mind-stopping occasion was half an hour before transmission time when we were due to open a 1920s musical show. There we were, sitting in our big dressing room, in cloche hats, low-waisted gowns and pointed toed shoes.... "Right," said Daphne, our head girl. "Let's go through the opening chorus, shall we...er-one, two, three, four..." We all opened our mouths automatically, and there was a dreadful silence, not one word or note could we remember. We dived for our musical copies with a screech of horror, and 'fa-fa'ed desperately through the maze of notes until we were called down onto the set.' As Daphne Bell recollects, 'If things went wrong, we made it up on the spot.'

All this work gave George and his singers a huge breadth of musical knowledge which stood George in good stead for his later flagship programmes, the *Black and White Minstrel Show* and *Around The World In Song*. He covered everything during these years from pop to grand opera. Irene Thomas recalled, 'George made us sing operatic choruses, Viennese waltzes, everything, and even though at times there were only twelve singers, the BBC engineers made us sound like fifty.'

Stung by ITV stealing one of its major assets, the BBC again gave the Glee Club its own radio show called *Rendezvous*. But this was just a single broadcast. Producer Dennis Main Wilson and Bob Luff were still fighting hard with the BBC to get the Glee Club another series. Dennis argued that *Twenty Questions* lost half their viewing figures to the 1950 *Glee Club* series and that the choir was now far more experienced. One of his strongest arguments was the fact that the choir featured high up in individual popularity indexes, generally coming second or third to huge stars such as Tony Hancock or Joan Turner. When such lists were confined to musical performers, they always came second to pianists Rawitz and Landauer, who were 'the biggest listening figure getter' the BBC possessed. It was a 'great shame the BBC never capitalised on the undisputed success of the first big *Glee Club* series four years ago,' said a BBC internal memo. But for some strange reason, the BBC still wasn't convinced. An annoyed George immediately put the Glee Club back on stage, featuring 'Tony Mercer, the sensational new vocalist from *Top of the Town* and *Star Bill*'. But still no new BBC series materialised.

Minstrel Magic

Another producer, still using the choir regularly, was Charles Chilton who had started it all off in *Cabin in the Cotton*. And in 1956, he introduced the choir into one of his and the BBC's biggest-ever successes. Written and produced by Charles, *Journey Into Space* had started in 1953 and quickly became phenomenally successful, with annual series. It was the last UK radio programme to attract a bigger evening audience than television. Originally, four series were produced, though the fourth was a remake of the first. Ever-keen to use the choir, Charles now managed to cast the singers as the 'Celestial Choir' in seven episodes of series three. The original magnetic recordings of the show were erased shortly after broadcast, and for several decades, it was believed that no recordings had survived. But in 1986, a set of misfiled discs was discovered, containing complete copies of the three original series, which enabled the BBC to rebroadcast the show in the late 1980s and release copies, first on audio cassette, and more recently on CD and internet download.

In February 1957 George turned forty, and the choir decided to make it special. Irene Thomas recalled, 'Fred Tomlinson made a beautiful arrangement of *Ye Banks and Braes o' Bonnie Doon* and as many of us as could be got together went to Levy's in Bond Street to make a recording of the song. On the other side was a collection of "endings", the sort of harmonic arrangements that we sang so often as the last few bars of popular songs, and Fred had written them in George's own style as an in-joke only he and we would understand.' Years later, George remembered the surprise: 'The party was organised by the Glee Club and included most of today's Minstrels. Sometime during the party, Dai Francis handed me an LP in a plain sleeve bearing the title *Life Begins at Forty*. It turned out to be a recording of some of my biggest hits they'd made in a studio somewhere, only they'd jazzed it up with cod lyrics all about me turning forty. Some of them were very funny indeed, and everybody had a great laugh at my expense. I suppose forty seemed positively ancient to them then, so I hate to think what I must seem now. Decrepit I should think.'

By now, both Tony Mercer and Dai Francis were working for George. Born in Sheffield and the son of Dave Mercer, England and Sheffield outside right, Tony started singing and playing the piano accordion in the Mexborough Grammar School Band. On leaving school, he joined Dot Stephens' Juvenile Troupe and later

Archie's Juveniles and toured in variety, playing the trumpet and singing. He sang with Oscar Rabin's band at the Hammersmith Palais, before joining the Royal Corps of Signals (Parachute Regiment) in 1940 and going through the Burma campaign. During this period he formed an eight-piece band, with himself as vocalist, to entertain the troops. Duties with the occupation forces in Sumatra followed, before demobilisation in January 1947. Back in civvy street, he toured the variety theatres for two years with *Hello*, before being associated with Lew Stone's band with whom he broadcast, later singing with the great bands of Roy Fox, Eric Winstone, Geraldo and Carl Barriteau. Tony's appearance with George in *Happy Holiday* in 1952 sparked letters in the *Record Mirror*, one of which said, 'I can give you a typical example of a real good baritone singer who is being misused by the BBC. The singer is Tony Mercer. This singer was apparently the Mystery Voice in *Top of the Town*. We well remember his rendering of *Old Man River* and can truthfully say that only Paul Robeson can equal that effort, but what have they got him singing now? Horrible things like *Whip Crack Away*. I realise he must sing numbers suitable for the choir, but this boy is more than good enough to have a series, either with or without the choir. I wrote to Tony recently and asked him why he was wasting his voice, and though he was very noncommittal, I gathered he had very little say in the matter and was supposed to sing old songs in the modern manner.' The same issue carried a letter from 'Another Mercer Fan': 'My record shop assistants are beginning to think I have gone crazy as I'm continually asking for recordings by Tony Mercer with the same result - "Sorry, we have that song but not recorded by Mercer." And I'm not an isolated case. I personally know dozens who have asked for such recordings.' Although there were rumours that Tony would soon be releasing a record, record producers wouldn't take a chance on him, fearing he sounded too much like Bing Crosby, though George always believed Tony was the better singer.

Dai Francis joined George in the mid-1950s. Born in Swansea in 1930, Dai learned more than two hundred Dixieland songs from his father, a music hall performer. Before he was ten, Dai was blacking up to sing in local carnivals. During his National Service he won first prize in a talent competition impersonating Al Jolson, and after leaving the RAF, he toured in the *Zuyder Zee* show, singing, giving impressions and playing the trumpet. He also worked in nightclubs and was featured at London's Pigalle with the Woolf Phillips Band, as well as at the Embassy Club as a singer and trumpeter, before joining George, sometime in 1955.

The third critical element in the success of the *Black and White Minstrel Show*, John Boulter, joined later than the Dai and Tony, in 1957. John, from Gillingham in Kent, was a lyrical tenor who started singing aged eight in HM Dockyard Church Choir before joining the RAF when he was sixteen. He studied for four years at the Royal Academy of Music, obtaining Recital Division, the Gold Medal and two other notable prizes for singing. After touring for the Arts Council with *Opera for All* and singing for Sir Thomas Beecham in Delius' *Irmelin*, he auditioned for George who snapped him up. During a programme on the Minstrels, which John narrated, George recalled, 'Cyril Fletcher rang me and said, "Darn good fellow in our summer show. I think you ought to hear him." So I said send him up, and that was John Boulter. He's a tremendous musician with a fantastically adaptable voice.' John remembers, 'George was lovely. He used me sporadically at first, then when he next asked me to join permanently, I said "yes" because I had several children to support, and went to Blackpool Opera House in the summer of 1958, then straight into the *Birthday Show* at Coventry followed by the pantomime there.' George described John 'as one of the finest singers on TV. He is certainly a great tenor. The amazing thing about him is he can tackle anything from rock to opera with almost equal facility.' John himself found settling in quite hard: 'Tony and Dai were both ex-Army, and they thought I was a soft touch. I was, however, ex-RAF so started to get my own back and not give an inch. It was difficult to come into the choir.'

Although John, Dai and Tony became known as the Three Musketeers, once the Black and White Minstrels took off, they were quickly joined by a fourth principal. Don Cleaver's first appearance with the singers was in *Sinbad* in Edinburgh in 1959. Don had never really wanted to do anything but tread the boards. As a child he had always run backyard shows and when old enough, began having singing and dancing lessons. He went from dubbing voices in a Tom Arnold ice show to the skating singing star of the *Ice Follies*. He joined the Carl Rosa Opera Company, then branched out to play opposite Jimmy Edwards and Tommy Steele in the delightful Rodgers and Hammerstein musical *Cinderella* at the London Coliseum. Now he joined the Mitchell empire where he stayed until 1971. He said in 1968, 'It pays to stay loyal to such a grand outfit. I've travelled all over the place for George - once as far as Yugoslavia and now to Australia.'

Other principals such as Les Rawlings, Bob Hunter and Ted Darling were already singing with the choir, Les and Bob permanently and Ted on an *ad hoc* basis as he had a successful solo career, as did Andy Cole who became a Minstrel principal in 1969. The final major player for George on TV and stage was Les Want who joined the London company in 1964. He had been a member of the high-flying Kentones but 'Rock and Roll wiped everything off, and we broke up. I wrote to George, as I knew he'd been impressed with the Kentones, and I started that week, without even an audition.' A great asset to the football team, he had to start in the show's chorus, despite extensive experience. He later said, 'There's nothing quite like the show. It offers wonderful schooling for youngsters entering the business. The management was always fair to me from the beginning, and I was always encouraged to prove myself worthy of a solo spot. That's what so unique about it. There's no big star complex. Everyone is treated equally, and if you've got the talent, you'll be given every opportunity to show it.' Dot supports this, 'Anyone could audition for George at any time if they fancied a solo spot.' Les became a tremendous asset to George from then on, despite some upsets along the way.

CHAPTER 11

Although no one knew it at the start of the year, 1957 became the second turning point for George's career. After seven years of trying to get them back on the radio, George and Dennis Main Wilson were overjoyed when the BBC gave the Glee Club its own television series instead. But this new series, which took George's success to new heights, wasn't a conscious decision on the part of the BBC at all. In fact, the whole thing very nearly didn't happen.

Dennis turned up on his first day as a television producer and Ronnie Waldman, BBC Head of Light Entertainment, said, 'How would you like to jump in the deep end and learn to swim quickly?' Dennis said, 'Sounds all right, what?' 'A show's fallen out,' said Ronnie, 'I've got seven half hour blanks. *Radio Times* goes to press in two weeks. Can you do it?' Always ready to try anything, Dennis quickly agreed: 'I'd never handled a TV show in my life. Luckily I remembered what I'd done in radio - I'm mad about choirs - and I'd used the Mitchell Singers. I rang George, we had a hurried meeting. The only studio we had was Lime Grove's Studio G, a long thin corridor with a knob on the end. Can you imagine, we put in twenty-four singers, eight dancers and an orchestra and moved them. This is where BBC TV is breath-taking. I knew nothing about how to do it. Everyone guided me through and blow me down, we did it.' One paper recorded, 'George is just a little worried, but he says he feels comforted when he thinks of his producer. After many years in radio, it is his first TV production.'

One other newspaper reported, 'BBC viewers will see something they have never seen before - the *George Mitchell Glee Club* .... the twenty men and women singers who are the cream of the two hundred singers now on George's payroll, together for the first time in their first television series. And for the first time, George himself will be on view for a few minutes to his viewing public as he conducts. Why is he not always in the limelight? Explains George, "I don't shun publicity: as a showman, I know its value. But I think I suffer from an inferiority complex." '

Minstrel Magic

George chose ten men and ten girls, among them Daphne Bell, Maryetta Midgley and Irene Thomas, to form the Glee Club for this series, together with a select four, including Dai and Tony, who formed the Jackpots. Irene Thomas remembered, 'We would start each show in the same way, with a song that sounded like *Maryland, My Maryland* but wasn't. George wrote the tune and I wrote the words.' Billed as 'a show of songs for all lovers of music', it used everything from skiffle to the *Hallelujah Chorus*. Still firmly believing that music shouldn't be compartmentalised, George resolved to include, in one programme, a sequence leading straight from a 'beat' number into *Tell Me Pretty Maiden* to a rock 'n' roll piece, finishing with *Greensleeves*. It actually worked.

But trouble quickly surfaced with the sound. How do you manage to get singers dancing, yet leave them with enough breath to sing? Charles Chilton came up with the answer - pre-record the music, with Equity approval. Charles recalls, 'I don't think Dennis Main Wilson had ever pre-recorded music before, as he came to me to see how to do it - but lots of people felt they were being cheated.' But this solution was kept from the public, with George and Dennis going out of their way to fudge the issue, much as happened later with the Minstrel shows. The press were left thinking that 'the Glee Club has been concentrating on its sound reproduction, using special microphones and pick-up systems. George Mitchell says the result has been startling.'

But the solution brought its own problems. Adrian Stocks, BBC TV Sound Supervisor, recalled, 'The playback for miming was from fragile lacquer discs. We had the usual straightforward Mitchell rehearsals; suspiciously smooth perhaps because on the live show I had a repeating groove in the middle of a number. I like to think my ready-poised ever-alert finger eased the pickup into the next groove in the twinkling of an eye and that the choir never faltered for a moment in their rhythmical swaying.'

The publicity departments at both the BBC and the Mitchell organisation went into overdrive. Unusually the press were invited to rehearsals. *Reynolds* reported, 'Blondes Daphne Bell and Irene Thomas and redheads Betty Murphy and Peggy Allen have been on television hundreds of times. But because they belong to the always-heard-never-seen George Mitchell Singers, we've never seen them, except sometimes as shadowy parts of the background. A pity. Because like all the George Mitchell girl singers, they're good to look at. And the male singers are handsome too. I write

Minstrel Magic

from the experience of watching a choir rehearsal in one of those Hammersmith pub lounges which, out of licensing hours, are now serving as BBC overflow studios.'

Another newspaper to visit was the *Oxford Mail* who reported, 'Twenty voices rose in a crescendo of sound fit to crack the glass roof of the hall where the Glee Club was rehearsing. "That sounded fine," I said to six-foot choirmaster George Mitchell. But Mr Mitchell mopped his brow and replied lugubriously, "You wouldn't think so if it was the twentieth time you had heard it." A twinkle in his tired eyes indicated that the gloom was not to be taken too seriously although the most ardent music lover could be forgiven for wearying of *You're Wonderful* at the twentieth rendering, and music is George Mitchell's life. "I'm very lucky to be able to earn my living at the thing I love best," is a sentiment he was still able to express after the twentieth *You're Wonderful*! I had caught George Mitchell at the end of a seven-hour rehearsal on a steaming hot day. He stood out from the rest of the company not only for his height but for the fact that he alone had kept to the formality of collar and tie and dark grey lounge suit - he hadn't even discarded his coat. The friendly atmosphere was unmistakable as the singers romped joyously through their numbers. "They're always like that," said George Mitchell. "There's no discipline, there's no need for it. They're a grand bunch."'

George and Dennis' nerves were in shreds by the time 6.45pm on July 19 came around. There'd only been a couple of weeks to rehearse the first show, the others would have to be managed in the seven days between shows. This first one was staged as an Anglicised version of an American campus. George was deeply affected by seeing his singers in this first show: 'It gave me an odd qualm. The first time they dressed that way was for a concert at the Cripplegate Institute in the City of London in 1943, when the bombs were falling around. That was the beginning of my choral work and every time bomb blasts drowned our singing, I thought it would be the end of it!'

The girls' basic choir 'uniform' was blue blouses and skirts whereas the boys wore traditional blazers monogrammed *GM*. The girls generally made four changes each show, so although it looked peaceful on screen, the turmoil off set was something to behold. Their dresses waited on hangers, and TV dressers moved this wardrobe on wheels to where it was needed next. These frantic quick changes gave everyone some hilarious moments. Maryetta

Midgley remembers, 'We did one song in choir uniforms, then straight to the next set which was *Bless This House*, then we were to go into *Old Ark* where we were all dressed as animals. Daphne [Bell] was a penguin. Daphne forgot about *Bless This House* and changed from her choir uniform into her penguin costume; when she realised, she tacked onto the end of the line for *Bless This House*. George said, "What????" We were all streaming tears, and Daphne was wiping hers away but with a yellow flipper.' Irene Thomas recalled 'a line of girls in frothy tulle dresses gazing upwards and singing a romantic song....very elegant, except that one of them was still wearing the cowboy boots she hadn't had time to change from the last number. A lot of the care that went into our costumes and sets was wasted [because the show was in black and white], but as we became known to various theatrical costumiers, and trusted by them, they let us wear some genuine garments from their stocks of Edwardian and 1920s and '30s clothes.'

The BBC was inundated with letters from all ages, praising the programme and the evident enjoyment of the singers. One moving letter came from Peggy Skinner who wrote, 'I am only a poor old working woman and my opinion does not count for much, but your programme was superb. After listening to the so-called music we are forced to endure, I was beginning to wonder if all was lost and there could be nothing more to look forward to. Your beautiful music gave me a glimpse into your world of harmony, and I thank you from the bottom of my heart for the pleasure you gave me.' Eleven-year-old Elizabeth Aldred wrote, 'I enjoy the different types of songs. I also like the dancing, and I wondered if you could include some ballet.' And it wasn't just humans who liked the show! Dorothy Moore wrote, 'I live alone with a Scottie pup. We shall be your constant admirers.' Old friends from the early days, such as Major F McDermott from the RAPC, wrote he was 'really delighted to see you now have your own television show. It was grand, calculated to suit all tastes and I thoroughly enjoyed it. But why did we never see you except as a back view? It's your show, and you really must bring yourself forward more.'

Press reaction was equally rapturous. All papers reviewed it, with *The Weekly Sporting Review* perhaps summing it up best: 'One of the BBC's more commendable efforts, but like most good ideas, it has to be spoilt in some way. In this case, it comes on the air at the rather ridiculous time of 6.45. So refreshingly different is this show it deserves a peak viewing time. There are no big names and few soloists, as the choir is featured as a team, but so good is the programme that I always make a supreme effort to watch it.'

It quickly became the most popular music show on TV, with one of the biggest audiences. Both public and press demanded that the BBC double its length and move it to a more accessible time slot. George said, 'This is the chance I had been waiting for, for years - putting into the TV picture all that we have tried to do ever since Dennis Main Wilson and I first launched the Glee Club in the Light. It is incidentally also the retort to all those TV fans who have been asking, "Where's George?" Until July 19, I never appeared on TV. And then it was only the back of my head. I don't like the limelight for myself. Until I showed the back of my head, I hear that amusing stories went around that there isn't really any such chap as "George Mitchell".'

When the series ended, everyone was very disappointed. Even though George too was deflated, he philosophically said, 'I have no ambitions because everything I set out to do, I have already done.'

Little did anyone know what was just around the corner.

With a sigh, George returned to arranging music. Singers worked in summer seasons and pantomimes, radio and television shows, with stars like Ted Ray, Arthur Askey, Harry Belafonte, Tommy Trinder, Bernard Bresslaw, Vera Lynn, Eddie Fisher, Semprini and Jack Hulbert in shows such as *Words and Music, Dancing Years, Century of Song, Hi Summer, Black Magic, Perchance to Dream, Carousel* and *Show Time*.

Harry Belafonte, one of the most successful Caribbean American pop stars in history, and later social activist, and at the height of his fame in the late 1950s, proved an important connection for George. His was the first million-selling album by a single artiste. He became one of Martin Luther King's confidantes, strong in the Civil Rights movements. Now, he desperately wanted a black choir for his new BBC series, but when he failed to find one, producer Ernest Maxin inevitably suggested George's singers. Harry liked what he heard and so the choir was booked, but it caused a last minute panic for George. As George recalled, 'I thought it would just be an average size group. A few hours before the show I heard the BBC wanted a 32-piece choir.' With three hundred singers on his books, George easily fulfilled this last-minute request, except he had no suitable high soprano. Swiftly arranged auditions produced 16-year-old Maryetta, who later became the first female soloist with the Black and White Minstrels. But the main benefit for George was in the friendship he forged with Harry's musical director, Robert de Cormier, who became the only man George would ever trust with his choir.

The Belafonte series was called *Songs from Many Lands*, which meant the singers had to learn songs in a variety of languages, including Hebrew, Spanish and French, all good training for the future *Around The World In Song* and a doddle for the talented singers. Belafonte was that rare show business specimen – 'a one-take man' – though this, of course, was the norm for Mitchell Singers. George recalled, 'While we waited a few minutes for the tape to be checked, he flooded us with funnies. I remember one quite well. A Texan landowner awoke one night. Sure he heard something outside, he dashed out with his rifle, tripped over his son's bicycle in the doorway, broke his ankle and realised there were three men on camels on his lawn. He tried to get up but his ankle was too painful, and he yelled, "Christ!" The man on the nearest camel said, "Hey, that would be a great name for the kid!" Then they slowly disappeared into the mist on their long trip to Bethlehem.' John Boulter also remembers the jokes: 'We were standing in evening dress on rostra. Harry Belafonte walked back towards us, and sotto voce said, "I don't care whose star you're following, get those camels off my lawn!"' Harry was a passionate believer in black rights. 'For *Chain Gang*, we were wearing black shirts and trousers,' recalls John. 'Harry went mad, saying we looked nothing like a chain gang, we were too smart. I learnt a lot from him – he felt very deeply about Negro spirituals and what they meant.'

Producer Charles Chilton, who used the Mitchell singers whenever he could, was also developing a new series for them, built on his love of American history. In BBC TV's *Battle Cry of Freedom*, Charles profiled the songs of the North in the fascinating but tragic war between the States, among them *Tramp, Tramp, Tramp, Marching Through Georgia* and *Glory, Glory Hallelujah*, all songs which appeared later in one of the Minstrel show's most popular conducted sequences. Later, George reunited with Charles Chilton in *The Blue and the Gray* which attempted to show that both sides in the American Civil War had some fantastic music. This programme was repeated endlessly over the next few years and a second series made in the late 1950s. In 1961, Charles

Chilton moved his talents to the First World War, profiling its music in *The Long Long Trail*, again with the singers. Written and produced by Chilton in memory of his father whose name was inscribed on the memorial at Arras, the piece ended up as a radio documentary that used facts and statistics juxtaposed with reminiscences and versions of songs of the time, as an ironic critique of the reality of the war. Irene Thomas remembered the programme as 'one of the most moving radio programmes [we] took part in. It was hard work, anything up to fifteen numbers for a half-hour programme and never was good sight reading more essential.'

Gerry Raffles, manager of the internationally prestigious Theatre Royal Stratford East, heard the broadcast and proposed developing it into a stage musical. He took the idea to his partner, the hugely influential Joan Littlewood, but she hated the idea. Gerry took Charles to meet her and eventually she began to see its potential. In 1963 *Oh, What a Lovely War!* premiered, taking the theatrical world by storm. Filmed in 1969, it is revived again and again onstage, the latest such revival being in 2014. And all because of Charles and the Mitchell Singers.

Busy with these and many other radio and television shows, George was also asked to provide singers for several of the shows being broadcast from the annual Earl's Court Radio Show. The big event of this year's show was BBC TV's *Birthday Party*, starring Jack Benny and produced by Ernest Maxin, when the BBC celebrated twenty-one years of transmissions. Other programmes from the show included *Toast of the Town, Golden Age,* produced by Charles Chilton and also starring Benny Lee, and another in the *Pantomania* series for BBC Television, *Closing Night*, with Eric Sykes with the choreography and production in the hands of Ernest Maxin.

Hidden among these was a routine, run-of-the-mill request from the BBC for twelve Mitchell men for a show to be called *The 1957 Television Minstrels*. The show's producer was George Inns, who had first met George Mitchell a few months earlier when they were both involved in the *Ted Ray Show* for BBC Television. George described their association as 'an instantaneous mutual admiration society. We've built a kind of rapport that never goes awry. We understand one another. He's the greatest friend and supporter I've ever had in my work.' Like George, Inns was a perfectionist, always full of energy but never happy with a show.

This rapport spilt over into their private lives, as Dot Mitchell recalls: 'They made a great partnership, going to bars, dinner and on holidays together.' Eric Maschwitz was adamant that much of the (Minstrel) show's success lay with George Inns himself 'with his uncanny flair for what the public wants. He retains a basic simplicity of outlook to which may be added his dynamic energy, his gift for picture-making, plus the all-important quality of leadership.'

Born in Hammersmith London, George Inns took a keen interest in the theatre from an early age. Despite early ambitions to become a comedian, he joined the BBC in 1925 as a messenger boy, later joining their Dramatic Society. After transferring to the Effects Department, he joined Hermione Gingold in a mother and son act, before moving into television in 1932. After the war he briefly returned to radio, producing shows for Ted Ray, Jimmy Jewel and Ben Warriss, before transferring back to television in 1952. Having worked as assistant to John Sharman and Harry Pepper of the then famous Kentucky Minstrels, his dream for years had been to produce a television Minstrel show, so he grabbed the opportunity the Radio Show offered to stage his own Minstrel show. Years later, George Mitchell said, 'George was highly amused to be asked to do a Minstrel show, as he was the first to admit he had Van Gogh's ear for music! Although he'd worked on the Kentucky Minstrel show, they were actually the BBC Staff Chorus, and the nearest George got to them was pulling the microphone cables about.'

Minstrel shows had been around for well over a century, though there is some dispute over how and why they began. The earliest shows originated in the Southern States of America and were staged by white men, who blacked up their faces, though no one now knows why. The modern politically-correct theory is that this was to give white men, many of them slave owners, the chance to ridicule their black slaves, though no one has ever satisfactorily explained why white owners, or indeed anyone else, would want to do this. It would seem quite a bizarre pastime for rich Southern gentlemen. Another theory suggests that slave owners wanted to portray their slaves as leading happy lives, which of course most of them did not, and took such shows to the North to prove that the South could produce great music, as well as well-run and happy plantations. One parallel and perhaps more sensible theory is that slave music was so impressive that white artistes wanted to be associated with it, blacking up to seem more authentic. According to this theory, the makeup was in imitation, rather than ridicule. Whatever the actual origins - and it's probable there was a mix of motives - it's known that black artistes also donned black makeup to appear in such shows. Black artistes, free or slave, were banned from appearing on the stage, so wearing black makeup was one way around this prohibition. In many early shows, even female artistes blacked up, though the famous Minstrel shows of the late nineteenth and early twentieth centuries used only male performers. Whatever the real reason for the development of Minstrel shows, their popularity rose with each passing decade and ensured the survival of great black music, which led to jazz and ragtime. Whatever their intent, the early shows were certainly racist in format and content. Jokes continually poked fun at the black man, making him out to be dim-witted and always grinning. Even so, African Americans flocked to watch the shows, identifying with many of the jokes which the white audience failed to understand.

But by 1957, entertainment had changed dramatically and, in reviving the Minstrel show, George Inns knew exactly what he wanted. As far as possible, it was to be a traditional minstrel show, though using both black and white performers, filled with traditional music but stripped of its racist elements. George was asked to produce a background chorus of twelve men, billed as the Mitchell Minstrels, who were to sit on rostra and sing two three-minute spots. The traditional Mr Interlocutor and Mr Bones would be present, but not the original corner men. 'Very easy but very boring' was George's verdict, 'just another variety show.'

The show's stars were Kenneth Connor, GH Elliott, Isabelle Lucas and Jerry Desmonde. Connor first appeared on the stage at the age of two and by eleven had his own act. After periods at drama school and the army, he returned to the stage, but found most success in radio comedy, particularly as comedian Ted Ray's brother-in-law in *Ray's a Laugh*. He joined the *Carry On* regulars when the films started the following year. GH Elliott was one of Britain's best-loved blackface entertainers. As a child, he became a star in America. On his return to Britain, he quickly became an elegant, sophisticated music hall star. Isabelle Lucas was a black Canadian-born actress and singer, who had arrived in Britain in 1954, performing in film, television and the West End stage. She continued to support the Minstrels as late as 1983, with no mention of thinking the show was in any way racist. Master of Ceremonies Jerry Desmonde had built a career as a song-and-dance man both in Britain and America, joining with Sid Field to become one of the most celebrated comedy teams ever to appear on stage. Other black entertainers who appeared in the show were Rita Stevens, Jim Rich and Randolph McKenzie, the last two of whom had been three of the original Kentucky Minstrels, together with Ike Hatch, who had often appeared with the Mitchell singers over the previous decade.

Everyone, even the band, had their faces blacked up, except for Jerry Desmonde, singer Mary Naylor and the twelve Television Toppers, who, under the direction of Larry Gordon and breaking with tradition, were brought in to provide the necessary glamour. George chose traditional Minstrel songs for the show, including *Ring Ring the Banjo, Dixie, Oh Susannah, Coal Black Mammy, Polly Wolly Doodle, Some Folks Do, Li'l Liza Jane, Nellie Bly, Golden Slippers, Miss Lindy Lou* and *Campdown Races*. Most featured consistently in Mitchell Minstrel medleys for the rest of the show's existence, many being turned into the sequence which closed every stage show and the last show of every television series.

Although no one saw this as anything other than a one-off show - another in the long line of programmes involving Mitchell singers - evidence of sensitivity showed from the start. George Inns had already stripped out all racist connotations, such as the jokes and sketches, and insisted on proper pronunciation, changing, for example, *Dem Bones* into *Them Bones*. Though this remained the case for most of the Minstrel show's life, it didn't extend to Scottish, Irish or French songs, which were always sung with the appropriate accent - an interesting reflection on how racism was then viewed.

The show was allocated two days' rehearsal - easy for Mitchell singers - and televised on Monday, September 2, at 8pm. But it was to flag. The *Birmingham Mail* reported, 'When TV takes us to the Radio Show, we should expect top entertainment to match the new technical achievements of the industry. The BBC's *Television Minstrels* would not have sent a potential set-owner rushing to sign his name on a hire-purchase form. It was a programme of spirituals without spirit, seemingly over-produced to a characterless refinement. Even the George Mitchell men singers failed to make up with quality what they lacked in numbers. They made far too formal approach to minstrelsy.' The *Star* agreed: 'There were plenty of well-blacked faces but the script was the most pallid I've heard for a long time. It was worth watching only for singer Isabelle Lucas and the Minstrels whose contributions were sweet but far too short.' The reaction from BBC audience research panels was mixed too. Some complained there was too little in the true Minstrel tradition and too much modern music, which gave 'a most boring, weak and very dull programme', which only a few thought worth repeating. The majority reaction was temperate, with viewers thinking it pleasantly enjoyable but not outstanding, though the Minstrel flavour 'made a nice change'.

This uncharacteristically lacklustre show was quickly forgotten. Disappointed though George Inns was, George Mitchell shrugged his shoulders, saw it as a less successful programme tucked firmly in among hundreds of successes and carried on with all the other work piling up on his desk.

Helping to bury the memory even deeper was the very welcome news that the BBC had quickly bowed to public and press pressure and re-commissioned the *Glee Club*. Five months after the last programme in the first series, the *Glee Club* was back with a longer series of ten shows, plus a special May edition to usher in the holidays. In a popular move, it shifted to Mondays in the even more prestigious 7.30pm slot, though the twenty-minute length still wasn't popular with anyone. This time there were no guest stars or compères - *Radio Review* said, 'The Glee Club believe they can carry it off by themselves' - and some of the twenty-four singers featured in small groups. Tony Mercer and Dai Francis were both named soloists, together with the Jackpots and Dai's wife, organist Elsye Monks. The singers invited viewers to join them 'with songs old and new'. Film shots were sandwiched between songs – there were fleeting glimpses of a parachute drop, a train puffing through the countryside and a rocket being fired into space (accompanied by a muted rendering of *Auld Lang Syne*), most of which puzzled viewers. During the closing credits, the choir members came towards the camera in lines of four, with camera captions giving their first names. This innovative feature was very well received by the press, who called it 'all very pleasant and chummy' and 'emphasised the friendly easy atmosphere of the whole programme'.

In complete contrast to the reception given to the Minstrel show the previous September, the press was ecstatic. The *Aberdeen*

Press & Journal said, 'There has been no BBC TV programme to equal this.' The *Glasgow Evening Times* called it a 'real showstopper – or would have been if it had been given half a chance to overrun its time. It was a change to see choral singers making such clever use of the stage instead of standing around woodenly in a depressing-looking huddle.' The *Star* gave the choir an unexpected accolade: 'Lime Grove gave us two treats – those super singers the *George Mitchell Glee Club* and those super showmen of basketball the Harlem Globetrotters. Both teams are wizards in their own way.'

The series soon proved the most popular of the week. Letters arrived from starry-eyed viewers, usually for Dai Francis or Tony Mercer but also for many of the girls. As the series progressed, press praise mounted. The *Wolverhampton Express* wrote, 'It's gone from strength to strength and is in no danger of losing its place at the top of the variety poll.' The *Bournemouth Daily Echo* praised Tony: 'In Tony Mercer, the Glee Club has a leading singer with great appeal, and there are several other members who are first-class soloists. Long may they sing!' Music to George's ears, of course. But the perfectionist in him would not have been happy when eagle-eyed reporters said, 'Surely the members could take more care with their dress. Some wore bow ties, some wore long ordinary ties. To be on the safe side, two people wore both at the same time.'

By March 1958, the show was approaching the end of its run, much to everyone's dismay. But it had one more trick to play. For some time, Dennis had wanted to include a Minstrel-type sequence. He remembered, 'When we'd produced the Glee Club on radio, one of the most successful routines had involved Stephen Foster songs. George and I were keen to incorporate this into the televised *Glee Club*, but couldn't see a way to do it.' As the *Glee Club* was live, it was impossible to put on the right makeup. Lightning quick costume changes were one thing, but new makeup?

Henry Burke was a junior designer on the show. Twenty years later, he recalled this landmark series: 'Charles Carroll, a somewhat flamboyant character, supposed to be designing this weekly series, for some reason decided to let me have one or two settings on my own. These were black and white days of course, and I created some fairly conventional but effective enough sets, using white outlines against black drapes. They had no in-between grey shades at all. It would never pass muster on television today, and I wasn't very proud of it then. But everyone seemed happy, and Charles Carroll asked if I could be left to do the next week's programme [the last but one in the series] on my own, while he was on holiday.' Henry remained firmly, but almost inevitably wrongly, of the opinion that it was his black and white sets which made Dennis want to incorporate a Minstrel sequence. Twenty years later, Henry was still bitter, blaming the show for his subsequent jobs at the BBC. Ignoring the fact that the *1957 Television Minstrels* had already happened, he remarked, 'That's how the *Black and White Minstrel Show* was born. Nobody believes today it was largely my fault. Somebody at the BBC never forgave me. I was taken off the *Glee Club* and put to work on historical plays with splendid titles like *Thunder in the West* and *Ordeal by Fire*.' It's anyone's guess as to why the BBC would have wished to punish Burke at all at this time, so maybe there's a degree of political correctness in hindsight happening.

Reluctantly Dennis shelved the idea as impossible to pull off, until one day a bright makeup girl had an idea. Dennis again: 'We were sitting in the bar at Lime Grove when the makeup girl said, "I've just had a bloody good idea. I put a very light green makeup on everybody, with slightish white lips and slightish white eyes, but keep the contrast ratio between the light green and the white, minimal. Stick a red filter on a camera, what happens?" Under normal lighting, the cast appeared with their usual (in those days) white faces, while in the studio they looked like men from Mars. Then the Minstrel sequence began, and all the lights in the studio changed to red. For the first time, the Mitchell Singers appeared black faced!' The trick was risky. 'Let's say we're hoping to turn them black,' said Dennis to the press, never one to turn his back on an experiment, particularly if it involved Mitchell Singers, 'because it means using special makeup and special camera filters. This, of course, means that all the scenery and costumes will come out in shades of black, white and greys throughout the show – different from those you would normally see. We'll just have to wait and see what happens.'

Henry remembered the set designs for this show very well: 'Dennis Main Wilson asked for another sort of black and white palace setting, this time for a Viennese number. There were the usual platforms for the choir, a set for the band, and also an elaborately painted backcloth some 40' long, depicting a sort of stylised city. For some reason, although the cameras were black and white, the design was a riot of colour, but, looking at it today, I would unhesitatingly describe it as disastrous. Studio G at Lime Grove was restricted in size, so, while the cameras were directed on whatever was going on in front of the awful backcloth, studio hands were to 'strike' the palace and set up in its place a minstrel theatre – dummy proscenium arch and footlights and a background, all set in front of black drapes. In this setting, the George Mitchell Singers would appear singing Stephen Foster songs. For the background, I designed a large riverboat – the first of hundreds that have been used for the programme since. Funnels were stock columns, the railings were from a Terry Scott show the previous week, and there was a large painted paddle-wheel.' Dennis closed the previous sequence on a close up of Dai Francis (still in 'white face'), then cut to a long shot of Dai surrounded by the others, now 'black faced' singing *Mammy*. The whole thing worked like a dream and received blanket press coverage for its innovation, with people clamouring to know how it was done.

There was general dismay when the series ended. The *George Mitchell Glee Club* was obviously the flagship programme of the Mitchell empire and well on the way to becoming the flagship programme for the BBC. The *1957 Television Minstrels* were a distant memory, and no one was in any hurry to resurrect them.

CHAPTER 12

Until, that is, another 'accident' influenced George's career.

Eric Maschwitz, newly appointed Head of Light Entertainment, discovered a scheduling gap on Saturday, June 14, 1958, and asked for suggestions. George Inns, still mulling over the relative failure of *The 1957 Television Minstrel Show*, now leapt at the chance to produce a studio version. Maschwitz accepted with relief, giving, according to John Boulter, both Georges a huge budget, saying, 'I'm sure you'll make a success of it. If you do, that's wonderful. If not, we've all lost our jobs.' There was one condition - George had to agree to do another series of the flagship *Glee Club*. George agreed delightedly, and both Georges sat down to see what could be done with the show.

Everyone agreed it hadn't worked at Earl's Court. That had been little more than a run of the mill variety show. To capture an audience, it needed movement and colour, even if it was going out in black and white. The new show - now to be called *The Television Black and White Minstrel Show* with the Mitchell Minstrels - was to be broadcast from the Television Theatre which, though small, gave producer George Inns far more scope for creating an exciting production. So he scrapped the entire cast, retaining only the Minstrels, Toppers and Kenneth Connor. But not as brave as Dennis Main Wilson, he couldn't bring himself to abandon the stylistic format of traditional Minstrel shows entirely, so the Mitchell Minstrels remained, as usual, as background to the real stars of the show, though now they were given some dance movements. In came pop singing sensation Dennis Lotis, plus Peter Kavanagh, the Big Ben Banjo Band and Don Arden, the young singer and impersonator.

Now that his twelve singers were also moving around the stage during their segments, rather than sitting in straight lines as they had at Earl's Court, George had to think about how to manage their voices. But this was an easy decision. The problem was the same as he had had with the *Glee Club* and the solution was the same - use pre-recorded sound. As George Inns said in 1963,

'Without miming, you would not have had Fred Astaire and Ginger Rogers.' This was normal practice in films, so why not use it to make television programmes more appealing too? The Television Theatre was so small that both Georges agreed they could only realistically use twelve men on stage, as they had at Earls Court, but as they were miming, George could bolster the male voices on the soundtrack, by using sixteen men to record the music weeks beforehand. It also meant that he didn't have to use the same men who had recorded the sound, in the show when it went out from the Television Theatre. As John Boulter remembers, 'Some of the men turned out not to be photogenic or couldn't move well, so they were changed. For television, we used thirteen men and thirteen girls, with one on standby.' Equally, he was now free to use many of the same singers on the sound track throughout the show's history which not only ensured the sound remained the famous Mitchell sound but meant the soundtracks could be recorded in more or less one take, as everyone was experienced in what George wanted.

George now had the opportunity to use female voices, to add yet another dimension to the music. But there was no room for these female singers to appear on the stage, and they couldn't replace half the Television Toppers as they weren't trained dancers, so someone had the bright idea of letting the Toppers also mime to the soundtrack. Dot Mitchell, who started life as a Topper before becoming a Mitchell Maid and then a principal, remembers how it worked: 'They didn't have all the girls as singers because they wanted more movement on stage and it was difficult to get good singers who could dance that well. The boys were just doing basic movements, marching, step ball changes, or passing hats and didn't need to be stunning dancers, but they had to be able to lift us.' The men were never expected to be dancers, but they had to be able to move in a routine, though they never needed to lift the girls very high, mainly because they couldn't risk their black makeup coming into contact with the girls' costumes. John Boulter recalls, 'The routines were quite hard, it was an athletic process.' No wonder George needed to replace any man who couldn't move properly. Glyn Dawson is full of praise for the show's choreographers: 'They did such wonderful work and had the knack of finding the right moves for us, without asking anyone to do more than they could enjoy. Their dedication blended the dance with the music and our voices, and it was a pleasure to learn new movement for both the stage and television shows.'

However, the potential for things to go wrong with the recorded sound was great, so backup procedures were needed. Pat Heigham, posted in 1962 to Crew 3 as a Junior Sound Assistant, remembers, 'My job was to keep the standby tape in step with the master playback so that if that failed, a crossfade could be effected and hopefully no break would occur.' However, such insurance didn't always prevent problems, as the years would show.

Comic Don Arden opened the first show with an impression of a blackfaced Al Jolson, and closed with one of Elvis Presley, having done an Eddie Cantor impersonation in between. Among other songs, George chose *Song of the Dawn* which the choir sang with Don Arden, *Dinah, Carolina* and *Alexander's Ragtime Band*. There were still no Minstrel soloists, though Dai Francis was once again in the chorus, joined by Tony Mercer who had now decided the show had a future.

George held his breath that June night the first reworked show was televised. But this time he needn't have worried. The show captured everyone's imagination, the revamp had worked. The BBC's audience panels raved about it, with comments like 'very much above the usual Saturday night variety', 'went like a bomb from start to finish,' 'really first class, just the thing to keep us at home'. Press reporting adopted the same tone. The *Stage* said, almost disbelievingly, 'The hour-long show achieved something of which few others are capable. It made this critic wish for more.' *Punch* concurred: 'I shall be a regular customer. Moreover, I shall be very disappointed if a great many of the younger generation don't join me. I am glad most of the creaking conventions of old-time minstrel shows have been dispensed with. This is a delightful hour, always attractive pictorially and with some excellent period singing.' *Reynolds* said, 'If one must view on such a lovely evening, the end-of-the-pier touch of the BBC's *Minstrel Show* was the best kind of television - a glimpse of the real minstrel tradition.' One reviewer caught it 'by accident' but stayed to see the entire show, 'Two minutes was enough to convince me this was going to be well above average and I stayed switched on. Let's have more.' BBC's audience panels also liked this show better than the previous year's. While some didn't like the pop element as 'not fitting this sort of show', the Minstrels themselves were particularly praised, with their singing 'particularly clear and controlled, even for so accomplished a group'.

But jazz musician Humphrey Lyttleton was enraged. In a review out of kilter with most current public sentiment, he thundered, 'One day perhaps an electronic device will be invented which, at the touch of a lever, will send a stream of tomatoes simultaneously into the studio, the control room and the governors' or directors' boardroom. Had such a gadget been available last Saturday, I would have been happy to unleash the entire stock of Covent Garden. It's time the minstrel show, which invites us to laugh at the physical appearance, the alleged childishness and stupidity of large numbers of our fellow men, went the same way [as Jewish jokes]. The time to dig it up as a quaint historical record will be when apartheid, social discrimination, the banning of coloured people from hotels and dance-halls are buried in history too.'

Undeterred, a delighted BBC commissioned a second Minstrel show, shown in August, two weeks before the Notting Hill riots. Although these riots are remembered as being white versus black, in reality it was more complicated by far. As most black men who came to Britain initially were single men, they weren't eligible for council housing and as such were forced into private rented houses. Unscrupulous landlords, like Peter Rachman, kicked whites out of areas such as Notting Hill, which had been sinking into decay and crime for decades, and packed blacks in. A neighbouring area was home to the extreme right. Add Teddy Boys into the mix, who would fight anything and everything, and the inevitable happened in late August. For the first two nights, the blacks didn't retaliate, but when no police help was forthcoming, they took matters into their own hands, supported by many white residents. Although the riots were triggered by race, they were not about the skin colour of migrants. They were equally about the conditions of white working class lives and their sense of exclusion.

Into this atmosphere, the second Minstrel show gave its audience a chance to see blacks from a 'safe' distance. In a third show at Christmas, George included a minstrel medley, Christmas songs and music from the Twenties, closing with a Jolson finale.

Both Georges could hardly believe what was happening when they were asked for a further three shows, shown monthly in early 1959, before adding yet another one in April. Although filming commitments meant Kenneth Connor couldn't compère it, he had

Minstrel Magic

enjoyed doing the show so much that he made time to fill the guest spot, allowing Stan Stennett to be brought in as compère. These all went out under the final title of *The Black and White Minstrel Show*, though no one can now remember how the name came about. George reported, 'Simple. It was black and white TV, colour wasn't around.' However, another version says it was because the men were 'black' and the girls 'white'. By the time the extended run ended, the show was receiving publicity as 'the fastest show on television'. The Minstrels, now the most popular element in the show, had sung over four hundred songs during the seven-show run, which neatly worked out at 'a song a minute', a publicity tag that never left them.

Although press and audience were sad to see the show ending, shades of later thunderclouds were already showing. The *Manchester Evening News* was puzzled: 'One thing I cannot understand. In the *Black and White Minstrel Show*, it has a talented fast-moving production that never cloys. It has lost nearly everything of the minstrel show, which was the first conception, and retains just one old-fashioned and quite irrelevant touch - the blacking of the Mitchell Singers' faces. By the time it comes back, the decision should have been made to let them be themselves.' But the *Daily Mail*, which had originally agreed with the *Manchester Evening News*, had a change of heart: 'I was wrong to ascribe the black-face gimmick to laziness. I now see it helped to preserve anonymity and hence the speed of the show. But I still think it's terribly silly. Any kind of uniform would produce the same effect as the black faces, without robbing the male singers of their identity. If I were one of them, it would be very bitter to know that, however well I sang, nobody would be able to recognise me under a coating of shoe polish.'

The Minstrel show was now firmly part of George's repertoire, but only twenty-four of his singers were involved in it, a very small percentage of George's empire. No one had really yet foreseen the heights which this show would reach, and how it would totally dominate George's life, to the exclusion of everything else, though Bob Luff was already thinking far ahead. But for George, it was still business as usual at the end of the 1950s, with regular shows and one-off specials still using Mitchell singers on both radio, television and the stage.

Minstrel Magic

But he began to realise he might have stumbled upon something very special when the BBC commissioned another Minstrel series, this time of eleven shows, which started in September 1959, a mere five months after the previous series had finished. This was the turning point for the show. The previous series had been successful, but few had expected the show to return so soon, or indeed at all. But both public and press were clamouring for more and the BBC was only too happy to oblige, particularly as they were gearing up to improve their own television offerings, having realised at last that TV was here to stay. The new Director General Hugh Carlton Greene wanted to cultivate a new mood of creativity, innovation and enthusiasm and saw the Minstrels as a major part of this attack. The show was about to create new television heights.

Once again, the show was revamped, ending up in its final format. It was cut from an hour to forty-five minutes, with the extra acts now playing second fiddle. The audience reaction reports had consistently reported that the Minstrels were the most popular part of the show so now they were promoted to become its stars. Each show had five big production scenes and one static item - the conducted sequence - which preceded the finale. Guest stars still featured, such as Joan Hinde and ventriloquist Daisy May and Saveen, but the show was now said to 'star' the Mitchell Minstrels. Stan Stennett and Kenneth Connor took it in turns to compère, dipping in and out as the pantomime season took them elsewhere. Stan said later, 'Now I'm a comedy-song man and do very little gagging. Before I joined the Minstrels, I only sang in my bath, but now I'm so confident I sing in the garden as well.' Margo Henderson, also booked for the series, likewise left for pantomime. The final regulars were George Chisholm's Jazzers. Chisholm recalled, 'Stan Stennett was instrumental in getting me in. He asked George Inns to give me a shot, so I decided to ham it up. I asked George Inns how long I had so I could prepare my slot. He looked at the Head Topper and asked, "How long do you have to change from the blue to the pink?" She said, "One and a half minutes." So that was how long I had. Hence why my routines are always so fast.' George Chisholm achieved a huge reputation for comedy on the show, occasionally reducing the cast to such helpless hysteria that the show's smooth running would be jeopardised.

The Minstrel segments concentrated on the 'good old songs'. Over ten years of arranging music for his singers in almost every show going had given George a huge knowledge of the popular music of the past century. It had been the most fantastic apprenticeship which in hindsight had been steering everyone towards the culmination of the Minstrels. He later said, 'The choice of songs was simplified by the fact that most of the tunes I like best seemed to be those which the majority of viewers also preferred. My colleagues know how much I love Wagner and Schumann and they also know how enthusiastic I can be about the Minstrel songs which to me are just as good in their own category. A lot of good songs are still being written, some for films and stage musicals. The beauty of the Minstrel show is that any good pop song can be used and the only reason that current songs (other than items from the big musicals) are rarely used is because one can usually think of an older song which fits the routine just as well and has a much better tune and lyric. But I don't believe that any music which has survived for many years can be bad - whether it be classical, folk music or pop. The letters I receive from viewers of all ages convince me that most of them are happy with the choice of songs and I do in fact include dozens of titles suggested in their letters.'

During a series the singers needed to learn about five hundred songs, and as George said, 'I've probably worked my way through ten times that number before making a final selection. Songs must flow along naturally without untidy tempo changes or unpleasant modulations (referred to by the singers as "diabolical gear changes")'. He used about a dozen songs in each sequence, but only snippets of each song were used. Irene Thomas, who sang on the soundtracks, recalls, 'Every tune we sang was short – seldom more than sixteen bars of anything, with one song sailing smoothly into the next, thanks to George's superb talents as an arranger, so the result was a fast, tuneful, good-humoured show.'

Sequences were themed, such as music by a particular composer, or from one show. Sometimes, the link would be trains, or farming, or maybe music halls. Sometimes a whole show was themed. The second show of this new series, for instance, had a food theme, with songs such as *Food, Glorious Food, Bangers and Mash, Gorgonzola* and *Boiled Beef and Carrots*. George even managed to include whelks and kippers somehow. Often George concentrated on a country, such as Spain or Scotland, or a particular time of year to suit the transmission date. Christmas always produced a show filled with seasonal glee, often including as the conducted sequence, the Canadian Indian Huron carol *'Twas in the Moon of Wintertime*, which became a particular favourite.

George explained: 'A typical bright routine would probably have three peaks - the opening, a centrepiece using the attack of Dai, and our traditional big finish involving the entire group. Between these items my other principal soloists Tony and John are admirable contrasts in style.' A typical sequence might have started with *Yankee Doodle Boy*, featuring Dai, followed by *Pasadena* with John and into *Old Nebraska* with Tony. *Old Kentucky Days* would have come next, then *Kentucky* with Margaret Savage, *San Francisco, That's My Home* and finishing with *Birth of the Blues* with Don. Or it could be a quieter romantic piece, starting with *Violetta* with John and Don, *Mandolins in the Moonlight* with Don, *Man with a Mandolin* featuring Dai, *Stars Shine in Your Eyes, How Wonderful, Hear My Serenade* with John, *Meet Me at the Masquerade* with Margaret, and ending with *Mardi Gras*. George tried to vary the pace of the sequences, with a quick, bright one usually being followed by a quieter, more romantic series of songs.

Visually the sequences often didn't have obvious tie-ins with the music. Original choreographer Larry Gordon would frequently produce dance routines which had nothing to do with the song. 'For instance, take a tune like *Swanee River*,' he said. 'Anything might come into my head. It could be hospitals and doctors. That means we could have the boys and girls pushing one another around on stretchers and trolleys.' Goodness knows what the viewers thought of this, but it obviously worked.

Although most arrangements were reasonably simple four-part harmonies, George gained plenty of contrast by using soloists, male voices alone, girl voices alone, a mix of the two, plus smaller groups, particularly the Jackpots, four senior singers. Initially, the choir provided most of the singing, with soloists being used sparingly, though none is mentioned for any of the shows in the first two series. Where they were used, they merely stepped out of the chorus line and returned to it afterwards. In later series, as the years progressed, the soloists left the chorus and came more and more to the fore, as George sought changes to keep the show fresh. John, Dai and Tony, who quickly gained the nickname of the Three Musketeers, gained 'spotlight' sequences, both on TV and stage. Dai's spot became famous as the Al Jolson routine, John's

Minstrel Magic

were always beautiful romantic sequences, and Tony's were inevitably very relaxed. In later series, particularly towards the end when George was using eight soloists, the choir had virtually become background to the soloists, who dominated most sequences.

The Minstrel soloists, for the first time named as John Boulter, Dai Francis and Tony Mercer, quickly caught the public's imagination, even if they still weren't altogether sure which one was which. The *Daily Mirror* printed a letter asking for the name of the tenor soloist and a further letter asking to see the face of the 'plump singer with the Crosby voice'. The paper duly printed a picture of Tony Mercer, reporting him as saying, 'He doesn't mind being faceless - "Not at all. People remember me for being so big. I make far more money than when I was with the bands - and I work fifty-two weeks a year."' One woman asked George to settle a family argument: 'There is doubt as to which soloist is Dai Francis. I say he's the one that sings similar to the late Al Jolson and my parents say he is the tubby one. As we are Welsh, Dai is of special interest to us.'

During this third series of shows, someone also dreamed up the conducted segment, which became one of the show's most popular features. It became the still heart of the show, a welcome contrast to the fast moving, spectacular sequences which surrounded it. This part of the show gave George a chance to show off the more accomplished nature of the choir, with a more complex arrangement of just one song. Initially, this segment involved only the men, usually standing in a triangular pattern on stage, with the soloists at the front. The only movement allowed was occasional on the spot marching, though arm movements were also used. The men were usually dressed in white without hats, to reinforce the choir aspect of the spot.

George Inns forced George to appear on screen in this segment, albeit with his back to the camera, while he conducted the miming choir in a huge variety of music. Good old standards, such as *Blue Moon, Song of the Dawn* and *The Road to Mandalay*, alternated with nursery rhymes like *Three Blind Mice, Old MacDonald* and *The Frog and Mouse*. Old English folk songs such as *Greensleeves, Clementine, Sixteen Tons* and *Widecombe Fair* frequently appeared, as did tunes like *Onward Christian Soldiers* and *Ode to Joy*. He occasionally used some of the more accessible pieces from operas such as *Aida*, or glorious arrangements of songs like *Battle*

Hymn of the Republic or *What Now, my Love?* And of course, George used his favourite spirituals such as *Old Ark, Noah Found Grace, Dem Bones* and the all-time favourite *Michael, Row the Boat Ashore* which probably became the unofficial anthem of the show. Surprisingly George chose *Born Free* for the final television show when most viewers would have expected *Michael*.

It was about ten years before the Toppers, miming to Mitchell Maids' voices, featured in the segment, except for one Christmas show and one occasion involving Maryetta Midgley, which was 'the first and only upset with him really.' She explains, 'I was the queen of the Ooooos, which I did on the *Legend of the Glass Mountain*. Daphne Bell said, "By the way, they won't need you in the studio for that live show. A Topper can do the Oooos." After a tussle with Daphne and then George Mitchell, I offered to do it for nothing, saying, "It's not fair, they're my Oooos." ' She got her way.

These early shows were transmitted live before an audience in the Television Theatre in the Shepherds Bush Empire, an old converted music hall. This tiny theatre had proper scenery flies, enabling swift scene changes, but also providing a challenge which typically both Georges turned to advantage. The stage area was so small that there was only one foot on either side out of camera vision. Dancers and singers had to leave the vision area past the cameras and stop dancing immediately to avoid falling off the stage. George Inns recalled, 'During transmission, you can see dancers jamming themselves against the wall to keep out of camera view. Often some people have to get back to the changing rooms by crawling along the floor under camera view. A few inches either way and they'd be seen.'

George Inns made a virtue out of this small stage area, by letting the main camera go up and down the centre of the theatre on a crane arm - Eddie Stewart was the No 1 cameraman who rode this high crane. This made it look as if the cameras were moving forward through masses of dancers and singers. The camera crew was vital to the show's success. George Inns said in 1966, 'It's time Camera Crew Three got the credit they deserve. They know to an inch exactly what's wanted. One false camera move and all the glamour would go.' One incidental advantage - for the cast at least - was that there was a space beneath the mounted camera, where sound engineer Pat Heigham remembers sweets being put, to which the girls helped themselves.

Minstrel Magic

Nerves were at snapping point on show day. This show was fast becoming the No 1 BBC show, and a lot rode on the back of it. To make it even more stressful, senior BBC personnel and Board members watched every show from the theatre.

The *Radio Times* caught the excitement: 'Red plush seats in the Television Theatre. Toppers swoop down in swallow-flight behind the cameras to seize ribboned tambourines or perhaps flower-entwined hoops of cane before flitting into the spotlights again. Minstrels, blazered and bow-tied, queue at the trot for beach balloons, or snatch at 'property' trombones, and are back once more in the fray. Between rehearsal spots, there is George Mitchell stalking around on the stage, all smiles. I met Larry Gordon, leaping around in a white sweater. "Never moved so fast in my life," he said. "And never worked with a friendlier team. Five changes of dress in forty-five minute. Average changing time - two minutes." I heard more from Mary Woods, the wardrobe mistress. "We have a dozen quick-change dressers in the wings," she said. Minstrels are quicker off the mark than Toppers. They are more trouble, though, to Toni Chapman, the girl who does their makeup. "One blackened face, including barrier cream, takes twenty minutes," she said. "And that's without the ears. Ever tried blackening an ear?" '

Each show involved about one hundred and fifty people. To the orchestra of sixteen and the cast of twenty-four were added a couple of solo artistes, and a crew of technicians, wardrobe and scenic assistants a hundred strong. Add the regular production team, and the show became the largest single production team working on any BBC Television programme. One programme entailed three hundred and twenty-eight hours of sewing, fitting and quick-changing by dressers and wardrobe assistants, three hundred and thirty-six hours hammering and scene making by studio carpenters, one hundred and four hours of work by studio painters on the colourful sets, three hundred and sixty-nine hours put in by the set erectors, ten and a half days' work by the designer, fifteen days' work by George Inns, and ninety-five hours on rehearsals and actual transmission by the camera crew. And that's without the work George put in before any show could begin to get off the ground.

CHAPTER 13

No one knew it, but all the Minstrel jigsaw pieces were now present and would remain together for years. But just what was their secret?

George had strong views as to why the show was so successful: 'It's tuneful, colourful, harmless and good quality entertainment - that's why it has stood the test of time and the Race Relations Board. We're not old hat. We don't merely rely on the safe and familiar and the old evergreen favourites. Every season we have thirty new songs never heard before. We have tunes from every new Broadway musical, and we often have them before anyone else. Usually, we're accused of things we don't do. Once there was a complaint "Oh no, you're not doing *Hello Dolly* again." Actually, it was the first time we had included the number.'

For George Inns, it had a similar three-fold appeal: 'Nostalgia, people love a trip down memory lane, secondly speed, it must never for one minute lag, third, the show must have lots of pretty girls smiling at you and making you feel good. They're a great invention, pretty girls, I don't know where we'd all be without them.'

Inevitably Bob had a much more commercial view: 'To succeed, you need five things - a great show, very lavish, secondly a family show, appeal to the whole family. Thirdly you must gear your show with a view to being right for people who can't speak the language. Fourthly, the right prices through long runs. Fifthly you must publicise well. Our publicity machine is powerful, and people come to London just to see them.'

George Inns was never tired of stressing that the secret lay in teamwork. From the cast on stage and the singers in the recording studio, to the backstage crew and the orchestra, the show worked as one. The Mitchell Singers had always been a happy family group, and this shone through in these early Minstrel shows. It just became a bigger family. Although the BBC publicised the show 'like a Hollywood extravaganza, expensive, studded with top talent, with glamorous girls and glittering costumes', they also pushed the fact that 'in one respect the comparison is invalid: in the Minstrel show there are no individual stars. The cast work as a team, have tremendous loyalty to the show, and pack in tremendous zest to make up forty-five minutes of the fastest show on television.' George always supported this view, saying, 'I promised them they'd be the first chorus to top the bill and they believed me. In all the years I have never discovered a star. I work with a group, and it's team spirit as well as talent that I'm after. The Minstrels' success was that they were 100% in favour of the group rather than themselves. They were not employees, they were all friends of mine. It was never a show of stars. There were acts, but the stars were the singers, and that's what it was all about. I tell the Minstrels it's better for us all to light the lamp together because if they go out on a stage alone, they mightn't light the lamp at all. They run the risk of finishing up in the dark. People need melody and liveliness, and we give them both, with dashes of sentiment and thrilling music. Three numbers which are in great demand sum up the formula - *Dry Bones, Bless This House* and *the Nun's Chorus*. Stephen Foster always creates a stir. To put the mixture over on television, I must have a top-notch crowd. The more the merrier, because I like numbers, masses, to give a full, round sound. Besides having voices, my minstrels must be good looking in black paint, as well as naturally. They must move attractively, rhythmically. They must be intelligent because they have to work their heads off in intricate numbers. Beyond that, they must enjoy themselves. Well, they do - and it shows.'

George Inns thought the same: 'We don't have star names - which means that everybody connected with the show will do exactly what we ask them, without having to worry about personal reputations. We're a team. It all boils down to one word - enthusiasm. That's just what the George Mitchell Singers do. They bring to your screens a wonderful feeling of enthusiasm and excitement about everything they take part in. That's the secret of our pace. We put the whole show through a series of gear changes so fast, yet so smooth that the viewing public never even gets the chance to lose interest for a moment. One small flaw in the planning could throw the whole schedule out. Timing is calculated right down to the applause. Two minutes are allowed for this. If the audience looks like clapping too long, Eric Robinson gets a signal to start playing the next number over the top.'

Minstrel Magic

It was, of course, this 'team effort' that was the cornerstone of the show's success. Nearly all contemporary features mention the show's family feel, echoed by almost everyone interviewed for this book. Later soloist Ted Darling recalls, 'There was a family atmosphere backstage. The chorus was treated well and regarded as the mainstay of the show, which they were.' Minstrel Peter Clare recollects, 'We were one family, together 24/7 so we all got on so well. If you didn't, you didn't last. You left, or your contract wasn't renewed.' Later soloist Les Want recalled, 'That's what's so unique about it. There's no big star complex. Everyone is treated equally, and if you've got the talent, you'll be given every opportunity to show it.' A singer on tape but never on stage, Maggi Lawler echoed this, 'We were so close as a family. We were all so good – no drugs, no playing around, no one-night stands. Not show businessy at all.' Tight discipline ensured that little was allowed to disrupt this family feel, which all publicity reinforced. Peter Clare recalls, 'If Bob Luff heard a hint of an affair, one or other wouldn't have their contract renewed. Swearing would lead to suspension. If you were late and you missed the 30-minute call, you'd have to put on full makeup and costume but sit in the dressing room for the whole show. You didn't do it again.'

The team feel extended to the production team. The television series ran for twenty-one years and was to have only three producers, two choreographers and one orchestrator. The production routine never varied. It started six weeks before transmission, on a Sunday morning when the two Georges met at the Mitchell house where they sorted out the music and talked through the visual effects. Quite often routines were decided on the telephone. George explained: 'He thinks out a scene, describes it to me, and I produce the music. Often he just rings up with a costume idea for an eight-minute routine, and I arrange the songs. Four or five phone calls like that, and we have a show.' Once the routines were set, George spent the early morning hours whittling the initial forty or so songs for each segment, down to the eight or ten which best fitted the chosen theme, which might be hats, shoes or railway stations. Then he started arranging, again at night: 'By writing at night when it's quiet, I get more done. Most of my music is written between 11pm and 3am according to how I feel. Scoring music for the show gives me great pleasure because I know that a superb presentation of every song is assured by our exceptional combination of talents. Every effort is made by the production

Minstrel Magic

team to exploit each routine to the fullest advantage, and although one might think after each TV performance that every possible variation had been used, the show seems to provide a perpetual challenge to produce something new for the next programme. When you've done thousands of arrangements, it's hard to be different, especially opening a show.' Asked for the secret of their success, he said, 'I don't know – I suppose it's originality. I like to do the songs in a certain way - my way. I don't listen to other people's versions of songs. I think the show calls for a positive style and I try to give it that.'

Perhaps programmes for the later stage show said it best: 'The reason for the unprecedented success of the show has been assessed as the fact that it combines the pace, sparkle, tunefulness and above all, split-second timing of the TV show, with the colour and glamour of a live stage performance. Many ingredients contribute to this happy combination: the care and judgement that goes into choosing the singers so that the voices blend perfectly, and the equally high standard required of girls joining the delectable Television Toppers; the constant rehearsing and re-rehearsing; the taste and brilliance of design that goes into the making of the fabulous costumes, the clever amalgam of ever-popular tunes, good singing, dancing and comedy; the zest which each member of the cast puts into every performance, and the overall care and discernment that moulds the show into the finished production.'

The heart of the show was, of course, the music. Everyone loved George's arrangements. Maryetta Midgley thinks 'they were surprisingly simple, but they worked'. Ted Darling recalls 'his ability to arrange things that sounded good, though they weren't necessarily by the book. A serious arranger might have found a few flaws in the arrangements but they sounded superb, and everyone enjoyed singing them.' Ann Mann who sang with the choir and later produced the Minstrels on radio, says, 'He was so great at medleys and choosing songs to follow each other. His was a brilliant gift.' Carl Ewer was also a huge fan: 'His arrangements were easy to sing and easy to listen to. If I listened to *Sing Something Simple* (with the Cliff Adams Singers), I would always want George's arrangements. You couldn't see the join slipping from one song to the next.' And this brilliance extended beyond the actual medleys. Early singer Eve Blanchard feels, 'There were very few who could arrange for voices - he got it exactly right and could hear the tiniest thing wrong. He was very talented with harmony for voices. The US were good, but he was one of the very few British people who could do it. He created beautiful arrangements. They were commercialised with the Black and Whites, more singalong, arranged nicely but nice simple arrangements.' Irene Thomas remembered George's exceptional arranging skills: 'He was a fine musician with what is much rarer - impeccable music taste. His choral arrangements were simple and deceptively easy to listen to, each under-part forming a "tune" on its own which is most unusual.' Maggi Lawler agreed: 'All his harmony lines had good tunes to them.' Later Maid Julie Morgan could still recall whole sequences, over thirty-five years later, because 'he was so good at flowing one song into the next'. Comedian Don Maclean is adamant that 'George was the finest vocal arranger in this country'.

Once the arrangements were finished, usually after a week, George placed them in an outside loo where a motorcycle courier collected them, taking them to orchestrator Alan Bristow. Alan, who had already collaborated with George on the *Glee Club*, was on board from the first show and remained so for the rest of Minstrel history. George is on record as saying he never had to tell Alan what he wanted for any particular piece, Alan knew intuitively. Alan also worked fast, usually taking only a week, together with a second orchestrator Ray Terry, to finalise the orchestral parts. These major players had unbounded trust in one another's abilities. As Alan said, 'There has never been a cross word with George Mitchell. He really is the easiest person to work with.'

Little rehearsal time was needed before recording the sound. George explained, 'I know what each person is capable of and write accordingly. The boys and girls know what they are doing, and you don't have to spend two hours telling them a routine. Time is always limited, but through the years, many shortcuts have been evolved which have increased speed and efficiency. Details which waste rehearsal time such as breathing marks, style of diction, dynamics and phrasing are all conveyed by various methods on their vocal parts; the main job is interpretation but here again, my style is so well known to them that they know what I expect after one run through. It sounds silly, but we record our LPs in a two- or three-hour session.' John Boulter recalls, 'Some while before the show, we all received our singing parts. We all read music, so no great rehearsing was needed - we were just called together for perhaps a four-hour session, while the singing is recorded.'

Learning the dance routines took longer. Rehearsals took place all over London, at places like the Sulgrave Boys Club, the Aeolian Hall and a Maida Vale venue, though they usually rehearsed in a Kensington church hall for a week before transmission. They then moved into the Television Theatre for one day's rehearsal, before live transmission the following day, when everyone worked from 10.30am till finale. George recalled, 'We rehearsed and rehearsed until it was pretty near foolproof. By using the more complicated props early on in rehearsals, we tried to get the gremlins out of the show long before we reached the theatre.' Despite this, the gremlins occasionally won. George Inns remembered, 'One day when we were doing a candelabra scene, a scene shifter came into camera range holding a damn great candelabra in his hand, and looking surprised. As well he might, for there were ten million viewers looking at him and knowing that something had gone wrong. Another day we were let down by a million to one chance. We had a snowball scene with all the guys and girls throwing balls of cotton wool about the stage. By a million-to-one shot, one ball thrown at the camera got stuck in the lens. It was just the right size, thrown from just the right angle....and it blacked out the show completely!' A 1974 show had one sequence set in a Russian nightclub. To make it look smoke-filled, the props guys pumped a mixture of water and glycerine into the air. The trouble with this combination is that it's slippery and once it settled on the studio floor, no one could keep their footing. The idea was quickly shelved.

The Television Toppers, under the direction of Larry Gordon, were always the dancers of choice. Jackie Joyner, the Toppers' leading lady, was with Larry from the start. He said, 'She's a wonderful judge of character, and in selecting girls for the show, she's an absolute wonder.' Girls needed to be excellent dancers - and tough enough to stand the strain of Minstrel work - but almost more importantly, they needed a 'vital personality'. Later features reported, 'The girl needs to light up when you speak to her. They had to dance well but were chosen more for their friendly personality.' The producers wanted 'girls next door', allowing audiences to imagine the girls were 'just like them'. The girls were also carefully chosen for their height - they had to be between 5'5" and 5'7" tall - not so tall that they towered over the men. The girls' hair was also carefully matched - half were always blonde and half brunette - though of course, the exact matches owed more to hair dyes than nature! The continued use of the Toppers caused problems for their director, Richard Afton, when he took over the production of the later Friday night favourite *The Charlie Chester Show*. Because they'd been seen the previous evening in the Minstrels, the BBC refused to let them appear. Odd, given they used Mitchell Singers endlessly. 'So I can't even use my own girls in my own TV show,' moaned Richard. A very disgruntled Richard remained bitter. Years later, after his links with the Toppers had ended, he was to say, 'I was distressed to see how they have deteriorated. Once there were only twelve of them, six blondes and six brunettes. They used to do three routines a week and were the finest group in the country. Now they are no more than an average, slightly untidy set of dancers who do very little real dancing.'

As with the *Glee Club*, it was the sound which gave both Georges the most hassle. Despite the fact that the show was rapidly heading towards becoming the Number One BBC production, the BBC still refused to co-operate with George's requests. Pat Heigham, Sound Engineer with the show, remembers, 'George asked the BBC to guarantee the same music engineer each week. The BBC refused, so George said, "That's what I want. If I don't get it, I'll go outside." Which he did. Adrian Kerridge was the balance engineer at Lansdowne Studios, probably the most famous recording studios in London, where the Black and White tapes were made. 'I'd get these master tapes from Adrian,' says Pat, 'and make copies which were used as dance rehearsal tapes, and the singers used copies to learn their parts at home. We couldn't use the master tape for rehearsals as the Musicians Union said we had to pay the musicians for each day we used the tape. George said, "If we have to pay the musicians, we'll have them there." So the orchestra would be in the studios for transmission day, live in those days. We used the master tape that day, so the orchestra had little to do, except play the opening fanfare and accompany some of the musical bits in between the sequences, plus the live playoff at the end.'

Later the BBC tried to dispense with Lansdowne. Adrian Stocks, BBC TV Sound Supervisor, recalls, 'BBC Management were rather miffed that Lansdowne produced the distinctive Black and White sound and, despite what we suspected was determined opposition from Messrs Mitchell and Inns, a Minstrel session was booked in the new BBC Riverside Sound Recording Studio. The excellent Bryan Forgham was to mix the session, and we both knew beforehand we were on a loser as the studio was neither technically nor acoustically up to it. It was a total disaster, but George was so patient and understanding that I am sure he realised it wasn't our fault but that we couldn't let the BBC down by explaining why. The two Georges must have raised a suitable stink because I can't remember a second attempt.'

The orchestra in question was the Eric Robinson Orchestra, who remained part of the television show until it ended. George built up a huge rapport with the orchestra. Ted Darling again: 'The orchestra gradually increased over the years, from one trumpet and one trombone to three of each, or a full brass section. George loved that. He had a great respect for the band. If you respect someone's talent, you get it back. They all loved working for George. Musos are a tough bunch - they'd say in other places that they enjoyed working for him. There was no hassle, no shouting. Alan Bristow's backings were a delight.' But no Minstrel show, on television or in the theatre, ever used strings. No one quite knows why, though the reason was probably that they needed a strong sound. Keith Leggett thinks 'perhaps the brass-only orchestra was a cost thing - we always had the orchestra in the studio when we recorded which added so much to the sound of the minstrels which was full of vitality. We would have needed a lot of strings, and I think George and Alan liked the drive of the brass.'

Much of the show's glamour was due to the glorious costumes, though these weren't always so great. John Boulter recollects that the costumes started off poorly: 'They weren't top notch at first. We started with plain white jackets and trousers. The sizes varied too, with things like sleeve length being one inch too short or six inches too long. Everything was tarted up with sequins. The hats were the greatest - they were covered with sequins and painted - they looked so good.' George also remembered 'George [Inns] groaning about one set of (Minstrel) costumes. "I get the best line of girls on TV, and I've seen wounds dressed better." ' But things quickly improved and even black and white television didn't stop the costume designers going overboard, if only for the benefit of studio audiences. In the early days of the show, when George Inns was building up a wardrobe stock, the costume budget was £1,000

Minstrel Magic

(£21,000) a programme. A thousand items of wardrobe were needed for every programme, though not all costumes were new. Designer Mary Wood created certain basic costumes which could be adapted, almost unrecognisably, by a change of trimmings, headgear and accessories.

Mary's work began at the first planning conference, after which she would 'sketch tiny figures and work out dress designs on them'. Costumes had to be foolproof and were tested rigorously during rehearsals. If a costume didn't 'work', was easily damaged or if it was too difficult to get in and out of, it was thrown out, and an alternative design created. Colourings needed to match the scenery, the choreographer had to be consulted as to the requirements of the dance routines, and often George Inns would offer suggestions, such as, 'This is a South American sequence, Mary, and I don't want you to fall back on the old conventional costumes.' George Mitchell occasionally put his foot down about what he wanted. When George Inns once wanted full crinolines, George was furious. He wanted - and got - short crinolines, parasols and big hats. Once the costumes were approved, Mary 'shop[ped] for anything we can do ourselves, though about 75% of the clothes are made by outside costumiers'. All kinds of materials went into them, but they had to be tough and designed for lightning-quick changes. Fastenings were hook and eye tapes with very big hooks. 'We daren't risk zips,' said Mary. 'The girls loved bright colours. I was partial to hats, they added such a lot to the total effect.' But the Toppers sometimes had difficulty keeping the gorgeous hat creations in place. The problem was solved by stuffing the hats with foam rubber. Dresses were fitted nine days before the show, but the girls didn't snuggle into them until five hours before transmission. Often there were last-minute alterations. Mary said, 'After all, a Topper must not only look beautiful but feel comfortable.'

Another Mary, Mary Hard, worked on the costumes in the early '60s. She still recalls the period with great fondness: 'I worked for a theatrical costumier called De Milo Creations of Earls Court Road, 2nd floor above an antique shop. David Harvey Jones, an ex-BBC dresser, ran the place. We all sewed, making costumes for all sorts of shows, light entertainment, clubs, theatres, etc. Our bread and butter work was the Minstrel Show. Every two weeks turnaround. The dancers would have their costumes revamped, things put on, things taken off to recycle all the time. Every show had one set of completely new costumes. As old ones wore out, they were always replaced. It was a hectic schedule with only one fitting. Mary Woods would arrive with bales of cloth, lots of trimmings, leotards, etc, plus sketches and measurements for each girl. It was great fun, and each week we would dress up in the costumes and take photos of ourselves.'

The average costume change time was one and a half minutes, with one dresser for every two Toppers. The changing room was always deadly quiet. Jackie Joyner remembered, 'We were too tensed up to utter a sound. Sometimes there wasn't even time to reach the dressing room. We'd whip off all we'd got, down to the basic bathing costume in front of a "dead" camera and were into the next dress before the red light came on again.' Each cast member had a chair on which were piled in the correct order their twelve different coats or hats. 'Nobody has time to do more than grab the next coat and get back on stage again,' said Inns. 'One hat in the wrong order could mean chaos.' Nevertheless Roger Green remembers, 'We had to go off and back on with canes for one routine, but the stagehand didn't have one for me. I did the whole routine with a pretend cane, and nobody noticed. I expected George Inns to call "Cut" at any moment, but he never did.' Sometimes it wasn't the costumes' fault. Glyn remembers one of the very few things to go wrong. 'Bob Clayton had just come off stage from the cowboy routine in cowboy garb, guns, stetsons. I was ready to go on in the next sequence which was Romantica. Bob asked me to watch the time as he wanted to phone his girlfriend. I kept warning him, two minutes, then one minute. Still he kept talking until he suddenly realised they were playing the Romantica music and he had to go straight on still in his cowboy gear. He asked me afterwards, "Do you think anyone noticed?" '

Minstrel makeup was Max Factor Negro No 2, a pancake makeup with an ingredient of powder to reduce the shine. The BBC's Toni Chapman was in charge for most of the television shows, with Cherry Alston towards the end. Toni and her girls spent one hundred and seven hours per show involved in makeup. Seven assistants helped make up the thirteen men, who were dealt with in two relays over three hours. During lunch breaks, only faces were blacked up. During tea breaks, ears, necks and wigs were dealt with, leaving the men fully costumed and made up for the final run-through, during which they wore tissues round their necks to prevent the white shirts being marked. During

Minstrel Magic

transmission, the makeup girls stood in the wings, ready with running repairs to any faces smudged during the lightning-quick costume changes. Colds caused problems too if a man wanted to blow his nose. One reporter asked whether the singers minded having their faces blacked: 'Up came the answer in the shape of James Charlton, the Minstrels' "singing" manager. "We couldn't be happier, black or white," he told me. "The only snag is, once made up, we daren't show our faces outside the Television Theatre until the show is over." ' Often the men drew lots to be last. The makeup girls weren't involved in the removal process but as one feature says, 'They suspect it's not a long process. Towels and grease are left in their dressing room, and minutes later all that remains is a heap of blackened towelling.'

One strong argument as to the show's popularity was that the black makeup created uniformity amongst the men which added to the magical fairy-tale feel the show created. And it certainly came in very useful during one show, which produced not just a first, but a 'one and only' for the Minstrels when a female Minstrel took part in front of the cameras. One Minstrel, who wasn't happy with Geraldine Yates' choreography and frequently tried to get his own version in, stormed off set immediately before one recording, leaving a shocked George to try to rearrange the routines to cover his absence. But choreographer Geraldine had a better answer. She, of course, knew the routines inside out, so quickly blacked up and danced her way through the whole show as a Minstrel! And no one noticed!

However, many newspapers wondered about the effect of the makeup on the singers. The *Record Mirror* asked if the artistes suffered from the show's essential anonymity: 'Apparently, they don't. Said Tony, "True, many viewers don't know us by name. But our voices are all different, and they write in asking for pictures of - in my case - the fat one." ' The *Daily Express* reported, 'Few fans recognise them. They even have problems at home. John Boulter relates, "My small daughter Francesca used to think she had two daddies - the one she knew at home and the one she saw on television. When she was taken to see the show, I went to talk to her in the interval, and she behaved as if I were a stranger." Bass singer 44-year-old Tony Mercer, with a stomach that showed an appreciation for the good things of life, grinned. "Someone recognised me in Majorca last year at a swimming pool when I was just wearing a pair of shorts. They didn't know my face, but they

Minstrel Magic

knew me by the way I walked. I never break into a gallop." But is blacking up really necessary? Wouldn't the songs be just as nostalgic, the costumes just as vivid, the dances just as spectacular without it? "It wouldn't be the same," said Tony.' The makeup did cause issues among the cast occasionally. At the first dress rehearsals, the girls often didn't have a clue as to which Minstrel they were meant to dance with, though as one man said, 'Sheep know each other right away. So do we.'

Stanley Dorfman was responsible for settings which, he explained, 'set the designer a number of problems and a unique opportunity for self-expression. With its constant high-speed change of mood and pattern it's a challenge to the ingenuity, but of all my work in television, this programme has been the most satisfying.' With twenty-four singers and dancers, the stage had to be kept uncluttered, so effects had to be achieved boldly with a minimum of scenery. Sequences could range from a New Orleans showboat scene to a romantic spectacle featuring a single piano and chandeliers. Once Dorfman's ideas had been translated into sets, a scene-crew worked overnight before the first day of camera-rehearsal, to set up the scenery. During the two days between set-up and transmission, Dorfman dressed the set with props, which often included unusual ones such as veteran cars, a Victorian milk cart, and an American Pacific-type locomotive hired from Southend's Kursaal Amusement Park. On one occasion, he had to stage a jungle sequence which called for two stuffed monkeys, a deer, two leopards, a tiger and three zebra skins, all covered with diamante jewellery. Property men always kept a good supply of Victorian props, such as grandfather clocks and gramophones with big brass horns, as they knew George Inns was certain to ask for them. Dot Mitchell recalls, 'George [Mitchell] always knew what he wanted scenically. He had an overall picture of the stage. He said what he wanted, then the others went away and created it. If someone came up with a better idea, he'd take it. If necessary, they'd come back to him and say we can't do that, but we can do this.'

One feature never seen by the audience at home, but essential to each television show, was *Dibs Dibs*. Dreamt up by a superstitious Topper to ward off evil spirits, it preceded every single television show. It began like a nursery rhyme game, the Toppers forming a circle with the men behind. Then at a signal from the chief Dib-

Dibber, everyone broke into a chant. The words varied depending on who was leading it but usually ran something like:

Dib-Dibs, dib-dibs! Oinky-toink, oinky-toink!
It's gonna be good, it's gonna be smashing!
Hello, George! Where's Eric? Here come the Minstrels!
That's it! That's it! Bye-bye!

George was clear about its purpose: 'It had to happen. We were all convinced disaster would strike if anything prevented it. It gave a tremendous boost to us all, allowing the team to blow off steam at the crucial moment of tension before the red light goes on. It gave the stimulus that made the live show really lively and spontaneous. Their singing and dancing became natural and spirited, and the whole show benefited.' Principal Margaret Savage was adamant: 'You couldn't start a show without it. After Leslie Crowther had done his warm up, red lights were flashing, Elspeth Hands (Head Topper) would say the routine, the others repeated it, then we had a successful show. Otherwise, it would never have happened.'

By the time the second series ended in April 1960, the Minstrels were firmly embedded in the national consciousness. Audiences regularly topped eighteen million, almost unheard of then, even though there were only two channels to choose from. Newspapers and magazines clamoured to run features on them, focusing on all aspects of the show, from individuals to the makeup, from routines to romances. Every newspaper, national and regional, ran reviews of each television show, the vast majority of which were ecstatic, placing the Minstrels firmly centre-stage. The *Wolverhampton Express* called them 'a choir of superlative quality, by far the best musical group in the business', whereas *The Star* said, 'Mitchell's non-stop minstrels have given me more pleasure than any other musical series I can recall.' The *Yorkshire Evening News* talked about the singers' 'speed, energy, zip, vitality, captivating tunefulness. Nowhere are they seen and heard to better advantage than in the *Black and White Minstrel Show* which deservedly gives them star billing.'

But not everyone was happy. The *Daily Mail* scathingly said, 'It's nothing much like anything, a hybrid of half a dozen different styles and has painstakingly preserved the silliest elements of each. We had the sublimely idiotic spectacle of a dozen men with black faces and blubber lips dressed in the uniform of pre-1914

Hussars and singing a Viennese medley.' The *Daily Mirror* also had its criticisms: 'The principal defect is the black makeup. Unless the singers who dominate the show stage a genuine Minstrel song, which is rare, their traditional makeup looks out of place.'

But fans of all ages sided with the glowing reviews and wrote to the BBC and to George in their thousands. George was staggered by the amount of mail received and tried to answer as many as possible, though this became an increasingly difficult task. But he did what he could. One anonymous fan wrote to George, after being present at a television recording, to offer his 'sincere thanks for the most enjoyable evening of my life. It was most noticeable of the warm family atmosphere glowing among you all.' Sadly he told George that he only had a short while to live and asked for a photo, as well as more audience tickets, which George arranged to be sent. Douglas Milne received an autographed book of the girls and boys, meaning he could now follow them on screen - at least the girls, 'not so easy with the men!' One fan who years later asked George which albums he was missing, was flabbergasted to receive taped copies of two albums to complete his collection. This loyalty to fans extended long after the shows had finished. At least one fan in George's hometown of Falkirk was desperate to keep the show alive. In 1990 the *Falkirk Herald* published a letter from Robert Douglas who said he was desperately searching for a book or information about George so that he could write something on 'genius George' for the quarterly Minstrel fan magazine: 'He is so shy and unassuming that I've not had any luck. I chose the *Herald* for my appeal as George was born in the Falkirk area.' This letter produced a response which must have absolutely delighted Mr Douglas, as George himself answered. The cutting had been sent to him by his cuttings agency, but friends across Scotland had bombarded him with the information. He included cuttings and programmes to help Robert Douglas and, loyal to the last, wrote that he was not to be credited with his success and instead praised his hundreds of singers and dancers, considered by him to be personal friends. This led to the paper publishing a feature on George. In a further letter to the paper, Robert wrote, 'This is a great compliment to the *Herald*. George is a very private person and this information will be a big help to me.'

Fans saw themselves as heavily entwined in the show, and as part of one big family, an image promoted heavily wherever possible by everyone concerned with the Minstrels. Despite the precision and uniformity of the show, the friendly eyes and smiles of the cast came through the television cameras and across the footlights. For many fans, writing a fan letter was a new experience, one which the family-friendly nature of the shows encouraged them to undertake and tell George all about their own lives. Walter Butt, aged 76, wrote of his choral history since a boy, saying, 'My greatest delight is your television shows, and I wish I were one of them, for I still enjoy good health.' Pensioners Mr and Mrs Kenney from Leicester told of their life 'managing nicely' on £10 (£200) per week, and saying the show deserved 'all the Oscars that may come your way'. Joan Fletcher explained she had just come out of hospital back to her caravan 'to find a pipe had burst and I was flooded, even my bed was soaking. I am a widow so had no one to help me. I sat and cried. In despair, I turned the TV on and watched your show. I can now face up to things once more.' Widowed Elsie Day told George all about her two stepdaughters and how one had just visited her from Canada to enable them to meet for the first time.

The show touched across the generations. As was perhaps to be expected, older people loved the music. Mrs Morley Neale wrote, 'Being in my 78th year, I can hardly be accused of being a "fan" writer. However, I feel it is due to you to have a special word of appreciation for the magnificent show you are providing. To my mind, it stands supreme. To us old folk it is a soothing relief to hear melodious music conducted and put over by ones who so perfectly know their job; a really satisfying antidote after the semi-crying noise so often inflicted upon us under the guise of a song.'

But children were massive fans too, and George seems to have responded particularly sensitively to letters from youngsters. One touching example was sent by Ann Elizabeth 'aged 6½', reproduced with original spelling: 'I like all your shows. I like the costumes and me and my mummy and daddy woch your shows evry week. When I woch your shows I cuddle my mummy and I eat my swets and I share them round.' A young Jacqueline Huntley asked for a photo of the man who 'sings like Al Jolson. I like the way he waves his hands when singing. I am sorry I do not know his name but everybody talks about him.' Carolyn Lloyd, aged 10, wrote to say she was in bed with chickenpox and so couldn't watch the show, though she could hear it. She asked for - and got - cast photos so she could look at them as she listened to the show. Thea

Minstrel Magic

Suafara wrote about her little two-year-old boy, who had been a fan since he was one: 'In March last year, my little boy Aaron took a sudden fancy to the Minstrels and especially Dai Francis. It was after he was burnt and came out of hospital. He gets quite angry because Dai can't sing all the time. As he is now only two, he can't talk that much, but he tries to sing the songs and do what they do on the shows. He sits there and doesn't move throughout the whole show. I wrote to Mr Francis for a photo which he takes everywhere with him and shows everyone his Dai. I didn't like to bother Mr Francis again, but I was wondering if you had any old programmes or something with pictures in so that I can make a scrapbook for him.' George sent her a programme. Young Stephanie Corfield from Wolverhampton wrote thanking George for saying an earlier sketch of hers was good, though she now knew that 'it was not all that good', and sending him a further one illustrating *Shine On Harvest Moon*. Ruth Hetherington, aged 8, wrote that 'I have enjoyed watching the shows and so have Mummy and Daddy. We shall be very glad when the shows come on next autumn.' Although she didn't ask for them, George sent her photos of the cast.

Sixteen-year-old J Savage wrote, 'All my friends call me square because I never miss the show but I don't guess you can be a square watching because all the songs are love songs and were popular in the earlier days and I think when I grow up and have kids, they will say to me, "Oh I think Cliff Richard and Elvis Presley are awfully old-fashioned." ' The Minstrels had even younger fans. Brenda Bancroft asked for a recording of nursery rhymes: 'My little girl heard them singing, and since then, she wants nursery rhymes.' George duly obliged with a nursery rhyme segment in one show. RE Molsher asked for photos of the Minstrels, as she had a three-year-old daughter who is 'an ardent fan. It is the quietest forty-five minutes we get, nothing else can quite stop her from talking. She tells all and sundry that the Minstrels are her friends.'

Sadly George's response to a letter from sixteen-year-old Christine hasn't survived. She wrote, 'My boyfriend and I sit riveted together watching your programme, especially we like the rabbit. My boyfriend often sings. My mother says that I should ask you if you have a little opening for him somewhere? He is lovely and light on his feet which I have noticed when we go dancing every Saturday night. Also, we have a parrot. And we were wondering if you could suggest a song as he seems quite musical really. I realise you might be too busy to reply so we were wondering if you could let us know you have received this letter by scratching the back of your neck on your next show. We think that if you do this, nobody will realise except us and it will be all right.'

Many writers praised individual singers. Mrs D Bedlington wrote she was 'an OAP and I enjoy the show as much as my 16-year-old niece who lives with me. Would it be possible to have a signed photo of John Boulter, Anne's favourite, my own choice is all the soloists, they are smashing (Anne's words, not mine).' John was a particular favourite, with many, like 87-year-old Ethel Hopkins, praising his tenor voice as 'too divine'. Viewers tried hard to identify their favourites. Despite three years of the show, confusion still reigned! AM Licence wrote, 'We would like to say how much we liked watching Little Miss Saucy Face, one of the Toppers. She is the young lady who did the solo ballet dance to *Moonlight and Roses*.' People seemed hesitant to write but did so nevertheless, such as Mrs E Leathley who said, 'Forgive an old lady, but I'm really haunted by your wonderful tenor singer. My dearest wish is to know his name and see his face as they look identical in their makeup. Recently he sang *When I Grow Too Old to Dream*, it took me back to when my husband sang it to me.'

Requests poured in, mostly marked by a high degree of courtesy. One mother asked, 'Could you oblige my 12-year-old son by singing the *Dam Busters March*?' E Williams wanted '*The Old Rugged Cross* and the *23rd Psalm*. I don't know whether you have many requests or whether mine is a lone cry!' Some writers pulled at the heartstrings. Mr McKeoun went overboard, 'Why don't you take as your request sequence the immortal song *Roses of Picardy* and songs of that dramatic period of world history. I feel it's a homage to those that went through so much during their youth. The tragedy is emphasised today by the pensions that so many have to live off. The slaughter of youth in the 1914-18 war is something that I feel we are now having to pay the price for.'

People also often requested songs with no idea of the timescale involved. W Clegg from Dewsbury asked on February 14 for an obvious Al Jolson song: 'You must have our favourite *On the Banks of the Wabash* in the very near future - say February 28 - could you? Would you?' James Steele requested, 'Would you get the Minstrels to sing in their next show *Only a beautiful picture in a beautiful golden frame*. I think that is what it is called but you will understand the one I mean.' H Perchard expected instant results too: 'May I ask your very fine choir to sing *All in April Evening* the next time you're on.' Equally expecting instant results was Frank Hunt: 'With the approach of Easter it would be delightful if your singers rendered *Shepherd of Souls* from *The Sign of the Cross*. I can imagine your lovely alto, tenor and that profound bass excelling themselves, and also a violin obligato or descant in the background, and if orchestra were to be used, give them a large card of "pianissimo" as the many orchestras of the BBC programmes imagine it is their performance and not the singers' solo.' Some clearly expected George's knowledge of music to be even more encyclopaedic than it was. But it's doubtful that even George, with his vast database of songs, could help Rhoda Forrest, aged 86, who asked for two songs 'that I've never found anybody knows, one is about putting money into a gas meter, and one is about parents ending up in a court because of a fight'. George probably also struggled with the letter from R Smith of Doncaster, who sent in a 'request for a song of which I can only remember the first and last lines, but it means a lot to my wife and me'. Mrs E Bonny asked, 'Is it any use my asking for the choir to sing the old ballad title *The Volunteer Organist*. I have never heard it on sound wireless or television. My mother used to sing it years ago.' J Elliott requested, 'There is one I have not heard since 1920, it's called *Motherland*, it was sung a lot in 1914-1918 in praise of our colonial troops, so if you know the song, would you mind getting your party to render it for me for old time's sake.'

Many people sent in actual copies of their requests, hoping the choir would use them. Mary Ray enclosed 'two old songs, in the hope that you may either know of them or could trace them. Both are gems of their kind, the melodies haunting and as lullabies most effective. In your capable hands and with your truly superb rendering of any of these old melodies, I am sure you would give many of your older admirers a great deal of pleasure. In view of the recent Royal baby [Prince Andrew], a programme of lullabies might be a graceful tribute to him, and indeed may cause a revival of the old habit of mums singing their offspring to sleep! Bad for them? Rubbish!' Some people even wrote songs for the choir to try. Samuel Morrison sent two songs for 'any lady or gentleman vocalist to try private (not TV of course) to see how they clink?'

Just how George managed his workload can only be imagined. In 1959 and 1960 he arranged, rehearsed and recorded eighteen

Minstrel shows, as well as organising 170 other television shows and 157 radio appearances. Mitchell Singers were still involved in regular series such as *Vera Lynn Sings, Variety Playhouse, About Religion, The Ted Ray Show, Words and Music, Make Mine Music, Frankly Howerd* and *Hi! Summer*, as well as plenty of one-off shows. George reported, 'It's been tough recording all these shows. A tough year really.' Something had to give, and that something was stage work. George halved the number of summer shows and pantomimes his singers appeared in, saying, 'I just can't find time to get round them all. There's so much to do in London. For twelve months we've averaged five-and-a-half radio and television shows a week.' He had to force himself to delegate even more, mainly to Keith Leggett, who somehow was still managing to sing with the Mitchells as well. However, just how impossible it was for George to retain control of everything becomes clear in mid-September 1959 when his singers were rehearsing *The Ted Ray Show, The Harry Belafonte Show* and *The Black and White Minstrel Show*, all on the same day! Christmas Day this year set a record for Mitchell appearances. A special *Glee Club* was televised on Christmas morning, in which George used music dating from the C14th to arrangements by Gustav Holst. Given a Dickensian setting including a Georgian bow-fronted shop containing authentic early C19th toys, the choir sang twenty-four carols, including *The First Noel, The Gloucestershire Wassail* and *the Coventry Carol* - 'This is the most beautiful thing I have heard them sing,' producer Dennis Main Wilson said. George also included music with a Royal association, possibly because this programme was televised immediately before the Queen's Speech, which, only in its third year on television, had not yet settled into its now-customary 3pm slot. In a turnaround on Christmas Day the following year, the *Glee Club* followed the Queen's Speech. Producer Dennis Main Wilson was jubilant and went round saying, 'I've got the best announcer in the world.' The singers featured heavily in the traditional *Christmas Night With the Stars on Christmas Night*, when they backed several stars, before closing the programme with a special *Black and White Minstrel Show* - quite an achievement in only their second real year of existence.

CHAPTER 14

Bob Luff had had an outrageous idea. In August 1959, he calmly explained to George one day that he wanted to take the Minstrels into the theatre, making the show the first major BBC Television musical production to be put on the stage. George was shocked. Everyone else's reaction was incredulous as well. Take a television programme back to the theatre? There had only been seven shows so far, if you don't count the very first one at Earls Court. Who knew how long the public would continue to like it? Film and provincial theatre had both been badly hit by the rise and rise of television and were already shaky and likely to be killed off entirely shortly. Surely this was not the time to pour money into a theatre show? Pundits saw this as a hugely retrograde step, involving massive financial risks. Everyone, including their best friends, told George and Bob the idea was pie in the sky. But Bob wanted to produce a stage show which was ageless, classless and full of lovely nostalgic music – the *Black and White Minstrel Show* was the blueprint.

The hurdles were immense, not least convincing the BBC that this was a great idea. But this didn't worry Bob; as always, he relished the fight ahead. Over the years, he had won nearly every battle he'd fought with the Corporation, and he was convinced he could win this one too. Bob approached Martin Turnell, Head of Programme Contracts, asking for the stage rights for two or three years from April 18, 1960, at 'a nominal royalty of £20 (£420) per week'. As predicted, the BBC was vehemently against the whole idea, worried about an adverse impact on the television show. SG Williams, Controller of Television Admin, was 'very doubtful about the project. This is very important BBC property, and we should have very serious misgivings about handing over our rights for two or three years. It is very different from agreeing a limited season of two or three months with the BBC having a say and the security of knowing George Inns was the producer. If it would enhance the value of the programme by the publicity of a first class show for a limited period, then yes; if not, then it would be wise to withhold our agreement and reconsider when the programme has reached the end of its useful life.' Little did he know this 'useful life' wasn't to end for another nineteen years!

When someone pointed out that legally Bob could produce a stage show called '*the Stars from the Black and White Minstrel Show*', over which the BBC would have no control at all, the BBC began to worry that their rights to the show were much less definite than they had thought and swiftly agreed to put it on the road. Their only stipulations were that George Inns had to produce it, and they would only grant a greatly reduced time scale of April to September 1960 'but no longer'. Bob immediately asked for a fortnight's extension 'to cover the Blackpool Illuminations'. The BBC also wanted a percentage of the profits, though it was doubted 'he'll agree, doubt if worth pursuing'. Much as they'd expected, Bob threw his hands up in horror and told the BBC in no uncertain terms that paying a percentage was 'impossible', though he was prepared to increase the flat fee to £30 (£630). He argued he would have huge outlay and would probably be getting only 55% of the takings while carrying all the risk.

The BBC also thought it risky as it brought people into closer contact with a show which mixed blacks and white, albeit only via makeup. Britain had seen a huge rise in immigration over the previous eighteen months, mainly to beat the restrictions which were to come in with the Commonwealth Immigrants Act in 1962 which introduced a voucher system. People's main issues still revolved around relationships between black and white and here the show would put them almost within touching distance of audiences.

Needless to say, Bob did as he always did and won the battle. By October the BBC had agreed to everything he had originally asked, 'for the publicity', though they still refused him permission for anything beyond October 1960, as the television show would be back on people's screens by November. George Inns was allowed unpaid leave to produce the show. Never one to stop while he was winning, Bob was back again a few weeks later, asking for similar permission for 1961; in a face-saving exercise, the BBC refused, though they promised to 'look at it again if we are happy with 1960'.

They were difficult about the use of the Television Toppers too. Although Larry Gordon remained as choreographer, the BBC refused to allow the use of the name – they were to be billed as the

Minstrel Magic

Larry Gordon Dancers. At the same time, George Inns suggested the BBC might like to hire its costumes to the stage version, bringing the BBC great publicity and financial reward, though of course, it would also have saved everyone work and a large part of the set-up costs. But the BBC were determined not to let Bob have his own way over everything and refused, saying the costumes were recycled for other shows and would leave a huge hole in the Costume Department.

But the battle with the BBC was only the start of it. Producing a live show night after night, with two performances a night, was completely different from a fortnightly 45-minute television show. Just how would it work? It proved a nightmare, involving constant difficulties and huge start-up costs. George insisted that everything had to be brand new and of the best quality; he wouldn't make do with second-hand anything. For instance, the fans cost £600 (£9,600) each, and there were fourteen of them. (The first set were red; a couple of years later, he bought a second set in blue, then another set later on.) The start-up costs were eventually to reach £100,000 (£1.6m). Despite the risks, both Bob and George backed the show financially, with George remortgaging his house to raise 20% of the costs. Ossie Whitaker moved from George's business to the Luff Organisation specifically to handle the stage show and quickly became the pacifying link between the two offices.

The first issue was to decide the show's format. The television shows only lasted 45 minutes, but a stage show would last two hours. How to fill all that time? One option was just to expand the TV format, but everyone felt it was much too risky to let the Minstrels carry the whole show, so the show moved back to a 'variety' format. The first half consisted of Stan Stennett, Joan Hinde, 'glamorous girl trumpeter', comedian Ossie Noble and singer and comedian Penny Nicholls, with the Minstrels appearing only in the second half in eight Minstrel sequences, interspersed with the other acts. George chose a *Meet The Minstrels* sequence, followed by *Leslie Stuart Melodies*, *Thank Heaven for Little Girls*, *Your Requests* and *Ay! Ay! Ay!* One sequence involved an *Al Jolson Tribute*, featuring Dai Francis. The conducted sequence was *Memories of Stephen Foster*, with soloists John Boulter and Tony Mercer, and the show closed with *Doodah Day*.

Now that he knew the format of the show, George faced another dilemma. He needed to use his best singers if the stage show were to stand any chance of success, and audiences would, of course, expect to see the same soloists as on TV, yet this meant depriving the core group of many of its best members. It was obvious that John, Dai and Tony would have to join the stage show but what about the rest of the cast? George decided to use sixteen men on stage, though the television show was only using ten at this stage. There was still a lot of other television and radio work to cover, which needed the fast sight-reading skills of the core members. The only answer was to split the core. Some, like Alan Cooper and Les Rawlings, would stay in London to cover the other work and the rest, among them Keith Leggett, Glyn Dawson and relative newcomer Don Cleaver who had only been a Mitchell singer for four months, would go into the stage show which also demanded strong singers. In any case, George reasoned, Bob only had permission to do the show for five months, and so he would get the rest of the core members back before the Christmas rush.

Running alongside this dilemma was the even greater problem of how to reproduce the television show which the audiences would be expecting to see. Theatre is a very different medium from television – the audience is there in front of you, there is no chance at all of redoing a sequence if something goes wrong, and above all, it's live. The television shows were still going out live at this point, and so the cast was used to getting it right first time and also used to having an audience in close proximity in the tiny Television Theatre. But cameras could always avoid showing any mistakes that might be made and of course, the big plus was that the sound was guaranteed to be right on television as it had been recorded in advance to George's satisfaction. But just how could this work in a live theatre environment? And what about the sheer physical difficulties of getting the Minstrels to sing and dance at the same time? George recalled, 'It was very difficult originally. You had the choice of cutting all the choreography out and keeping them at the front of the stage, all down on one knee, or trying to make it look like the television Minstrel show. We tried everything under the sun – head mikes, throat mikes, all shocking, it wasn't going to work. It was all right for certain things like the finale as they all came down to the front and sang. The soloists were fine as they had very powerful voices and didn't need a mike at all, but it was the devil on the ensemble when they were dancing and jumping and very often with their backs to the audience.'

Minstrel Magic

There was of course only one practical answer. The Minstrels would have to mime on stage too. George recalled, 'I recorded the whole lot onto tapes, rigging fourteen speakers around the theatre, and it sounded marvellous. We put in three miles of cable fixing speaker systems along the stage which were controlled so the sound could be moved from side to side. But mechanical things can easily go wrong, so there was a standby tape; however, there was always a slight hiatus when one failed before they could switch to the second tape. We never hid the fact that the chorus work and indeed the solo work was pre-recorded.' It got them into trouble only once, when the show was in Melbourne in 1962, when an audience member left, saying, 'I didn't pay to listen to a load of miming'.

But hide it they did. Over the years ahead, there was much deliberate fogging of this issue, with George and the rest of the team occasionally agreeing it was recorded, at other times denying it outright. They kept it deliberately clouded, partly for fear of criticism and losing audiences, and partly to generate publicity. The cast got dragged into the controversy too, under pain of death not to disclose the truth, or that there were more voices on tape than on stage. When the show opened at the Victoria Palace in London in 1962, Maryetta Midgley reports, 'Eight of us girls had done the soundtracks. We were sworn to secrecy and threatened with the sack if it came out.' Much press comment rumbled around it for years. During the show's stay in Bradford in 1961, one reader wrote to the *Bradford Telegraph*: 'My friends say the show is partly mimed. I didn't think so. But they say they saw it in Scarborough, and they understood it was mimed.' And E Hancock asked, 'Will it be betraying a confidence if your theatre critic told the public whether the show is mimed?' Their theatre critic obliged: 'To avoid any over-fluctuation of sound which would otherwise occur during the singing of the large numbers, these items are vocally recorded and played over a specially installed and very costly amplification system. The recordings are made by the people actually taking part in the presentation. During the show these artistes do not mime but sing "on top" of the recordings, thus giving impressive weight to the melodies. George Mitchell himself told me, "There is no secret about this and no intention of fooling the public. The whole idea is to improve the musical balance which I think you will agree it does." ' In 1965 George Inns went public in the *Radio Times*, saying the singers

Minstrel Magic

sang at the Victoria Palace but the television singers mimed 'as required', whatever that might mean. More confusion arose when the *Melody Maker* reported George as saying, 'For certain parts of the TV show, we may use pre-recorded tapes, but no hard and fast statement can be made, as many of our production numbers contain "live" and taped music alternating several times during the course of a five-minute routine.' This certainly sounds unrealistically complicated and was presumably part of the efforts everyone made to conceal the fact that the sound was pre-recorded.

The *Manchester Evening News* learned how the Georges tried to insure against catastrophe: 'The complicated dance routines do not interfere at all with the precision of the singing. George Inns has developed the miming method so far that when the show went out on tour, the tape recording gear went along too and we had a chance to see just how exact the synchronisation was. His method? "A whole lot of rehearsal," says Inns. "Every number must be rehearsed over and over again until the singers are sure of every bit of phrasing." Then they can sing with confidence while the tape carrying the recording goes out. The words must be properly sung and if there is a lack of confidence it shows.'

With pre-recorded sound, the Minstrels could have got away with miming, but that just didn't work on the stage, any more than it did on television. John Boulter explains, 'It was tricky singing to the tape, but Tony, Dai and I all sang. It helped us focus for movement. If you didn't sing properly, you ended up looking like the proverbial goldfish. So we still suffered all the sore throats, loss of voice, and all the symptoms that a singer puts up with as an occupational hazard despite all the technology.' But there were major advantages too. It meant anybody could, in fact, go on stage and perform in the show, no matter what had happened to the original Minstrel. If personnel left, they were easily replaced with no need for lengthy singing rehearsals. And anyone suffering a cold could still perform. The soloists were always recorded separately – and allowed more licence in how they interpreted their solos – with the understudies recording their own tapes so that if a principal was ill, it was easy to pull their voice out and insert the understudy tape.

But of course, there was one huge disadvantage. Could they rely on the tapes twice a night, night after night, even with a standby tape? Surely at some stage, it would come unstuck. This was one reason why George needed strong singers on stage. If the tape failed, then the cast was expected to keep on singing, so everyone needed to be up to Mitchell standards. And this included the girls in the show. The Toppers were all reasonable singers – it was part of the audition process – but by and large, they weren't up to George's standards. So they decided to add several Mitchell Maids to the stage show so that if the tapes failed, the Maids could sing live. Although they appeared to be dancers to the audience, they were never expected to dance, and Larry Gordon usually kept them towards the back of the stage or up on rostra.

Head Topper Mary Oakley remembers one unexpected problem with the sound: 'On special occasions, such as New Year's Eve, we'd sing an extra song at the end. The audience would always be bewildered because the sound sounded much thinner than the show itself, where the live singing was enhanced by the tape. We'd always sing *Auld Lang Syne* and join hands with the stalls. George insisted we sang the correct words which are not what everyone thinks. When we checked, he was of course quite right. The last line is not "for the sake of auld lang syne" it's "for auld lang syne." ' Years before, the *Glasgow Evening News* had complained about a *Glee Club* in which they'd sung *Auld Lang Syne*: 'Already the annual crop of *Old Lang Zynes* is knee-high. Worst offender was George Mitchell. A few weeks ago he boasted to me about his many Scottish connections...yet his choir sang with a very pronounced "Z". Shame on you, George!'

As always, the Musicians' Union threw a spanner in the works, insisting that the orchestra had to be physically present in the theatre, though this of course covered any emergencies with the tapes. This meant it could only be between twelve and sixteen in number – old theatres couldn't cope with any more. But now of course, yet more problems cropped up. The audience could see the orchestra, so they had to play – it would have looked extremely odd otherwise! But keeping the orchestra in time with the tapes was far from easy. John Boulter explains, 'The musical director listened to a click tape through earphones, so knew when to come in. We weren't allowed to put the orchestra onto the tape because of the Musicians Union.' That this was achieved successfully night after night, year after year is nothing short of a minor – or major – miracle. After all, singers usually took their cue from the orchestra; now the orchestra had to start at exactly the right moment to keep time with pre-recorded voices, with no room for the slightest error.

This way of working was to cause difficulties in the years ahead. In 1966 all thirteen musicians in the orchestra were dismissed, apparently because it 'sounded tired'. The Musicians' Union demanded their re-engagement 'or the show will come off'. In an effort to escalate the dispute, the Union said it was soul-destroying for the orchestra to accompany tapes 'as none of the singers sing, and it's unfair to dispense with them now. The tape machines slow up in cold weather, and the musicians say they have had to retune because at times the recording is flat.' They told the theatre owners that they were likely to withdraw permission for members to accompany tape recordings anywhere in the future. But within weeks, the dispute had been settled, and the notices withdrawn. In a humiliating volte-face, Harry Francis, the Union's assistant secretary who had made the remarks about miming, was forced to recant: 'I made it clear, when I was talking about the show's dancers, that tapes are used to boost the voices of the dancers as they move away from the microphones. The explanation which I gave did not refer to the soloists who do not dance but sing live above the tapes and the orchestra.' George sent a letter to the press, stating why they used tapes: 'Faced with the choice of a true visual picture causing insuperable difficulties with the amplification system, or a true sound reproduction which involved a considerable reduction in the pace of the show, it was decided to augment the sound system with pre-recorded tapes. The tapes were made by the artistes you see on the stage. They do not mime but sing at every performance, the amount of augmented sound being under the control of an expert sound engineer. This system calls for exceptional discipline and constant rehearsal.' The matter wasn't to threaten the show again.

The next problem faced by the Georges was working out how the cast would cope with the sheer physical effort of performing the show twice nightly, even if they were miming and only providing the second half. It was a very fast-moving show, requiring a high level of fitness and George certainly didn't want puffed-out Minstrels on stage. The solution was to use a system called swinging. George cast thirteen men singers, plus John, Dai and Tony, which allowed everyone one sequence offstage each show. A later experiment found out that the cast were running the equivalent of a half marathon every night so fitness was essential.

Towards the end of the stage shows, the swing system was dropped to enable fewer men to be used in the company, so the cast ended up running even more every evening.

More minor problems were quickly solved. In the Television Theatre, the cast had dressers and makeup artistes to help them. Dressers were normal in theatreland, but each man now had to learn to do his own makeup. John recalls that blacking up normally took him twenty-five minutes, though he could do it in eight. Dai Francis held the record with a nail-biting three minutes, after he was held up travelling to the theatre one evening, though nothing remains to show how successful he was! According to later speciality act Clem Vickery, who blacked up to appear in Minstrel sequences, 'The makeup was really bad. The white was so greasy, it'd drip into your eyes. The gay boys spent ages getting it perfect. Me, I'd dob it on as quickly as possible.' One unforeseen advantage of the daily makeup was its protective element. Later soloist Jeff Hudson, sharing a dressing room with principal Don Cleaver, mentioned it was good for the skin, to which Don retorted, 'The only trouble when you do it day after day, you see another wrinkle.'

By Easter 1960, everything was ready. Bob had struck a deal with the powerful Moss Empire Group, and the show would open on Easter Monday at the prestigious 2000-seater Bristol Hippodrome, before a short tour both before and after a summer season at Catlin Empire's Futurist Theatre in Scarborough. It would play twice-nightly for one week in Bristol, before moving on to do a week each at Liverpool, Manchester, Newcastle, Glasgow, Edinburgh, Birmingham and Hanley. Fans unlucky enough not to be in Bristol that night could still see the Minstrels, however, as the last programme in the current series was televised at the same time. For the first time, the show was recorded in advance. Stan Stennett, resident comic with the stage show, was disappointed that these shows clashed, saying, 'It's the first I've telerecorded, and I was looking forward to watching it, but the stage show makes it impossible.'

By the time everyone reached Bristol on Easter Sunday, all the problems were behind them – or so it seemed. After arriving on Sunday morning, the cast rehearsed from 2pm until after midnight. But shocking news came through that evening. American rock sensation Eddie Cochran, who had just finished a week's run at the Hippodrome, had died that afternoon, as a result of injuries he received in a car crash at Chippenham on his way back to London after his final show. But everyone soldiered on, only to be faced with a catastrophe which threatened the entire opening night. George Inns remembered, 'I gave a theatre hand the job of starting up the recording. The whole company was assembled, the conductor standing with baton ready to strike up. We stood and stood – still nothing. Then I heard whirring, rustling noises that sounded ominous. I rushed backstage. There it was – recording tape spilling off the spools and tangled like cooked spaghetti, about 80,000 feet of it.' The tape was quite useless, twisted and torn. How on earth could they manage the final rehearsals? George tried to get a duplicate from the recording studio but this was Easter Sunday, and everyone was out enjoying themselves in the unexpected sunshine after an unseasonably cold few days. Panic set in and preparations were made to postpone the opening. After hours of trying, the studio boss was finally traced on Easter Monday morning. He rushed to his premises for a duplicate, and drove to Bristol, just a matter of hours before the curtain.

Everyone's nerves were on edge. Just how would the first television show to invade and capture the live theatre be received by the press and the public? George and Bob were even more nervous, sitting in the audience. George said, 'I was so keen to put the thing onstage, but I'd never have been able to organise it and fix everything, and he [Bob Luff] did a hell of a good job.' Keen he may have been, but typically George's diaries make the merest mention of this seminal event. The entry reads, 'Bristol Hippodrome Minstrels Opening Night'. His faith in Bob was about to be tested.

A later Head Minstrel Roy Winbow recalls the excitement: 'The night starts at 5pm when you make sure your costumes, shirts and gloves are in place and your wig looks good. You also ensure your shoes, one pair white, one pair black, are clean. Any changes of costume you need during the opening number you take to the wings and set them in your place. At the half hour call, you start to prepare, applying your makeup in your own order, some do eyes first, some do face and neck. "This is your fifteen-minute call" – the orchestra's warming up. Here it comes, that tingle, it's starting to build, the makeup's done and the wig pinned in place, into your first clean shirt, it won't stay white for long. Trousers next, then socks, then shoes. Get the bow tie or jabot in place, now the waistcoat, and into the tailcoat. "Your five-minute call" – now you really go up a gear, gloves on, hat in hand. "Overture and Beginners" – and off to the stage, now the adrenalin is really kicking in. Now you sense the audience, out in the dark, beyond the curtain, the chatter, the excitement and the rustle of sweet papers, programmes and clothes. "Places, please" – you go to your spot, the orchestra starts and here comes that burst of energy and excitement: Ladies and Gentlemen, it's the *Black and White Minstrel Show*. That huge rush of applause as your audience gets their first sight of the glitter and glamour, that kick into top gear and off you go, twice nightly for six days a week covering thirteen miles a night at running pace with, if you're lucky, a fifteen-minute break between shows. In between the eight numbers in each show, you're running up or down stairs changing costumes at the same time. "You must be mad," people say; well, maybe we are, but until you've experienced that surge, that lift, that wonderful all-encompassing feeling of achievement, love and warmth, you just do not know what it means, and it never goes away. Would we do it again? You bet your life we would, because we were the Mitchell Minstrels, Maids and Toppers, and we were the best show that the BBC and live theatre produced throughout the '50s, '60s and '70s.'

The show burst upon the Hippodrome stage in a riot of colour and glitter, thrilling an audience used to seeing it in black and white. The press loved it, with the *Western Daily Press* calling it 'excitingly good. The show is bursting with life; it is fast and funny, and at the same time healthy; it is spectacular in a dramatically simple kind of way. As holiday entertainment, it could hardly be bettered. The soloists frequently [do] turns to give force to the impression that this is teamwork. Skilful parodies are a highlight with Dai Francis paying a tribute to Al Jolson that is at the same time modest and superb.' The *Evening Post* agreed: 'Rarely have I been charmed by a variety show as I was by this one. There is every colour of the rainbow. The costumes are gorgeous, the settings simple and completely effective. I was completely captivated.'

George breathed a sigh of relief. The first hurdle was over. The show worked on stage. The week in Bristol ran its course, 'get out' was immediately after the second house on Saturday evening, with many of the cast helping. Six removal vans travelled through the night to Liverpool for the next week, and then everyone was faced with the 'get in', which could mean thirty-six hours without sleep for people like Wardrobe.

Press reaction everywhere the show went remained ecstatic. Scottish newspapers welcomed one of their favourite sons home with favourable reviews, such as, 'Superb on the stage. The pace is fast, the tempo ever-changing and the costume colours are a perfect foil to the black and white of the Minstrels' and 'I once wrote that TV was the perfect medium for this show. I was wrong; it is even better on the stage. Last night a holiday audience showed its appreciation by standing up and applauding. They wouldn't let the Minstrels off the stage.....happiness radiates from this company, and since happiness is so infectious, the audience just has to respond.'

But trouble was in store. Despite such a great press reception, audiences were by and large poor, with many of the best seats remaining unsold. After all, why pay to see the show when it was free to watch at home? But despite the Minstrels still haemorrhaging money – it had lost £13,000 (£210,000) in eight weeks - Bob stuck with it; he believed the combination of old familiar songs and pretty girls – or pure escapism – was what people really wanted, and he firmly believed that he now possessed the expertise to exploit it. He had already laid the ground with the BBC for a longer tour the following year.

Nevertheless, George and Bob knew the show somehow wasn't working after all. So they took a deep breath, gritted their teeth at the cost, and completely revamped it before opening in Scarborough on June 25. New tapes were recorded and new routines rehearsed. Though the Minstrels still comprised only the second half, they now also closed the first half, with a *Good Old Summertime* sequence. Only the *Al Jolson* sequence survived in the second half, which now started with *All Aboard the Showboat*, moved on to the *Grand and Glorious Twenties*, a Jackpots sequence, *In the Still of the Night* featuring Tony Mercer, then John Boulter took everyone *Down Mexico Way*, followed by the saved *Al Jolson* sequence, then John and Tony led the company in *Carnival Mood*. The conducted sequence was *The Battle Hymn of the Republic* and the closing was *Dixieland*. The last song of the show was to be *When the Saints Go Marching In*, which became their signature tune, even though it triggered an argument between the two Georges. George Inns wanted the standard fast jazz version of the song, whereas George was adamant that the slow version was the most suitable. George won, and so it remained for the lifetime of both stage and television shows, closing the last show of every series, as well as every stage show.

George hoped the revamp would reverse the still-disappointing audience figures. They now had to fill a 2000-seater theatre in Scarborough twice nightly for twelve weeks. It was the biggest indoor show in the history of the town with 288,000 seats to sell.

Nerves were stretched to the extreme on opening night before a specially invited audience, though George's diary is again characteristically low-key – 'Scarborough opening'. But they needn't have worried. The first-night audience gave them a rapturous reception, and the following morning the entire coastal road was blocked with cars and people trying to get to the booking office. The police had to be called out to control the crowds. George could hardly believe it: 'It just never stopped. It got absolutely ridiculous.' The show became 'easily the hit of the resort's holiday programme, playing before packed houses'. John Boulter remembers, 'It was a truly unbelievable experience. We had been playing to very disappointing audiences, and suddenly we were packed to capacity every single night. It gave the entire cast a tremendous morale-boosting lift.' 'Everyone was injected with renewed enthusiasm,' said Dai Francis. 'The whole cast, including backstage personnel, had worked so hard for this moment it was difficult for them to conceal their emotions.' Later principal Elspeth Hands recalls, 'It's very exciting when a show breaks through like that. The whole company responds in a most marvellous way. Because you're suddenly a hit and in demand, everyone performs better, and there's a tremendous feeling of exhilaration.'

Press reaction was equally ecstatic. The *Yorkshire Evening News* wrote, 'No audience anywhere could sleep through the second half. The show races through sixty-four different numbers with its cast of thirty-six crowding the big stage. It is happy, superbly dressed, delightfully danced and wonderfully sung.' The *Stage* agreed: 'A sell-out success since the first night – wonderfully sung – the Minstrels shatter the audience with an almost atomic presentation.'

George was baffled by this enormous success, on record as saying, 'It may be the girls, they look marvellous, sing well, dance well, but basically, I suppose it comes down to the music. The lesson seems to be that good, tuneful songs are always attractive.'

Minstrel Magic

Bob Luff was certain he knew what made the show so successful: 'The Minstrels are bringing the family audience back to the theatre. Television is giving a shot in the arm to the living theatre. The show on the stage is not the same as that which people have already seen on television. The formula is the same, consisting of modern interpretations of some of the loveliest popular music ever written, costumes which are a blaze of colour, and choreography which fills the stage with lively movement. The spectacle of the show lies entirely in the costumes as the scenery is reduced to a minimum, consisting of a cyclorama, against which an occasional decorative motif is displayed to create atmosphere. This leaves the stage free for dancing and gives choreographer Larry Gordon ample space for sweeping and speedy routine numbers. The girls and boys have the hardest chorus job in the history of light entertainment. They are the major attraction of the show.' Margo Henderson had no doubt as to the reason for its success: 'This is, above all, a team show, a kind of perpetual motion that has never before been created on stage. The success belongs to everyone in the show. It's a complete phenomenon in show business.' Record publisher Ben Nesbitt told the *Daily Sketch*, 'The Minstrels have been consistently the biggest money-makers in the business.' The paper added, 'Their earning power totals something which should stagger those who assume there's never been anything in all history quite like the Beatles.'

The show quickly settled into its summer run. Television, as usual in those days, broadcast an excerpt from the show in its *Show Parade* series and all three soloists featured in *An Evening at the Candlelight*, recorded at a Scarborough night club. Stan Stennett indulged his love of flying his four-seater Cessna as much as he could, returning to his Cardiff home every weekend. John Boulter had also discovered a love of flying and spent a lot of time in the air with Stan. But not everyone was so keen. Dai Francis hated the idea of flying, and although the whole cast persuaded him to go up with Stan, he backed out at the last minute. The cast enjoyed cricket and rounders matches and were invited to many social engagements around the resort.

They closed in Scarborough in mid-September, after which they started a provincial tour ending in Cardiff in late November. The allure of the revamped show hadn't faded. One Brighton critic wrote, 'What impresses most is the stamp of complete professionalism. Not even a long summer run at a Northern seaside resort or an extensive tour have dimmed the sparkle or pace.' Cardiff agreed: 'Not since Secombe and Shirley Bassey have I heard an audience cheering so loudly.' However, Blackpool critics weren't so kind, with one writing, 'While it wouldn't catch the crowds here during the summer (lacking a really weighty star draw), it makes an amiable evening's entertainment.' Time proved this critic spectacularly wrong.

But inevitably the technology unravelled. There should have been a slight hiatus before the standby tape could be activated, but Edinburgh didn't go according to plan. George remembered it well: 'We had a new Stage Manager. Tony Mercer was on stage, and one tape started to go wrong. The Stage Manager turned the other tape on straight away instead of turning down and fading in.' John Boulter remembers it as even more chaotic: 'The number one tape began to falter just as I was coming on. The reserve recorder was hurriedly switched on – but played at a slightly different speed from the first. Meanwhile, the music director – understandably thrown – was conducting at a third tempo. I coped by hurrying to the centre mike and singing full voice to set the tempo myself.' George Chisholm also left his recollection, though as he wasn't with the stage show, he's probably thinking of a later event: 'They all stood frozen, mouths open, wondering whether to sing another note or not. There was this silence for about thirty seconds, but that could have been thirty years. Then from somewhere towards backstage an unknown third or fourth tenor found voice again, the orchestra picked up and the chorus swelled. Backstage they were making good the broken tape, and any second now it would come live again and the amplifiers would blare out – but would we be anywhere near the same bit of the same tune? It certainly couldn't have been much of a miss for it didn't even get a dishonourable mention in the papers next day.'

Surprisingly the company was rarely treated to this sort of emergency. Dot remembers, 'Tapes only broke once or twice a year. Although the tapes were meant to be in sync, they never were, as after about twenty minutes, the heat would make one a bit slower than the other, as the tape slackened. We had two people on sound, so one would always be there to get the second tape to where it should be if the master tape broke. But a couple of times they got it wrong. Often one guy was local without the experience to really know what he was doing, and if the tape broke when the regular guy was off for coffee, that's when problems happened.

Often they'd skip a number which was better than going back. You couldn't tell the difference [between dancers and Mitchell Maids] until the tape broke, when the Maids went off stage to cluster around a mike to sing and hopefully drown the terrible noise coming from the Toppers on stage – they'd all be out of breath, trying to sing and dance at the same time. It didn't throw the stage routines, everyone just mucked in. It would always be the same four boys and girls who came off, so everyone knew what to do on stage. You just spread out, and no one noticed as long as the patterns and the show kept going. If a tape broke, whoever was on their 'swing' routine was out of that dressing room so fast and to the mike to augment the sound. You kept singing and dancing, and in less than thirty seconds, everyone was singing and dancing as before.'

Trying to synchronise the tapes didn't always work. Dot again: 'Once, we were doing *I've Never Wronged an Onion* on stilts in clown outfits and red noses. You need someone behind you to give you a leg up onto the stilts. So we came onstage singing on stilts, and suddenly the tape broke halfway through so we were screaming it at the top of our voices. We finished it and got off the stilts, ran round and four of us had gone onstage for the next number when *Onion* started again. We shot round the back, onto stilts and back on stage. Of all the places to break! The stilts were wooden and very heavy with rubber feet to stop us slipping, which was exhausting anyway, so to have to do it twice was shattering.'

The tape technology was threatened by a national electricity go-slow in 1963 which gave everyone some anxious moments, though in reality the tape only cut out on one occasion. George remembers, 'The Minstrels were marvellous. The stage mikes were turned up, they sang louder than ever until the recorded sound was restored and the incident passed off without comment.' However, they were not so lucky on the spring evening in 1964 when BBC2 started. The first warning that the Victoria Palace got of problems at Battersea Power Station was when the tape gradually began to fail, along with the lights, again with poor Tony Mercer centre stage. As the tape slowed, Tony's recorded voice got deeper and deeper until he gave up all hope of slow-miming, though Leslie Crowther recalled he tried, despite 'going absolutely ashen under his makeup'. Then the lights went out completely. Stage manager Laurie Bloom rushed upstairs – the tannoy system had failed as well – to fetch Leslie Crowther, the stipulated fill-in performer. Leslie recalled, 'Margo Henderson was in hysterics rolling on the floor. George Chisholm and I were clutching each other in laughter. Laurie said, "Listen, you buggers, get on that stage and keep the flag flying." ' In seconds, Leslie was pattering away to the audience, first by the light of the matches he struck, then by a cigarette lighter. He battled on for five minutes, then eight. John Boulter recalls, 'I'd just bought a brilliant torch, so I put this on for him.' Leslie didn't know who or what the light was until George Chisholm stood beside him, bowler-hatted and grinning like a Cheshire cat, shining the torch onto his own face. They carried on, each shining torches on the other, playing music and fooling around for fully twenty minutes until the lights went on again – only to reveal Leslie in the middle of the stage wearing only his underpants!

Battersea caused more problems in October 1966, when the show suffered a major blackout when the power station once again failed. The entire company was dressed and made up, the house was full and the show ready to go on, so go on it did. The company mingled with the audience and sang all their favourite songs. Some of the girls even sat on a few knees until every member of the audience was drawn into a happy sing-song. No one left, and no one asked for their money back. As Bob said, 'What should have been a disaster turned out to be one of our most successful evenings ever.'

Audiences obviously loved it when these sorts of things happened, though it wasn't always quite as noticeable. 'I am always worried sick in case anything goes wrong,' said George, generally present at opening nights, 'but apart from minor irritations, fortunately, things seemed to turn out well.' He had, of course, noticed the tape breakdown early in this show. This time the affected soloist was Glyn Dawson: 'The tape went off, so I sang *Serenade* right through it.' George did his own poll of the audience to see if anyone had noticed but no one had. George was interviewed later that evening by a magazine writer who asked him if he ever got scared about the mechanical side. George replied, 'I'm scared the whole time I sit out front. I'm that type of chap. But I must admit that I do keep my fingers crossed about the tape mechanics. However, a breakdown doesn't produce the disaster that one might think. The artistes just increase the volume of their voices, and few people know the difference. We had a breakdown tonight. Did you notice?' Of course, the reporter hadn't.

By the time the first tour ended in November 1960, George and Bob's faith in the show had been vindicated. A magazine feature later wrote, 'What decided perfectly normal men like Bob Luff and George Mitchell to risk large sums of money and personal reputations to stage a show like the Minstrels? A lot of risk and nerve! Britain was emerging from the Second World War, people craved for new experiences, and the new and exciting world of television was coming to the fore, so why put money in a show with no known stars and no dialogue? It takes a very special kind of person to persuade someone to work hard doing two shows a night six nights a week for little monetary return, plus rehearse a TV show during the day, and record it on a Sunday. If you also put in the fact that your real face will never be seen, hidden behind black makeup, you have to be nuts. But this quiet man called George Mitchell, backed by George Inns and Bob Luff, did it. It speaks volumes about the man.'

But Bob wasn't going to leave it there. Relishing another battle with the BBC, he'd begun his latest attack before the show even reached Scarborough. With typical Luff exaggeration, he had written to the BBC's Martin Turnell, saying the show had been 'having fantastic success with audiences. Although the advance in each town has not been exceptional, the merit of the show and the press criticisms have combined to build up a very good week's business, though had we played two weeks in each town, our overall average would have been higher.' In July he approached the BBC again, asking to add four weeks to the season. The BBC agreed but said, 'No more as they will be back on television.' But that didn't stop Bob, back again a month later, telling the BBC he wanted to do a provincial tour the following spring, following six weeks in Coventry, and another Scarborough summer season. He also tried to get the BBC to agree to a further four years on the same terms, which as usual led to endless internal debate at the BBC. When Assistant Head of Light Entertainment Tom Sloan told him he had no chance, Bob retorted that his outlay had been huge, without the actual running costs, and the show hadn't yet moved into profit. The Corporation realised that legally they were on thin ice, particularly as other commercial ventures were extremely interested now the show had proved such a hit.

This was yet another battle that the BBC was destined to lose. Realising they would have to agree if they were to keep hold of their star show, they changed tack and started to argue over royalties.

When Eric Maschwitz, Head of Light Entertainment, Television, favoured only asking for a modest fee increase, Tom Sloan spluttered, 'This is one of the most successful summer shows this year, grossing £6,000 (£96,000) per week at the moment. It is utterly unrealistic not to get more. George Inns is on a 1% royalty and is getting £60 (£960) per week.' The BBC was getting a fraction of that.

Bob wasn't giving anything away easily and fought hard. He offered £60 per week for the 1961 Scarborough season, but only the current £30 for the other venues. He also wanted two Minstrel companies, adding – possibly threatening – that he had 'had an offer to stage the show in a theatre many miles away'. Maschwitz was against a second company as 'they would hardly be likely to be up to standard' and tried to insist that in 1961 Bob used the same cast – dancers and singers – as in the winter television series: 'This will let us recruit first class dancers for the series and keep them in work throughout the summer before returning to television next winter.' In return, Bob would be allowed to call them the Television Toppers. But Maschwitz was overruled. Tom Sloan refused to agree to both years but 'would concede 1962 if necessary'. He also agreed to the second company, in return for which Bob conceded £60 per week royalties at all venues 'for the No 1 company'.

CHAPTER 15

Europe was beginning to feature highly in everyone's minds. The first *Eurovision Song Contest* had taken place in Lugano, Switzerland, in 1956, though without the United Kingdom which didn't join until the following year. George's singers had appeared in a programme called the *Festival of British Popular Songs*, the winner of which went on to the *Eurovision Song Contest* in Frankfurt that year. George had worked on one entry and later told the *Daily Herald*, 'I told my collaborator, "This is awful tripe" to which he replied, "The buggers only hear it once, George – there's no point writing anything good." ' It's hard to imagine perfectionist George settling for anything less than the best he could do, though he used one *Eurovision* winner *Tom Pillibi* in several shows later in the 60s.

By 1960, the BBC was staging three shows to choose the British entry, during which the Mitchell Singers backed stars such as Pearl Carr and Teddy Johnson, Ronnie Carroll, Bryan Johnson and Dennis Lotis. Most songs were slammed by press and audience alike. The British final was won by Bryan Johnson, with *Looking High, High, High*, which went on to come second in the actual contest, though without the choir as the rules prohibited backing groups accompanying the singers. The Mitchells retained close links with the song contest for years to come. In the 1963 competition, Mitchell Singers again took part in the programme to choose Britain's entry. Before each of the six songs, they sang a medley of past successes by the relevant composer. The winning entry turned out to be *Say Wonderful Things* with Ronnie Carroll, in which three Mitchell girls – Mary Moss, Maggi Lawlor and Penny Jewkes - clad in black cocktail dresses, moved furniture and planks around a raked set and posed on it, singing as they went. Maggi remembered, 'We each had a different sized stool for the routine, but somehow we all got the wrong sizes, so the routine wouldn't work and we had to make up our own.' In the final, staged at White City in London, where Britain came fourth, this inept staging had been dumped, and the girls sat in front of Ronnie, gazing adoringly at him.

Dutch television producer Jos van der Valk was also interested in George's singers for a Dutch television series. Jos clearly remembers what light entertainment was like on the Continent then: 'Holland had no musical tradition or stage entertainment as in the UK or USA. Songs familiar to UK audiences were totally unknown in the Netherlands. Then on TV, we saw shows from Perry Como and Andy Williams. It was completely new to us. I came to England often and worked with the Television Toppers.' During one of his visits, Jos caught a performance of the Minstrel show. He recalls, 'I was starting a monthly Saturday night series and to give it an international look, I thought music by the Mitchell Singers would be a good factor. I gave George suggestions for the music which was specially recorded in England, with the tapes, the group and George travelling to Holland every month to film the show.' The choir did two successful seasons, from September to May each year. These Continental shows were seen widely across Europe. Those for Dutch television were also seen in Belgium, whereas similar shows made in Vienna for Austrian television were seen by thirty million viewers across Austria, Germany and Switzerland. Half these shows were sung in English and half in German, which the choir learned phonetically.

Staging caused more problems here too. Maryetta Midgley recalls, 'We were singing children's songs, with hobby horses, and had to go down a chute. Everything was very big so we'd look young and small. Each girl had a boy at the bottom of the chute, who was to catch the girl and then they'd waltz off together. However, during the break, the cleaner polished everything, including the chute. We all slid down into a heap on the floor. We were going out live although the music was pre-recorded. No one was in their right place. I've never laughed so much. George was behind the camera, he put his hand to his head and walked away.'

Later Minstrel principal Ted Darling was one of the Mitchell singers who travelled to Holland every month. He recalls that George 'loved his food and his booze. When he was abroad – we did a lot of work in Amsterdam – he had a list of all the best restaurants. I was one of the fortunate ones invited to try them out with three or four others. I felt very honoured to be asked.' Reg Bracken, a friend in later life, remembers a rather less salubrious occasion: 'We ate out at a pub noted for its fish menu. It was quite busy, but we managed to find a table and ordered our meals. After quite some time, instead of being presented with our food, a loud voice called out from the depths behind the crowded bar, "Bracken, Mitchell". This was not quite what we were used to, but it made us smile and was a story often referred to.'

Work was still plentiful in Britain too. George welcomed an opportunity to record another series with Josh White, again with producer Charles Chilton, who also produced another major Mitchell series *Frontier America* which gave Chilton another outlet for both the choir and his passion for American history. Before this finished, Charles Chilton launched a major series with Bud Flanagan and the choir, *Bud Flanagan Remembers*, which came about following the earlier *Long Long Trail* when Charles realised Bud Flanagan had a lot of interesting music in his life. Charles must have been ever-present in everyone's lives as he also produced a new radio Minstrel series, *Mitchell's Modern Minstrels*; this series starred Tony, Dai, John and also Jeff Hudson, and ran for six weeks. Charles says, 'The idea was to convey in sound the same sort of impression as the *Black and White Minstrel Show* on TV.'

Much to George's amazement, he had been approached to record an LP of Minstrel songs, aimed at the Christmas market. Record giant EMI quickly saw the Minstrels' huge potential and EMI's recording manager, Wally Ridley, met George several times in July 1960 to persuade him to make the album. George was doubtful as he couldn't believe people would buy what they could hear freely on television. But Wally had no doubts, later saying, 'I always thought it was a good property though I never imagined we'd do this well.' George was eventually persuaded, but the timing was difficult. He could use London core singers instead of the Scarborough Minstrels but he obviously needed the regular soloists, and they were appearing twice nightly all the way north in Scarborough. And there was no time for rehearsal and precious little time at all if the soloists were not to miss any stage shows. George solved these problems by using the stage sequences and bringing down to London only the three soloists and five singers, including Don Cleaver, Keith Leggett and Glyn Dawson, augmenting them with London-based singers. The Mitchell girls were all London-based, including Maryetta Midgley, Mary Moss, Daphne Bell, Julia Whitaker and Maggi Lawler. George recalled, 'That record was made with absolutely no trouble at all. We came down one Sunday from Scarborough, made it in two smart sessions and were back for the Monday shows.' Glyn Dawson remembered the occasion well: 'We went down by train one Sunday to make the LP at Abbey Road. George took us for fish and chips, at a place where there were live fish swimming about in a tank.'

The publicity machine swung into action. George placed a large advert in many publications saying, 'George Mitchell thanks the Mitchell Minstrels for their loyalty, enthusiasm and co-operation, the public for their tremendous support (BBC TV over 10 million viewers every show, theatre over ½ million patrons in six months), the Press for their generous comments. And now another record – music from this fabulous show has been recorded by the Minstrels and is available now!' Very soon it achieved record sales, selling over 20,000 copies in its first week. By the end of January 1961, the album was 6th in the charts, bested only by Elvis Presley, *South Pacific*, Ray Conniff, Cliff Richard and the Shadows and Adam Faith. It occupied the Number One slot for nine weeks on and off from July until late autumn, never leaving the top six chart positions and staying in the charts for two and a half years. It achieved the then very rare distinction of a gold disc for sales of over a million, presented to George at the end of one television show. An EMI spokesman said, 'This has been one of our fastest-selling LPs – a truly remarkable achievement. It's the first album by any of our British artistes to reach six-figure sales.' George remained flummoxed: 'This success is ridiculous. I had to be persuaded into making this record because I've been so frantically busy since the whole thing started in 1948.'

Back in the recording studios the following year, the Minstrels spent a mere nine hours recording the second album *Another Black and White Minstrel Show*, released in October, followed by the EP *Christmas with the Minstrels*, which formed the basis years later for *The Magic of Christmas* album. This second album quickly reached No 1 in the charts, staying there for eight weeks and kicking its predecessor, *The Black and White Minstrel Show*, into second place. This gave George the accolade of becoming – and remaining – the only artiste in the world to hold the first two places in the British top ten album ratings simultaneously, beating huge names in the burgeoning rock and roll scene. The third album, *On Stage*, moved to the top immediately after its release in December 1962, only to be ousted, in the final week of the year, by the first album, which thus returned to the top eighteen months after it first hit it. Sales of all three albums remained phenomenal, with EMI reporting an all-time record for anything produced in Britain. As George said, 'Nobody had ever made 1st and 2nd before but to have 4th as well and considering one of those albums was three years old, it's going to take some beating.' In fact, it never has been beaten, in the British or American charts.

To heap further praise, the Gramophone Record Retailers Association and Record Retailer and Music Industry News presented EMI Records with the award for the Best Light Entertainment Vocal Record of 1961 – they won the same award the following year with *On Stage with the Minstrels*.

Albums became an annual event, eagerly awaited by fans, but never again were they to repeat the success of the early 1960s. The 1964 album, *Spotlight on the George Mitchell Minstrels*, made recording history when producer Wally Ridley recorded 'each unit individually so that their presence could be preserved as cleanly as possible. We can sort out our own sound specification, the boys from the girls, the tenors from the baritones, the band's brass section from its rhythm.' But this album, like the previous year's, could only reach No 6 in the charts. A similar but lesser fate awaited nearly every future album. Until, that is, 1977 when EMI released what was to become one of George's most successful albums. *The Black and White Minstrels with the Joe Loss Orchestra, Thirty Golden Greats* was launched with a huge £250,000 (£1m) advertising campaign, including TV commercials, which compared very favourably with the £300,000 (£1.3m) spent on launching the *Beatles at the Hollywood Bowl* album the same year. The TV ads were a departure, with the accent on a mainly black and white animated clip, to complement the black and white sleeve design. The album also broke with tradition, as it only featured a couple of medleys. Most of the album was filled with individual songs, many of which were contemporary, such as *Y Viva España, Consider Yourself, Paloma Blanca* and *Tijuana Taxi*, and ended with a most un-minstrel like *We're Gonna Rock Around the Clock*. One reviewer said, 'How can you begin to extol the virtues of two such entertainers? Both have long been regarded in high esteem in their respective spheres. The joining together of two such pre-eminent entertainers must surely be regarded as a momentous occasion.' But many reviewers thought it a risk to release this album, due to 'both the dated nature of the material and the fading appeal and protests against the show'. Nevertheless, it entered the charts ahead of the Rolling Stones' double album *Get Stoned*, and EMI said they would be 'very disappointed' if the record was not Number One by Christmas. Sadly, despite being featured as album of the week on the *Jimmy Young Show* on Radio 2, the album was destined to disappoint EMI's hopes, peaking at Number 10.

Before the Minstrels hit the touring road once again, George and Bob were able to add yet another accolade to the show's posters. When the European Broadcasting Union decided to hold a television light entertainment festival, to choose the world's best light entertainment show, many countries raced to create programmes specially to enter the competition. America, allowed to send two entries because of its huge viewing public, submitted two specially recorded entries, a *Perry Como Special* and a Fred Astaire show. But the BBC dithered about whether even to enter. Eventually, George Inns submitted a *Black and White Minstrel Show*, with George Mitchell saying, 'We're planning nothing special. This will be a representative show, relying as always on teamwork.' Future publicity would have us believe that this was a totally random choice, a tape casually removed from storage, but the episode George Inns chose was the sixth show in the recent series, which the critics had rated the best. It's inevitable that it was carefully chosen, but the 'random selection' story certainly brought great publicity. Although the BBC was proud of its entry, it was certainly far from confident. The opposition was formidable, including not only the two high-profile American shows, but a spectacular Italian revue, a Soviet entry featuring the famous Kirov ballet, and a hugely expensive German musical comedy. George thought their chances touch and go: 'Opposition will be tough, and I'm not too sure Continentals understand the concept of black-faced minstrels.' Several critics agreed, thinking it unlikely to do well because the Continent was unfamiliar with the traditions.

Both Georges, together with costumier Mary Woods and George Inns' wife, travelled to Montreux. Three and a half days of judging reduced the thirty-four entrants to a shortlist, with final judging taking place on May 27. The Minstrel team remained encouraged by the fact that the British show, screened early during the judging, was received with 'standing applause'. George's delight can only be imagined when they swept the board, winning not only the Golden Rose itself but also the Silver Rose, the Press award for the best show. They were now officially the best light entertainment show in the world. George recalled, 'It won by a mile. Talk about a clean sweep – little did I know it would run for twenty one years.' George Inns was delighted: 'This is a wonderful birthday present. No American will believe we do the show live. One of their entries, *The Fred Astaire Show*, took three months to film.' Noel Coward presented the Golden Rose to the BBC, which, beside itself with joy, dropped that evening's *Perry Mason* show to repeat the winning programme.

The stage show was currently in Bristol. The atmosphere there that night was tremendous, with even more verve and enthusiasm generated by this now internationally award-winning team. Topper Elspeth Hands remembers the occasion well, 'The call came through that we'd actually won, and the excitement was electrifying. During the night we travelled up to London. Mr Luff had given us a special allowance, and all the girls bought hats, and then met George Mitchell and George Inns at the airport, as they came off the plane carrying the Golden Rose.' An occasion long remembered by the staff there, as well as incoming passengers who were caught up in the reception. Surprisingly, the *Stage* disagreed with the result: 'It's difficult to see how this show won against competition from the inspired choreography in the *Perry Como Show*.'

Eric Maschwitz, BBC's Head of Light Entertainment, decided to share the £800 (£12,500) prize between the show's creators, saying, 'We believe in recognising the people behind the scenes. The Minstrels' show is pure television. It is always produced live, and it clearly had tremendous visual and oral impact upon the judges. I am very proud of George Inns and all the team who made the win possible.' George Inns received £200 with £165/3/1 going to George Mitchell; the rest was shared between Toni Chapman (makeup), Larry Gordon, Mary Woods (wardrobe), Stanley Dorfman (designer) and Tom Montcrieff (lighting). The following Monday the BBC's Board of Management recorded, 'It is a great pleasure that the *Black and White Minstrel Show* has won the award. Warm congratulations of Board of Management to the Head of Light Entertainment Television and George Inns for their part in this.' No mention of George or the cast! Director General Hugh Greene presented George Inns with a bound copy of the winning show's script. Inscribed in the book, which was in both

Minstrel Magic

English and French, were the words, 'Warmest congratulations and all good wishes.'

A few weeks later, George was back in Scarborough, overseeing the recording of the stage show, in front of an invited audience, which was televised next day as an 'excerpt from the 1961 stage presentation of the International Award-winning BBC TV series, starring the George Mitchell Minstrels.' This programme achieved the highest audience response of any television show ever put out by the BBC.

This win changed BBC attitudes towards light entertainment forever, from something they were forced to provide, into flagship BBC shows. Worldwide sales of the Minstrel shows rocketed, with countries as far afield as Japan snapping it up. Though the win had one slightly bizarre result - agent Jack Fallon told the national press that the idea for the *Black and White Minstrel Show* had been his and he was considering suing the BBC. Asked why he'd waited till now, he replied it was 'because they have won the Golden Rose of Montreux!' The Minstrel show was never entered for Montreux again, though *Music Music Music* with the Mitchell Singers was entered in 1969, and several future entries included Mitchell singers, such as The Charlie Drake Show in 1968 which won the premier comedy prize, the Special Prize of the City of Montreux. One Dutch TV show with the core singers was about to be submitted when Dutch Television discovered that German TV was submitting a Mitchell programme made for Munich TV.

Following the Golden Rose win, the BBC took the unprecedented step of publishing a commemorative book about the Minstrels. When the BBC wanted to send staff photographers into the studios to take production shots for the book, George Inns refused, arguing that the best people to take the photos were the camera crew. With bad grace, the BBC agreed. Pat Heigham, Sound Engineer, remembers, 'It was wonderful because we were never normally allowed cameras in the studios. I was dabbling with 8mm ciné, so I fired away with that, deliberately choosing whole numbers and covering them from two camera positions on the two dress run-throughs. I sought permission of the sound mixer, Adrian Stocks, to set it up in the Sound Control room one tea break, and showed the result to George Inns. He immediately brought the boys and girls in to view it. As the show went out live, none of them had actually seen it at all. And of course, it was in colour! To celebrate the book, the Corporation threw a cocktail party for the cast and crew, where George Inns wanted me to run the film. I was a bit scared as it was against the rules and of course, I had 'borrowed' the music tapes. Eric Robinson, the conductor, was consulted and gave the OK, so loudspeakers and a tape deck were delivered and I set up my little projector. On a signal, Len Mitchell, the Floor Manager, doused the lights without warning and the film hit the screen. When it finished, the current Controller of BBC Television, taken unawares, stood up on a table and said, "This gives a very good example of what our Light Entertainment output could look like once we start transmitting in colour – and ranks as the best example of unofficial enterprise inside the BBC!" So I kept my job and at George Inns' request, kept filming.'

Typically this led, once again, to yet another row between Bob and the BBC, which escalated to major proportions and threatened the show's television future. Never one to miss an opportunity for money or publicity, Bob objected that he hadn't been consulted over the book's references to the stage version, whereas he had consulted the BBC over the theatre's souvenir programmes. Certainly, the book got quite a lot wrong. Bob rang Eric Maschwitz, distressed by the BBC's 'grossly unfair' account of his theatrical association with the Minstrels. He pointed out he had begun negotiations for the stage show 'before the television programme was well known or popular' and of course, he was correct. Bob also complained the BBC hadn't credited him with giving the Victoria Palace broadcast 'for free' – this broadcast from the stage of the theatre had opened the latest television series. Tom Sloan, Head of Light Entertainment, pointed out the *Radio Times* had said the show had been 'televised by arrangement with Robert Luff Holdings' and he found it 'difficult to see what further credit could be given'. However, Bob insisted that he should have a screen credit and eventually Tom agreed. He also agreed to pre-record three studio productions 'using the Number 1 company on any convenient summer Sunday next year' so that they could start the new television season while this company was still appearing on stage. If these were used while the show was still on stage, then 'appropriate credits will be given'. The BBC was clearly getting annoyed with Bob for continually raising more and more changes to a contract he'd already signed.

In an extension to the row, Bob began to worry about the film possibilities. Internally the BBC accused him of 'behaving like a spinster looking for burglars'. Feeling was strong that Bob wasn't bound to continue the stage shows at all, and that if they agreed to needing his consent to produce any films, that was tantamount to giving him total rights in a hugely important BBC property. However, they also realised that practically nothing could be done without his permission as he controlled the stage Minstrels and George, so they offered to consult him before agreeing to any film. When Ancona Productions approached the BBC the following year, to make a film of the Minstrels for European audiences, the Corporation was fairly positively inclined towards granting permission as long as both George and Bob were on board. However, Bob was not at all keen for any transaction with Ancona, feeling that it was against everyone's interest for a film to be shown while the stage version was still running. At the same time, Bob pushed for worldwide rights for himself, but the BBC weren't having any of it and would only consider giving him first refusal.

But it wasn't to end there. Eric Maschwitz asked the Contracts department to 'investigate the peculiar credit to the stage production in the *Radio Times*. This is quite wrong and should be stopped. We only give credits when artistes are under exclusive contract to another management, and we couldn't get them without a credit. This could not possibly be so in this case.' The show was BBC property – or so the Corporation thought.

With glee, Bob quickly put them right. For the past eighteen months, unknown to the BBC, all the Victoria Palace artistes had been under exclusive contract to him until the stage show ended, with the principals contracted until 1965, and so not available for television without his consent. So he asked for the credit 'customarily accorded to a West End theatre manager in such a case'.

The BBC was stunned. 'I don't see how this could possibly be true,' fumed Maschwitz. 'We would never have leased rights if it could have had the effect of making a continuation of the television programme depend on the lessee surely?' But true it was. Somehow a clause normally inserted in contracts to stop this very situation happening had been omitted. 'Without such a clause,' raved Eric, 'there is nothing to prevent the producer of the stage show preventing the leading artistes in the television production from appearing on the screen.' Bob, quickly on the offensive again, complained that without such credits, the BBC was forcing him to break his contract with Moss Empires. The

BBC, backed into a corner, reluctantly agreed: 'As we did not raise it before, as it would embarrass him with Moss Empires, we will agree as an exception this time.' Once again, Bob had run rings around the BBC – his greatest coup over the BBC.

In spring 1961, the stage version of the show had returned to their first home, the Bristol Hippodrome, chosen, according to Bob, because 'everyone felt the Bristol press and public, and the Hippodrome Theatre staff, combined to give us a really wonderful send-off last year'. The Minstrels still only filled the show's second half, with Leslie Crowther, Penny Nicholls and George Chisholm, the Peter Crawford Trio and the Two Pirates, a well-known acrobatic act, providing the variety acts of the first half. Most of the men from the previous year's stage show returned, with the Jackpots now consisting of the three principal soloists plus Don Cleaver, though the four Mitchell Maids were completely new. Nearly half the Toppers were signed up again, augmented by among others Elspeth Hands who became Head Girl, appeared in most later Minstrel shows on stage and television and eventually became a soloist. Bob put in the same production team too. Jackie Griffiths added the role of Ballet Mistress to her onstage role with the Toppers. Ossie Whitaker was Production Manager, Laurie Bloom remained as Manager and Stage Director, George Steele was Musical Director, though Marie Worth became Wardrobe Mistress.

By mid-June, the show was safely in Scarborough for another summer season, which sold out from start to finish. To the delight of the opening night audience, George took to the stage to conduct *Dry Bones*. Once again, George had arranged and recorded two very different shows. Programme 1 consisted of *Meet the Minstrels* followed by Tony Mercer and *An Old Soft Shoe*, then *A Garden of Flowers, Those Were the Days, Songs of the Islands, Al Jolson* tribute, *Cowboys and Indians, Dry Bones* and finishing with *Doo Dah Dey*. Programme 2 started and ended the same way, and also had an *Al Jolson* sequence; in between the Minstrels offered *All the Fun of the Fair, Hooray for Hollywood, Latin American Way, Serenade in the Night, Square Dance* and *Old Ark*.

There was plenty to entertain the whole family as Bob always laid huge stress on the show's family nature. This was one thing both Bob and George could agree on. George 'always put something in for children – Cinderella, clowns, something for everyone in every programme,' recalls Dot Mitchell. The aftermath of the war had brought about an emphasis on traditional family life, but life was changing fast, with pop music sweeping the world with Swinging London its hub. Many people feared how liberal Britain was becoming. Hanging and flogging were abolished, attitudes softened towards homosexuality, abortion, divorce and censorship which led to shows like *Hair* and *Oh, Calcutta!*, both welcomed by many but also widely condemned by large swathes of the population. Nostalgia was one of the most powerful forces in post-war British culture, which was hardly surprising with the collapse of empire and endless talk of political and economic decline, all of which threatened the safe order of life.

In a period of change, the Minstrels offered a sense of reassurance and stability, appealing to all ages and projecting a familiar view of a world based on romantic love and family. Bob took advantage of this to promote the safety of the old songs and the clean-cut image of the show. He often said, 'I expect youngsters to lead a reasonably free life. But the two things I always crack down on are extra-marital affairs and swearing. If I hear a girl swearing for the second time, then she is out. One warning is enough. Exactly the same thing goes for marriage breakers. That sort of thing could wreck a happy company like mine, and I won't stand for it.' These rules weren't as rigorously enforced as Bob would have liked the outside world to believe – affairs certainly happened with no one being penalised. Roy Winbow recalls, 'It was inevitable really. You come off stage on such a high, and the people you really want to be with are miles away, and the loneliness just hits you. Of course, people are going to find comfort closer to home.' Keith Leggett reinforced this: 'There was always a great adrenalin rush. I remember feeling quite let down when the show finished as I was on such a high, and everyone just packed up and went – usually to the pub next door.'

The family feel was particularly important in summer seasons, which were the most lucrative part of theatreland in an industry which was seen to be slowly dying. Ninety-nine percent of companies now gave their workers two weeks' paid leave which most chose to spend at one of the traditional resorts like Scarborough. The theatre still played a major part in giving holiday-makers a great time, to encourage them to return next year in the face of the growing attractions of coach tours and the Costa del Sol. Only 4% of Britons took package holidays abroad in the early 1960s, rising to only 8% by the end of the decade, but the threat was there and became a reality once the currency restrictions on foreign travel were lifted in the early 1970s. Resorts were slow to respond, but one huge weapon was the glittering entertainment still on offer evening after evening in the major resorts.

The show often became an actual family. Any excuse for a party would do so it's no wonder that a real family feel and friendships - and more - bloomed. The long-running companies inevitably produced the usual engagements, marriages and babies, all of which were announced from the stage at the end of the show. George's organisation made the most of the attendant publicity. This trend had always been present in the Mitchell Singers, beginning way back as early as the late 1940s, when, as singer and long-time associate Alan Cooper recalled, 'Tom Burroughs married Stella Wood, Miki (Barbara Boyle) and Griff (Emyr Griffith) married too. Chris Matthews and Clive Harrington married and went to Australia, Daphne's boyfriend was Geoff Gooding, Frank and Elsie Cooper were married. Jose married me, and Olive married Ralph.' Dot explains, 'The twins (Jose and Olive) started the trend of marriage to the guys. There was virtually no social life outside the show. There was no time to meet anyone else. Working together day in day out, you see all the bad bits, so you know what you're getting, which is why so many of the marriages lasted.' George's right-hand man Keith Leggett, when asked why Minstrel marriages seemed to last, said, 'One of the main reasons is the age gap between the girls and the men. The girls usually joined the show at 16 or 17, while the men were in their 20s or 30s, so it means the men have plenty of time to get around before they settle down. They get used to working with glamorous girls too. They're never likely to be bowled over by a gorgeous mini-skirted secretary.' Many Minstrel couples, such as Peter and Jenny Dakin, John and Dana Asher and Peter and Nanette Kingston all celebrated their 40th anniversaries recently.

By the end of 1966, there had been over thirty marriages between Minstrel company members, without even counting marriages between other choir members, and newspapers fell over themselves to report them all. When dancer Jill Bradburn and Australian Minstrel Garry Hayes got engaged in 1966, Astraka of London presented her with a black and white striped faux fur coat, flown specially from America to Britain, which brought huge publicity for the show and Astraka. All these marriages led

Minstrel Magic

inevitably to lots of Minstrel children, the first 'all Minstrel' baby arriving in early 1965, born to Minstrel Michael Rowlatt and Maid Angela Langton. By the mid-1970s, there were over a hundred babies associated with the shows. Bob gave every new mother a pram and quite often stood godfather to the babies, occasionally throwing a party for all the children on stage.

After a hugely successful summer season in Scarborough, Bob once more defeated the BBC, and the show toured throughout the autumn, spending two weeks in most of its venues. Bob was proved right as they broke box office records everywhere they went, both for audience figures and for the amount of advance booking the theatres took, with most theatres completely selling out. In Bradford, theatre owner Gwladys Stanley Laidler placed ads everywhere, 'to thank Bob Luff and George Mitchell for the opportunity to present the *Black and White Minstrel Show* at the Bradford Alhambra. Thousands were turned away disappointed.'

The new television series was due to begin on Christmas Day, but the stage version was touring until the end of November. When on earth was the new series to be rehearsed and recorded? George had plenty of capable singers who could provide the sound in London, but his principals were all over the country with the stage show. There was only one thing for it – the television shows would have to be rehearsed wherever the show was appearing on stage and the sound somehow recorded. So George took to travelling. How everyone coped with the schedule remains a mystery. For instance, the tour was settled in Bradford for two weeks from September 18. On that day, they rehearsed the Christmas show, recorded the sound a week later, and filmed it over two days while they were appearing in Stockton. This sixty-minute Christmas special moved out of the Television Theatre and into Studio 4 at the Television Centre, gaining the second biggest audience of Christmas Day – 17.2 million. By October 2, they were in Nottingham for two weeks. On Friday, October 13 and Saturday, October 14, they rehearsed from 10am until 4pm, with Sunday given over entirely to television rehearsals until 9.30pm. In Brighton, they recorded the sound for a further three shows over three days – quick work indeed. And all this while performing two shows a night.

In June 1960 the BBC celebrated the opening of Television Centre by hosting a large-scale first-night party, and transmitting

Minstrel Magic

This is the BBC, an award-winning film about an imaginary day in the BBC's life. A cast of twelve hundred included Flora Robson, John Gregson, Beryl Grey, Richard Dimbleby, Richard Murdoch, Kenneth Horne, Jean Metcalfe, Cliff Michelmore, Cy Grant, Eamonn Andrews, Frank Muir and Denis Norden, as well of course as the Mitchell Singers. This was followed by *First Night*, the first studio production from the new Centre, which used Mitchell singers, as well as David Nixon, Arthur Askey, Richard Hearne, Leslie Mitchell, Elizabeth Larner and Irving Davies. Irene Thomas recalled, 'We had been rehearsing there in what was called the Canteen Block, although there was no canteen in it yet, just a vast bare room with nothing in except a piano, a trestle table and some clattering metal chairs. At last, it was ready to open, and we opened with a gala variety show. I can't remember a thing about the show, except that we and the dancers began the opening routine crouched down on our knees waiting for the orchestra to play the introductory chords and it seemed hours before the floor manager started the countdown, with consequent yelps and moans of simulated agony from us as our muscles became cramped.'

CHAPTER 16

Bob had also been busy. Determined to give the BBC no peace, he was soon back, asking for more. Even though he knew the next television series would be underway from Christmas, he had been negotiating with the BBC from early in the year to keep the Minstrels touring and to stage them in Liverpool over Christmas. Knowing the BBC had always vehemently opposed the show appearing on stage and television at the same time, he countered the expected opposition by telling the BBC, 'The touring Minstrels are different from the television Minstrels, and so there would be no effect on the television series.' He promised to replace the soloists with new ones for the Christmas stage season, although he had no intention of fulfilling this – he knew the public wanted to see the Three Musketeers - and the Television Toppers would once again be 'replaced' by the Larry Gordon Dancers. They were, of course, the same dancers, with the BBC having insisted on the name change in the first place. Bob also knew that George Inns had no intention of using Stan Stennett and the other regulars in the next television series and so they could easily be added to the Christmas season. Once again, he anticipated well – the BBC naïvely believed everything Bob promised and agreed immediately.

In mid-December George and the Minstrels moved *en masse* to Liverpool where they settled in for their first Christmas season at the Royal Court Theatre, opening on December 22. Despite Bob's 'promises', it, of course, starred the regular TV soloists John, Tony and Dai, plus the usual Minstrels and Television Toppers, along with Stan Stennett and Margo Henderson. In a departure, the show ran for three hours with one house at 2.30 and one at 7.30. The Minstrels closed the first half and once again took over the second half.

Both Georges, plus Larry Gordon, were present on opening night. The *Liverpool Daily Post* reported, 'It has all the verve of the popular TV show. The spirit, the vitality sweeps over the footlights, engulfing the audience in a satisfying warmth of pure entertainment. It succeeds almost effortlessly in being the best of its kind. Effortlessly? Perhaps not. Its most striking feature is the energy every member of the cast puts into it.' Perhaps they were trying to get warm? Kay Matthews, a Topper, remembers, 'It was a lot of work but a lot of fun too, though it was freezing cold and there was no heating in the digs.'

One further act joined the show – the Littlewood Songsters. A couple of years earlier, in 1959, Littlewoods, the major Liverpool family who had built up quite an empire involving mail order shopping and football pools, had approached George. They wanted his help to give a more commercial look to their in-house choir, a group of female employees known as the Littlewoods Songsters, who worked in local radio and theatre. The group were all aged between 17 and 25, beautiful, and a mix of blondes and brunettes, with one pair of red-haired twins. Littlewoods were keen to expand their work as this would keep their name in front of the public on the commercial-free BBC. George was initially very reluctant to take on this role and turned them down. He'd had his fingers burned in a previous partnership in 1956 when he went into partial partnership with Raymond Woodhead, the manager of Ashton Palais de Danse. The idea was for Raymond to audition singers, form groups and present shows under the Mitchell banner throughout the North West of England, an area which took in such major entertainment centres as Blackpool and Liverpool as well as Manchester. 'For the purposes of the North West, George Mitchell and myself are one,' said Mr Woodhead. 'I am to be musical director, organiser and co-partner. My own singing group, which in two years has made over a hundred broadcasts, will continue to be known as the Raymond Woodhead Choir.' A full-scale talent search for two hundred singers took place across the North of England, with the aim of setting up a Northern section of the Mitchell Choir. Whatever George hoped would happen, the only collaboration was later that year when the Raymond Woodhead Choir combined with the singers to appear in *Blackpool Night*.

So George was in no hurry to repeat the experience, but Littlewoods persisted and eventually, they entered into a two-year agreement with George, appointing Bob as their agent and getting permission to use George's name in any publicity. Nevertheless, George decided to stay at arm's length and asked one of his right-hand men, Fred Tomlinson, to take on the job. Fred moved to

Minstrel Magic

Liverpool – Littlewoods paid his removal expenses – and set about turning the choir professional.

By April 1961, George had decided Fred was more useful to him back in London and asked singer Harry Currie if he'd be interested in replacing Fred. Canadian Army soldier Harry had joined the singers during his posting to Britain in the late 1950s, to gain more experience in topline commercial music. When he was sent back to Canada, 'George said if I should come back to England, he'd have lots of work for me.' Harry had just returned to Britain and recalls, 'George was as good as his word, and I was working in sessions of all sorts almost immediately.' Now George was offering Harry a great opportunity to run his own group. He quickly agreed and as he remembers, 'I wrote arrangements for the choir, hired a choreographer, got new hairstyles and performing clothes, used contemporary music as well as standards, and the choir blossomed, and we did tons of work on stage and for BBC Manchester, all in the North.' One Songster, Wendy Faulkner, recalls, 'We appeared on radio, stage and did most of the TV variety shows eg Harry Secombe, Dicky Valentine, David Whitfield, Morecambe and Wise, Ken Dodd, etc, plus a weekly radio show with the BBC Northern Dance Orchestra.'

The BBC was keen to use them more, in programmes aimed at the North, so the girls made a trial television programme. The BBC's Barney Colehan asked George to review this programme, but George wasn't too happy with what he saw. Writing to Eric Maschwitz, he said, 'Both the vocal and visual aspects show that they tried to be too ambitious and their efforts have got them nowhere. I still think you will agree that the idea of the programme is basically suitable and that for a first attempt the girls did pretty well.' He told Eric that he had now put the 'very capable' Harry in charge of the Songsters, where 'he has improved the vocal side 100%'. George was worried that the BBC could lose 'what might be a potential low budget show for Northern viewers – their enthusiasm is tremendous'. Eric refused to watch the pilot, as 'it was generally considered not to be up to standard' but to keep everyone quiet, promised to see if another pilot might be recorded.

Now at Christmas 1961, the Littlewoods had joined the successful Minstrel stage show for the six-week stay in Liverpool. Harry remembers, 'Somewhere along the line, I was introduced to George Inns, and the two of us got along very well. We kept in touch, and when the *Black and White Minstrel Show* was coming

[213]

to Liverpool, George Inns suggested we incorporate the Littlewoods into the show. We got the whole treatment – four sets of costumes, makeup, hair, choreography, two individual spots in the show plus working in the opening and the closing. It went very well.' Much to Harry's delight, the theatre programme credited him as Musical Director. He felt he had earned the title, even though George was the one being paid as Musical Director. According to Harry, Littlewoods paid George £60 (£930) a week to supervise the choir. Fred and Harry were each paid £30 (£466) to act as MD to the Songsters, plus a £10 (£150) a week expense account, so 'it was a pretty good deal at that time.' All seemed rosy.

The Songsters' success in the show was so great that, according to Harry, 'George Inns called me a few weeks later and told me of a new musical variety show that was being scheduled for BBC TV for the new season. He was the producer, and he said the Littlewoods would be perfect. He asked me to get new photos done, some new recordings, and he set up a meeting with Tom Sloan (newly-appointed Head of Light Entertainment). The Littlewoods people were so excited that they insisted on having a new wardrobe done for the choir. The day arrived, and I was in London for the big meeting, armed with all the goodies to sell the choir. I walked to the desk at the BBC and asked for George Inns. I was told that the meeting with Tom Sloan was cancelled and I was to call George Mitchell immediately. I did that, and George said, "Oh something's come up, old boy, and I think you should come to the office and we'll talk about it." Bewildered, perplexed and very disappointed, I headed for the door through the BBC lobby, when a voice called out loudly, "Harry, where are you going?" I turned, and there was George Inns, hastening after me. "Where are you going?" he said again, "We're late for our meeting with Tom Sloan." Confused, I told him of the call from George Mitchell, and George Inns said, "That's strange, this is nothing to do with him. The meeting is still on. I don't know what George is talking about."

'We got to Tom Sloan's office, where I had a brief thrill of being introduced to Eric Maschwitz, the lyricist of *These Foolish Things* and *A Nightingale Sang*, before I felt a chill at our reception. Tom couldn't have been ruder if he'd tried and I'd barely said hello. I looked at George Inns, and he seemed shocked. Tom grabbed the new professional photos, scattered them on his desk, muttered, "Not very photogenic, are they? Well, I suppose we must hear them sing." He slapped the tape into a player, heard about one minute, shut it off and said, "This is not what we are looking for," and I was almost shoved out of the office. And this was a group that regularly broadcast with Alyn Ainsworth and the BBC Northern Dance Orchestra. George Inns was stupefied. "What the hell is going on?" ' he asked. "Tom was all in favour of hiring them sight and sound unseen after what I told him about the group and having worked with them. They are perfect for this show. I just wanted him to see for himself." He took me to the BBC Club in the building, ordered me a stiff drink, and told me he'd be back. About thirty minutes later he came back, ordered himself a stiff drink, then said very quietly, "Well, it seems as though your boss George Mitchell wants you to do very well, as long as it's not competition for him in London. He persuaded Tom Sloan to turn down the Littlewoods." And that was that. I was so angry that I couldn't go near George Mitchell or even talk to him for several weeks. Littlewoods had been hoping for a major breakthrough like this for years – their choir on a major weekly BBC TV show. When I told them what had happened, I'm sure it made them lose faith in George and this undoubtedly contributed to their decision to close down the Littlewoods a few weeks later, though I know there were other factors.' Littlewoods did indeed close the Songsters down very shortly after this, though whether that was a decision made in the Littlewoods board room or in George's office will never be known. But there was obviously no major bust-up between the Liverpool firm and George because they gave him a parting gift. Dot recalls, 'They gave him a fabulous dark brown leather three-quarter coat with a big fur collar and a sheepskin lining, to wear in his open top car, as a thank you. He still had it up to his death.'

Harry remains very bitter about this, although Dot is adamant this is highly unlikely to have happened: 'George just wasn't like that. He would never leave a meeting with a nasty taste. He'd rather talk it through and sort it out. He'd always try and get his singers work with other organisations if he had no work for anyone. And in any case, he would at the very least have done well financially out of such a show. He had lots of groups working under different names, so I can't see he would have been worried about the success of yet another one. And after all, George had been handling the group for over two years now, so he would have been pleased if they had broken through into the big time.'

Wendy Faulkner was one of these Littlewood Songsters. She remembers the times with affection: 'Maureen, Jeannie and I met up when I was 17 in the Littlewood Songsters. George took us over and sent one of his chaps as our musical director, Fred Tomlinson, one of the early Minstrels. The troupe was disbanded and Mo, Jeannie and I, together with two others, went to London where George took us into the Minstrel family.' This doesn't sound too much like someone who just abandoned the Littlewoods in a fit of pique. Keith Leggett, George's right-hand man and still singing on stage, recalls the Littlewoods fondly: 'Margaret Wilson and Jean Price-Hughes were both Littlewood Songsters. Wendy Faulkner who was also one of the Songsters went to Australia with the show in 1962. Jill Graham joined the Victoria Palace cast as a Television Topper, and Kris Keyhoe worked with Stan Stennett a year or so after the show – both ex-Littlewoods.' George obviously set quite a lot of the Songsters on the road to a life in show business.

The new television series was now running at peak viewing on Saturday nights, pulling in regular audiences of well over sixteen million, a third of the adult audience. The *Radio Times* quoted George Inns as saying, 'Terrific speed and attack – that's what we're aiming at. Lashings of new ideas, a new look in costumes, and more gimmicks like those that made the show a sell-out success on tour this past summer.' Despite Bob's 'promise' to the BBC, Stan Stennett remained, to be joined by Leslie Crowther, poached from *Crackerjack*, who was to stay with the show, on stage and television, for years to come. He'd been spotted in a concert-party 'because I could twitch my eyebrows individually, in time to the music. George Inns thought this ideal, and if I could do that, I could do all sorts of other things.' Also new to the line-up was Benny Garcia, a Scottish tap dancer. George said, 'I know it's out of fashion. Well, we've got Scots dancer Benny Garcia to start everyone tapping again.' But it proved technically difficult to slot him in live and eventually his tap dancing was pre-recorded.

It was the final show of this series which started a long-standing Minstrel tradition. Cameraman Eddie Stewart well remembers, 'George Inns said we were going to pull a stunt on George, just because he didn't like publicity. At the end with everyone on stage together, everyone else would walk off and leave him alone. But George Mitchell thought, "I'm not having this," and walked upstage to the treads, leaving his tambourine in the centre of one tread. Camera 1 panned onto the tambourine as the closing shot, and this became the standard closing for years.'

CHAPTER 17

Big news broke before the Liverpool Christmas run ended. George and Bob were gambling once again by moving the show into London's West End. John Boulter remembers it was Dai Francis who suggested to Bob that the Minstrels went into the Victoria Palace: 'Bob thought it a silly idea, but later it came out as Bob's 'brilliant' idea.' Initial doubts that the show would be able to go into the Victoria Palace – the theatre was rumoured to be closing because of the new Victoria Underground line – were soon laid to rest. The famous theatre had been home to the Crazy Gang since 1947; however, their last show there was to be on May 19, and the Minstrels were to open a week later for a five-month run.

The Liverpool cast were ecstatic; this guaranteed work for many of them throughout 1962 but more importantly, it took them into a West End theatre. But trouble was brewing. Even knowing the show was to open in London, Bob had now exercised his long-held option to produce a second Minstrel stage show and so needed twice as many Minstrels and Toppers and three more principals. The company was in uproar. Kay Matthews, at Liverpool, remembers, 'Ossie wanted to put his own girls into the Victoria Palace and send us all to Morecambe. We were so cross because we'd done the tour and expected to get the Victoria Palace and then to think we were being done out of it. We rebelled, I became the spokesman. George Inns came up and reversed the decision.' But George insisted on having seasoned Minstrels and dancers in both productions. Eventually, some of the existing company agreed to go to Morecambe, and the rest went to London.

This was just as big a gamble as in 1960. Even though the show was now a proven stage success, at least in the provinces, London could prove tougher to crack. What would they think of the miming, for a start? And set up costs were astronomical in the capital. George mortgaged his house – for the second and final time in his career – to pay for the scenery, costumes and lighting. To minimise tape problems, the theatre was equipped with entirely new amplification, with two men monitoring every show.

Minstrel Magic

The figures for the wardrobe alone are staggering. For the first time, all the costumes were made new and for specific people. As far as possible, zips were eliminated. As Head Wardrobe mistress Marie Worth explained, 'Zips always jam at the worst possible moments' so she equipped the thousands of costumes with hooks and eyes for high-speed safety. However, there must have been some zips as one singer remembered 'with eight fast changes of costume per show, zip fasteners are a constant source of worry. The number of girls who have gone through a routine on a pin and a prayer must be legion!' The show needed 10,000 sequins a week – two women had a permanent job, sewing them on. Each finale gold hat took a week to make and used two thousand sequins hand-sewn by London Wardrobe Mistress Billie Brenchley, who must have been seeing them in her sleep! The Toppers' long gloves became the biggest wardrobe casualties, as the sequins on the banjos the girls 'played', played havoc with the sheer silk gloves, which only lasted two weeks. Laundry bills were astronomic. Each Minstrel got through twelve shirts and collars a week, and their white gloves and socks were in constant need of laundering. Wardrobe staff had to daily wash thirty shirts, sixty collars, thirty pairs of socks, four ballet dresses, a dozen washable costumes and an endless stream of ties and handkerchiefs. The girls had eight pairs of shoes and two pairs of boots each, which only lasted six weeks. Wardrobe was constantly occupied with running repairs as well as keeping the washing machines on the go. Marie Worth became a phenomenon within the show, managing to keep track of the thousands of wardrobe items, as well as memorising everyone's measurements. Legend has it that while watching one show, she realised one Minstrel had shoe problems. By the next sequence, she had produced replacement shoes, recalling his shoe size from memory.

Twenty dressers were brought in to keep the show going. Although the men changed costume for every sequence, the dancers' changes were even more extensive. Dancer Chrissie Westall recalls, 'During the course of the day, you get up, get dressed, go to work, change nine times, have an interval, get changed nine more times, get dressed, go home and get undressed again. We were forever taking off and putting on clothes.' Elspeth Hands, head Topper, recalls how hectic it all was: 'We'd get to the theatre about 4.30pm, gather any notes, do our makeup and get our costumes ready, then be ready to start at 6.15. The dressing

Minstrel Magic

rooms were at the top of the theatre, with four flights of stairs to them. And we always had complete changes of shoes, hats, gloves, as well as the actual costume.'

George and Bob were confident enough by now to allow the Minstrels to appear throughout the entire twice-nightly show. The speciality acts were spread out between the Minstrel segments. Leslie Crowther returned, backed up by Margo Henderson and George Chisholm, with international comedy trampolinists the Schaller Brothers added to the ensemble. George used mainly long-term Mitchell singers, some of whom, like Don Cleaver, Ron Urquhart and Gordon Gray, had been in the stage shows from the start, and were now joined by several new Minstrels. George also included six Mitchell Maids, including Ruth Baker, later to find fame as Ruth Madoc.

The Luff Organisation did a vast amount of pre-show publicity, as usual managing some unexpected events. *Vanity Fair* used two Minstrels and a female model in a photo fashion shoot, while a photo feature for *Honey* magazine consisted of the Honey-girls versus the Minstrels at ten-pin bowling. The Minstrels easily won and were presented with a 7lb jar of honey by designer Teddy Tinling. George promptly challenged them to a return match, offering to provide the prize – for the losers! Tickets prices were kept deliberately low. The Crazy Gang had charged 17/6 (£14) for a top-price ticket, but George and Bob were determined to make the show as accessible as possible. Opening ticket prices were 15/- (£11.50) for a top ticket, a price which remained unchanged for five years. All this meant advance bookings went through the roof. Booking had opened in February and by the end of April had taken over £100,000 (£1.5m) in advance bookings.

Everyone began rehearsing like mad, daily from 10am till 9pm. Harry Currie's fury with George over the Littlewoods hadn't lasted too long, and he was now drawn further into the Minstrel fold: 'George asked me to train the Victoria Palace chorus. I worked every day for six weeks solid, getting them ready to record the stage show. George came in for the last rehearsal of course and conducted the recording.' As usual, this included far more voices than were going to appear on stage but George saw no need to change the practice which had worked so well for the past four years of the show.

Excitement was intense on opening night. Good luck telegrams poured in, including one from the BBC's Bill Cotton Jnr. Many of

George's core singers, involved in the soundtrack but not on stage, and under pain of death to keep that quiet, were in front row seats. Maryetta Midgley recalls, 'On the opening night, George and Irene were in the box, but Daphne (Bell) was in the same stall seats as us, which we thought strange.' Everything went superbly, and the audience went wild. George and Bob breathed huge sighs of relief.

Not so Harry Currie, also in the audience. He may have moved past his earlier upset with George, but they were about to come to blows again. 'I was thrilled to have played a major part in this production,' he recalls. 'I scanned the theatre programme, confident I'd see my name as chorus master once again as I had in Liverpool for the Littlewoods. I must have looked carefully for thirty minutes and came to the realisation I wasn't mentioned. "You really didn't expect to be, did you?" said Dai Francis, later. "George would never want anyone to think someone else had anything to do with the singers. He wants all the credit." ' This is hard to understand. Harry must have seen the Brighton programme, where the show had previewed before opening in London, and he wasn't mentioned there either. The Liverpool programme the previous Christmas had credited Harry as Littlewoods' chorus master, and future Australian programmes credited him as choirmaster for the Australian shows, so George obviously had no issue with giving Harry the credit. He decided to say nothing to George, but this was only the start of yet another contentious period between George and Harry.

The next morning, the critics raved. The *Stage* said, 'Fine singing, supremely fine production and a policy of continuity which makes no allowance for breaks of any sort combine to make a show which puts every other in the shade. Professional to its fingertips. One comes away, exhilarated and happier. One might imagine that a stage version of the excellent television show could hardly add anything but here one would be very wrong indeed. Stanley Dorfman uses the minimum of scenery, just vital sections, his main décor effects coming from eye-catching costumes by Mary Wood, cleverly uniform, the majority in Persil whiteness, highlighted by clear-cut reds, greens and blues. The show is a model upon which light entertainment must base itself if it is to have a future. No audience could possibly fail to respond with immediate warmth towards such spontaneous joy.' Even critics who didn't want to be present were converted. The *Yorkshire Post's* critic wrote, 'I went with a strong prejudice against it but there is no better evening of light music and nostalgic charm to be found in London.' Rather uncharitably, the *Bristol Evening Post* tried to be critical: 'So television spews back into the theatre what it stole from it. It doesn't really. The frame is larger, that's all, and you get some bright colour. The show is directed with a battering slickness which emphasises the impression of something pre-digestive and canned. Contact with the live theatre is momentarily established by Dai Francis's creditable impersonation of Al Jolson. Last night's ferocious applause suggests that no one is going to be saddened that the decorative banjos are unplayable and the one in the orchestra cannot be heard.' The show was obviously carrying all before it.

The left-wing *Guardian* tentatively raised the spectre of racism but just as quickly pushed it aside: 'One wonders what a solemn sociologist would say of this whole phenomenon in the newly colour-conscious Britain of today. But it certainly went well.' The *Times* edged closer: 'They have kept an air of anonymity, of being all-round entertainers rather than specialists, which gives charm to this evening. They are helped by the uniform of top hats and tails and by a common makeup. Mr Mercer's deep voice and his shy indication of friendliness do as much as anything to make the audience wish to turn minstrel too.'

One major pre-show worry had been what the sophisticated London audiences would think of the miming. Certainly, it sparked some controversy. *Disc* thought, 'The miming, far from spoiling the show, gives it a tremendous lift.' *Record Mirror* said, 'It could have been messy and contrived. It could have been too obvious. It isn't.' The *News of the World* agreed: 'Despite the mechanics of pre-recorded voices, George Mitchell's magnificent troupe can't miss with tambourines, chocolate-and-cream smiles, that old soft shoe and sentiment on their side.' The *Daily Express* also had no problem with the recorded sound: 'What a pleasurable romp it is. Well-paced, tuneful and colourful, the show breaks new ground with its sound system. Could run for years.' However, the *Daily Telegraph* recorded, ' "Are they really singing?" asked a spectator. The answer was yes and no. They were singing all right. We had the conductor's personal assurance of that. But it was their voices amplified from the tape that most of us were actually hearing; a sort of booster, you might call it, and no small triumph of synchronisation. Although it rendered the words wonderfully clear, the technical soon began to wear thin, exposing the essential tinselled hollowness of this whole bright, noisy, cheerful but monotonous entertainment.' Both Georges were swift to answer. In a letter printed in the *Evening Standard* and the *Daily Mail*, they wrote, 'Mr Shulman, in his review (in the *Evening Standard*) said, "They are merely miming to a pre-recorded version of the songs." This is untrue and misleading. The artistes do sing – they sing their hearts out. While we do not wish to divulge the technical details, the show is carefully monitored throughout, and the synchronised sound of the artistes' voices is added during active routines to ensure complete sound coverage in all parts of the theatre.' Milton Shulman couldn't let them have the last word, adding, 'It may be true that they sing but would Mr Mitchell tell us whether we could hear them without the recording?'

The show quickly became the hit of the London season. Although it was still expected to close in November, Leslie Grade, of the prestigious Grade Organisation, had asked to transfer it to the Prince of Wales Theatre where he said 'it would run for five years'. Leslie MacDonnel, managing director of Moss Empires, said that the Minstrels were 'the hottest proposition in music hall today and if it could have been left at the Victoria Palace indefinitely, it might have run for two years'. He was soon proved to be pessimistically wrong. When all tickets for the five-month run at the Victoria Palace sold out, it didn't take much to persuade everyone to extend the show's stay at the theatre. Advance bookings rose and rose, with November figures breaking records, for takings per house. Tickets became impossible to get for any house, any date. Ultimately the run was extended again and again, and it didn't close until May 1969, only to reopen six months later and run for a further three years.

Surprisingly overlooked the previous year despite their Golden Rose win at Montreux, the Minstrels' impact on the West End was recognised this year at the highest level when they were invited to close the first half of the *Royal Variety Show*, for which they wore sparkling new black and white costumes. John Boulter said, 'We can't really believe it. All of us are delighted of course, but we're so busy at the moment that we haven't really had time to think about the honour.' Singer Mary Moss remembers it well: 'It started snowing. Everyone was late for rehearsal, and we were live that night. However, we managed to do the show, then the snow froze and didn't melt for six weeks.' The *News of the World* wrote, 'One act surpassed every other performance in this glittering cavalcade.

It belonged to a bunch of artistes whose faces are barely recognisable once they've wiped off the makeup. Yet they've confounded the know-alls by becoming within five years the country's greatest box office attraction.' The *Stage* later carried an advertisement from Bob and George who wished 'to thank all members of the *Black and White Minstrel Show* – artistes, production and executive staff – who, by their untiring efforts, splendid co-operation and wonderful team spirit have made this great honour possible'.

Offers to tempt the soloists away flooded in, but none was interested. Earning over £5,000 (£75,000) a year, with the possibility of even more in the year ahead, John was reported as saying, 'I earn more than the Minister of State but less than the Minister of Works.' And as Tony put it, 'Things are really only starting to happen. Not that money matters too much. We're happy, we like the people we work with, and we like the music we sing.'

Never happy to leave matters as they were, Bob wasted no time and was immediately back negotiating with the BBC. He once again pleaded poverty, asking the BBC to extend his licence for the next four years and keep their royalty payments at £60 per week. He argued that the BBC had gained from the stage show and that George had remained loyal to the BBC, despite commercial temptations. Predictably Eric Maschwitz objected, arguing that the Victoria Palace had already generated huge advance bookings. The BBC claimed they now needed 5% royalties, though internally they agreed to settle for 3%. In an implied threat, they also said that George Inns should now get 2%, given that they weren't 'certain how long they could keep on releasing him'. Whatever either side was saying publicly, obviously both Bob and the BBC realised that the show had a long term future on the stage. After a lengthy negotiation, Bob got his licence for four years but had to give the BBC 5% royalties and the right to televise three shows from the 'Number 1 company', plus royalties of 4% from the provincial show. For once, the BBC had got the better of Bob.

The Morecambe show now claimed all of George's attention. As always, this second Minstrel company was based around a nucleus of seasoned Mitchell singers, but George needed to find new principals, as John, Dai and Tony had obviously gone into the London show. Usually, he found new soloists from within his existing ranks, but he broke with tradition for Morecambe, bringing in three new soloists. He flew to Guernsey specifically to see Jeff Hudson perform before inviting him to join the Morecambe cast. Eric Whitley had already tasted major success, singing with big bands, such as Carroll Gibbons, Jack Hylton and Geraldo, and occasionally appearing with the Mitchell Singers. He'd spent four years as singing lead with the Crazy Gang, then became Entertainments Director with the US Air Force. George persuaded him away from that role and into becoming a Minstrel principal.

In perhaps a surprising move, the third soloist – and chorus master for Morecambe – was Harry Currie, still bitter about the omission of his name from the Victoria Palace programme. Morecambe wasn't about to improve their relationship: 'George and I were speaking by then, and he told me to come back to London – he'd have lots for me to do within the Mitchell organisation. He then asked me to train the chorus for Morecambe. Jeff and Eric had been signed to do the Tony Mercer and John Boulter roles, and I was to pick up Dai Francis' parts, except the Jolson sequence, assigned to comedian Stan Stennett. This was so they wouldn't have to pay me a full soloist salary, just give me some solo titbits and a bit extra to be chorus master. But I held out for a better salary and got it, though not as much as Jeff was getting.'

Others who went to Morecambe included Wendy, Maureen and Jeannie, ex-Littlewood Songsters, plus Margaret Savage. Wendy remembers, 'We palled up with Maggie Savage to rent a bungalow and had a great summer together. Mags is a very funny lady, her Scottish accent adding to her humour.' Margaret, of course, became the show's major female vocalist for years to come. She first auditioned in Glasgow 'when I was 16 years old in the mid-'50s. Although George liked my voice, he suggested I gain some experience. Five years later I came down to London looking for work. Along I went to Dinely's studios to audition for him once more. He remembered me from Glasgow and asked would I like to join the Morecambe show. That was the beginning of a long and happy union.' George remembered Maggie's persistence: 'She wouldn't take no, she kept on at us all the time. In the end, she had her audition and joined the happy band. A very versatile girl is Maggie, with a fine voice. She also has a terrific sense of humour. She and Dai convulse each other. It's a miracle they ever get through some numbers. They are great characters to have around. No matter how dreary and tired one may turn up at the studio, they cheer you up. I've seen them helpless with laughter at something that has amused them. They sober up for a moment, then catch each other's eye, and off they go again. Yet when the red light shows, they are spot on cue. Even today after working with them for so long, I am amazed at the way they can cut out the laughs and turn in a perfect performance.'

All three Morecambe principals sang on the soundtracks for the current television series. Jeff appeared in the series as well: 'We rehearsed in a church hall in Kensington for the BBC TV shows before we went to Morecambe, to introduce me to the scenery, George Inns and Larry Gordon. I did solos on TV - *Champagne Charlie* and *Every Morning*. At the end of *Champagne Charlie*, I raised a glass as a salute. Dai said to me afterwards, "Well done, that's the good news. The bad news is that it'll never be seen. They'll cut it out." They had to because of the timing.' The Morecambe show was rehearsed during the day at the Victoria Palace, which, as Harry remembers, 'made sense - the sets were identical'. As was the majority of the show. The only real difference was that the London company sang *Dry Bones* as the conducted sequence, whereas Morecambe used a medley of Stephen Foster numbers. This duplication obviously made it much easier for George - and Harry - to produce a second show.

The touring companies often rehearsed at the Victoria Palace where they used to frequent the Stage Door pub in Allington Street, near the theatre, at lunchtime. In 1970, the company that was moving to Paignton for the summer got to know the resident pianist and it developed into a lunchtime sing song which often meant the regulars stood and applauded them as they left to return to rehearsals. When cricketer Basil D'Oliveira dropped in one day for a quiet pint, he was welcomed with a magnificent rendering of *Hello Dolly*. On the last day, it was bottles of champagne and the whole bar joining in some of the most professional and inspired pub singing ever heard in London.

Harry soon wished he hadn't accepted George's offer: 'My next shock was when we arrived (in Morecambe), and I discovered that only Eric and Jeff's names were displayed as soloists – mine was missing. They either forgot or deliberately didn't change that when I took on all of Dai's parts. I simply said I wouldn't perform unless they fixed it - I was tired of being shafted - and very quickly they produced enough display material with all three names.' Yet another tiff averted. To be fair, Jeff Hudson didn't remember this, and neither does Keith Leggett, who appeared in this show to keep an eye on things for George.

But Morecambe itself was unhappy. In an echo of the row with BBC producers years earlier, people were indignant at being fobbed off with what they thought was inevitably going to be an 'inferior show' as there were now two Minstrel companies. Ossie moved swiftly to defuse the situation, saying the formula for both shows was the same, with the singers and Toppers divided between the two shows. Despite this row, or perhaps because of all the extra publicity it brought, advance ticket sales were excellent. During the winter and spring, the theatre's marketing manager had organised huge publicity drives, which resulted in coach parties coming from far and wide. After a spectacular gala opening on June 23, the show played to packed houses, breaking all records at the Winter Gardens.

Minstrel Magic

John Laird,
George's grandfather

Barbara and Robert Mitchell,
George's parents

George as a baby with his
mother Barbara

George with his first wife, Irene
on their wedding day

A family outing

The original RAPC Choir with George at the back

Minstrel Magic

George, the choir and their old bus, probably in Aberystwyth

The early George Mitchell Singers

Minstrel Magic

The George Mitchell Glee Club

On PS *Royal Eagle* on the Thames

Minstrel Magic

The Mitchell Singers in Holland

A very early Christmas Minstrel show - note the wonderful baggy striped trousers!

Minstrel Magic

The Early George Mitchell Minstrels with Tony, John and Dai at the front

The Minstrels and Toppers in the 1970s
Dot Ogden at the front kneeling

Minstrel Magic

The Minstrels on the Victoria Palace stage

Minstrels and Toppers with (l-r) Penny Jewkes, John Boulter, Tony Mercer, George, Dai Francis and Margaret Savage

Minstrel Magic

Dai Francis   John Boulter   Tony Mercer

Below: Ted Darling, Bob Hunter, Les Rawlings, Les Want

Minstrel Magic

Above left: Dot Ogden
Above right: Margaret Savage
Above: Bob Luff with a photo of the Futurist Theatre
Left: George Inns

Minstrel Magic

George conducting a choir sequence at one opening night

Presentation of the third cheque by Bob Luff to Bill Binning of the Guide Dogs for the Blind

Minstrel Magic

Around the World in Song - (l-r) Dai, Tony, John, with Les Rawlings, Bob Hunter and Don Cleaver
Country and Western Show with Don Cleaver centre front, Les Rawlings middle left, Bob Clayton middle, Bob Hunter top right, Ted Darling middle right

Minstrel Magic

The much-enjoyed outing on the Isle of Wight Ferry

A typical scene from the Television Minstrels

George and son Rob with his OBE

George with his second wife, Dot on their wedding day

Minstrel Magic

The first reunion
Front row l-r Dot, George, Stan Stennett
Back row l-r Rob Mitchell, Joan and Neville King, Glyn Dawson, John Boulter and Ruth Madoc

CHAPTER 18

Bob was about to shock George and the BBC again. Not content with running two stage versions of the Minstrels in the UK, as well as the television series, he proposed taking it half a world away. George was initially horrified – how could he keep control of standards when it was all happening 12,000 miles away? But as usual, Bob ploughed on regardless and approached the BBC with the proposal. He knew the BBC would object fiercely, as they always did, and tried to forestall them by saying the proposed show would 'include some former principals which won't affect the UK show as they are no longer appearing in it'. Quite how this fooled the BBC is anyone's guess as up until Morecambe, there had only been three principals and they were all safe with the show in London. But Bob had a stronger argument. The proposal had come from Kenn Brodziak, Managing Director of Australian production company Aztec. Bob was able to add the sop that Aztec wanted to show the television series on Australian television, an area the BBC was finding it difficult to break into.

This wasn't the first time outside production companies had shown interest in the show. Earlier in 1961, Hillcrest Productions asked permission to film the show for worldwide distribution. The BBC's Ronnie Waldman said they weren't interested in co-financing but wanted guaranteed payment and a percentage of income. In a complete reversal of their earlier reluctance, the BBC thought, 'We do not want to do anything to prejudice the stage production.' Eric Maschwitz thought it 'increasingly doubtful' it was a good idea; he felt strongly that if the film were bad, it could only do harm; if good, it might badly overshadow the stage version 'which may have years of life in it yet', so the BBC refused Hillcrest permission.

But another stage version? That was a different proposition and one the BBC quickly became interested in. After some initial resistance, during which the BBC investigated Aztec, they gave in and granted the Australian licence, to run from September 1961 until March 1963, agreeing to give George Inns six weeks' unpaid leave to produce the show. Bob had once again won with an outrageous idea.

After lengthy negotiations, a six-month tour schedule involving the Tivoli Theatre circuit was agreed, with the Minstrels opening in Melbourne for three months, followed by stints in Sydney and Brisbane. However, exporting a successful musical wasn't nearly as easy as it sounded. Although George wanted as many British cast members as possible, so he could mix experienced and new singers, Australian union laws demanded that local singers and dancers were used, meaning George could import only his leading artistes, including his principals.

But he had no intention of yet again tying up long-serving core Mitchell singers in a production of the other side of the world. He needed them in the UK but still needed to ensure that any new recruits would maintain his extremely high standards. He found the perfect answer. Put three new soloists into Morecambe where they could prove themselves and learn how a Minstrel company worked, then send them out to Australia in the autumn. Harry Currie, however, had a hard time deciding if he wanted to go out to Australia, particularly as he was still deeply unhappy with George: 'George asked me to train the chorus out there and if I wanted, remain for the tour. I didn't feel George played fair with me and I wasn't sure I wanted to remain part of the organisation. Eventually, I stayed because I thought it was an opportunity to see a part of the world I might otherwise never get to, and we were told we'd be there six to ten months maximum. Stupidly we signed a run-of-the-show contract, not realising how that would affect us.'

Harry left the Morecambe show in early August and flew to Australia to start recruiting new singers and dancers. But the show was totally unknown in Australia so singers had no concept of what they were auditioning for and Jack Neary, the Australian entrepreneur and star maker, had trouble recruiting female singers: 'I wanted two singers for the chorus line. I even offered jobs to girls who had never been on stage before. Here was a tremendous opportunity for youngsters to learn the business under some of the best show business names in the world. They knocked it back.' So George was allowed to send out three Mitchell Maids – Wendy Faulkner and Maureen Wilson, ex-Littlewood Songsters, plus 18-year-old Shirley James.

Dance Director Jackie Joyner also left the Morecambe show and flew to Sydney with Harry. She had more luck with recruiting dancers than Harry had with singers. She told the press she needed 'dancing girls who can sing and singers who know how to

Minstrel Magic

move. It's hard to get the combination.' As usual, standards were high, and Jackie auditioned four hundred girls to find the sixteen she needed, among them twins Margrette and Elizabeth Hurley. However, when they learned their long hair had to be cut, Margrette agreed, but Elizabeth refused, turning down a place in the show. Another successful auditionee was Pamela Steele who had been deaf since she was four months old, after contracting meningitis. Unable to hear the music, she could feel the drumbeat and dance by feeling the music's vibrations and watching the other girls out of the corner of her eye. Her sister Rondell also successfully auditioned, which meant she could coach Pam with the words. All of this lent itself to great pre-show publicity, badly needed if the show was to succeed.

Harry and Jackie soon moved to Melbourne, where they were joined by George Inns and his wife, Stage Director Laurie Bloom and Musical Director Billy Merrin. The show's speciality acts arrived later. Penny Nicholls was already a Minstrel stalwart, Bob Andrews was an all-round entertainer who also covered the Al Jolson spot, and completing the line-up were comedian Eddie Mendoza, acrobats The Balcombes and jugglers the D'Angolys, all experienced Minstrel speciality acts. Once the Morecambe show finished, Keith, Eric, Wendy, Maureen and Shirley flew straight into Melbourne rehearsals. The show was basically the same one as the soloists and girls had been singing all summer in Morecambe which gave them a head start. The show was to run for two and a half hours, longer than the British stage version; because of the length, it was impossible to run it twice nightly as in London, so each performance started at 8.15, with matinées on Wednesdays, Saturdays and holidays at 2pm. It began with the usual *Ring Up the Curtain* sequence, then *Meet The Girls, Al Jolson*, a London sequence, with a Latin American segment closing the first half. The second half started with a Hollywood sequence, followed by a Gilbert & Sullivan medley, *Along the Navajo Trail, Sweethearts' Serenade* and closing with the usual *Doo Dah Dey* finale. The conducted sequence was the ever-popular *Dry Bones*. Much of this was identical to previous British shows, with only one or two sequences that were new to the stage anywhere in the world.

Blueprints of every part of the show, including scenery, props, costumes and lighting, had already been sent to Australia. As usual, the scenery was minimal, with no set changes, just variations in suspended lights of different shapes and fabric, plus filigree backdrops, with moving clouds, moons and flames projected onto the backdrop. Laurie Bloom decided to re-floor the stage, which needed treating with special paint to get the right lighting effect. The entire theatre was rewired with hundreds of lamps and miles of wire. Even the dozens of multi-coloured lampshades were dyed with a special durable fluorescent paint to ensure they didn't lose their brilliant glow during the season. The latest electronic equipment was imported from Britain so that the same reinforced stereophonic sound could be reproduced.

All the costumes, designed by Mary Woods, were made in Australia and became the greatest undertaking ever handled by the Wardrobe Mistress, Winnie Gill, with six hundred costumes being made in nine weeks, as well as three hundred and fifty hats. Thousands of ostrich feathers were used, along with hundreds of yards of gold and silver lurex, crystal nylon and satin, plus hundreds of thousands of specially shaded sequins imported from Milan. For the South American sequence, the stagehands hand-painted the fabric in rainbow stripes, while the *Serenade in the Dark* dresses had skirts of five different-coloured crystal organza, with sequins the same colour. The Red Indian sequence used six hundred ostrich feathers in each headdress. Special paint had to be chosen for parts of the costumes and shoes featured in one of the spectacular numbers. Speedily though these costumes were made, they needed to be sturdy – the longest costume change was two and a half minutes! The sixteen changes of costume were done in the wings, with an army of dressers to get the dancers in and out of their costumes. In the most intricate change, crinolines were suspended from wires, the girls lined up underneath, a stagehand lowered the wires, and the dresses fell over their heads. In a departure for Tivoli showgirls, the dancers had their hair cut, then half were bleached pale blonde and given a specially devised tint called Silvery Frost. The brunettes had colours ranging from Jet Black, Dark Brown and Auburn to Black Tulip and Burgundy, which contrasted well with the blondes.

Everyone was afraid the audiences would stay away, as the show was completely unknown in Australia, so Bob swung his flair for publicity into action. Every airport arrival was reported, and endless publicity opportunities arranged for the principals, including wine contests, cabaret engagements and school visits in full costume and makeup. According to press reports, Penny

Nicholls travelled to Australia in the black cocktail dress in which she had been given a send-off in London. Totally impossible and impractical, obviously, given the length of the flight, but it provided yet another marvellous photo opportunity when she landed. The girls had weekly hair do's, using local salons on tour, again generating great local publicity. Harry Currie turned out to have an excellent flair for unusual publicity himself. Jeff Hudson recalled, 'When Harry started wearing contact lenses, he wrote to Kleenex, mentioning the show, and said their tissues suited him best. They sent him a crate. Volkswagen gave him a car, and he also got a washing machine for the girls.' Cast members packed sweets for distribution at the Christmas party they held for two hundred and fifty orphan children, and sent a Christmas cake to the Victoria Palace, though the London cast took two years to reciprocate! Harry even used the fact they had to leave the rehearsals rooms next door to the theatre on day one when everyone was kicked out of them to make way for workmen who were doing alterations. At least it gave everyone a chance to get to know one another in a local coffee bar.

George and Jeff Hudson, the third soloist, left London for New York in mid-September. George had asked Jeff to fly with him: 'He liked company. He paid my fare, and I paid him back at £5 (£100) per week.' Harry recalls, 'Mellowed by several drinks, George talked to Jeff about how lucky he'd been. He acknowledged he wasn't much of a musician or arranger, that he knew just about enough to "get away with it" and that he knew "both Fred Tomlinson and Harry Currie are better than I am, so I have to be careful about who knows this." ' This sounds more like typical modesty, and Jeff himself didn't remember the conversation, though he did recall George saying, 'Trouble with people like Bob Luff, they don't realise the work that goes in, but they realise what goes into the bank.'

Just before they left, the BBC sprung a surprise on George when he innocently attended a 'George Inns party'. The following day, he wrote to Tom Sloan, thanking him for the 'most kind and unexpected presentation last night. When you commenced your speech, I was waiting with my friends on the production staff to applaud a star personality, and you can imagine my consternation when I suddenly realised that you were referring to me. I know that my singers will feel this is also a tribute to their efforts.' Such a letter shows not only George's modest nature but also how supportive he was of his singers.

The lengthy journey to Australia was far from easy in 1962, and there were a lot of stopovers. After a night in New York, they flew to San Francisco, staying two nights at the Sir Francis Drake Hotel, before leaving for Honolulu which Jeff recalled fondly, 'We stayed at the Hilton Hawaiian Village where *Hawaii Five O* was filmed. Sitting on the beach, I had my guitar and sang to a group gathered round us.' Qantas flew them to Sydney on September 22, arriving there at 6.45am the following day, and leaving for Melbourne on an 8am flight, seven days after leaving London.

George arrived in time to conduct a week of final rehearsals and the actual sound recording. Harry says, 'After all, we were the George Mitchell Minstrels, even though all the work was done by someone else.' That 'someone else' was, of course, Harry himself. However, Harry had little cause to complain this time, as the Australian programmes credited him as 'choirmaster'. In a rare lapse of organisational skills, the show nearly became the Red and White Minstrel Show! At the last minute, George Inns found the Negro No 2 makeup they normally used was far more red in Australia and quite unusable. Luckily Eric Whitley had brought some from Britain, and that was sent to Max Factor Australia, who made up a batch to match and called it Negro No 2 (English), though the Minstrels were forced to use light brown at the final dress rehearsal.

George obviously hadn't had enough of flying. Despite the heavy workload the week before opening, he decided to 'pop over' to Papanui, near Christchurch, New Zealand to see an uncle and cousin he hadn't seen for thirty years. He flew from Melbourne at 10am on Friday and returned on Monday 'not even out of breath', to quote a local newspaper. While in Christchurch later when the show played there, Jeff Hudson stayed with George's cousin, who, Jeff remembered, was really wrapped up in the show: 'Pre-show, we went to the pub. George's cousin wore black and white gloves and costume.'

Friday, October 5 came round all too quickly. For the charity Gala opening, the Tivoli foyer was decorated in black and white, with an exhibition of black and white cartoons, and the theatre offered prizes for the smartest black and white ensembles. James Buchanan and Co provided miniature bottles of Black and White whisky for the men, and small bottles of Worth perfume for the ladies.

It's hard to imagine the degree of nerves backstage. No one in the audience had any idea what was about to hit them, as negotiations between the BBC and Australian television channels had stalled over money. But once again the worries were unfounded. Wave upon wave of applause filled the theatre, with four encores. The newspapers fell over themselves looking for new superlatives, 'There are hues in the sets the rainbow hasn't yet heard about', 'Outstanding impression is one of colour' and 'honey-like entertainment at its best'. The *Melbourne Herald* enthused, 'It's slick, superbly staged and abundant with song. The pace leaves you breathless and the colour leaves you dazzled', with the *New Musical Express* forecasting 'It will occupy Australian stages for a long, long time.' Jeff Hudson remembered, 'I don't know how we did it but we were sensational from the start.' Stage Director Laurie Bloom recalls, 'The day after opening, we were sitting upstairs in the theatre offices reading the reviews, when somebody shouted, "Hey, look out of the window." And there was the most enormous queue of people you've ever seen in your life. Word had got around that the show was good and people flocked to see it. It was simply marvellous.' George said, 'Suddenly I became an honorary citizen of Melbourne with a gold badge to hang on my necktie.'

The cast members found themselves treated like stars, overwhelmed by warmth and hospitality. 'There was a party every night,' said Laurie Bloom, 'Sometimes two or three.' Jeff Hudson remembered parties where he played guitar and Keith Leggett sang. One such party had welcome repercussions for Jeff: 'We were invited to Billy May's home – he made Maton guitars, the Australian Gibson. At the party, he said if I could use a guitar on stage, he'd give me one. So I added the guitar to the opening of the *Navajo Trail*. He told me afterwards it was better publicity than normal advertising.' Such guitars were legendary; George Harrison used one, and Christie's recently sold one for £100,000. The *Navajo* segment, which also featured at the Victoria Palace, opened very quietly with only two or three men on stage for the first number, during which Jeff played the guitar. After this slow opening number finished, the scene immediately burst into life and colour and became a barn dance. It called for impeccable timing.

The cast quickly became heavily involved in the Melbourne social scene. Jeff remembered they frequented one particular club, the Muso's Club: 'This led to a cricket match between us. They turned up in full cricketing whites, while we were in casual gear. The match was a draw, and I won Man of the Match – 22 not out in both innings. The Muso captain was very indignant because they felt they should have won, whereas we really didn't care.' Some cast members attended the Black & White Provincial Cup dinner dance in late October, and also attended the Players' and Playgoers' Association's cabaret ball in late November. Many were guest speakers at the Players' Association during their stay. Foys Department Store featured black and white window displays, with daily black and white fashion parades, and Minstrels sang in-store and appeared in the fashion parades. They also did a tremendous amount for charity – the iron lung ward at Fairfield Hospital asked for one artiste to entertain, and nearly the whole cast volunteered!

As always, celebrities flocked to the show, producing more great publicity. Henry Fonda, the entire English cricket team and members of the Royal Household in board the Royal Yacht *Britannia* all saw the show, (the Queen was in Australia to lead the 50th jubilee celebrations of the naming of the capital Canberra), as did the famous Lesley Ross Singers who celebrated their latest record release by visiting the Tivoli show. In a first, the theatre management invited a group of Ballarat children to see the show and later invited a group of Young Farmers from Kilmore. Thirty-five mentally disabled children and their teachers also enjoyed the show as Tivoli guests.

So successful was the show that there were talks about a second Australian company. Some people saw the show twenty or thirty times, and two or three return visits was easily the norm. But audiences differed from the usual Tivoli attendees. Theatre management saw a fall in bar receipts and a rise in ice cream sales, Over half a ton was sold each week, with low use of the cloakrooms, as many of the audience were more used to attending films!

Breaking with tradition, the Tivoli kept the show over Christmas, cancelling its usual pantomime, and extended the run to March, when it was to be forced to close to make way for the National Theatre's production of *Show Boat*. But in March, they were still turning away record numbers, so the theatre decided to keep the Minstrels in Melbourne until May, moving *Show Boat* to

Sydney instead. The Minstrels eventually gave the theatre its best run ever – 31 solid weeks – breaking a 62-year-old record, attracting more people and making more money than any other Tivoli show.

Only meant to be in Australia for six months and to visit Sydney and Brisbane as well as Melbourne, the show's schedule was now thrown into chaos. Bob returned to the BBC, asking for an extension but the BBC was having none of it. Part of the attraction for the Corporation was the chance to break into Australian television but, despite renewed negotiations, the show still hadn't been seen on television, because of the sky-high price the BBC demanded. As their prime reason for allowing the licence in the first place seemed to be fast vanishing, the BBC now demanded that, given the show's huge success, they should get more money. Inevitably Bob opposed this, repeating that the success had opened the door to Australia, but his argument was now seriously weakened. Eventually, the BBC reluctantly granted Aztec's request to do a live telecast from the show as 'there is now little prospect of selling shows to Australian television'. Ironically this resulted in television channels fighting to screen the show. But at this point in the face of Bob's determined opposition to giving them more money, the BBC decided their legal position was weak so took what they could get and granted the extended licence. Once again, the BBC had backed down.

But this brought problems. Jeff Hudson recalled, 'Expecting to be there six months, I left my children in Britain with my wife', so he refused to stay unless he could bring his family out. 'George was lovely about it, sending me a personal letter. My wife came out with the children, and our third child was conceived in Australia.' But Harry certainly doesn't remember this amicably: 'Jeff, Eric and I decided we should reap more of the huge payoffs going to Kenn, Bob and George, so we held together and got a reasonable increase, certainly nothing exorbitant. George was drawn into the dispute and wrote letters asking us to be reasonable, and we certainly were, though we had definitely incurred his displeasure.' George, never involved in the financial side of matters, would have done what he could to keep the company running smoothly.

The show itself didn't always run smoothly, though the company's efficiency meant there were few hiccups. Discipline was tight, with everyone under strict orders to watch their weight, as any changes meant costumes didn't fit. Five minutes late for rehearsals meant a fine. Five minutes late for a performance meant you didn't get paid. Jeff Hudson recalled, 'Once I turned up a little late and Keith Leggett had to do the opening. I had a 10/= fine.' One girl didn't lace her shoes properly, and one of them sailed into the audience when she kicked her leg. She had to wait while the shoe was passed from the back rows to the front, which raised quite a few laughs on and off stage. Tape problems were, fortunately, few and far between. Keith Leggett recalls only one: 'At the beginning of *Dry Bones*, the tape ran slow – "*Nooow heaar thee woord of theee Lorddd.*" We were doing the movements in slow motion – quite hysterical – I did a slow shuffle off to the wings to see what was happening. The tape operator was a young lady, and an admirer of hers was leaning on the machine and making the tape go through very slowly. With a few choice words from me, he stopped leaning, and things returned to normal.'

The show eventually ended its first visit to Melbourne in early May 1963. The cast were given a farewell party at a leading Melbourne nightspot, before flying to New Zealand, to a welcome from the Te Pataka Maori group, who, after rubbing noses with them, performed the *wero* and *powhiri* ceremonies of welcome. Although the cast arrived safely, the props didn't. Carried aboard the *Koromiko*, the ship didn't dock in Wellington until the day before opening. Now, instead of the required three days to set up, they had just over twenty-four hours, which meant everyone working overnight right up until the 8pm opening on May 20.

Their popularity had preceded them, and police had to hold back enormous crowds on opening night. Demand for tickets was unprecedented, with one New Zealand paper explaining, 'The show's triumph is that teenagers are caught up as well as their elders.' Reviews were wonderful, with the *Wellington Evening Post* reporting, 'Trying to describe the colourfulness of the production is as hopeless a task as trying to photograph an auroral display on black and white film – suffice it to say that the stage resembled a vast ever-changing kaleidoscope. It was the Minstrels who really stole the show with their infectious happy-go-lucky charm as they took the audience on a nostalgic journey.'

The show moved to Auckland in late June, and then to Hamilton and Palmerston before crossing into South Island for six weeks at Christchurch. A Christchurch paper carried an opening night review: 'Spectacular effects of a standard never before achieved in Christchurch. A resounding success from the first ovation to the last of the six curtain calls.' The show played Dunedin, then Invercargill, everywhere receiving the same ecstatic reception. Keith Leggett remembers, 'When we arrived in some of those little towns it was like the Wild West when the rodeo hits. Strangers knew all about us, and it was a really big event. You should have seen the crowds waiting at the airports. We almost felt like the Beatles.' They found to their astonishment that although they were booked for a week in many of these small towns, they were actually only expected to give one performance. No touring show, they were told, had ever run more than one night, nobody would come for the other five. 'We proved them wrong,' says Keith, 'We played to packed houses every single night.'

The adulation may have been great but Stage Manager Laurie Bloom groaned over the conditions in some theatres. Dressing rooms were often one room with a single bench: 'The girls were trying to do six costume changes in the middle of what was the only thoroughfare. As for the lighting – it was so hopeless in one place, we chartered a plane to fly in a full set of electrical equipment. It couldn't have been worse in the local church hall.'

In mid-October, the show's contingent of seventy flew to Sydney. Once again, Bob pulled out the stops with pre-opening publicity, which included a parade by the Wentworthville Marching Gun and Pipe Band, dressed in black and white, while Sydney's premier department store, Grace Brothers, promoted black and white fashions, using the dancers in a big advertising spread. In a departure, the theatre inaugurated theatre-party suppers in the foyer, at which the show's stars joined the patrons.

The gala preview show, held by the Black and White Committee of the Royal Blind Society, went like a dream but reality hit the next day. After the previous adulation, some reviews shocked the cast. A major newspaper called it 'lacking in heart', blaming the need to synchronise with the tapes. But even critical reviews agreed with the *Daily Telegraph's* reviewer who predicted 'the Tivoli will find it difficult to take it off before the middle of next year'. In the end, the show outshone even Melbourne, playing for 37 weeks, the longest run any Tivoli theatre had ever had. Before it closed in August 1964, it was seen by 582,400 people.

Adelaide welcomed the show just as extravagantly, after which they returned to Melbourne for what was intended to be a further six-week run. In the event, they stayed for four months before leaving there in February 1965. Keith Leggett recalls this farewell to the city which had supported them so strongly: 'On our last night, the audience was standing on the seats and singing with us. You've never seen anything like it.'

The final stop on this two-and-a-half year tour was Brisbane where it stayed until mid-April. When the show closed on April 15, 1965, the company sadly disbanded. Jeff, Harry and Eric, along with Keith Leggett and Laurie Bloom, returned to a changed Britain. Laurie recalled, 'When we got back to London we suddenly found there was nothing to do. I'd go back tomorrow, I think all of us would.' Keith returned to the Mitchell fold – he'd been an integral part of the organisation, both on stage and in the office, and had been sadly missed. However, the soloists weren't so lucky. Harry is still bitter: 'I called the office, and Daphne said George would want to see me the next day. We had a pleasant chat, a drink, he thanked me for all my work, but when I asked what I would be doing, he said, "There's nothing that I can see, old boy. I'm having enough trouble keeping the people here working." I told him that by leaving Britain for over three years [sic] on his behalf, I had closed the doors with the people I had worked with in the business, that I would have to start all over almost as an outsider. "That's part of the business, old boy," he said, and with that, I left and never saw him again, and they certainly never called me. I found out later that the same thing happened with Jeff and Eric, and they never worked for him again either. We were properly punished.' Harry is convinced that the main reason for this punishment was the album the three principals had made without George's permission while they were in New Zealand. But George certainly used Jeff again, later on, so he at least wasn't being punished for any misdemeanours in New Zealand.

Characteristically Jeff saw it in a kindlier light: 'I went to see George and asked what was going on? George said he'd had people working with him over lots more years and he couldn't push them out. He had no work for me. It didn't concern me too much. He was over a barrel with work after Oz, so I understood. Light entertainment was changing, and there weren't the theatre shows then. He had done me a huge favour. I'd been earning 14 guineas (£300) per week, and he put me up to £90 (£1,800) per week when he took me on. And he paid my fare to Oz.'

CHAPTER 19

Back in 1962 when the company left for Australia, life on the work front looked rosy. Not content with two stage Minstrel shows and the regular annual Minstrel television series, George now dreamed up a summer series which became the show of which he was the proudest. Essentially a resurrection of the Glee Club, *Around The World In Song* did just what you would expect from the title. George wanted to do a folk song show, 'a unique show, with a wide appeal throughout the world but it won't be folksy, no folk singers or instrumentalists, but traditional music presented commercially.' He suggested songs from various genres such as folk, world and cowboy songs, like *Didn't It Rain, Walk Together Children, Dance Boatman Dance, Hava Nageela* and *Ox Driver*. Busy with the Minstrels and about to fly out to Australia, George wanted someone else to take on this project – and he knew just the man. Robert de Cormier, Harry Belafonte's musical director, with whom everyone had got on so well a few years earlier, was approached to become Musical Director and swiftly agreed. This was the only time George handed his choir over to another musical director – he later said, 'Bob de Cormier was the only man I trusted with my singers.'

Staged by famous choreographer Douggie Squires and produced by Travers Thorneloe, it featured core singers – eight girls and twelve men – using as main soloists John, Dai, Tony and Don, though most of the singers performed solo at some point. Like the Minstrels, the sets were virtually non-existent, usually a bare stage with perhaps some steps or a few chairs. Most songs were backed by a small orchestra of two guitars, flutes and rhythm, but often they sang unaccompanied, though, as Mary Moss recalls, 'The show had really energetic routines, you were exhausted.' The singers loved the series, particularly Maryetta Midgley: 'I loved it. It only had a short rehearsal time, but it was written in such a way that nobody was put upon. Douggie Squires was so patient. We rehearsed in an army place which was very wide; the set was narrower, so we'd put sticky tape on the floor to mark out the set.

Then Douggie would say, "Cut out the first three steps and start in right, not left." It was very confusing, and there was many a debacle.'

Viewers knew many of the songs, such as *Where Have All the Flowers Gone*, *There was an Old Woman* and *Big Rock Candy Mountain*, but lots were completely unknown, and the singers needed new skills. For instance, *The Cuckoo Song* was sung in Polish, though apparently, the meaning of the words was self-evident. Irene Thomas remembered, 'Much care was taken to get the pronunciation right, and many a startled announcer from the World Service in Bush House was shanghaied into our rehearsal hall to drill us in his native language – Polish, Czech, Serbo-Croat, Spanish. Our favourite was the smart young Japanese who not only told us how to pronounce the words of the cherry-tree song *Sakura* but actually sang it to us in an excellent light baritone voice. Our baritone section fetched an extra chair and tried to make him join us permanently. Some songs we had already done with Harry Belafonte, like the charming lullaby from Indonesia *Suliram*, but some were new to us, and there were fascinating American examples of how old English songs crossed the Atlantic with settlers throughout the centuries and came back again with words and tune slightly changed. Altogether, the programmes were a delight to us and Bob the most considerate and kindly of conductors.'

The phenomenal amount of press coverage was, as usual, mostly complimentary. Praised for itself, many compared it with the Minstrels, often to the latter's detriment, thinking it more technically accomplished. But the old problem of how to stage a choir for television proved the bugbear once again. You had to give the viewers something to watch as well as listen to, but many found the routines a distraction from the music. The *Listener* was quite disbelieving: 'I looked at – or rather gazed open-mouthed at – the George Mitchell Choir. The spectacle of umpteen gentlemen padding about in evening dress in meaningless patterns while they sang of the misery of life down a mine looked like being one of the more priceless television moments until they promptly capped it by trotting around in excited circles and giving voice to an all-yelping Russian song. Even they, I noticed, couldn't keep the grins off their faces.' The *Television Mail* agreed: 'Mincing through the pick-axe rhythm of *Sixteen Tons* and the long-oared sweep of *Michael* and an Arts League of Culture-type choreography for

Waltzing Matilda produced more than faint embarrassment – and oh dear, that attempt at an Ukrainian folk dance!'

But viewers loved the series. Some thought it a pity 'such a well-trained choir should squander their talents on such undemanding trivialities', others regretted the inclusion of 'so many American songs', but the vast majority thought it 'quite delightful' and 'impeccable'. One feature that pleased viewers immensely was the old *Glee Club* trick of naming the singers individually as they approached the cameras at the end of the programme. And of course, now they could see their favourite Minstrel principals without the black makeup. Fan mail for John, Dai, Tony and Don rocketed.

There were howls of disapproval when the show finished in late September. To keep people happy, an *Around The World In Song* album was recorded, using John, Dai, Tony and Don as soloists, with several other singers, such as Mary Moss, Glyn Dawson and Bob Hunter, contributing to several tracks. One Australian newspaper reviewed the album: 'The very thought of a BBC choir performing some of the world's most stirring folk songs appalled me until I heard *Around The World In Song*, a magnificent new record that blazes with infectious tunes and lively imaginative singing – far from the usual BBC approach.'

It was 1965 before the series returned, to the initial delight of millions of fans. But many were to be disappointed as this return placed it firmly on BBC2, still inaccessible to many viewers. Shown in Holland before running in Britain, it was so successful with those who could see it, that the BBC repeated six of the thirteen shows immediately the series finished. The first show included Pete Seeger's *Turn Turn Turn*, followed by a greeting song from Kenya, a comic West Indian ballad, a poignant Scottish song and a patois song from south-western France, plus an Elizabethan madrigal in the middle. BBC2's Controller reported to the Board of Management, 'A first rate programme having all the charm of the Black and Whites although produced on a very much smaller budget.' No wonder the Corporation liked it! As before, it featured John, Dai, Tony and Maryetta Midgley, plus Ted Darling and Les Rawlings, and occasionally Don Cleaver once the touring show had a break. Other occasional soloists included Julia Whitaker (Ossie's daughter) and Vanessa Howard. Vanessa, then barely seventeen, was quickly courted by the London stage and later Hollywood. Although George tried hard to keep her, offering a starring role in the next Minstrel series, she decided, firstly to go to the West End stage, then later moving to the States, where her first film was *I Could Go on Singing*, with Judy Garland and Dirk Bogarde. Hollywood loved her, and by September 1969 she had made five films including *Here We Go Round the Mulberry Bush, Mrs Brown You've Got a Lovely Daughter, Corruption* and *Death's Head Vampire*.

The workloads for everyone in these early years of the 1960s were phenomenal, particularly in 1962. George and Bob were coping with a new stage show at the Victoria Palace, overseeing the existing touring version, settled for the summer in Morecambe, and organising for a complete show to open in Australia, in the days before easy Internet communication. George was also working on the music for *Around The World In Song* and the new album, *On Stage with the Black and White Minstrel Show*, recorded with their usual speed in three sessions in June. And Mitchell Singers were still involved in other shows such as *Variety Playhouse, The Long Long Train, This is the Place* and *The Singing Years* for radio, and various television series such as *It's a Square World, The Andy Stewart Show* and *The Singing Summers*. George was still producing groups for other stage shows - he was involved in eight this year, unsurprisingly far fewer than previously but nevertheless time-consuming. To top it all off, a new series called *Mitchell's Modern Minstrels* ran on the Light programme.

True, George still had enough singers on his books so that many were involved in only one or two of these ventures but for George, the core and the principals, this was a ridiculous amount of work. Take just one week. On Monday George rehearsed *Around The World In Song*, continuing on Tuesday morning. That afternoon and evening they recorded the Morecambe stage music – this gave the Three Musketeers some time off. On Wednesday, the company and George moved to Morecambe. The sound for the first *Around The World In Song* was recorded on Wednesday, in George's absence with Bob de Cormier in charge. On Thursday they rehearsed the second show, recording it on Friday. Back in London at the weekend, George was once again rehearsing *Around The World In Song*, which went out live on the Sunday, together with recording the next Minstrel television series, due to start in October. Once *Around The World In Song* finished, everyone concentrated on the television Minstrel series, which took huge amounts of everyone's time. Rehearsing one week for six days from 10-5, those involved in the stage show then dashed to the Victoria Palace to do the evening shows. On Sundays, they recorded the television show in the studio for transmission the following Sunday. The following week they spent having costume fittings for future shows, and the whole pattern started again.

Principals John, Dai, Tony, now joined by Don Cleaver, were involved in both television shows, both musically and in vision, as well as appearing nightly on stage. Certainly many of the core singers sang and were in vision in *Around The World In Song* as well as on the soundtrack for the TV shows, though spared the work of being in vision as well. This certainly spread the load somewhat for most singers, but the four soloists' workload was unbelievable. George and this core were rehearsing and recording seven days a week, sometimes the *Glee Club*, sometimes the Minstrel show - it's a wonder they remembered what they were doing! Good memories were never more important.

George had no qualms about the amount of work he was putting his singers through. Indeed some of them wanted more. Some stage Minstrels were upset that they weren't used on television. However, George explained, 'What you've got to remember is that the TV was voluntary. We'd put a notice up, asking if anyone wanted to do the television shows; well, everyone wanted to, so they were rehearsing from 10am on Monday, finishing at 5pm, to the theatre until 11.30, then back in the studio again in the morning. They were in the television studios Sunday, recording right up till 11 o'clock at night, so it was a seven-day week from 10am until 11pm. But they were all young, making a few bob out of it and none wanted to miss a show.' The soloists were glad to be back on TV. Dai agreed that the television shows made 'a breezy break from theatre routine', adding that 'they also bring in the fan mail'. By now, John and Dai at least were getting around three hundred letters a week. Tony said, 'Tired of the show? Not on your life! We love it. If we didn't, we couldn't carry on. We're a happy crowd, and there's lots of laughter on that stage.'

Singer Mary Moss vividly recalls this frantic period: 'There was a lot of stress because I was doing the Victoria Palace twice nightly and also doing thirteen *Around The World In Song*. We'd rehearse all day to 5pm because we had to be at Victoria Palace by 6.15, then do the live show on Sunday. We'd rehearse the sound

Minstrel Magic

Monday and Tuesday, pre-record it on Wednesday morning, rehearse the vision from Wednesday to the live transmission on Sunday. Most difficult was getting to the theatre on time, it was a mad scramble.' As John said, 'It was a lot of fun but terribly hard work. You met yourself coming back. We were working fourteen hours a day, seven days a week.' Keith Leggett has similar memories: 'The television shows meant one hell of a workload as we had to be in the theatre by 5.40 and we often rehearsed until 4.30 at West Kensington. A mad dash to Victoria, quick pint in the Stage Door pub, then get the black face on.'

This occasionally produced some hilarious moments. Minstrel Roger Green remembers 'one Saturday during a technical rehearsal for the TV cameras, it was necessary for us to don the traditional minstrel makeup. This particular Saturday nothing went according to plan, and instead of finishing in good time to get to the Victoria Palace, George Inns eventually called it a wrap much later than usual, leaving us with little time for our journey. To save valuable time, we were told not to remove our minstrel makeup but to change into civilian clothes and head straight to the theatre. Four Minstrel colleagues and I travelled with Tony Mercer in his bench seat Rover, three in the front and three in the back. We were so preoccupied with getting to the theatre in record time that we were unaware of the special interest we were attracting from other road users. That is, until we pulled up at traffic lights. The astounded looks we got from fellow motorists and pedestrians were nothing short of hysterical. Had we had more time, we would have loved to have continued our journey seeking out more traffic lights!'

Just to add to this phenomenal workload, the core Mitchell Singers were also involved in the new 1963 Tommy Steele film *It's All Happening*. The four soloists all appeared in the film, with John, Dai and Tony having set piece solos and Don having solos within chorus numbers. The film's premise - Tommy Steele's character's efforts to raise money via a charity show - provided a natural format for set pieces by a number of well-known singers. The Mitchell Singers' segment towards the end of the film gave the audience a typical *Glee Club* sequence, which started off in an office setting and metamorphosed into a seaside holiday. Recording of the soundtrack for the film - composed by Phil Green – was interspersed with recordings for the Minstrel programmes, involving the same singers. The last week of January was entirely given over to shooting the production sequences for the film, for which Douggie Squires had done the choreography. Mary Moss remembers Douggie getting very cross with her as she needed to sit down a lot - he hadn't realised she was pregnant! The film was released in June at a special launch in Brighton, with other seaside pre-releases following before its general release in London on September 1. It was generally well-received by critics and audiences alike.

Although a second Dutch television series was already planned for the autumn, Jos van der Valk was now keen to produce a series based entirely on George's singers, to be done live, from tourist places, with more music, a bigger group of singers and no presenters. George involved the same core group, including Don Cleaver, Alan Cooper, Bob Hunter and Les Rawlings, as well as girls including Daphne Bell, Maggi Lawler, Maryetta Midgley, Mary Moss and Joyce Rawlings. Pleased with the result of this film made in Holland, George decided to repeat the experiment the following year. Producer Jos van der Valk remembers that 'George was thinking of basing it around South German castles. The plan was that we would shoot and produce this, and my broadcast company would spend one hour's fee for television. Once I'd done that and one repeat, George would have full rights to it.' The Dutch producers and agent made the trip to Germany but decided it wasn't the right place; eventually, someone hit upon filming in Yugoslavia. George flew sixteen singers out to Yugoslavia for two weeks in August, plus producer Jos van der Valk and choreographer Tommy Linden. Mary Moss remembers they took a small plane after landing in Yugoslavia, then a bus along a twisting coastal road before reaching Dubrovnik where they filmed enough for three thirty-minute programmes, before taking a boat to the island of Korčula, where they stayed on the boat as well as using it in the film. The minimal wardrobe - mainly shorts and T-shirts or peasant dresses for the girls, plus slacks and shirts for the boys, all in red, orange, yellow or green - accompanied them as well. The basic plan of the programmes remained the same - some mixed segments à la Minstrel style, plus solos, interspersed with local dancers, groups and choirs. All of the singers sang solo at some stage, even if it was only one line, with main solos being taken by John Boulter, Don Cleaver, Les Rawlings and Margaret Savage.

Alan Cooper remembers the day they arrived: 'We saw crowds of people walking uphill to the church. They were all praying for rain, they hadn't had any for about six months, and yes, we got it. It rained heavily for about three days, of course curtailing the filming. Both locals and tourists stood around for hours watching us film.' Mary Moss remembers people wandering around and across takes. It was still raining by the time John arrived, so they had to use light reflectors to make it look sunny. However, these were to cause problems, as John remembers: 'Margaret and I were on a rock doing a duet. I was singing away when George shouted, "Shut your mouth." I couldn't understand what he meant. I'd spent a lot of money at the dentist's before I flew out and had a lot of gold fillings at the back of my mouth. The light from the reflector boards was being reflected back from my fillings!'

Alan Cooper also ran into problems. One routine began with the singers out in the harbour, two or three to each little rowing boat, which they then rowed back to shore, before jumping up onto the quayside and continuing the routine ashore. As Alan remembers, 'as we got back to the harbour steps, I missed my footing and went straight to the bottom. Luckily I came straight up. I rushed to our coach, and the wardrobe mistress changed me, but I soon dried out as the weather was so hot by now.' Mary Moss remembers that the filming 'was a bonding experience' and John recalls it as 'wonderful'.

George visited Killarney in Ireland twice the following year, hoping to make yet another foreign-based programme. He was so enthralled by his first trip that he doubled the length of the proposed programme, intending to have the choir singing Irish melodies at places like Muckross Gardens, Aghadoe and Ross Castle. But disappointment at the sales of the first two films meant this Irish plan never materialised, though the other films eventually received an airing on both Dutch and British television under the title of *George Mitchell's Wandering Minstrels*.

Once the Minstrels exploded across both television and theatre, George had neither the time nor the singers to service the usual vast number of seaside shows. Nevertheless, he still managed twenty-six summer shows and pantomimes in 1963, as well as a lot of radio and TV work. The long-running *Variety Playhouse*, taken off after eleven years, was replaced by the virtually identical *Starlight Hour* which also included Mitchell Singers, while appearances in the new *Billy Cotton Band Show* series and *The Good Old Days* meant Mitchell singers were appearing in prime time shows two Saturdays out of three. More jingles for Esso, as well as jingles for products as diverse as Ruben, Glengarry Whisky and Smartest, provided work for some Mitchell Singers, as did *Your Kind of Music*, a new series of *Secombe's Here*, a return of *Star Parade* and three Andy Stewart shows.

But this was an age of huge changes in light entertainment and work once more fell off. It was the era of the Beatles and the Rolling Stones, screaming pop fans and huge outdoor concerts. Equity made matters worse by insisting that singers were paid as much for a day's backing work as for a week's work in the theatre, so most backing work dried up, and many backing groups disappeared. Other singing groups had begun to fill the gaps created by George concentrating on the Minstrels and this upset George. Many of his core singers, loyal for years, were not involved in the Minstrels, other than on the soundtracks, and keeping them employed was fast becoming a major problem. Many left him as the attraction of guaranteed work was no longer there. No wonder there was no work for Jeff and Harry on their return from Australia. George hated letting people go and tried everything he could to find them other work. Those he desperately wanted to keep, such as Les Rawlings, he moved to the Minstrels, even if they had only appeared on the soundtrack in the past.

Meanwhile, he dreamed up yet another format for a television show to occupy his singers. Convinced country and western music was about to make a huge come-back, he developed The *Country and Western Show*, which did exactly what it sounded like. This time George chose to use his reducing number of core singers in vision as well as on the soundtrack. Soloists were the experienced Don Cleaver, Australian Bob Clayton, existing Mitchell singers Ted Darling and Les Rawlings, together with Eve Blanchard. Don was still in the Victoria Palace show, so his workload was once again comparable to the previous summer's heavy schedule. Many of the Minstrel production team were brought on board, including producer George Inns. The show was compèred by Canadian Gordon Lightfoot, then at the start of what remains a stellar career in North America. The Mitchell Men were teamed with the Prairie Flowers, a 'glamorous team of cowgirl singers' comprising blonde and brunette Mitchell girls, including Penny Jewkes, Mary Moss, Maggi Lawler and Margaret Eaves, and led by Eve Blanchard and Liz Paul. They were supplemented by dancers, the Hickory Sticks, led by Topper Jackie Joyner who said, 'The *Country and Western Show* is quite different from the Minstrels. We don't change costumes so often, but we're more acrobatic.' In an attempt to distance the show from the Minstrels, advance publicity stressed that George had brought in 'new faces, with the notable exception of Don Cleaver, who "to get the feel of the set-up" smuggled himself into the last Minstrel series'. Most publicity concentrated on Don who had of course been with the Minstrels for years; he was obviously becoming a firm favourite with fans. *Radio Times* dedicated a feature to him: 'Born in Bow twenty-eight years ago, he was a great one for throwing himself about. "While singing I love to move around and dance." He has been asked for his autograph several times recently which came as a pleasant shock. "With a black face, you sink your identity. I quite forgot people would pick out my real face in the Western get up." '

And the singers weren't all that people could spot. The show had a genuine country feel. Choreographer Douggie Squires recalls, 'Dancers, guest stars, chickens, horses, name any farmyard animals and we had at least one on the show. There was chicken shit everywhere. We had guests riding horses, feeding chickens and just being cowboys and Indians.'

Although some viewers and critics thought the show a pale replica of the Minstrels, most loved it, thinking it 'tuneful, attractive and well balanced', as did BBC Board members. Press reaction was just as positive: 'Cheerful unsophisticated entertainment, with characteristic zip and zest', and 'It has the unmistakable touch of George Mitchell magic. A real hum-dinging toe-tapper.'

The first three *Country and Western Show*s went brilliantly. George remarked, 'What interests me is so many viewers are taking again to old favourites they'd almost forgotten, *like Colorado Trail* and *Beautiful Ohio*.' Eve Blanchard loved the show: 'It was a wonderful show, even in the summer, traditionally poor for television series. Its very high ratings were even better than the Minstrels.' The hit of the summer it certainly was, but trouble lay ahead. The music and choreography for the eight-show series were finalised and as Douggie says, 'On paper it looked really healthy'. But after three shows, the BBC moved George Inns into a new series - Douggie reports, 'He was a champion at getting new ideas into action' - and with the series running successfully, the BBC thought another producer could easily manage the rest.

But they thought wrong. The new director arrived or more accurately, didn't arrive. Day after day he couldn't be found, so Douggie rehearsed the fourth show as planned. The new director eventually turned up on the last rehearsal day, and 'So began a pattern,' says Douggie. 'He'd enter, usually drunk, to see a run through, during which he'd read a newspaper, hardly looking up and then say, "I hate it. Get ready for changes." Everyone found this so dispiriting and utter chaos ensued. After the new director had left the studio, there was a rapid rescue job to be done as no one knew where they were. Somehow everyone did their best, and the show went out.' To make matters even worse, he brought in his own set designer, replacing Stanley Dorfman with Melvin Cornish. Two shows later, he trashed the show again. Douggie recalls, 'Twenty-four hard-working faces fell to the floor. I decided it was time to speak, "But everybody has worked so hard – it looks great, and we are in the studio tomorrow!" "If you don't change it. I'll get my wife to do it – she's a real choreographer," he replied. The shit hit the fan as the Americans so delicately put it. I left the rehearsal room angry and humiliated.' An emergency summit meeting was held and Bill Cotton Jnr, Head of Light Entertainment, quietly removed the would-be choreographer's drunken husband from the series - in the nick of time. The last shows used producer Johnnie Stewart, though as Douggie says, 'Despite the second producer's reputation, he completed his contract with the BBC, with the help of its supportive crews. Dear old loyal Auntie!!'

None of this turmoil affected the show's popularity, whatever it was doing internally to George and his singers. But many of the guest stars, which included Frankie Howerd, Stan Stennett and Alma Cogan, proved unpopular. The press were particularly critical of Max Wall's appearance, writing, 'How the producers ever thought (his) act would fit in with the delightful music and singing of the Mitchell Men beggars description.'

Another *Country and Western* series was strongly contemplated. However, nothing materialised, which Eve Blanchard attributes to the popularity of the Minstrels: 'The BBC had sunk so much money into the Minstrels they needed to keep it going.' Perhaps there just wasn't the money to run two such spectacular shows. In 1966, America showed interest in the series, and George asked Eve to return to head it up. As she said, 'I had to think hard but didn't go.' In the end, this American series never materialised.

CHAPTER 20

The pattern was now set for decades to come. A Minstrel television series in the winter, a virtually permanent stage version in London and touring versions in Britain and Australia. Unchanged it may have been, but George wasn't happy to rest on his laurels, saying, 'I'm always trying to improve the show. If it's as good as last year, it's worse. We used to play a lot of music in the style of the Twenties and Thirties. I don't do that anymore because so many people came along afterwards and flogged it to death. The music we play is a good mix. We play the old with the new and often feature pieces that have never been heard before in this country. If it's played and presented to the standard our audiences have come to expect, then there is no way it can be killed off.'

The conundrum facing the Georges was to keep the show the same, yet change it. George's first move was to persuade the reluctant BBC to move it to one show every three weeks, rather than fortnightly because he didn't want to oversell the show. George Inns agreed, saying, 'It's best to float on and off the screens at intervals and live to a good old age than be a one-year wonder and die.' The soloists and many of the singers were pleased by this move too - two shows a night at the Victoria Palace, as well as rehearsing and recording the television series, was taking its toll.

Both Georges worked hard to keep the television show fresh. George Inns explained that 'from being an adventure in the early days, the going now becomes tough. I want to give the programme a new look without altering the basic approach.' In Maschwitz's words in 1962, 'Even now, when [the show] has found its feet, George Inns needs to work tirelessly to keep those feet moving. The programme is too valuable to be allowed to slip.' It certainly was. The *Scottish Daily Mail* reported, 'Down in Commercial TV's jingle-land, they call it Black Saturday. There are two every month in the winter when 17,000,000 viewers are solidly with the BBC. It is the brightest jewel in Auntie's tiara. It zips, crackles and zooms.' ITV thought it had winners when it pitched *The Avengers* and *The Morecambe and Wise Show* against the Minstrels one season, and even reviewers thought the Minstrels would suffer by comparison, but the Minstrels easily beat both.

George always tried to introduce changes to each television series. In a very popular move, a high-profile female soloist in the person of Margaret Savage was brought in. Previous shows had occasionally used Maryetta Midgley as female soloist, but she never had the consistent profile now given to Margaret. John Boulter describes Margaret as 'the most photogenic girl I'd ever seen. Put her on a screen, and it comes alive.' Critics approved, with the *Aberdeen Evening Express* calling her 'an excellent vocalist who can hold her own with the big male guns of the Mitchell Singers'. Maggie was to be joined later by Delia Wicks, the Singing Topper, and Penny Jewkes who had been with George for some years. Delia created interest of her own as she had recently come out of an eighteen-month relationship with pop legend Cliff Richard, joining the Minstrels as a dancer shortly after he ended their affair.

The principals were 'whited up', one by one, in one series so that the viewers could see 'the man beneath the makeup'. John became white to play the part of the Prince in an *Alice in Wonderland* sequence, while Dai Francis was unmasked to sing a favourite song *If I Were a Rich Man*. Later principal Karl Scott was washed white for his first television appearance and introduced by George to the public in white tie and tails. Producer Ernest Maxim said, 'Since then, the phone hasn't stopped ringing. Everyone is commenting on his voice, which is just like Howard Keel's, and raving about his smile, his hair and his personality. It seems he's going to be the pin-up of the show.'

A second innovation was the introduction of a Family Request spot when John sang viewers' requests, in response to the thousands of requests which had flooded George's office and the BBC, asking to hear more of John. This proved so popular that George retained it until John left the show in 1972. One final innovation was to flash the words of some of the better-known songs onto the screen as the minstrels sang them. One critic reported, 'Care needed to be taken to ensure the couplets didn't block out the lavish settings but it's an idea worth persevering with.'

By 1967 the traditional pattern of five sequences and one conducted sequence per show was changed to allow longer segments, such as the one based on the songs of Broadway and

West Side Story. This opened with an eighteen-minute spectacular based on the building of New York, from *A Hammer and Nail* to *Rhapsody in Blue*, in which the Toppers took part in a baseball game and a mass tap dance. In a later show, a fifteen-minute sequence covered all four seasons with the girls appearing in spring outfits, bikinis and Russian snow costumes. One show included a lengthy segment of songs about London, during which the Minstrels were joined on stage, in a spectacular appearance, by the Coldstream Guards. A sequence of songs of England done in Elizabethan costume generated hundreds of letters of support, such as the one from Doris Wood who wrote, 'this England set in a silver sea could do with a little boost put over in a musical way by you and your company. Please, Mr Mitchell, for England, Elizabeth and St George.' A future edition included an aquatic display in a 5000-gallon tank, though no Minstrel or Topper went into the water! As George Inns said, 'we wouldn't get the Toppers dried off for the next number, and as for the Minstrels, we don't want them bleached!' By the end of one series, the Minstrels had sung their way through numbers featuring fairground scenes - one of which had a real roundabout - railway stations complete with locomotives and carriages, live animals, a hospital ward, and a Spanish sequence set in Covent Garden just because oranges from Seville were marketed there! George even managed to incorporate the *Grand March* from Verdi's *Aida* in one show, without anyone 'bursting a gasket', as George put it. Some sequences had become so complex they couldn't fit into the normally live programme, so Equity agreed to allow 10% of the programme to be pre-recorded and slotted in during the broadcast. Tom Sloan, Head of Light Entertainment, later said that '(pre-recording some sequences) was one reason for its freshness after seven years' exposure. We have learned how to harness technical gimmickry to its own advantage.' George even experimented with the conducted segment, though no one wanted too many changes to this spot. The results included a hauntingly beautiful *Blues in the Night*, using John and Don, and a stunning *What Now, My Love?*, another modern song. In a further departure, he used Margaret as the lone soloist in a soulful version of *Blue Moon*.

In a shake-up, one series did away with a resident comedian. The first such show was the Christmas special and was entitled *Max Bygraves Meets the Black and White Minstrels* which exactly described the show's new nature. Out went linking acts such as

Minstrel Magic

Leslie Crowther, George Chisholm and Benny Garcia, replaced by star compères, such as Ted Ray, Don Arrol and Norman Vaughan. Some editions were based around particular themes, such as that compèred by Ted Ray which used old music-hall numbers. His impersonations of George Robey, Will Fyffe and Max Miller were thought by one critic to be 'excruciating', though others said this was Ted Ray at his greatest. In contrast, Norman Vaughan's appearance was welcomed by viewers and critics alike. However, this was one innovation that didn't always work, and a permanent linking comic was swiftly reintroduced.

A new dance director Roy Gunson was brought in who livened things up and remained with the show until it finished. Les Rawlings recalled that the Minstrels 'used to be more static and hefty, now they move around more'. A new set designer was introduced - Lionel Radford remained with the show until his untimely death a few years later. Some of his more surprising sets featured the Minstrels inside a hotel and in circus ring (a sequence which also featured Tony Schaller, who, as one of the acrobatic Schaller Brothers, was with the show at the Victoria Palace).

Of course, it was impossible to please everyone. Viewers wrote in their thousands, with every praise and complaint possible about some of the changes that were tried. A word of warning was sounded by Mavis James who, although glad to see the show back, said, 'I am sure that there is a great number in your audience who would like to hear something new. As a member of the public with my ear to the ground, I know that unless the Minstrels can branch out a little more this series, there will be a drop in the audience figures. You are faced with the question - whether to satisfy the tastes of the several hundred diehards, or whether to gauge the tastes of the remainder, and I would ask you to think seriously about this, as I, for one, would not like to see this show go the way of so many others and become an institution.' George didn't reply to this warning!

One show caused more comment than most when George included a segment built around Gilbert and Sullivan songs. People were outraged at what they saw as sacrilege, though many others wrote to say how much they had enjoyed it. The Daniell Family, who had previously asked George to include some Gilbert and Sullivan, were horrified at the result: 'Please not any more like that! To us, it was sheer desecration. The singing, yes, every time, but not the gimmicks. The excessive movement obtruded onto the singing, instead of complimenting it.' Miss K Muskett, on the other hand, thought it 'sheer delight. It was a near miracle to hear John sing *A Wanderin' Minstrel*. I did not hear it properly, I was so amazed.' Joan Coleman also belonged to the happy category, writing 'You portrayed these gems in a new light but musically were still in the true style - a truly enjoyable addition to the show.' The *People's Journal* wrote, 'Up above, Sir Arthur Sullivan may have worn a little frown while he looked down on Gilbert and Sullivan as presented by the Minstrels - but I bet WS Gilbert loved every new twist.' The overall reaction must have been favourable as Gilbert and Sullivan sequences became staples of the show.

Although the Minstrels themselves were generally immune from criticism, some writers damned with faint praise, such as the strange letter from Frances Mitchell (presumably no relation!) from Durham: 'I still hold the view that Dai is a living example of prostitution of the arts - only once has he been given a real baritone song to sing and that was in one of your *Around The World In Song*. The man has a voice, and it's such a shame he has to use it in such a raucous fashion by imitating Al Jolson, who used to set my teeth on edge. I wish you had the courage to forget the Music Hall for once and give us sentimental songs without the eye rolling, hand waving technique. Also for your songs about ladies, we might be treated to some about more refined types. I know you're scared stiff of your public but surely, out of forty-five minutes on TV, we middlebrows might be allowed perhaps five minutes of drawing room memories. I'll write the durn things for you if you haven't the time. If I could just hear Dai opening his mouth once or twice from North to South instead of from East to West, I'd quit carping. John, of course, is beyond reproach, and I suppose the money he earns compensates for the muck you make him sing - great pity. We females call Tony Scoopy —-I guess you know why - and I'm afraid you wouldn't be able to use him on anything other than his present selections but he's pleasant to listen to, and that's something these days.' One would love to know what George made of this letter!

A letter from 'Sally Sourpuss' in the *Aberdeen Evening Express* disapproved of the Toppers: 'Now we are having more and more of the dancing girls routine with scanty costumes. Pretty dresses are gradually giving way to the more run of the mill leggy chorus. True, it would take more than this to distract from the Minstrels, but it seems nevertheless ridiculous to cast aside a successful formula.' The paper agreed to some extent: 'These new look minstrels seem to be going more and more for dancing routines and cutting down on the song-a-minute set-up of earlier shows.' H Chick of Mountain Ash who wrote that 'with the dancers' costumes seeming to get briefer each week, this isn't like the old presentation which all the family could enjoy.' Joan Mather indignantly wrote that 'you have recently introduced four almost naked women. What a great pity! You have no need to seek that type of popularity.' Inevitably some viewers thought the opposite. One wrote, 'I consider the show has changed a lot in the past few years - at least as far as the girls' dresses are concerned. At one time they performed many of their routines wearing only skimpy briefs and bras. Since the advent of Mary Whitehouse, however, the girls appear to have done a complete cover-up. This change might be welcomed by maiden aunts but has surely been regretted by most of the country's male population.' His complaint provoked outrage. Mrs Wedge thought he 'has a colossal nerve to suggest the show should discard those gorgeous dresses in favour of briefs and bra. The thought of a Viennese waltz served up as he suggests take some digesting.'

But some changes were nearly disastrous. The BBC moved the show from Saturday to Sunday evenings in late 1962, in what proved to be an unpopular move with large portions of the Minstrel audience. Letters of complaint poured in to the BBC and to George, with everyone saying they wouldn't be able to watch the show as they would be in church. Some people also complained that it wasn't a suitable show for a Sunday evening, though audience figures hardly dropped at all. Despite these complaints, the BBC retained the show on Sunday the following year, though the year after, in a move calculated to appease the many church groups who had complained, the BBC moved the show back to Saturday evenings, only to return it to Sunday in 1966 as part of their plan to conquer that evening from ITV. One vicar found a way around the problem: 'Because the Rev John Abbott has made a pact with TV fans in his congregation, from next Sunday they will be able to attend Evensong and still watch their favourite programme. For Mr Abbott, vicar of St Peter's Church, Gorse Hill, Stretford, is to bring forward the service by half an hour to six o'clock. "My congregation has been getting smaller at Evensong, especially every third Sunday when the *Black and White Minstrel Show* was on," said Mr Abbott. "It's a first class show - I often wish

I could see it. But I'm not giving in to TV. Why have a clash of loyalties when people can do both quite happily?"

This move wasn't the only near disaster. Lack of space at the Shepherd's Bush Empire Television Theatre meant that the BBC moved one Christmas show into two enormous studios at the new Television Centre, with a huge stage area, a number of additional cameras and the very latest technical advantages. The show looked marvellous, but no one was really happy with the situation, so the show returned to the Television Theatre for the next series. However, the following year, the Corporation wanted to try the same move again. The *Billy Cotton Band Show* had already made the move, a couple of weeks before the new Minstrel series started, but with disastrous results and quickly returned to the Theatre. Nevertheless, the planned move for the Minstrels went ahead, and they took over the mammoth Studio One, the second largest in Europe, where every inch of space went into making an even better show - faster and more sophisticated, with longer-ranging camera shots. Once again the studio audience was dropped to increase the available space. George Inns explained that 'this means we can stop after each number and make a complete change'. But the Corporation was worried, and Board members were asked specifically to watch the first of the series. With typical Mitchell magic, the Minstrels seemed able to overcome the studio difficulties, and Board members thought the series 'got off to a very good start, very well produced, dressed, designed and conceived'. But the lack of an audience caused serious concern to the Board. The Head of Light Entertainment explained that if the show lacked anything, it was not so much the applause but the vitality of the performers performing to an applauding audience, together with the reaction. The fear was that the new format might have introduced a certain chilliness into the programme which now lacked pace, with the beautiful studio technique no substitute for human action and reaction. The Board discussed dubbing in some applause but decided against it as 'you can't dub in vitality'. 'We had all the room and the finest facilities in the world,' recalled George Inns. 'Yet after only four programmes, we returned to the miseries of the old Empire. The studios had robbed us of the spiritual life of a live audience, and that was what had given us the freshness and zest from the start. So back to the Bush and back came our gallant six hundred to the stalls and circle. Sigh of relief. We had almost made a major mistake.'

Never one to learn from its mistakes, the BBC moved the show back to Television Centre in 1967, again unsuccessfully. The Bradford Telegraph summed up a general feeling about the lack of audience: 'While this might be an advantage with some shows, it is a real deficiency in this one. Quite apart from applause being a stimulant to the performers, viewers would, in this instance I feel, like to have a studio audience expressing appreciation of the sequences. They almost demand acclamation.' But in the Television Centre it was to remain.

CHAPTER 21

Crowds were still pouring into the London show. Bob was paying out a fortune in advertising, both in Europe and America and also on airlines, which certainly paid off, as, in the summer months, nearly 40% of the audience were foreign. Every show was filled to capacity including standing room. They pioneered the idea of organised coach parties and had two men working full-time on the project. Bob later estimated that nearly three-quarters of the audience arrived by coach. A deal with British Rail proved very successful. A new all-in rail ticket for Thursdays included travel from Brighton, a visit to the show and a fish supper on the journey home. Tickets cost fifty shillings (£50) First Class and forty-two shillings (£42) Second Class.

The show broke record after record on the stage and was overwhelmingly popular. As the *Daily Sketch* was to write, 'The Year of the Beatles (1963) was not entirely geared to the guitar and the Mersey Sound. Indeed no, it was an entertainment, old hat even in the last century, that tickled the nation's palate and quickened its pulse. While under-twenties fainted in queues, their parents were breaking records at the Victoria Palace.' By mid-1963 the Victoria Palace booking was extended until February 1964 as so many people were asking to see it over Christmas. Very soon there wasn't a seat available for Saturday nights until late January, and none for any second house shows for any night until August.

Extended again and again, the London show reached the first of many milestones in November 1964, when it became the longest running show at the theatre, even outstripping the Crazy Gang. It reached its three-year anniversary in May 1965, and George received a telegram of 'Congratulations and many happy returns from George Inns and the production team BBC'. With the second house on June 9, 1965, it notched up its 2514th performance, making it the longest-running musical in the world, and with a record audience of 3,400,000, passing *Oliver! Oliver!*'s management shrugged it off: 'If it makes them happy, I'm not worried, but their claim is not really true. Although you could argue that any show with music is a musical, the Minstrels don't have a plot.' This record-breaking second house was broadcast live to twenty-three hospitals via a GPO land line. The show had been broadcast to local Bristol hospitals during its opening run in 1960, and this link was remembered as the record-breaking occasion drew near. The Bristol Hospital Broadcast organisation agreed to send a team of four - two commentators and two engineers - to cover the event, which meant that eight thousand Bristol hospital patients could also enjoy the show. The show itself celebrated with a 'top hat' cake and champagne at a party at the Victoria Palace after the second show on June 7. Bob Luff attended, as did Leslie MacDonnell, Managing Director of Moss Empires. The Moss Empire staff at the theatre and at Head Office presented Bob with a silver cigarette case and a scroll to mark their 'long and happy association'. George kept the telegram that Bob sent him, saying 'May I congratulate you on this historic occasion and thank you most sincerely for a very happy and successful association. Long may it continue as ever. Bob.' Remarkably, Bob himself threw financial caution to the wind and funded a party with champagne and a two-foot cake decorated like the posters, to celebrate the 3000th performance. Soon they also passed *My Fair Lady* for the number of seats sold - 4,322,172! During 1968 it created yet another world record of 4354 performances before 5½m people.

Records tumbled around the country too. In 1966 the Bristol Hippodrome management said, 'We have banked record advance takings for this 54-year-old theatre. It's unprecedented and quite amazing. I wish we had the show until Christmas.' In Liverpool for four weeks, it broke all previous box office records before the show even arrived. Within the first ten days after the box office opened, over ten thousand seats were booked, and it created a record for any twice-nightly show at the theatre. In Coventry in 1967, in the week before booking even opened, the box office received more than 10,000 postal applications and had to take on extra staff. Unprecedented demand for tickets meant it was a sell-out even before it opened. In Birmingham, the theatre had never known anything like it since the Beatles' appearance there - and they only did a one-night stand! As was becoming the norm, the show broke all theatre box office records by the time it closed. The same story was repeated everywhere the touring show appeared.

Those who managed to get tickets wrote in raptures. Mrs Palmer said, 'I really cried with delight. It will live in my heart forever. My favourite is Tony Mercer. My husband bought me a golliwog, what have I named him? Yes, "Mercer".' Mrs Henderson had got the men's autographs during her visit and planned to pass the book to her grandchildren, 'as I know they will cherish it'. A large base of regular visitors was developing, such as June Haskill who had seen the show four times, and ET Bisset who wrote he had watched every TV show, had all the albums and the book, had seen the stage show both summers and now wanted to know where the show would be in June. But some fans obviously didn't quite understand how it worked. Percival Hall, who had been trying to see the stage show for months, had finally succeeded for October 21 and hoped George could do *Ave Maria* for the choir spot, while Douglas Milne hoped George would meet him between houses on October 15.

By 1968, Bob owned the Futurist Theatre in Scarborough and records continued to fall. In one week that year, they created a new record at the Victoria Palace with standing room only at every performance. The same week, the touring version, in Scarborough for the summer, created a house record - twenty-four thousand people saw the show that week, with full houses for each of the six nights. More money was taken at the box office than ever before for any Futurist summer show.

The London cast had by now settled down for what looked to be turning into quite a run. Any long run is in danger of growing stale, but George kept everyone up to scratch with weekly rehearsals. Every show was watched by a member of management so matters could be corrected before any mistakes got out of hand.

As with any long run, hitches occurred, though surprisingly few mishaps are recorded, given the show's speed. Several singers remember one: 'Two minstrels were carrying a Topper down stage when her underskirt fell to the boards. Nothing daunted, one of the minstrels picked it up and went off waving it - much to the audience's delight.' Glyn Dawson recalled, 'One blonde dancer wearing a crinoline skirt fell off the stage into the pit onto the drummer. Because of the crinolines, the girls couldn't see the edge of the stage. I wasn't far from her, so I jumped into the pit after her to see if she was all right. We stayed there till the sequence ended. A few weeks later she did it again - I didn't jump again!' Roger Green has a similar story: 'We were in the middle of a Latin American sequence, which involved leaving the stage and dancing on a raised narrow catwalk around the orchestra pit in close proximity to the audience before returning to the stage on the opposite side. Unfortunately, one dancer misjudged the catwalk width and fell headfirst into the orchestra pit. One of the percussionist's drums softened her fall, and like a true professional, she climbed back onto the stage and continued the routine.' The Topper involved in one of these events, Gillian Parsons, recollects her reactions: 'I only half fell in and was pulled out by one of the minstrels, who shouted, "Don't worry, my lovely", but I would rather have disappeared altogether than face that audience.' Topper Elspeth Hands remembers it was Gillian's first night and she got over-excited. She reaped the benefit, however, when Talk of the Town impresario Robert Nesbitt sent her a bottle of champagne after the show. Gillian fell over a few more times while wearing the massive tent dresses, though on at least one occasion she made it to the wings before falling over completely.

The boys' chief trouble was with their woolly wigs, occasionally lifting them off with their hats, revealing perhaps red or blond hair. Russell Stone recalls, 'We were all in a line, passing top hats off one way, then boaters on. James Earl Adair's wig came off when he took his top hat off, and it went all along the line inside his hat. James had long hair, fashionable at the time, but orders were he had to put it up in a hairnet under his wig, so this is what the audience could see! The front row of the stalls were laughing really hard and having a ball.' Keith Leggett remembers this same incident: 'There he was fully exposed as a blonde with a hairnet on! The poor lad got a bit of a roasting all round and probably never got over it.' Les Want remembered something similar happening to John Clements: 'His hat was too big, so wardrobe had stuffed it with foam. On stage, he took off the hat to pass it along the line, and his wig stuck to the foam, revealing his hairnet and curlers! He had to stay like that until his boater reached him. Nobody kept a straight face!'

The sets, although minimal, also caused the occasional problem. John Boulter recalls, 'One piece of scenery was up high, right across the stage, 25' long, 3' or 4' deep, depicting notes on a stave. I was on stage alone, singing something in the middle of a medley once, with these notes above me. The audience was dead quiet, then there was a collective gasp. I had no idea why and carried on. When I got off, I said to a stagehand, "What did I do?" He explained the note above my head had dropped a foot, stopping about one inch above me.'

John seems to have attracted mishaps. On another occasion, when he was singing alone on stage, he heard a curious hissing sound behind him: 'When the curtain lifted, I stepped back into a small waterfall.' A water main had burst in the wings, and a deluge was spurting thirty feet into the air, showering down on the company as they danced in from the wings. With cast and stagehands frantically trying to stave off the floods with brooms, 'we didn't have the faintest idea what was causing it, but we made the decision to press on and hope for the best. It took ten minutes before the engineers finally blocked off the water supply and by that time we were practically swimming through the routine. The audience loved it of course.'

George went out of his way to make sure the cast was well-looked after. Cast members were paid if they were off sick, almost unheard of in theatreland. A doctor visited weekly because, as *Woman* reported, 'A sort of lather from the black makeup gets into their ears and causes temporary deafness; the doctor syringes their ears. Then for the next few nights, they complain of being deafened by the applause!' George was well aware of the high degree of fitness such a show demanded and did all he could to protect the singers and, more importantly, the dancers who were under even greater physical strain. George said, several years later, 'We've had hundreds join the cast and leave - because they couldn't stand the pace. Unfortunately, there is high wastage among the girls, but new people are soon infected and work with the enthusiasm of the old troopers, often within a fortnight. I have a terrific bunch of singers at the moment. Marvellous soloists don't grow on trees, but I can count on nine altogether. Their talent is so well-laced that I always have someone who can do whatever is demanded and that gives me colossal scope.'

The cast were certainly hard-working, but there was also a lot of fun to be had backstage. Russell Stone, who joined the Victoria Palace cast, remembers the show well: 'There were two dressing rooms, one gay and one straight. I used to hang out in the gay dressing room even though I was straight, as it was much more fun. The lift to the dressing rooms took so long that no one used it. At the end, you'd have your hands behind your back undoing your cufflinks and buttons, then there was a rush for the stairs. At the Friday call, we were always told please wait for the curtain to come down before running off the stage.' Leslie Crowther remembered Christmas parties on stage at the theatre: 'They were so successful that we took over the whole theatre and God knows what shenanigans went on in the stalls and the boxes. We had to apply for permission because there were so many people on stage, the fire authorities were terrified it would collapse. The atmosphere was amazing, the stage staff, the front of house, box office, ticket collectors. There was a lovely dressing room of gay lads, and they gave one another the most amazing presents.' Clem Vickery remembers at the New Victoria in 1973: 'We had tremendous laughs with the gay Minstrels. I told one gay dancer that our drummer Keith fancied him. Keith, who wasn't gay, played up to it and everyone really enjoyed the joke, even the dancer.'

The huge audiences flocking to see the show, which, said one critic, 'puts every other in the shade, it is supreme entertainment', included Prince Charles and Cary Grant, who so enjoyed the show, joining in every chorus, that he telegraphed congratulations from his London hotel afterwards. American chat show star Ed Sullivan was crazy about the show when he saw it, and the theatre also welcomed a returning royal fan, when fourteen-year-old Princess Anne, together with school friend Susan Babington Smith, her governess Miss Peebles and a detective, saw the show from a box. Incredibly Minstrel folklore - and John - insists they remained unrecognised until ten minutes before the end when the theatre manager was called to the box because the princess had decided she wanted to see backstage. John recalls, 'There was a knock on the dressing room door, and someone said it was Princess Anne. We thought they were kidding, but there she was, a sweet-looking girl. But while we were shaking hands, her eyes were riveted on the wall behind us. She asked loads of questions, such as, "Did the makeup harm the skin? Is it easy to take off? How long does it last?" When she'd gone, we realised she'd been staring at a nude pin-up calendar I'd stuck on Tony's mirror for a joke. Well, they should have warned us, shouldn't they?' Next time she visited, she asked to watch from backstage. Lord Mountbatten of Burma was another fervent fan. The Duke and Duchess of Kent and Sir Malcolm had also visited secretly and often returned, frequently bringing friends from all over the world. Charlie Chaplin, his wife and family cheered from the stalls during their visit. Football fanatics among the cast were delighted when the wives and girlfriends of England's 1966 World Cup squad watched the show the night before the final, in which England famously beat West Germany.

The theatre show now had its legions of regular visitors. One fan had seen the show one hundred and sixty-five times, and hundreds had seen it twenty times or more. So impressed was George by EL Bond, who had brought fifty parties to see the show, thus booking nearly three thousand seats since the show had opened, that he even sent him Christmas cards. These were designed specially every year and were always based around a minstrel theme.

Perhaps the best-known fans were Christine Vick and Eileen Morris, who eventually saw the show seven hundred and ninety times each, seeing it twice weekly for seven years. Christine remembers people said she was wasting her money 'but I asked them if they smoked or drank. They always did, but I didn't.' The cast called them The Clappers - 'We used to shout "More" to encourage the audience. The audience didn't really need any encouraging, but it helped.' Christine recalls how they met: 'I usually sat in Row D middle gangway aisle seat because I wanted to be near the stage, but once, it was sold. They offered me A13 and Eileen was in A14. After that, we sat in those two seats regularly, they kept them for us at the box office. We'd go to the stage door before the first show to say hello to the cast, then we'd have a coffee and return for the second house. Afterwards, we'd pop round to say goodnight. Everyone was very friendly, though some of the cast would stop and talk more than others. Dai was very shy and would go through the crowd without anyone spotting him, though he always said goodnight to us.' Both Christine and Eileen watched the company more than the show and could always tell 'when Dai had new shoes or a new relationship started'. They kept lists of births and birthdays, sometimes giving cast members little presents. Once the show closed in London, the pair spent their week's summer holiday wherever the show was resident: 'We went twice per night every night and also to every matinée.' In 1971 the *Radio Times* featured a double-page spread on them, to publicise the new television series. The accompanying photo was shot in the stalls at the theatre, with Christine and Eileen in their regular seats, with all the soloists and many Minstrels and Toppers in full costume on stage, in the stalls and in the boxes. After the *Radio Times* was issued, Mrs Softley wrote enviously to George, 'I hope they realise how lucky they are. I would love to meet John

Boulter and shake his hand and tell him how much I enjoy his singing.'

Dustman John Ranstead was another regular, sitting in the seat next to Christine and Eileen. He saw the show a thousand times in ten years, sometimes going four times a week. John Boulter has one particular memory of John: 'He'd brought a pork pie, and he was down to eating the crust. Everybody was looking at him.' Another loyal fan, Lawrence Grassi, saw the show five hundred times. Some fans made almost superhuman efforts to be part of the show. Roy Winbow, later Head Minstrel of the touring version, remembers David: 'He'd still be at the theatre at the end of a get-out, we'd leave for the next venue, and he would still get there first to welcome us and help with the set-up.'

Charlie Tanner and Cyril Evans travelled the land taking their holidays wherever the show was, as well as being regular visitors at the Victoria Palace. From January 1963, when they first saw the show in London, they went twice weekly, at a cost of over £10,000 (£168,000), as well as seeing the touring version wherever and whenever they could. Cyril said 'every show is different. The audience makes a difference to each show, as does moving it from one theatre to another.' Tony Mercer presented them with Minstrel ties after their five hundredth show. They had a wardrobe of suits to wear to the show, including two white tuxedos and a pair of maroon suits with black lapels, which Charlie had seen while passing through Norwich. He travelled all the way back from London on the next train to buy them - he had seen John wearing an identical suit in one show. They were often late for work at Victoria Coach Station because they considered it disrespectful to leave the house if a Minstrel was singing on the radio. They even wore black curly wigs and burnt-cork makeup to watch the shows at home. When they saw their 1126th performance eleven years to the day after they saw their first, national press made a great fuss of them. Interviews with the pair and endless photos showed them dressed in the white dinner jackets and black and white striped shirts with lace fronts that they wore to complement the Minstrels on this visit. In January 1976, they gave up a week's holiday in Amsterdam to spend the week in Coventry, seeing the show on every possible occasion, once they realised it coincided with their 1500th visit. They took with them seven dinner suits each and forty-six different dress shirts. Ted Darling, Les Rawlings and Les Want welcomed them, with Ted saying, 'We're really knocked out by the way they follow us. It's always good to see them again, they're great guys.'

But not all fans were so welcome. In 1970, John was plagued by a lunatic fringe of women admirers, so much so that he had to get his then-wife, Lorna, to deal with them, to convince them he wasn't interested. He even had to call the police on one occasion to deal with a woman who became a regular intruder at the theatre. Another fan, the wife of a well-known London man, became a real nuisance, so much so that John had to ring her husband and appeal for help to stop her molesting him. The husband said, 'I wish I could. I'm sick to death of hearing your voice. My wife has bought every record you've ever made and plays your music from morning to night.' So the next time she tried to make a nuisance of herself at the theatre, John slung her out.

CHAPTER 22

The touring version was just as popular. From 1964, when Morecambe again won the battle, mainly, so George said, because of the hospitality extended to the 1962 show, every seaside resort fought to present the Minstrels in summer season, until the final shows finished in 1987, thirty years after they had started. Morecambe welcomed it back with great delight, with heavy bookings for months beforehand: 'We are the luckiest resort in Europe to have your wonderful show presented to our visitors.' Inland cities tried desperately to get them over Christmas or at the very least a few weeks during the spring or autumn tours. Bob and George rewarded loyalty, returning the show time and again to places like Bristol, Morecambe and Scarborough where they had been welcomed and feted with open arms. But although resorts were crying out for them, and Scotland welcomed them time and time again, Wales proved trickier. Bob tried negotiating with Cardiff's New Theatre for a six-week season, but the New Theatre thought a twice-nightly show would be too risky as this would 'involve 60,000-90,000 people coming through the doors, one fifth of Cardiff's population. Too much of a gamble.' One wonders at their short-sightedness, particularly as the show had been spectacularly successful during its previous visit in 1960.

George had learned his lesson after using Eric, Jeff and Harry as brand new principals in Morecambe in 1962, prior to them taking the show to Australia. From 1964, he reverted to using established Mitchell Singers as principals in the touring version, choosing Don Cleaver and Glyn Dawson, both very experienced core members, and Australian Bob Clayton, who, along with Don, had appeared as soloist in the recent television series. The *Evening News and Chronicle* wrote, 'First George Mitchell made John Boulter, Dai Francis and Tony Mercer. Next came a step up for tenor Don Cleaver...then another brisk credit - for baritone Bob Clayton. And it's Don and Bob who are in on the birth of a new Big Three formation with Merthyr man Glyn Dawson the third. All belong to the busy London set-up. Says Glyn, "Going solo is just great."'

Full houses and lengthy box office queues became the norm wherever the touring version stayed. Records once again tumbled. The hugely popular touring version opened in Sheffield where it had completely sold out before opening, and city centre traffic ground to a halt on opening night. It did even better in Leeds the following month, breaking every existing box office record. They even opened to record advance bookings when they played Blackpool Opera House, a 3000-seater theatre and one of the largest in Europe, also breaking all Opera House records for the money taken in one week. Soon no seats were available for second houses and very few for the first house.

Even adverse publicity couldn't halt the bumper sales. In Newcastle for ten weeks, it practically sold out beforehand despite the *Northern Echo's* campaign against them when the paper realised it wasn't the London show. Their critic reported, 'I think it's disgraceful, passing us off with a second-class show. I'm sure all those people packing the theatre every night are angry about the deception.' So he tried to find someone who was dissatisfied but failed; everyone he asked said, 'I've heard it's absolutely fabulous', or 'I'm not really a Minstrel fan, but I enjoyed every minute of it. I'm recommending everyone in our office to go and see it.' Audiences certainly didn't care. As one said, 'Nothing wrong with that. The Sadler's Wells Opera in the North is not necessarily the same as in London. Nor is there anything wrong if it enables more people to see entertainment of this standard.' The theatre received no complaints though company manager Frank Jarram said they'd had three people who had been disappointed not to see Dai Francis. But it's obvious there was rivalry between the two shows. Jarram went on to say, 'We think this is a rather better show than the one at the Victoria Palace. Quite a number of people who have seen both shows have said so.' He stressed Don had had solo billing in both radio and television Minstrel shows, as well as in the *Country and Western Show* and *Around The World In Song*, both Bob and Glyn had appeared in the Minstrels on television, and Bob had also appeared in the *Country and Western Show*.

As with many constantly touring companies, accommodation often proved a problem. With increasing industrialisation, many of the old theatrical digs had been redeveloped, and suitable low-cost places were now few and far between. Caravans solved the problems for many company members, which cut the costs of living on tour. Glyn was a leading light of the caravan brigade, though he'd earlier had a less conventional sleeping place. While the show was at Leeds in 1960, he bought a motorbike, and the following week in Shrewsbury, a three-tonne van: 'This bike was carried in the back of the van, even when taking any of the company who wanted a ride to the next venue for five shillings each! I used to live in the van on tour and travelled all over the country in it.' Don Cleaver was another caravan fanatic, saying, 'We have a lot of our social life in caravans. When we move from one place to another, it's like a wagon train.' But even this didn't always help. When they visited Birmingham in 1967, many of them had already failed to find sites for their caravans within three miles of the theatre - Glyn had parked his van in Coventry, twenty-one miles away - and arrived there the day before opening to start searching.

Even those who wanted more conventional digs had problems. In 1966 one cast member had a shock, trying to find accommodation in Bristol. He wrote to his first choice while the show was still in Scarborough and was rather taken aback when a letter came back saying, 'We are sorry, but we do not take coloured people.' Birmingham proved difficult: 'We're nothing but sophisticated gipsies,' said Douglas Pearson, Head Minstrel. 'Most of us can't find accommodation at any price, but we had been warned about the acute situation before we came. Many of us are so desperate we will take anything as long as it's got a roof. I just don't know where many of them are going to sleep tonight.' Fourteen out of the eighty-strong company were still searching. The problem was the same in Eastbourne in 1971 and in Bournemouth in 1973 where the Luff organisation had to appeal for accommodation for the Toppers. It seems as if Bournemouth landlords and landladies intended cashing in on the Minstrels' success as Roy Winbow recalls: 'Everyone put their prices up for digs and we couldn't afford them'. They were inundated with offers, with over a hundred people writing to offer lodgings. Bob wrote to the local paper to thank them for running the story and to thank everyone who had responded. Great free publicity.

The problem - and the solution - were different in Norwich in 1973. Because of global petrol shortages, the cast needed to be close to the theatre, as the show finished too late for them to use public transport. The cast came up with a variety of answers. Four of them parked their caravans in the theatre car park, including

Head Minstrel Roy Winbow. He recalls, 'we loved it, it suited the kind of life we led perfectly. We were completely self-contained.' But others were more adventurous, led by principal Andy Cole who stayed on a boat, as did fifteen of them on a total of six boats on the river at Brundall, including Peter Kingston who had done the same two years earlier. Dancers Joan Illingworth and Tessa Blackburn said, 'when we heard about the boats, we just had to try it.'

Loyalty to George was so great that the touring company had very little changes in personnel. The show toured constantly, so the lure of permanent work also contributed to the majority staying put. This gave a real family feel to the cast which inevitably shone across the footlights and embraced the audiences. Soon offstage activities developed and the cast was quickly absorbed into the social and charitable life of wherever they were playing, particularly when it involved lengthy summer and Christmas seasons. They challenged local sides to cricket and rounders matches, organised by Minstrel and later principal Glyn Dawson. They played darts matches and opened fetes, attended garden parties and sang in midnight matinées.

Most cast members tried to get home at weekends if at all possible. Glyn, in particular, would set off in his trusty van, still in full costume and makeup, and drive home to Cardiff after the second show on Saturdays. But trying to get home from Aberdeen one weekend produced a memorable moment for both Glyn and resident comedian Stan Stennett. Both men liked to get home to South Wales at weekends, but could only manage this from places as far north as Aberdeen because Stan owned his own plane. One weekend, he and Glyn flew down to Cardiff. Stan recalls, 'We couldn't fly back until Monday afternoon because the weather was so awful. The first show started at 6pm, and I was the one who said, "Ladies and gentlemen, it's the *Black and White Minstrel Show*." Eventually, we left after lunch and were meant to fly to Edinburgh, but were diverted to RAF Leuchars, where we were told there was a train to Aberdeen at 4pm. We caught it by the skin of our teeth, only to discover it was a stopping train, so we got to Aberdeen about 5.40. I ran to the theatre, getting there just as the opening music was playing. I ran on, said my piece, then sat down for five minutes to get my breath back.' There's sadly no record of whether Glyn managed to get his makeup on in time!

Minstrel Magic

Loyalty extended to the specialist acts as well. George used the same ones time and time again, and they were equally happy to stay with the show. Comedians Stan Stennett and Leslie Crowther spent years of their career on stage and television with the Minstrels, as did jazzer George Chisholm. Stan took the Al Jolson role as well as producing his own spots in the touring company, though it was this that eventually caused him to leave the show. He told George that his face was getting raw after so many washes every night - twenty-six per night for his eight different parts in the show, including the Al Jolson spot. He quipped that 'it must have made me the cleanest comic in the business!' Don Maclean also spent years with the show in the 1970s, on TV, in London and on tour. The final comedian of any note was Keith Harris who combined the roles of comic and ventriloquist. Keith said, 'To be associated with success like that was absolutely incredible. I was inventive, they could see I was doing something different each week. It modernised the show.' George was always keen to have a ventriloquist in the stage company. Initially, this was Saveen and Daisy May, but Neville King quickly became the most famous ventriloquist with his Old Man act, remaining with the show for many seasons and marrying a Topper. Famous husband and wife xylophonist act, the Mistins, toured endlessly, lending an even greater family feel to the show when their daughter Dana became a Topper, eventually marrying Minstrel John Asher. Acrobats were also firm favourites, such as Warren, Devine and Sparks who went to Australia with the show as well, the Schaller Brothers, and the Seven Ashtons, a famous Australian acrobatic troupe.

Clem Vickery, who became a regular performer with the Minstrels on stage and television from 1971, blacking up for seven years, ran a group called Clem Vickery and the Vellum Stompers, whose banjo playing skills fitted in perfectly with the show's format. As he recalls, 'I was only seventeen but had been introduced to Ernest Maxin when I worked for Clifford Essex Music. When I joined, I was on £30 (£420) a week between the four of us which actually was poor money for the West End, but it was so good to be associated with the show, and I thought it might lead somewhere which it has. Thirty years later, I've never been out of work and people still book me specifically because of the Minstrel show.' After he started appearing in the television show, Clem recalls that '*Opportunity Knocks* rang me. They needed an extra act one week, and offered to pay me £100 (£1,400) per

Minstrel Magic

minute for a three-minute slot! The BBC agreed I could appear. We won the studio show and waited to see what would happen with the postal vote. I rang to check the following week and was told we were neck and neck with a New Zealand singer. I got lots of people to vote for me, but ITV said we didn't win. It was, of course, rigged so they wouldn't have to pay me again!'

It was thanks to George's personal intervention that Clem Vickery and his group were signed for the stage show when it opened at London's New Victoria Theatre in 1973. As Clem recalls, 'By now, all the speciality acts had been signed, so there was no room for us really, but George wanted us in the show.' So it was arranged that the group would appear blacked-up within the sequences, sitting on haystacks and pretending to play to the usual pre-recorded tape. However, this wasn't to be a success, at least from Clem's perspective. He 'hated it. It was soul-destroying, miming all the time. Musicians can't "play", like singers can "sing".' Clem did all sorts of things to relieve the monotony: 'I'd swap places with the drummer, just to stop the monotony. Once I was sitting on a hayrick, with the girls around me. I'd been to Tommy Cooper's joke shop in Slough and bought a severed finger. All the girls were looking loving and adoring while listening to me "playing". I suddenly said "ow", as if I'd hurt myself and let the severed finger drop into a Topper's lap! Somehow, she kept on smiling, and everyone else struggled to stop laughing.'

But perhaps the most problematic of the acts were those involving animals. The Wychwoods were a performing poodle act who joined the show several times over the years, often spending the intervening periods performing overseas. When they first joined the show, they had just returned from an appearance on the famous *Ed Sullivan Show* in the States. Although they'd only spent two days in America, the dogs still had to endure quarantine but had special dispensation to perform with the show. They stayed in RSPCA kennels and were taken by special transport every night to the theatre which became a quarantine area while they were there. They had to be confined to the dressing rooms, only let out twice a night for a walk in a walled back-court, and then rushed back to RSPCA kennels after the show. Fortunately, the only problems the poodles developed were upset stomachs which unfortunately happened while they were on stage. At the start of the next sequence, two Minstrels sang and danced their way off stage in its opening moments, returning with brooms to sweep up the mess. The audience were convulsed with laughter.

The audience was further amused by the poodles on a different occasion when the dogs caused chaos on stage. Roger Green recalls, 'During the *Romantica* sequence, we were on stage dressed in beautiful purple and white costumes and swaying to and fro while holding candelabra. We were suddenly aware that the audience were amused and had begun to laugh audibly. It appears that one of the poodles had escaped from the dressing room and was running amok on the stage. It took some time before the poodle was brought under control and returned to its sanctuary, but not before the audience had enjoyed its escapade of weaving in and out of the legs of the unsuspecting Minstrels.'

The friendly family feel of the show spread to the dogs and one year, the inevitable happened. One of the poodles gave birth backstage to a litter which unusually included one black and white puppy. All previous pups had been pure white, so they called this one *Jolson* and presented him to Dai Francis.

A greater threat to everyone in the company was the time floodwater burst from a manhole backstage and swamped the dressing rooms and a corridor. The entire performance was threatened, but in typical Mitchell/Luff style, a way was devised to keep the show going. The Fire Brigade, who had sent a pump rescue and a salvage tender, realised that the rising floodwater could endanger the electrical apparatus but that using a mechanical pump would have drowned out the music and the show would have had to stop. So the fire team formed a bucket chain to keep the water level safe until the final curtain. They also carried the Toppers to the stage over a line of duckboards. But the poodles provided their own emergency as they disappeared one by one down the manhole! Luckily the firemen rescued them too!

It wasn't just dogs that caused chaos. George hated bird acts but was persuaded to use an act called Anna-Lou and Maria, which involved Chihuahua dogs jumping through hoops, birds flying about the stage and large Alsatian dogs running around. The act culminated in a host of doves being released from a basket at the back of the upper circle. The birds would fly down to Anna-Lou and Maria on the stage who would deftly insert them in a basket. One opening night, the inevitable happened! The birds flew from the top of the theatre to the stage at the start of their act, but one over-excited bird 'spotted' George on the way, all over his brand new dress suit! 'I hate bird acts!' was Georges succinct comment.

He was probably to regret hiring this act even more as the season progressed. Minstrel Greg Oxnard remembers 'the minstrel number which followed ([the bird act] had a Spanish theme and it began with a single trumpet heralding the start of the *South of the Border Down Mexico Way* number. We all had to be completely static while the lights slowly came up behind the gauze and the lone trumpet played. The men were revealed frozen in suitably Spanish-like positions, and the women were in excruciating back bends complete with fans and mantillas. We had to hold this position for about thirty seconds while the gauze went up and everyone was in a fixed position. One of the Toppers Sharon Nicholls had a particularly large chest (which she hated because it made it really uncomfortable when doing certain dance moves). She was bent right back holding the Spanish pose when a lost dove flew down onto her chest and started to strut back and forth, pecking her chest and ruffling its feathers. Of course, we all started to laugh, and she did too, and the more she laughed, the more her chest bounced up and down, and the more active the bird became. But she couldn't move because of the freeze. The audience was transfixed by this bird and Sharon's mobile chest. Maybe they thought it was all part of the number?'

The television shows weren't exempt from animal problems either. One series used a macaw twice; the second time he appeared, the bird refused to say his lines as rehearsed and ended up doing what birds do all over the back of Leslie Crowther's costume.

CHAPTER 23

From the start, George was always a huge supporter of charities, particularly eye charities and local hospitals. He served on committees and never missed a chance to attend fetes or fundraising events, such as a Christmas Fair at the Manchester City Hall, where he met thirty-one children selected from the local Save the Children Fund Junior Club. George and the children toured the fair, after which he said that he would like to buy something for the children to use at the club. He selected a beautiful pedal motor car which was presented to the visitors who cheered loudly as they were assembled around the wishing well. He was equally supportive of local charities, saying, 'I enjoy living locally because people are prepared to give up their spare time to support a worthwhile cause. I don't get much spare time, but when I do, I make it my business to come along and support functions like this. I am impressed with the work that has gone into this fete, and I hope I can be present next year for the third year running.'

Reg Bracken was a long-term friend: 'I was a police officer stationed at New Malden and first met George and his wife through my police duties. They and their daily help Mary made me most welcome, and over a period of time, we became good friends. At the time of the Molesey floods, [1968], the local police raised money for the relief fund and George, together with a number of other local well-known people, agreed to sign autographs for 5p (£1) a go. After his first wife died, George introduced us to Dot, and she also made us feel so welcome. When we visited, George would sit one or other of our children on his knee and draw pictures for them on manuscript paper. They were very proud of their pictures from "Mr Mitchell". George was a lovely man, and we had some great times together. My wife, our girls and I were privileged to call him "friend". He is truly missed, but he lives on in his music and television recordings which, over many years have brought us tremendous pleasure.'

But there was also a purely practical side to this philanthropy. As Dot explains, 'It was expected of you to do this sort of work then, but George would have wanted to do what he could to help anyway. He always allowed anything for charity, as long as it was through him. And there was another practical reason. George saw it as a good rehearsal hall. You could see how a song worked, then you could change it around if necessary.' So invitations to appear at midnight matinées, garden parties and charity concerts were quickly accepted.

This was one area where George and Bob were in complete agreement. Bob expected the singers to do all they could to support charities, particularly during the long summer and Christmas seasons, saying, 'Life isn't just a playground. My youngsters [the casts] go into hospitals and old people's homes and do their bit, and I believe it makes them more responsible. The Army taught me to be responsible for others, and it's one thing I insist on in the cast. I don't have to promote the thing - it just snowballs. But I believe they are less selfish as a result. I'm very proud of them.' Known for his extreme parsimony, Bob was also more than happy to give albums and tickets away and always made a great fuss of the winners, entertaining them royally when they visited the Victoria Palace.

Sometimes supporting a charity caused huge logistical problems. Take one Sunday in 1951. They appeared in the *British Film Festival 1951* from the stage of His Majesty's Theatre, in which all the stars appeared and re-enacted their roles, rather than using film clips. Big as this show was, the logistics of this day must have been completely horrendous as the same singers were also appearing at the Drury Lane Theatre in a charity performance for the Equity Club. This five-hour show starred the tops in entertainment - Jessie Matthews, Elizabeth Welch, Evelyn Laye and Stanley Holloway, among others. It contained extracts from various shows and musicals, such as *Bitter Sweet, White Horse Inn, Happy & Glorious* and *The Admirable Crichton*. Several other acts were also doubling up at both Drury Lane and His Majesty's, so a fleet of cars was arranged which took stars from one to the other as their acts ended, often passing on the way.

Fundraising for disasters was always strongly supported. John, Dai, Tony, plus Head Minstrel Arthur Lewis, were all vice-presidents of the Gentlemen Songsters, a choir based in the Rhondda's Tonyrefail, which they'd 'joined' after a party from the Victoria Palace travelled to Treorchy in the Rhondda, to play against Cardiff RFC. Organised by Arthur, the match was in aid of

Minstrel Magic

the Cambrian Colliery Disaster of 1965 when thirty-one men had died. A year later, the Songsters were fundraising for their proposed American tour, and Arthur offered a cricket match. Richard Williams, the Songsters' Musical Director, said, 'This is a wonderful gesture. They have proved the most active and helpful vice-presidents.' A few weeks previously, Tony Mercer had provided a raffle prize - show tickets, a backstage tour to meet the stars and hotel accommodation. Arthur Lewis visited again in May, bringing a message from John, Dai and Tony saying, 'We are all very proud of your tremendous achievements in reaching the semi-finals of the BBC European Male Voice competition.'

The Minstrels were deeply affected by the terrible Aberfan disaster in October 1966, when a coal waste tip collapsed onto a school, killing 144 people, 116 of them children. The cast felt it particularly deeply, because the night before the tragedy, two coaches had travelled from the Aberfan area to see the show in Bristol. Glyn remembered, 'I'd seen them in the foyer and had sung to them. Next day we heard one of them had been killed and a 14-year-old had had his leg amputated.' The Minstrels immediately collected for the Disaster Fund and discussed plans for a soccer match between the Minstrels and the TV All Stars before a gala show in aid of the disaster fund. Initially, they intended staging this show straightaway but felt, 'It will take a long time for the grief to wash away and we don't want to inflict our merriment on people who are not receptive.' Head Minstrel Arthur Lewis visited Merthyr in November to make initial arrangements for the show, now planned for the following spring. It was hoped local boy Glyn Dawson and Swansea-born Dai Francis would star in the show, the main aim of which was to express sympathy. As Arthur said, 'We want to show the people we feel for them. The money raised is secondary.' However, Glyn remembered, 'Later we had a message from Bob to say we couldn't do the tribute show because the touring show's commitments were too great.' It's rather odd they weren't allowed to do the show; Bob had allowed others, such as the one for the Cambrian Disaster Fund the year before, and it was very unlike him to ignore such a publicity opportunity.

Once the Minstrels got into their stride and were constantly touring Britain, fund-raising really got into its stride. Initially, they played sporting fixtures - mainly football and cricket - against local sides. Often they persuaded sporting stars to join them, such as one visit to Blackpool when Keith Leggett, who was the 'sporting Minstrel', succeeded in signing a friend of his, Barry Knight, the Essex and England all-rounder, for the Minstrels' cricket match against Great Eccleston in early August. The teas laid on by the local teams had the added advantage of feeding the Minstrels and Toppers who were surviving on very low wages. Roy remembers these Sundays vividly: 'I don't know if we ever won a game but that was not the point of playing. Glan was our demon wicketkeeper, and we had some good batsmen and fielders in Peter Pennington, Peter Clare and Richard Archer. Our secret weapon was our deadly bowler John Asher, he never missed an opposing player. We were always treated very well by the local cricket clubs, which were sometimes a fair distance from our base. The high spot was the afternoon tea breaks where the team's wives would put on a spread for us that would sustain an army for a week. Lots of the Toppers came with us and usually went around collecting or selling raffle tickets; that always went down well with the local studs. We didn't let the girls play the game, feeling it was better to keep the injuries down to those inflicted by the Minstrels.'

Just occasionally, these matches were threatened from unexpected quarters. In 1968 the Lord's Day Observance Society called the police to a match which was being played on a Sunday between the Victoria Palace soccer team and QPR players. The police took names and threatened prosecution. Keith Leggett, who was Captain of the Victoria Palace team, said he believed they were being summonsed under the Sunday Observance Acts of 1625 and 1780 which carried a maximum penalty of three shillings and fourpence (£2.73)! He observed, 'It all seems so silly to me. We've been playing soccer and cricket on Sundays for the past eight years - the funds are all for charity.' But support came from unexpected quarters too. The Secular Society condemned the attitude of the Observance Society and encouraged everyone to do all they could to ensure that the Sunday Entertainment Bill, currently before Parliament, was passed.

One early charity which received long-term support from the touring show was Cystic Fibrosis Research. After they learned that Ann Wetherby, a young cystic fibrosis sufferer, was a fan of the show, they decided that the money collected from their cricket matches throughout one summer season was to be given to research into Cystic Fibrosis. Keith, Derry Daniels and Susan Lynne visited Ann in hospital. She was so excited when they visited and gave her presents including a Minstrel doll that she could hardly speak. 'I have seen them on television, but I never thought I would meet them,' she said. By the season's end, they had reached their target of raising over £500 (£7,300) for the charity, having played eleven cricket matches - they won six - two darts matches - they lost both - and enjoying quite a few social evenings and coffee mornings.

Gradually as the years progressed, one charity dominated their fundraising. One summer season, it became public knowledge that the mother of one cast member Peter Kingston, had been blind for over thirty years. Four local women immediately began organising a coffee morning for the company to raise money for a guide dog for her. The dog was estimated to cost £250 (£4,000), and they hoped to raise more than that to get more guide dogs. After the cast started collecting silver paper, members of the public inundated the theatre with bags of foil. Peter explained, 'We sold it to a woman in York, so anyone who went over to York had to take his car absolutely loaded with the stuff.' By September the silver paper collections alone had raised between £30 (£500) and £40 (£700), and the coffee morning raised another £88/10/- (£1,500).

The success of the first coffee morning gave the cast the idea of holding one at the theatre, so on September 10, they served coffee and biscuits on the flat roof of the theatre to raise the remaining £20 (£330) they needed to get the guide dog and to start a running fund for another. They also took collections during the two houses of the show and raised so much that they managed to sponsor two dogs, one to be called *Scarborough Minstrel*, and the second *Topper*.

Such efforts were deeply appreciated by the towns where the show was resident. Towards the end of one run in Scarborough, the *Scarborough Evening News* published two letters. Allan Branagan, Vicar of Newby, thanked them for everything they had done: 'I want to pay tribute to the concern and interest shown by the company for the countless activities beyond the confines of the stage on which they act. There must be very few good causes in our neighbourhood which have not benefited by the willingness of these young men and women to join in all that went on, whereby they provided pleasure for those members of the public who came, acted as perfect guests to their hosts, and swelled the coffers of the charity concerned. All this they must have undertaken at no small cost to their personal life and pleasure. Put this alongside the zeal and reliability which they displayed at such events, and we have a great deal to rejoice over.' The second letter, from Constance Ogden, echoed this theme: 'May I say a big thank you to all the members of the show for all their kindness and work so willingly given to help local charities and coffee mornings, cricket matches, etc. I am glad we have had the chance to help their guide dog fund. It is good they have passed their £250 mark. May they soon reach their next target.'

The Guide Dogs charity remained a favourite of the Minstrels. When the show was in Eastbourne, they once again decided, driven by Head Minstrel Douggie Pearson, to hold a good-cause coffee morning at Devonshire Park, the entertainment complex containing the theatre. This event, the first of its kind staged by a summer season company at the theatre, turned out to be one of the most successful charity events ever staged in Eastbourne. The company had hoped that five hundred people would attend; in the end, nearly two thousand people paid two shillings to enter, with queues snaking around the complex and people overflowing into the theatre foyer and the park itself. Coffee and biscuits were served by the Minstrels and Toppers, and Minstrels and other company artistes, including the Three Monarchs, served as waiters. They also manned various stalls and sideshows, which did a roaring trade. Inside the Congress restaurant, queues formed for the palmist booth run by Minstrel Chris Fox. Minstrel embroidery expert Michael Farndale had made twenty cushions for the event and sold them for £33 (£540). Toppers Mandy Zebcuikas and Jackie Murdoch sold kisses for 6d. Douggie's golden retriever Simba proved a huge draw, as he wandered around with a collecting box strapped to his back – he collected £30 (£500)! Ultimately they collected £300 (£5,000) which was split between their Guide Dog Fund, which had now raised enough to support two more dogs, and the Christ Church Tower Restoration Fund. Sensibly the company had decided to support one local charity as well as their own chosen beneficiary. A supporting collection during both intervals one night raised another £250 (£4,000), with the total amounts being handed over to the Guide Dogs Association by Douggie on stage at the end of the season. The Minstrels asked that this third dog be called *Luff*, after Bob; the Association in return handed over a framed photo of *Eastbourne Topper*, one of the other dogs they had funded.

Minstrel Magic

Two years later, Douggie wanted to repeat the successful coffee morning of two years previously. He expanded his plans this year, enlisting the help and co-operation of the local council in getting the use of the Winter Gardens, next to the theatre, for a Saturday morning fair in September. Everyone pitched in with a wide variety of ideas and odd items, and most of their spare time was taken up pursuing their own projects for the fair. Mitchell Maid Anne-Elizabeth Stephenson came up with the idea of making little minstrels and Toppers out of odd pieces of cloth. Both the public at large and the show's wardrobe department provided an amazing array of material, from black velvet and cloth to lace and gold lame. Any sequins that fell off costumes were secreted away to use on the dolls. According to Roy, 'Anne proved that not only was she a very good dancer and singer but she was an exceptional seamstress, as she designed and plotted the outline pattern for the bodies and the trousers and jackets. She also cut, sewed and machined most of the pieces together. The rest of us were at her command and had the delightful job of stuffing the things with kapok. These sessions became known as stuffing parties (no comment), lots of boys and girls came round to help, and the final result was incredible. We made over a hundred, and they sold very well.' Support from the community was amazing. The theatre received a steady flow of gifts and donations beforehand, such as two feather beds to fill the cushions Minstrel Michael Farndale made, and the offer of free icing of the Minstrel logo onto a Dundee cake baked by another Minstrel.

The whole event was a roaring success. As two years earlier, there were astonishing crowd scenes, with the public queuing before opening time and continuing to pour in as the morning progressed. Ticket sellers ran out of tickets, and they had to open extra doors to allow people in. Ultimately two thousand people attended. Douggie's dog again came along to collect for his favourite good cause! Tony Everts-Taff and Suzanne Jones sold kisses, and there was a huge Minstrel dummy as a prize in one competition. One resident said, 'I think it is extraordinarily good of them to give their time like this.' Another said, 'It's a splendid do. They are delightful people, and there is a wonderful relationship between show and town.'

More money for the Guide Dog Fund was raised backstage throughout this season. They persuaded the new publican of the old pub the Lamb, around the corner from the theatre, to empty his cellar of any stock he didn't want, which the cast raffled off at the theatre. As Roy Winbow remembers, 'Fortunately he was also a fan of the show, so a few complimentary seats sealed the deal and allowed us to hold weekly raffles backstage for some, at times, fairly potent brews.' So much money was raised throughout the season that they exceeded all expectations. They had hoped to raise enough for the full purchase and training of one more guide dog. In the end, they raised £1,000 (£15,000) and bought and trained four more guide dogs, one of whom was named *Mitch* in honour of George Mitchell. Roy, later to be Head Minstrel himself, says, 'It was a true tribute to Douggie and his organising abilities and dedication. I can truthfully state that Douggie was the best head boy for a chorus I ever worked with and I could never have followed that act, no matter how hard I tried.'

As well as their chosen Guide Dogs charity, the Minstrels always chose a local charity to support. While at Eastbourne in 1982, the St Wilfrid's Hospice Appeal was the lucky recipient. The pre-season charity show, dubbed the public dress rehearsal, had raised £500 (£1,700) which was handed over on opening night. A collection point was set up in the theatre foyer, and in less than a week, it had raised £1,000 (£3,400), which by the end of June had topped £1500 (£5,100). Their target of £3,500 (£12,000) was boosted by a couple of coffee mornings, for which Production Manager Sandy McFarlane launched an urgent SOS for gifts and prizes. The event was widely supported and raised £515 (£1,800) for the appeal, which now stood at over £6,000 (£21,000). Most of the cast visited the hospice, and the final cheque, handed over by Head Minstrel Michael Farndale and Head Topper Dorothy Barsham on the show's closing night, was for an astonishing £8,226 (£28,500).

Most company members took part in these fundraising events which produced a lot of fun for everyone. But a dedicated core of Minstrels and Toppers encouraged a more serious side to their seasons by linking up with local churches. The theatre always had a resident chaplain so it was easy to arrange matters and most seasons ended up with a religious service at the theatre's chosen church. The service was usually arranged by the Minstrels and Toppers themselves who often performed specially rehearsed numbers. In 1967, a dozen cast members delayed leaving Coventry for a day so that they could lead the worship at the People's

Minstrel Magic

Service at the Cathedral. The Toppers performed *Message in Mime* to illustrate *The Happy Prince,* and seven Minstrels plus one Mitchell Maid sang Bach's choral prelude *In Exaltation My Heart Rejoices*. Freddie Williams who had arranged the event said, 'This is not a stunt or a sort of celestial *Black and White Minstrel Show*. We are very sincere about this. We are giving thanks for the ability we have.'

In January 1974 in Norwich, they chose to do a similar service along the theme that, just as the Wise Men from the East were welcomed at the cradle of Christ, so all men of whatever race or colour, nation or class were always welcome because to Jesus Christ there are no barriers. At the end of the last reading, a small child began to whimper. At that moment, two Minstrels stepped forward to sing *There but for Fortune* which begins *Hush little baby don't you cry*. By the end, the child had stopped crying and didn't cry again, which Canon Westwood, who was also the theatre chaplain, commented indicated the power of music. People usually packed these services for a chance to see the Minstrels in a different light, so such services often included a fundraising element to swell the coffers of the Minstrels' charity appeal. One such service at Eastbourne, attended by more than 500 people, raised £225 (£800) for their charity appeal for the hospice.

The BBC got to hear about the religious side of the companies and occasionally took advantage of the Minstrels' presence in a town to use them in a religious broadcast. This tradition had started quite a few years earlier in 1955 when in quite a departure, BBC Television broadcast *The Epilogue* from Blackpool, with 'evening prayers conducted by the Rev Geoffrey Gower-Jones, the Actors' Church Union Chaplain at Blackpool, assisted by Variety artistes working in the town'. The choir's singing must have added considerably to the beauty of the occasion. Surprised critics nevertheless thought the experiment a success. The *Church of England Newspaper* reported that 'Mr Arthur Askey read the lesson and the George Mitchell Choir, who are known for their swing-singing, sang the hymns....congratulations to the BBC for successfully using jolt tactics in a religious programme and for doing so in a quiet, reverent way, with no trace of sensationalism.' The *Birmingham Weekly* agreed: 'It must have surprised many viewers last Sunday night to find Arthur Askey reading the lessons during *The Epilogue* and the George Mitchell Choir - in the choir. But it was another excellent example of the power for good that can be transmitted among so many thousands through the medium of television.'

Now the BBC was back and taking advantage of the Minstrels' presence. A special *Songs of Praise* was broadcast in 1969 from the parish church of St Martin-on-the-Hill, Scarborough, featuring John, Dai and Tony, who, with the Minstrels, sang *Praise to the Holiest in the Height, At the Name of Jesus, Kumbayah, What a Wonderful World, Dear Lord and Father of Mankind, He who would Valiant be, Guide me, O Thou Great Redeemer, Jacob's Ladder, Were You There?, Christ in Glory Reigning* and *Onward Christian Soldiers*. The choir was conducted by George himself. The BBC liked this programme, thinking it provided a good answer to ITV's *Stars on Sunday*. Of course, it nearly didn't happen when Equity got involved, but the union soon agreed that as long as there was no contractual obligation for the singers to turn up, there would be no standard fees payable. However, the choir could turn up for free, after which the BBC could make a payment if it so wished!

The programme was a hit with press and public alike. Papers all over the country printed letters from viewers praising the show, and both George and the BBC were inundated with praise. Typical was a letter from Mrs D Berry of Ilford who wrote, 'A really entertaining half-hour. The Minstrels were never better, and one could see the congregation were thoroughly enjoying themselves too. How sorry I was when it ended, it really made my day.' Miss M Lunn suggested that George should 'make a record of it'. In fact, he did just this in 1975, when the choir released *Glory Glory Hallelujah*, a collection of 'twelve sacred songs ranging from hymn-book favourites and spirituals to chorales and religious ballads'. The popular *Onward Christian Soldiers* was included as was *Sound Ye Trumpets, Jesu Joy of Man's Desiring* and *The Battle Hymn of the Republic*.

CHAPTER 24

The Minstrels dominated the BBC's schedules - and everyone's entertainment - throughout the 1960s. In the days before video recorders and catch-up TV, it wasn't unknown for people to refuse social invitations for the Saturdays the Minstrels were on TV and event organisers knew better than to arrange their event for such a Saturday. Though occasionally it worked the other way around. One viewer to ITV's famous quiz show *Take Your Pick*, who had entered their Box 13 draw, wrote to the quiz saying she would be out on a particular Friday night when her number might be called. She ended her letter, which host Michael Miles read out on air, by saying, 'Should you wish to phone me during your programme, would you please be good enough to phone me in the audience at the Victoria Palace?' One wonders how they could have done this in the days before mobile phones. In any case, Miles commented, 'I'd be delighted to, but I'd hate to be responsible for stopping a show that has had such a long run.'

The highlight of the Christmas schedules was the Minstrel show, as whole families settled down around the set to enjoy their favourite programme.

1967 marked the tenth anniversary of the very first Minstrel show at Earls Court. The BBC honoured the show in an hour-long programme on radio when Leslie Crowther told *The Story of the Black and White Minstrels*, covering these first ten years of their existence. The final show in the 1967 television series on August 19 was a 'highlights' show. Broadcast almost exactly ten years after the very first show, it brought back Leslie Crowther as a special guest. In what was their 102nd television performance, the Minstrels featured an opening sequence which reprised many of the songs used in that first show. The second segment was taken straight from the 1961 winning Golden Rose of Montreux show, and it was followed by a sequence of requests. In a unique conducted sequence, George put together snippets from their most popular conducted songs; starting with *Old Ark*, it continued with *Old MacDonald, Clementine, Michael, My Bonny, Dry Bones* and

Minstrel Magic

Without a Song. Ironically, one of Leslie Crowther's contributions was a skit in which a BBC official failed to find the Golden Rose they had won six years earlier. This was to come true prophetically years later as the BBC did its utmost to airbrush the show out of history.

However, in 1967, the BBC was still firmly behind its star show. The Board of Management paid tribute to the 'dedicated work of George Inns during a successful run which was now ten years old'. The Head of Variety Light Entertainment Television also emphasised the very high professional standard of 'his work as producer of one of the best-directed shows on television. He knows how to inspire designers and technical staff to do their best work because he cares about this as well.' They all agreed it was a magnificent finale to a superb series.

But as the Sixties wore on, the press gradually turned against the television show, although the stage show continued to receive plaudits wherever it played. The television shows were seen as tired. Despite George's efforts, critics thought nothing had changed. But viewers still loved it, and audience research still produced exceptionally high response rates. The show was always used to mark important events. On July 20, 1969, a momentous day in broadcasting history, the BBC showed a *Black and White Minstrel Show* as a prelude to the BBC's coverage of the moon landings. One show went out on an Election Night providing, according to the *Stage*, 'a delightful prelude before the highlight of last Thursday evening, the election results. The George Mitchell Singers shine more in this programme than in any other. I found last Thursday's programme easy to watch...charming to listen to and with the right touches of humour. An excellent show this.'

But had the show reached the end of its life? A saviour was, however, on the horizon, in the form of colour television. Still at the forefront of innovation as ever, both Georges were looking towards colour television which, George Inns said, 'contrary to our title, will bring out a rainbow of colours'. Everyone including the BBC was taking it for granted that the show would be around for years to come.

As long ago as two years earlier, in January 1965, the BBC had experimentally filmed the Minstrels in colour in a trial run for their new colour cameras. The test runs went well, and everyone was thrilled to discover that colour television made the show look like 'a million dollars'. George reported 'once you've seen the show in colour, black and white looks dull and stale'. In a move which underlined the BBC Board of Management's support, the new Minstrel series was chosen to be the first programme officially shown in colour on BBC2 on December 3, though it meant once again risking the move from the Television Theatre into the biggest studio at Television Centre. Now audiences at home would be able to see what theatre audiences had been privileged to see for the past seven years.

At the end of the final show of the 1967 series, the last made in black and white and specifically for BBC1, Leslie Crowther announced that they would return 'in the autumn on BBC2 in colour which can't be bad, can it?' But viewers were outraged, writing to George and the BBC in their thousands. Many areas couldn't get BBC2 at all. Where it was available, less than 100,000 people could watch in colour, as few people could afford new televisions. Colour sets cost about £300 (£4,000). It was estimated that there were only twenty thousand colour sets in use, many of which were still in dealers' showrooms. No one was quite certain about its impact. Much like when television had started originally, many critics didn't expect the new-fangled invention to last. Ansells' Brewery didn't share their pessimism as they had installed colour TV in some of their pubs. The licensee of the Raven in Coventry said, 'They were queuing up as if they were going to the cinema. This television is drawing in still more people, especially shows like the *Black and White Minstrels*.' However, the licensee of the Red Lion in Rugby reported no change: 'Unless there are lots and lots of *Black and White Minstrel Show*s on BBC2, I don't think colour television will make the slightest difference to the trade.'

Many pensioners, like S Beaumont and Grace Wale, were devastated that 'we shall not be seeing your fine show again'. The *Sunday Sun* gave a guinea for the best comment of the week to F Mitchell for writing, 'I am shattered to learn that BBC1 is to be deprived of one of its best winter shows. The majority of old people can't afford the changeover, so they are being penalised. Surely it would be possible to repeat it the following night on BBC1?'

Once again, everyone was stepping into unknown territory, driven by fears that the move was the wrong one for the show. George Inns approached the use of colour cautiously: 'I aim at contrast from one sequence to the next. I'm not trying to be colour-mad but will keep a certain dignity about it. The secret is delicate pastel hues with perhaps one outstanding colour in each scene. I just want people to see the show as it is now but in colour which makes it twice as enchanting.' In the end, apart from the opening sequence, the rest of the first show used pinks, greys and silver for the girls' costumes, while the sets and the men remained dressed in black and white. George praised the BBC for 'performing miracles on its budget to maintain the standard of the shows, and the coming of colour has bumped costs through the roof'. Most of the extra cost per show - a third more on the budget - went on stronger lighting, which raised the studio temperature to 105F!

But once again, their fears were groundless. The press fell in love with the show all over again, and everyone breathed a sigh of relief. Many critics applauded the restrained use of colour, ratifying George Inns' decision to tone it down. The *Daily Mirror* thought 'the technicians are to be congratulated for their avoidance of throwing in every colour they could find and instead, making much more impact in a subtle kind of way'. BBC2 had shown *Billy Smart's Circus* in colour which most reviewers thought dire and the colours 'so flashy and artificial', while the later Barbra Streisand programme was also condemned for its flashy use of colour. The *Sun* wrote, 'colour is at its most ravishing when it's black and white. The Minstrels cooled it with some straight black and white routines, indulging itself no further than a little glitter of silver here, a small dazzle of diamante there. If you want to see colour television at its finest, take a look at their next show.'

However, colour brought about a whole new set of headaches for designers and producers alike. George explained, 'For instance, in a normal show if someone loses a piece of costume or headdress, something can always be knocked up. As long as it's the same shape, nobody notices. But in colour, everything has to match, every mark or flaw in the costumes and sets will show up. There are incredible problems with ostrich feathers and hair pieces under the much stronger lighting, which searches out the tiniest variation in colour.'

Makeup also had to change from black to brown which produced unexpected results. Whereas the singers had been quite anonymous under the previous black makeup, the new colour, coupled with new colour cameras, seemed to highlight the singers' features, making identification, particularly of the soloists, very much easier for viewers at home. But many were less happy: 'I do not like the white lips, the change tends to make it look as if they are wearing false teeth over their own!' Even George had to be made up now. He needed a dull pancake, not only on his face and neck but also on the backs of his hands as they were in close-up while he was conducting.

A newspaper cartoon in mid-August, of a couple buying a colour TV, shows the far-reaching effects of the Minstrels on the national consciousness: 'Yes, it's lovely, but will we be able to get the Black and White Minstrels on it?' The *New Statesman* seemed surprised to find itself supporting the show: 'No other light entertainment show has been quite so successful as this one, and no other long-running TV programme has revealed so few signs of staleness or kept anything like so much genuine gusto. The show has the wit to appear fresh every Saturday night while actually remaining almost exactly the same. It cloaks its rigidity in a swirl of attractive bustle. It makes its wheezing elderly gasps look like the breathlessness of youthful zest. The programme's pace is astonishing. It only needed the arrival of colour TV to make it as permanently irritating a part of British life as Black Rod himself.'

Such was the difference that colour made, that George was overwhelmed with offers to take the show to America, Canada, South Africa and most Continental countries, as well as Japan where they had now seen the television shows. The Japanese said they 'simply must have the show visit them' and talks were taking place to send the Australian company to South Africa. Perhaps strangest of all was an offer from the States. Although Broadway managements had been over in force to sign them up, extolling the show as 'a gem' with 'nothing like it in America', nothing eventually came of this. But George Inns visited Los Angeles in 1968 and returned with a remarkable feather in his cap. Despite the race riots throughout the States, and the assassination of Martin Luther King, with the explosive race situation made still more so by the Presidential election campaign of Governor George Wallace, Las Vegas wanted the show. George was invited by the Flamingo Club to bring over the entire cast for live performances - black faces, striped costumes, the lot! The owners said they were happy to risk the consequences. But despite all this interest, nothing ever came of such offers, partly because George felt it impossible to maintain his impeccable standards with companies spread all over the world, though Bob was also fearful he'd lose control.

The show may have been given a new lease of life with the advent of colour television, but storm clouds began to gather elsewhere, ignited by the revealing nature of the new makeup. From the very first show, there had been those who had criticised the perceived 'racist' aspect of the makeup. Most press and viewers had dismissed such allegations as nonsense, citing the theatrical traditions of makeup, used from the earliest days to transform perfectly ordinary-looking actors into beautiful young girls, high-handed matrons, villainous rogues or kings of England. Indeed for centuries, only men were allowed on the stage and so had to transform themselves via makeup into women. Since the late seventeenth century, actors have used white makeup to transform themselves into Pierrot characters, much as the Kabuki theatres in Japan still do, and no one deems this to be racist against white people or women.

Transforming makeup is also traditional outside the theatre. Morris dancers, particularly around the border between Wales and England, still black their faces. Explanations for its use vary from evoking the faces of miners covered in coal dust to chimney sweeps covered in soot, or poachers blackening up to conceal themselves in darkness, or workers disguising themselves from their lords, or poor farm workers hiding their faces while begging in winter when asking for money was illegal.

Recently, however, our hypersensitivity around this issue has caused some spectators to hurl abuse at such dancers, accusing them of being racist, without knowing much if anything about the true origins. This has led some festivals to ban troops using full black-face makeup, in a bid to appease these outraged groups, though inevitably this has led to others complaining angrily that their old traditions are being ignored and forgotten.

In the Netherlands, Black Pete is Santa Claus' helper. He has hundreds in attendance at the annual parades which mark the start of Christmas in Holland. In 2016 critics questioned whether the makeup was racist and many participants toned it down to a dark grey, but over 90% of Dutch people questioned said it was merely a traditional part of Christmas with nothing racist about it.

One theory as to its origin is that it is linked with chimney sweeps who helped Santa deliver presents down chimneys.

In South Africa, the Cape Town Minstrel Carnival, or Kaapse Klopse, originated with the visit to South Africa of Christy's Minstrels in 1862. For decades, black participants would black their faces and add the traditional white around the eyes and mouth. The very competitive festival is now a huge tourist attraction in January. One of its features is still the makeup which, although now expanded to include every colour under the sun, still features a majority of whitened eyes and mouths.

Back in the 1960s, the issue of the 'racist' aspect of the makeup continued to puzzle people. The *Bristol Evening Post* felt 'for reasons which I find hard to comprehend, there are not a few people who take exception to this show. They talk about shades of Uncle Tom because a handful of pleasant white singers cover their faces in something black. As though that would cause an upswell of prejudice. With all the white girls involved, it looks more like an attempt at furthering the cause of integration. No, they are nothing more than light entertainment.'

People remain puzzled to this day. 'So blacking up to play a black man is racist?' asks Roy Winbow. 'By that logic, only gay actors can play gays, otherwise it's homophobic? Is straight Eric McCormack homophobic for playing the gay Will in *Will and Grace*? What about drag artistes? Are they offensive to women? What about Andrew Sachs playing Manuel in *Fawlty Towers*? Does that make him racist for pretending to be Spanish? And whereas the Minstrels only extolled the virtues of black men and wonderful music, it could easily be argued that Manuel poked fun at the Spanish. Why is it racist for a white man to play a black man but not homophobic for a straight man to play a gay? Why isn't it equally racist for a Briton is play a Spaniard and turn him into a figure of fun? And what about *Come Fly With Me*? Why is no one complaining about Matt Lucas blacking up to play a Caribbean woman, and even worse, portray her as fat, lazy and idle? If this is still acceptable, why is it not all right for the Minstrels to portray black men as brilliant singers and dancers with no hint at all of mockery? Why is it acceptable if it's done in the name of comedy with its inherent mockery but unacceptable if it's done in a musical context?' As Don Maclean said, 'The Minstrels in no way ridiculed black people any more than panto dames ridicule women or Frank Spencer and Mr Bean ridicule people with learning difficulties.'

Back in 1967, critics raged that the show encouraged people to view blacks as 'capering simpletons'. Supporters strongly refuted this claim, arguing that the show involved some of the best music produced over the past century. It also introduced Britons to the idea not only of blacks as a normal part of a population unused to this, but also of integration between whites and blacks, particularly in terms of inter-racial relationships. It was strongly argued that the show was gorgeous to look at and to listen to, leaving audiences in a better place, so what could possibly be insulting about any of that? The men danced and sang beautifully, the sets were glorious and as for the girl dancers.....if anything, it was argued, it could do nothing but enhance the general population's view of a different race.

But the ever-critical *Daily Mail* sneered, 'How far-reaching the extra information conveyed by colour can be was indicated in the *Brown and Pink Minstrel Show* last night. The function of the black makeup was to confirm anonymity and thence speed. In colour, the anonymity goes; pointless, the brown looks silly and rather nasty.' Typically the *Guardian* went on the attack again: 'More offensive and a fault which is heightened by colour is the sight of white men imitating jolly chocolate-coloured coons. This is really offensive to coloured people.' However, the *Evening Standard* was supportive: 'One niggle advanced by some critics was that the chocolate colour of the male singers made the show an even more offensive anti-Negro show than it had been. The thinking is shallow. This light-hearted show depends on the songs that are sung, and most of them have the rhythm, exuberance, atmosphere of the American South. Eliminate the traditional minstrel element, and you change the show into something entirely different. Those who argue that the show should be banned are in the same league as those who protest about *The Merchant of Venice* and *Oliver Twist*, and those who booed Synge's *Playboy of the Western World* because of its picture of Irishmen. Indeed if anyone had cause to protest about this innocuous and pleasing entertainment, it would be the white racist who should be apoplectic about those beautiful white girls being fondled by their pseudo-Negro companions - and obviously loving it.' SE Bushnell wrote to the *Spectator*, 'Surely nothing but the highest reflection is cast upon West Indians by this world-acclaimed show, and anyone who thinks otherwise must indeed have a warped mind.'

Mixed race relationships were still seen as the greatest taboo, with white girls being stigmatised if they were seen with a black man. Twenty years earlier, matters had been different. The government's Mass Observation project, started during the war, recorded great competition among young white factory girls to dance with blacks because of their superb sense of rhythm. Now here was a television programme showing just that, week after week. But dancing with them and marrying them were seen as completely different things, though the show played its part in making people accustomed to seeing such pairings. Even so, the BBC ran into trouble with many viewers when in one 'wedding' sequence, a Topper bride was seen 'marrying' a Minstrel groom. This was a step too far for many of the audience, and BBC sensitivities ensured that it was never repeated, though obviously George and the cast had no problem with it.

Every previous protest had been exceptionally minor and easily countered. But in 1967 in a move that shocked both Georges and the BBC, a more serious threat arose. The Campaign Against Racial Discrimination (CARD) presented the BBC with a petition signed by two hundred people, requesting that the show be withdrawn for its misrepresentation of black people. CARD had been created by a number of middle-class Caribbeans, including show business personalities and white liberals and clergy, after Martin Luther King's tour of UK in 1964. But it had no roots in any community and was now on the point of collapse, proving there was as yet no appetite among blacks to create a national organisation. 'It depicts my race as singing, dancing, laughing, idiotic people,' said Clive West who organised the petition. 'The show provides a hideous impersonation, is offensive and causes distress to most coloured people.' Its chairman Jamaican Dr David Pitt said, 'All (the show) is intended to do is to caricature coloured people and stereotype them.' Pressed by reporters, he soon agreed, however, that it was probably an exaggeration to say it caused distress to most coloured people.

George was shocked by the allegations: 'The petition came as a shock to me. When there are so many things you could pick on in the way of racial discrimination...well, I'm a bit surprised they jumped on this. You could go out and get two hundred signatures that there shouldn't be mixed bathing in the Serpentine. I don't think it amounts to much. There's not the slightest suggestion of anything to run down coloured people in the show. Until this cropped up, I don't suppose any of us really thought about it. It was just like clown's makeup. This may sound like a publicity story, but I've never had a letter from a coloured person saying they were offended. In some towns, we've had hundreds of coloured people in the audience, and they're not coming to be offended. Unless someone plants it in their minds that we're taking the mickey, I don't think they are going to object at all.' Dot recalls that 'I think he was a little bit hurt, in fact I know he was. It had never cropped up before, it would never have entered his head and I know for sure it didn't enter anybody else's.'

Certainly, the rest of the cast were equally shocked. Dai Francis was later to say, 'At the time, you must remember these ideas were looked upon almost as the lunatic fringe.' Keith Leggett says, 'To be honest, we were innocent about that. We were providing entertainment, and if we were going to take the racist aspect, all I can say is it's an insult to the British public who turned up in their droves to see the show, including black people who did enjoy it.' Principal Bob Hunter was equally adamant that the show was never meant to be racist: 'I think a lot of people wondered why it would offend when the whole of the West Indian cricket team would go into the Victoria Palace and watch the show.' Leslie Crowther went on record as saying that 'from the racial point of view I can only tell you that some of the greatest fans were the West Indian cricket team who sat in the front row and adored the show. Wes Hall actually laughed about it, and he was a feared West Indian fast bowler, and I think probably a clear-thinking man. He always used to say all he needed was a bit of toothpaste around his mouth, and he could join us because he was quite a good singer. So I can't see the problem. I just think everyone is so oversensitive these days that you can't say anything about anything anymore.' John Boulter also recalls the West Indians: 'The entire West Indian cricket team came into our dressing room at the Victoria Palace and we all had great fun together. Indeed it was that other great West Indian cricketer Sir Leary Constantine, speaking out in defence of the show, who said it was the most wonderful part of integration and coined the phrase *The Black and White Integration Show*. Quite simply the show was a fantasy land image, not meant to be a caricature of anyone.' Later soloist Ted Darling agrees: 'The West Indies cricket team filled up the first couple of rows. I had a letter from a young girl, *Dear Mr Darling, Mummy brought me to see the show, and I thoroughly enjoyed it. I'm black too.'* Bob Luff said, 'There is a lot of humbug talked about it. You'll find that those who shout the loudest have never seen the show. There is not, and there never has been, anything in it which could be the least offensive or embarrassing. We regularly have coloured people in the audience - and on our staff, working backstage. So far I've never received a complaint from any of them.' A later Head Minstrel Roy Winbow thinks 'they conveniently forgot the show was very stylised, formed around a very tried and tested format. Both George and Bob would never have been racist, they were both wealthy businessmen, especially Uncle Bob. If they had felt there was purely a commercial value in having black people in the show, then that would have happened, but instead of that, it was important to them to keep the show's format and style, and racism never came into it. I was aware that we received "letters" of complaint, even on tour, but they were not the sacksful that some people, even today, would have us believe. Friends at the BBC confirm most of the mail was in praise of the show, both on stage, TV and on tour. Our bosses were very proud of what the show was and that our audiences covered all groups and never catered for any specific type or race. You don't stay popular for twenty-five years plus and get TV audience rating figures regularly in the area of eighteen million, and for one Christmas TV special over twenty two million, putting *Coronation Street* into second place. Nor do many shows, even today, see the *House Full* boards out night after night, for both the Victoria Palace and touring shows unless there is something very special the public want to see. Nor do you have huge record sales and receive International awards and accolades.' *Time & Tide* supported the show, reporting that it was 'one of the cleanest and most popular programmes on British Television. One of the most nauseating stage shows of today is *Hair*.' The *Daily Sketch* wrote, 'Is there anything more ridiculous than the outcry against performers blacking their faces for minstrel acts? I suppose the next thing will be that someone will complain because an actor blacks his face to play Othello. To abolish all minstrel shows, which is what it amounts to, would be to deprive the stage of one of the nicest of its productions.'

Ironically a year earlier, CARD and the Africa Bureau were forced to hire the Victoria Palace when they failed to persuade any other theatre management to provide free housing for a fund-raising concert. The *Sunday Telegraph* now rather gleefully reported, 'It must be a bitter pill for them. The theatre is at present staging an entertainment which, although ironically suitable, they regard as anathema.'

Despite Dr Pitt's partial climb down, the petition caused headlines. The press and the country erupted in fury. Letters poured in everywhere - to the BBC, to George, to the newspapers - the overwhelming majority backing the show and objecting to the power wielded by what was a small organisation. N Charlton from Manchester fumed 'surely this is racialism gone mad?' Mrs R Shelling thought it was 'a great show and depicts coloured people as happy, musical and intelligent.' Many blacks also wrote in support, such as V Bedford from Southampton who said 'I have been watching the show ever since it started. To me, it is the happiest and most swinging show on the TV. I have yet to find something which could harm the coloured race. It provides a happy-go-lucky image of the Negroes, and that can't be bad surely. I will continue to watch the show with even greater interest. How about a show every week instead of every fortnight?' An anonymous Londoner pointed out a danger for CARD: 'As an African, I appreciate the struggle that right-minded people are making against racial prejudice. But CARD will be in danger of bringing themselves into disrepute if they dabble in trivialities like protesting against the show. I have always enjoyed this show and can find nothing offensive in it. Where will CARD's sword of justice next fall? Will it be aimed at Peter Sellers for his Indian roles in films?'

Many papers thought the petition ill-founded and badly timed, as new legislation was already planned in the wake of the Political and Economic Planning Report which had discovered widespread discrimination in employment, housing and services. The *Manchester Evening News* was so inundated with letters that they ran a special letters page. Perhaps 'ML' summed up feelings best: 'I think it is all nonsense! I fail to see how it can give offence. As regards "caricaturing" coloured people, that is just plain silly. It is a happy show enjoyed by many so let it go and continue to give pleasure.' FG Taylor agreed: 'This class of entertainment is certainly no hideous impersonation. On the contrary, I would say the shows are a compliment to coloured talent. The two races are equally and harmoniously impersonated and the absence of smutty humour, so prevalent in some other presentations, makes the *Black and White Minstrel Show* much more appealing.' Many pointed out that the show followed a strong theatrical tradition. J Hill wrote, 'What is the matter with these knowledgeable people or should I say lack of knowledge? The Minstrels are a continuation of a wonderful line of entertainment based on the coloured people themselves and are a credit to them. Racial my foot!' VE Sheridan said much the same: 'A hideous impersonation? What rubbish! They should be flattered that we try to impersonate them and their undoubted gift for music.' The *Northampton Telegraph* wrote, 'I think most of us are quite unmoved by the racial debate a few misguided do-gooders have waged about it. In any case, what Negro would be ashamed to be associated with the singing of the standard these minstrels adopt?'

The BBC's public response to CARD was cool: 'We have a strict attitude about the presentation of racialism in programmes, and we do not think that the *Black and White Minstrel Show* in any way offends this. It is a traditional show, enjoyed by millions for what it offers in good-hearted family entertainment.' But there was a flurry of activity behind the scenes. The day after the petition was presented, and perhaps as part of a concerted attack on the show, Chief Accountant Barrie Thorne sent a memo to Oliver Whitley, Chief Assistant to the Director-General, Sir Hugh Carlton Greene. He was dismayed at the continuation of the show: 'It is underlyingly offensive to many, no matter what the outward gloss and size of audience prove to the contrary.' He suggested asking the National Association for the Advancement of Coloured People and the Urban League for their opinion, as well as asking American television stations what the reaction to the show might be there. Oliver Whitley replied that 'it seems absurd to imagine that people who are not already racially prejudiced could possibly be in some way contaminated. People who are already racially prejudiced are more likely to be exacerbated by the protest itself than the object of the protest. The protesters are wasting valuable ammunition on a comparatively insignificant target.'

The Board of Management discussed the issue in May. The meeting felt that the subject had been helpfully discussed on *Any Questions?* The Director General reported that the secretary had sent an 'admirable letter' to the Chairman of CARD and no further action was necessary. In late July the Controller of Programming (Television) told the BBC's Board of Management that he could not agree with Stuart Hood's view that the programme should be taken off 'in the interests of race relations'. The matter came up yet again at the Board of Management meeting in August, when the Director of Television drew attention to a fierce attack by Elizabeth Thomas in the *Tribune*. Dai Francis later said 'the BBC thought this didn't represent the views of the nation and they were probably right at the time and therefore they ignored it.' Within a few weeks, Tom Sloan, Head of Light Entertainment, received a letter from Elizabeth Duben, currently touring the Caribbean as a singer, who wanted to tell the BBC that 'one show which is watched with absorbed attention and great enjoyment by the local people is the *Black and White Minstrel Show*.'

In a move obviously inspired by the CARD petition, local Paignton resident Brian Hutchinson wrote to a local newspaper asking 'townspeople with any spark of social conscience in them' to boycott it as it was 'a hideous impersonation'. He said, 'I have nothing against the show as a show, but it does cause offence to some people, even if only a minority. This is a blot on the nation, and I am only trying to get people to examine their consciences.' Paignton Council's Deputy Entertainments Manager Bill Preston maintained there was no racial prejudice in the show: 'If anything, there is racial integration. How much more integration can you get than the title?' No one seems to have supported the boycott; if anything, the speed of bookings increased and the show's summer season at Paignton became a record-breaker.

Complaints of racism weren't confined to Britain. The television show had been screened in Kenya the previous year and taken off at the end of the year, after proving to be one of the most popular of Voice of Kenya TV programmes. This had led to a number of appeals for its return, from viewers of all races. In May it was scheduled to return to Kenyan screens but didn't appear, the television company blaming the film's late arrival. It eventually started a week late. The critic of the *East African Standard* wrote, 'Sunday regained its old attraction last week. This programme is popular with African as well as European and Asian viewers in Kenya. It is odd that its return should coincide with a protest in London that it is racial - a complaint which is not made in Africa itself. Only the hyper-sensitive could find anything offensive in the show.'

However, Marvin Schiff of the *Sunday Nation* disagreed. After praising the show as 'highly polished, slickly produced and ultimately professional', he went on to abuse it on racial grounds, saying it was a 'racially defamatory form of entertainment'. Controversy followed. A letter from Nairobi said, 'What a pity he [Schiff] had to add to the currently fashionable torrent of abuse falling on the programme. Such a point of view is pure bias. An equally good argument could be made for saying that the programme is advertising 'black supremacy'. Or perhaps it advertises racial integration - black and white working and relaxing together in harmony, and what harmony! No! No! No! Away with such trash. This is pure entertainment with no other motives. I recently played a scoutmaster on stage and a vicious caricature it was, yet no one accused me of being anti-Baden-Powell.' Other letters agreed, pointing out that 'it does not poke fun at Negroes, or try to bring them into disrepute in any way.' Yet another critic responded, saying, 'I did some research and found that the general consensus is that these criticisms are nonsense. One of my African friends who says he considers the show the highlight of the week even went so far as to suggest that the critic might have written what he thought would be 'acceptable' which again is a harsh judgement. I've never seen one single item in any of these shows that could be considered a sneer at anyone - of any race, colour or creed.'

In a scathing attack, Clive Jenkins, the prominent trade union leader, called it 'a revolting disgrace', adding, 'At a time when the coloured peoples of the world are demanding their rights and their dignity, it is a cultural obscenity.'

The show was sold to Mauritius and Trinidad this year and was on the air in Rhodesia for several weeks in October and November, and again in 1968. Other countries enjoying the show included by now West Germany, Hong Kong, Malaysia, Malta, Nigeria, Cyprus, Sierra Leone, Gibraltar, Greece, Eire, Holland, Switzerland, Hungary, Poland, Portugal, Monaco, Singapore, Austria, Denmark, Yugoslavia and Czechoslovakia.

CHAPTER 25

The BBC was forced to reconsider its stance on the show in 1968 when the race situation in America escalated sharply, following Martin Luther King's assassination in April. The Head of Light Entertainment Television expressed anxiety as to whether 'the programme's format is still valid, in view of the seriousness of the colour situation and the rapidity with which events were moving.' However, his colleagues thought the series should continue either because it bore so little relation to the realities of the political situation or because it would not appear to be something which caused trouble.

But the show always seemed to be unfortunate in its timings. The first shows had coincided with the Notting Hill riots, and the first show in the 1963 series was broadcast just weeks after the bombing and race riots in Birmingham, Alabama, which left at least six children dead. Although this too raised awareness of the race issue, the only comment linking it and the show came from the *Sunday Times* and even that wasn't condemnatory: 'We called them the nigger minstrels in innocence and affection and no one on the pier ever suggested we were fascist hyenas. Now they call them the Black And White Minstrels, which is more tactful. Even so, it's only a matter of time before the old format becomes a matter of affront to educated susceptibilities. It will be the Mitchell Minstrels before we're much older, I shouldn't wonder; all whiter than white. There's a neat touch of unpremeditated irony in the return of this splendid old show tonight after a week in which it was impossible to escape from contemplation of the Negro problem.' In later years, the touring shows were to visit both Liverpool and Bradford at times of heightened racial tension.

But the same year as Martin Luther King's assassination, other trouble was brewing in Africa. The draconian laws in Kenya against Kenyan Asians had forced thousands to seek a home in Britain, causing Enoch Powell to make his famous *Rivers of Blood* speech. The speech provoked outrage in Parliament and marches in London. In January the BBC broadcast a discussion programme

Minstrel Magic

on BBC2, about prejudice against blacks in the media. It mentioned *The Jazz Singer* and Al Jolson but made no mention of the Minstrels. The *Guardian* was to say 'television's own furthering of the pernicious myth, the Black and White Minstrels, was left out of the discussion. One wondered if its omission was ignorance or just good manners.' Amid growing unrest, the Government rushed through the Commonwealth Immigrants Act in March, restricting the number of Kenyan Asians who could enter Britain to those with a relative who was already a British resident. Opinion in the press was fiercely divided over the legislation, and inevitably the Minstrels were dragged into it all. *Greenock Telegraph* wrote, 'Some people whose opinions I respect are even critical of the Minstrels for what they call its racial overtones. And some there are who smell similar tendencies in Noddy - because black Golly is invariably the villain of the piece!' Jazzman George Melly who was famously critical of the show, now said in the *Observer*, 'Surely even the Minstrels are more a question of bad taste and lack of imagination than of deliberate malice?' The *Daily Mail*, in a long polemic against the proposed Act, wrote that 'the right of a man to say what he likes, within the laws of libel and obscenity, is fundamental to the British tradition. It is the bedrock of our democracy. There is a real danger that this freedom may be seriously impaired, if not destroyed. One does not have to take sides in this distressing controversy to see that this is so.' The paper went on to question how far matters could go. 'No doubt we shall still be able to tell funny stories about the Englishman, the Scotsman, the Irishman and the Jew. But where will coloured people stand? Let us not forget that objection has already been raised to the *Black and White Minstrel Show*. This is the sort of thing that goes on under dictatorship.'

Despite all the controversy, its inclusion in the Royal Variety performance in 1968 before the Queen Mother showed that it was residing firmly at the heart of the nation. For their contribution, which closed the first half, George chose *Dixieland, That Old Soft Shoe* and *The Twenties* sequences. The Victoria Palace closed for the night - the one and only occasion - with the theatre management themselves bearing the losses. However, controversy lay ahead. Also chosen for the show were Diana Ross and the Supremes, the ultimate black trio from the States. Diana Ross had already caused difficulties for organiser Bernard Delfont when she wanted to use her own words for *Somewhere* from *West Side*

Story. This row was averted when Delfont allowed her to include a reference to the late Martin Luther King in the song, which she said had formed an essential part of her act since his assassination, though the inclusion caused a minor sensation on the night.

Rehearsals went well at first. Les Want, one of the Minstrels, remembers that 'we were all in our makeup and excited about Diana Ross and the Supremes, really thrilled to be on the same bill. We're all standing on the side of the stage or sitting in the auditorium, and she came on to do their rehearsal. She spotted us and refused to carry on until we'd completely cleared the auditorium and the stage. And as we left, she gave the black power salute which upset me, and I was going to talk to her, but Keith Leggett pulled me back and stopped me doing it.' However, Keith remembers it differently: 'I remember them being unhappy about the black face and they did get into dialogue with some of the Minstrels, asking questions about why we did it. I told the boys not to get too intense, but I don't remember her not letting us be in the stalls while they rehearsed or physically restraining Les. My recollection is that much was made of a small event. Most of us just enjoyed doing the show where we were a great success.'

After the show, the soloists were presented to the Queen Mother, Princess Margaret and Princess Anne, who said how much they had enjoyed the ten-minute spot and 'could see why we were so popular'. Of course, all three were already avid fans of the show; Princess Anne had seen it live on several occasions, and it was well known that the Queen Mother never missed a television show. On one notable occasion, the BBC received a phone call from a member of the Queen's Household, after one television show, asking, on behalf of the Queen, how they could be heard clapping during the conducted sequence when they were all wearing gloves! The Duty Officer at the BBC solemnly informed the Royal Household that other cast members were, in fact, standing in the wings, providing the clapping sounds!

It must be said that Diana Ross' reported reaction accords with Keith's version. She later said, 'I didn't see their act. During the finale, one of them was standing alongside me, and I had such a strange feeling. I wouldn't say I was upset by them, though. Really it didn't bother me. What difference does it make if a person's face is black - or painted black? But it's so old-fashioned. It gives me a little sadness and pain to think of the old days, although I don't dislike the act itself. I'm glad they're not going on much longer.' One of the Supremes, Cindy Birdsong, said it was the first time she'd seen anyone blacked up like Al Jolson, 'You can imagine the shock I got when one of the Minstrels asked me for my autograph.'

Diana Ross may have tried to dismiss the incident, but the press wasn't about to let it go, though the criticism was all of Diana Ross. *Disc Scene* said they made matters worse and themselves look stupid. The *Evening Standard* said, 'the biggest disappointment of the night turned out to be Diana Ross and the Supremes, who, while looking perfectly delectable, sounded badly balanced and out of step on occasions.' The *Record Mirror* printed a letter from Jeffrey Watson: 'I must protest about the exhibition made by the Supremes. What's pop music coming to when such a high-rated group protest about the makeup of the harmless Minstrels? But to crown it off, in the middle of their act, they deliver a sermon on racial integration.'

More potential trouble surfaced the following year when black singer Gloria Stewart auditioned for the show. An American who had been appearing in the musical *Hair* since it opened in London the previous year, Gloria had now left the show and decided she wanted to join the Minstrel show. She had already auditioned once and had been turned down. As Keith Leggett, now heavily involved in all aspects of the organisation, recalls, 'She didn't have the right sort of voice, she only had a range of eight notes and she couldn't sight-read.' Perhaps her aim was always to discredit the show, or maybe she just decided to get her own back for what she saw as an unwarranted rejection, but she saw an opportunity to claim she had been turned down on racial grounds. As John Boulter remembers, 'She had a lovely voice but couldn't sight-read, so when she was turned down, she decided to demonstrate against the show.'

Whatever her original motives, she certainly took advantage of the situation to get herself some publicity. She let it be known that she and the rest of the cast of *Hair* were going to re-audition and protest at the same time. Television and radio people waited outside George's offices in Marylebone High Street, which were next to the studios where George was auditioning. Such closeness enabled the office staff to go from one to the other via the roof. As George, who of course knew this protest was being planned, recalled, 'They were all there waiting for this big parade. It was all a bit of a joke, it was her and I think, two fellas.' Daphne Bell, who auditioned all potential singers, recalls, 'We knew there was going to be a deputation from *Hair*, and all the cameras were waiting for George to come through the front door of our offices. I'd gone into the studios over the roof as usual, and Keith was with me. We insisted on auditioning them, as that was what they said they wanted, but we made them come in one at a time - they weren't expecting that, and it deflated them.' What happened next deflated them even more! George reported, 'I said to Keith, do us a favour, go down there and tell her I'm just going down to the Genevieve for lunch, would she like to join me. Keith said, you're joking. No, I'm not, I said, just tell her. She said, all right.' Over lunch, they asked her to explain her objections to the show. George recalled, 'I said I appreciated her views but she was in another country, and we quite liked the show, and we certainly didn't intend to cause anyone any offence. Goodness, the government banned *The Mikado* in 1915 because we were trying to trade with Japan and we still do *The Mikado*, and that's a darn sight worse than anything I do.' Keith remembers, 'It wasn't too traumatic; her argument was the same as we heard many times afterwards - making fun at black people's expense. She talked about it being an insult to her race, and we explained that it was a traditional makeup and that certainly no offence was meant and that the message, if any, was that black and white worked together in harmony. We had blackface men holding hands and singing love songs to white women - so I would have thought that it might cause a backwash from the hard-bitten south of America.'

A television reporter, present when Gloria left, asked her if she'd had an audition. She replied that, yes, she had, but they weren't accepted for various reasons: 'They just said there weren't any parts for us at the moment.' The reporter asked if she really wanted a part, to which Gloria replied, 'Yes, that's why we came here.' Pushing for a story, the reporter asked if this was also a protest in some way. 'Yes,' said Gloria. Still probing, the reporter asked, 'Against what?' Gloria's reply was, 'Against the blacking up of faces and against the fact that it's the Black and White Minstrels with no black people in it. There are coloured artistes in Equity who need jobs too.' Nobody seems to have noticed the contradiction in her replies. If she really wanted a job, this would have entailed her dancing with blacked-up boys, which is what she was reportedly protesting about. In *Time Shift*, a later BBC programme about the show, black music critic Stanley Crouch

Minstrel Magic

said, 'There's a kind of madness that overcomes people, particularly on the anti-racist front, people get into campaigning, and they follow a particular logic which makes them think of something utterly mad, like trying to get a part in the show. Yes, the logic is that black actors ought to be able to act in anything but wait a minute, so you want to act in that?'

Keith believes that 'Gloria and her friends actually added to racial tensions in the UK. The average person in the UK at that time accepted people of any race, colour or creed and worked alongside them in harmony. Yes, they may call them names, but usually, it was just a nickname like you might call a Taffy or a Jock. I myself was called a pommie bastard many times in Australia, but I can only remember once being upset at the way it was said. What does cause racial tension is when a person has been used to viewing his or her favourite programme, and there is talk of taking it off because some people, whatever their colour, new to the UK, don't want it on. The reaction then is, "Who do these people think they are, coming over here and telling me what I can watch and what I can't." I certainly don't believe that the taking off of the *Black and White Minstrel Show* added anything to racial harmony in the UK.'

This view was supported by everyone at the time. George said, 'I've never had a complaint from a single coloured person. No one's ever written to me or said anything about it.' In *Time Shift*, Dot explained that 'people only got into the show if they were good enough. If there'd been a black person who was good enough, they were in, and we did have two or three black boys; unfortunately, we never got a black girl. I don't know why we didn't but we never did but it wasn't because of being black, because George would have loved six black girls and six white girls - it would have been wonderful, he'd have loved that, but as it turned out, they didn't come with the right talent.'

Upset by this racial unrest, George went to the BBC and said, 'Look, do we really need the black makeup? Why do we have it?' For once, the BBC didn't need much persuading, anxious as they were to export the Minstrel show to the States but realising it couldn't be done in its present format without fear of causing offence. So early in 1968, an experiment was recorded. Called *Masquerade*, it was effectively to be a white-faced Minstrel show, with the black face replaced by a black glittery Venetian mask across the eyes. This, it was hoped, would provide the same anonymity as the black makeup but without any possible offence. The singers, principals and comedians were exactly the same as in a standard Minstrel show. Dai said, 'It will make a wonderful change for us, working like this. The makeup used to take about twenty minutes to apply.' Tony agreed: 'Blacking up is such hard work, particularly under the studio lights. I wouldn't care if I never had to black up again.' The same production team was also on board - Roy Gunson as choreographer, Alan Bristow doing the orchestrations, George and Eric Robinson conducting the orchestra, and Martin Collins as designer. A Minstrel show indeed, by any other name! The idea produced a skit on *Points of View* in May when the programme asked, 'Is this proposal an example of colour discrimination on the part of the BBC? The *All-White Minstrels* has a rather racist sound.....'

Once the news got out that *Masquerade* was being made, many papers objected strongly to what they saw as the BBC giving in to a vocal minority. The *Sunday Express* said, 'These being sensitive times, the BBC has decided to take the Minstrels, bleach them and put them into a new white show. The idea, of course, is not to offend immigrants. How silly can we get?' The *Derbyshire Times* agreed: 'How spineless of the BBC to pander to a minority group of Black Power in their ridiculous demand that the Minstrels shall in future be staged "all white". Over the years that this most popular musical show has been televised, not one single insult or lampoon to the coloured race has occurred. In point of fact, quite the opposite technique has been employed throughout the production - always beautiful white girl minstrels on intimate and loving terms with their opposite 'black' minstrel numbers. The BBC has so far never divulged the cause of the complaint which in itself casts grave suspicion on their decision.' The *Morning Star* in a double-edged comment, said, 'This action is, of course, a complete admission that there may be racialist implications in this makeup; but does it also mean that British audiences are regarded as less sensitive to the subject that those of the US? Or will the BBC now get rid of this offensive makeup which has marred an excellent show for such a long time?' The *Sunday Times* reported that 'the present show stands a long way from those of the C19th with their vicious digs at Negro attitudes. The mere fact of *Masquerade*'s existence, however, is an indication of the BBC's unspoken hopes that it could one day replace the Minstrels without losing an audience of eleven million.'

Masquerade was eventually screened months later on BBC2, to be repeated on BBC1 the following April. Officially the BBC said the delay was because it was too good to waste on low summer audience figures but behind the scenes, there were talks about making the next Minstrel series in the same format. However, Bob quickly pointed out that the Minstrels were contracted for a further series and a Christmas special so it would be some time before any permanent change could happen.

But this experiment was to fail. Bob Hunter said, 'Generally it was felt, "OK, it's novel, it's different, but it's not a substitute for the makeup we're used to." ' Les Want recalled, 'The show was successful, but it didn't pull in the viewers that the Minstrel show pulled in. I think it was the mystique of the black faces.' The use of masks was not popular; a later critic said, 'When they had the black faces, there were eyes that were opening, there were expressions in all these faces, but if you put a mask on, it's like looking at something dead on your mantelpiece. There's no emotion there.' The *Manchester Evening News* wanted to know, 'Are the BBC trying to get rid of this show or not? If this is not part of a phasing-out process, why the masks? And why even make an attempt to change, even only slightly, what has become a very successful formula? Perhaps it is about time they were given a last grand hand-clap for services rendered, and then rested.' The *Sunday Times* was equally critical: 'They left off the blacking and adopted tatty masks. Strangely enough without the makeup, the men seem more anonymous, not less. Now one sees revealed the pettiness of the performance, its reduction of music to the dimensions of the merry-go-round. The basic pattern element of black and white, grotesque though it may have been, imposed a formal design on the proceedings which one now sees to have been as arbitrary as a pair of stays.'

The critics obviously didn't like the experiment, but viewers seemed to. The BBC's Audience Research Panel produced a very high Response Index of 86, higher than the Minstrel series earlier in the year which only reached 83 at its highest. Reports to the BBC show that the decision to abandon the black makeup was very warmly welcomed by the majority for the opportunity it gave them to see their favourite singers as they really were, saying, 'The interest in seeing singers in their true colours added considerably to the pleasure'. There was a widespread feeling that the half measures were a bit pointless and could be dispensed with.

Viewers stressed that 'the appeal lay in the invariably impeccable performance of lively tuneful music by artistes who could always be relied on to give of their best whatever the colour of their faces'. The overwhelming feel was that it was considered outstanding and polished, a triumph of teamwork. The format, without introductions, was thought ideal. The only adverse comments concerned the comedy spots which struck a sizeable minority as only moderately amusing; many would have been happy with just the music.

Maybe the BBC had already decided that *Masquerade* wouldn't work, despite its clear popularity with audiences. Two days after it screened, George started recording the soundtracks at Lansdowne for another new series, using his favourite twenty-two singers. *Music Music Music* was yet another step away from the blackfaced shows, as even the mask was dispensed with, and the men shown in all their white-faced glory!

The new 'all-white' *Music Music Music* began transmitting on BBC2 in January 1969 and ran for ten shows. It starred the usual team - John, Dai and Tony, as well as Margaret, Penny and Delia. George asked Maryetta Midgley to join the principals, but she had a few questions of her own first: 'I asked if I'd have as many solos as John. He said, no, but you'll have enough. I still refused to do it.' George then drafted in Pauline Whitaker, though Maryetta remained part of the chorus on the soundtrack. The rest of the team remained the same, with Roy Gunson handling the choreography, Alan Bristow the orchestrations, and this time, Mel Cornish the settings. Guest stars were also used, such as the Karlin Twins, and pop stars Ronnie Carroll and the Scaffold, though the links between items were only done as voice-overs. One show, which was a tribute to George Gershwin, also featured guests Miki and Griff, by now very well known in their own right, after leaving the choir.

Although the basic premise of the show was similar to the Minstrel shows, George used far more of each song. As producer George Inns recalled, they sang 'not just half a chorus but the whole thing, often with the verse as well. In a Minstrel show we used to get through seventy numbers, but in this, we average around forty.' Other aspects of the show needed altering too. George explained, 'We can't get away with putting the boys in blazers and flannels anymore. They've got to have glamorous costumes too.'

The BBC was impressed with the programme. Bill Cotton, Head of Variety Light Entertainment Television recalled that it was he 'who originally felt that the anonymity was the key to their success' but said that he had thoroughly enjoyed the new format. Tom Sloan said it had come off satisfactorily but wondered what the public would think, as one feared to change a winning formula. Some weren't happy with the linking narration, feeling it didn't match the elegance of the production and was full of stilted clichés. However, they thought it worked without makeup, though Bill Cotton reported that he had heard, from outside the BBC, many comments expressing disappointment at the singers' appearance without makeup. He felt that George Inns had gone so far out of his way not to imitate the Minstrels that all the faults of *Music Music Music* were those that the Minstrels avoided. What wasn't much liked was the way George himself had got in among the performers. Tom Sloan asked Board members to watch the series as they needed to make a decision soon, 'most carefully' about its future.

The show, which went out fortnightly at prime time on Sunday evenings, faced stiff opposition from both *The Forsyte Saga* on BBC1 and *Tom Jones* on ITV, at the same time, but was generally well liked. The research collator reported that people 'were clearly gratified to discover that, to all intents and purposes, it was the *Black and White Minstrel Show* without black faces and all the better for that, according to not a few, as it was "nice to see the men singers as themselves". ' It seemed to have 'all the attractions of the Minstrel show, blending into a pleasing and exceptional kaleidoscope of music and movement'. The BBC was so impressed with the show that they chose one programme as their entry for the Golden Rose of Montreux. However, despite this proving that they considered this series probably their best of the year, the BBC never re-commissioned the show.

CHAPTER 26

In a move which shocked fans and press alike, George and Bob announced at the end of 1968 that the Victoria Palace show would close on May 24, 1969 'as it enters its eighth record-breaking year, with a new world record of 4354 performances and 5.5 million visitors. We think it's time to give the public a new and even more spectacular presentation of this wonderful show.' The show would go to Scarborough for its only appearance outside London, so Bob Luff said, 'before a world tour in 1970'. Much of the current success was due to low ticket prices; although top seat prices had risen to 16 shillings (£13) by now, that was still lower than the 17/6 which the Crazy Gang had charged over six years earlier. Other theatres struggled to keep their top seats at less than £2 (£32).

Perhaps the break was a good idea. It must have been sometime around now that John endured possibly the worst nightmare of any soloist. As he remembers, 'I went on stage with a girl from stage left to sing *Ramona* and started 'Ramona' - and couldn't remember any more of the words. A good job it was recorded. I got through it and thought it'd be all right at the second house. But the same thing happened. I came off stage and looked at the Stage Manager's book, and I'd sung it 4000 times! I had to learn it all over again – it came back a little bit once I started to learn it again but not fully.'

Never a paper to miss an opportunity to snipe at the show, the *Guardian* wrote, on the morning of the last show, 'What confusions of racial attitudes give such popularity in 1969 to an entertainment built around white men made up as black men singing songs written about black men by white men some forty years ago? An African I spoke to in the audience told me that he didn't find anything offensive about it. "It's just a show," he said. But that was predictable; if he had found it offensive, presumably he wouldn't have gone. [The reporter seems to have overlooked the rather obvious fact that nevertheless, this African had gone and didn't find it offensive.] One American matron who had "just loved it" said, "They won't let us sing *Dixie* back home no more,"

Minstrel Magic

and then, in a near stage-whisper, "You know if they sang some of those songs back home, they'd be put in gaol." Perhaps massah's not in de cold, cold ground but alive and well and in the audience of the Victoria Palace. Is this the explanation of the show's popularity? That it's not just nostalgia, but that it also harks back to the old days when race was not an issue. A lot of people seem to find it absurdly over-sensitive to object to golliwogs and *Ten Little Nigger Boys* and *Little Black Sambo* and this show. Perhaps it is, but surely this is an issue where we should be over-sensitive.'

On May 24, the Victoria Palace show finally closed, with a ceremony backstage to mark the closing, at which Leslie McDonnell of Moss Empires handed Bob Luff an inscribed silver salver. Thirteen thousand people had applied for tickets for the last night, which proved to be a show to remember, with all sorts of unscheduled appearances and unexpected costumes. The cast played visual jokes on one another and on the soloists, which of course didn't interfere with the actual running of the show. There had been fifteen weddings between Minstrels and Toppers, six babies had been born, and Bob Luff was honorary godfather to them all. In another 'end of an era' move, dressers Lily Ingram and Nellie Cotter retired. Lily, now 90, and Nellie, 77, had worked together at the theatre for years, though their joint history went back to 1927. Bob gave the show's costumes to charity as he couldn't bear to sell them and 'then see them in another show at the end of a pier somewhere'.

But the Three Musketeers were to be no more, once the summer season closed. In a shock to George and fans, Tony Mercer announced he would be leaving the show. In the first major change since the show's inception, the three soloists would no longer be together. Tony had had a disastrous few years and after overworking himself to pay back his debts, was now suffering considerable ill health. The end at the Victoria Palace gave him the impetus he needed to leave.

His troubles began in 1966 which wasn't a good year for Tony. In April his home was ransacked by thieves who stole jewellery and other property worth £300 (£4,000). The same month he and friend and hotelier Bernard Coleman opened a West End restaurant and club in two adjacent premises in Beak Street, off Regent Street. Tony said that he'd had the idea because so many people wrote asking him to recommend somewhere to wine and dine before and after the show. As he said, 'After you finish the

[325]

night's show, you're all keyed up. You can't just go home and go to sleep without having something to eat and drink and relaxing, so I might as well do it in my own place.'

But more was going on behind the scenes. This was the era of the infamous London gangs, with the Krays and the Richardsons dominating the club scene. Entertainment and crime combined to make a glamorous and exciting world in 1950s and 1960s London and it was almost impossible not to have at least some contact with these gang bosses and their henchmen. The Krays asked ventriloquist Neville King to do a show for them. When he refused, saying his wife was down for the weekend, the answer was, 'it's not a request'.

One relative newcomer to the scene was Joe Wilkins, whose reign was short-lived but who was greatly feared. He had fingers in many pies but specialised in clubs and the entertainment world. There was serious money to be made here legitimately, but it was all heavily regulated, so gangsters such as Joe dreamed up ingenious ways to get round the rules. He owned several successful escort agencies and clubs, such as the 800 Club in Leicester Square, the Islet Town Club in Curzon Street and the Crazy Horse Saloon in Marylebone. In highly dubious circumstances he took control of a very fashionable club called Winston's, which was certainly frequented by Tony and the Kray twins. As Keith Leggett, George's right-hand man at the time, remembers, 'Joe Wilkins was a real hard man. I met him quite a few times, he terrified me and all his henchmen.'

Keith recalls, 'Tony was a lovely man who trusted everybody within minutes of meeting them.' Whether Tony came up with the restaurant idea, as he himself remembered, or whether Joe saw the potential of a great front man, too naïve to realise, initially at least, what was happening, will never be known. But certainly Joe took advantage of the situation, and common knowledge was that Joe owned the club. Tony put up £7,500 (£100,000) but for months, £30,000-worth of rebuilding (£400,000), designing, furnishing and fitting went on. Bernard Coleman probably put up some of this, but the bulk would have come from Joe.

It certainly provided an impressive setting. The walls were covered in red and white silk, the chairs were black and the tables covered with black and white tablecloths. The ceiling caused the most comment. UV lighting played on white strings under a black ceiling, giving a tiled effect. Specialising in South American dishes, the restaurant featured two specially invented dishes, Escalope de Veau Minstrel which cost 17/6 (£15), and Minstrel Special, a honey and brandy flavoured ice cream at 7/6 (£6.50). A black accordion player dressed in a minstrel costume played for dancing until 2.30am, the waiters all wore Black and White Minstrel costumes, and the menus and wine lists were set in record sleeves of *Magic of the Minstrels*. A nightclub operated out of the adjoining premises, where the Peter Crawford Trio were resident and Tony himself often sang, on the very many nights he went there after the show. Tony's father gave up his job with a Sheffield steelworks company to become resident director, and he and his wife moved into a flat over the club. He had the use of the flat, a Bentley and £2,500 (£33,500) a year tax-free.

The venture opened with a glittering star-studded reception in April 1966, with the opening ceremony being conducted by June Elliott, widow of GH Elliott, who unveiled a portrait of her late husband, the famous minstrel. The place received good reviews and by August Tony had added 'girls in the cage', a girl disc-jockey and two floor shows, the second of which started at 2.15am and was the latest in London. By now, he was in partnership with Aldo Ramella, one of the West End's most celebrated room-enliveners. The floor show was under the control of Keith Leggett who sang a number or two himself, then moved out of the way for other acts, such as the Oriental Gypsies and the remarkable Zari, who lay full length on a circle of six inch nails while a customer stood on her.

For weeks it was the place to go, and many stars would pop in but soon the money ran out, and Tony was under serious pressure from Joe. It quickly became a clip joint with 'girls' getting customers to order bottles of drink at very heavy prices; any problem and the customer was taken into the kitchen and 'dealt' with. Both Tony and his father hated it, but they were in too deep.

Joe and his henchmen paid several visits to the Victoria Palace to see Tony, terrifying the stage doorman. Bob Luff got wind of their visits and stormed round to the theatre during one visit, telling them in no uncertain terms to get the hell out of his theatre and not to come back. As Minstrel Frank McFadden reported, 'Luffy was afraid of no one, and these guys would have been carrying guns, which just goes to show what a gutsy character he was. It must have been his army background as even the police themselves were frightened of Wilkins.'

Even with the 'backing' of Joe Wilkins, the restaurant only traded for eight months, being compulsorily wound up in the High Court in January 1967, on the petition of Bumas Estates of Kilburn who were owed £531 (£7,000) for rent. Tony publicly attributed the failure to insufficient working capital, too low prices, and the effect of the Government's economic restrictions. The restaurant had counted on expense account diners but then came the credit squeeze and the consequent reduction in businessmen's expenses. Tony had also been incredibly generous to friends and colleagues, such as Margaret Hunt, someone Tony had known in Lincoln in the war. She asked Tony if he could get her tickets for the show; he gave her and her husband front row seats, then took them for a meal at the restaurant afterwards.

But it got worse still for Tony. Unsurprisingly Joe Wilkins had made sure that his name was nowhere near any of the paperwork or finances. The gangster had 'persuaded' both Tony and his father to act as guarantors for the restaurant which led to a hugely embarrassing incident for Tony while he was on stage. While he was singing *And the Band Played On*, private enquiry agent Barry Quartermain served him with a High Court writ alleging debts to Snows Hotel of £752/1/3 (£10,000). It looked for a moment as if the band might not 'play on', but everyone kept going, even Tony. He pushed the writ into his pocket and finished the song. He said afterwards, 'I thought it was a student rag. People often hand us things on stage.' Quartermain said they had chosen that time 'because it was the only time and place where we knew it could be done. I'll give Mr Mercer his due. He was a trouper and kept on singing as he took the writ.'

A creditors' meeting in February, where the venture was put into liquidation, was told the restaurant had debts as high as £37,000 (£485,000). Assets were put at £80 (£1,000) though there were ongoing enquiries about missing kitchen equipment which was valued at £4,000 (£52,000). Tony put himself forward as a creditor, saying he was owed £7,500 (£100,000) for a money advance. He told *The People*, 'I'm nearly broke. The restaurant cost me £7,500 - all my capital. I have lost everything. It was to be something to look forward to when I gave up show business.' At his bankruptcy hearing in April, Tony's debts were estimated at £12,600 (£165,000) and his assets at £582 (£7,600). Yet worse was to come, with friends and colleagues horrified, and Tony heartbroken, when his father died that summer, a death almost certainly caused by his hatred of what the restaurant had become.

1968 wasn't to prove any better. Tony's son, eighteen-year-old Tony Jnr, one of Britain's champion ten-pin bowlers, was killed in July, after being thrown out of his car when it was involved in an accident at Northampton. He had been travelling alone in the car which went out of control, slewed broadside across the road and skidded tail first into another car. The offside door flew open, and he was thrown out of the car and into the path of a mini-van. The now-driverless car continued on down the road and collided with a parked car. Tony received about three thousand letters of support, mainly from young people.

Tony, still struggling with grief, went into work overdrive, in an effort to pay off his creditors. His wife helped with fees from modelling clothes, and they cut back on the way and the numbers of people they entertained. Well known for his drinking, Tony also cut down on his drinks bill, even giving up altogether for nine months. They stopped eating out so often, and Tony swapped his Bentley for a smaller car. He added Sunday concerts to his Victoria Palace work and issued a solo album which sold about 70,000 copies. All this became too much for his health, and he often had to miss Victoria Palace shows, with Dai taking over his role. A thrombosis, probably caused by overwork and the stress of the restaurant venture, put him out completely for three weeks. So after much deliberating, he decided to quit the show, saying, 'I feel in a rut. I'll do cabaret and theatre work. I'm already doing Sunday concerts, and it's becoming a bit too much for me. It will be a wrench to leave the show and to leave Dai and John, but the break will be final. I talked to a lot of friends in show business before I decided to make the break - people like Frankie Vaughan and Donald Peers - and they advised me that it would be best to leave now while I am still young enough to try something new.' But his health was slowly deteriorating. After the London show ended in May, Tony spent a week in a private London hospital having tests to find out what was wrong with his right leg. Eventually, they told him he had diabetes, which had already been diagnosed. Once in Scarborough for the summer season, he had electric treatment at a local hospital, to which he responded. It was only afterwards that the doctors told him they had known all along that he was at risk of the muscle withering and that he could have ended up paralysed down one side.

Minstrel Magic

With Tony still on board, the London show moved to Scarborough for the summer season while the touring version opened in Eastbourne. Scarborough was delighted to welcome the original cast back to their first summer home, and the summer flew by with parties and celebrations.

On the last night in Scarborough, which was to be Tony's last night with the show, the entire company played a practical joke on him. They decided for the finale that they would all wipe the black greasepaint from their faces and trot onto the stage, white-faced.....everyone, that is, except Tony. The question was: how could they keep the secret from Tony? After hours of thought, they hit on a brainwave. Someone would have to keep Tony occupied. So the plan was for Les Want who understudied John, to keep Tony talking in another dressing room while every other Minstrel washed off the black. It worked like a dream. When Tony realised what they had cooked up for him, the music had started, he was already at the front of the stage and they were into the finale. Dai said he 'would never forget his blacked-up face as long as I am a Minstrel. Talk about being the black sheep of the Minstrel family firm, he was really on his own that night and didn't his home-country audience roar! It must have been the best-kept secret in the friendly Yorkshire seaside resort as the rest of us put on a happy, white face.'

As ever, George already had a replacement for his bass-baritone star. Forty-seven-year-old Andy Cole already had a successful solo career, appearing in hundreds of programmes such as *Melody Time*, *The Blue and the Grey* and many other Charles Chilton productions, often working alongside the George Mitchell Singers. He had sung in the last of the famous CB Cochrane's reviews in 1949, before appearing in *South Pacific*, *The King and I* and *Rose Marie* in the West End. A veteran of many television and radio shows, Andy had also had several series of his own, as well as numerous albums to his credit. He brought a whole lot of new fans to the show, including his most faithful fan Freda from Morecambe who wrote to him four times a week. He and George knew each other well and George saw him as the natural successor to Tony. And so it proved, at least for a few years.

London had now spent six months without a Minstrel show, but that changed in November 1969. Planned to return to its home at the Victoria Palace, it was to be called *Magic of the Minstrels*, a 'spectacular new £100,000 show'. Even before the first show closed, the new show had taken over £25,000 (£550,000) in advance bookings. By July, all Saturdays for the first year were entirely sold out, and they were already booking into 1971. By November, even before opening, they had already covered the show's costs, which by now had reached £100,000 (£2.25m), with £30,000 (£675,000) being spent on costumes.

The company moved into the theatre on November 3, before opening on November 24. Main billing was given to John and Dai, together with Margaret Savage, whom George had persuaded back into the show as the female lead. Andy Cole replaced Tony, though with lesser billing than the other soloists. The company included eighteen Minstrels and eighteen Toppers, with speciality acts including juggler Robb Murray, acrobats the Seven Ashtons, and the comedy harmonica players the Three Monarchs. Leslie Crowther had left the show for commercial television, so Bob Luff recruited comedian Peter Kaye. The Minstrels crammed ninety-five songs into the show's running time of two hours and five minutes, so no one could say it wasn't value for money; the first half closed with a tribute to Irving Berlin, and the conducted sequence was surprisingly *Jacob's Ladder,* which, while popular, had not often featured on television. Top ticket prices had risen but were still only £1 (£16), far lower than every other London theatre.

Nerves were as great on opening night as they had been in 1962 when it first opened in London. In the light of the rising criticism of the show, they expected to be on the receiving end of a huge amount of knocks from the critics. Letters of support and good wishes for the opening night had poured in from fans, which must have helped, but it was a very nervous George who sat in the stalls. Before the show started, the audience was overjoyed to be introduced to Tony Mercer who was sitting in a stage-side box with his family, about to watch his first-ever Minstrel show.

George's nerves were misplaced. Nearly all of Fleet Street saluted them. The *Courier* reported that 'It is many years since we heard such a first-night reception given to a new show but it well deserved the ovation and curtain calls. Here is a show which will once more break all records and one which you could keep going to see. It is a glorious feast of colour and music; indeed, it's magic, spell-binding and irresistible.' Another unnamed paper said, 'It is as critic-proof as the Brigade of Guards but better drilled and better dressed.' The *Sunday Mirror* thought it should run 'just slightly short of forever', while the *Daily Telegraph* called it 'overwhelmingly cheerful and faultlessly wonderfully drilled. Strange that so regimented a show should be as popular as the freewheeling Crazy Gang.' *Crescendo* wrote, 'They could hardly have chosen a more apt name. I stand in awe of the technical achievement - particularly the integration with a live orchestra in the pit.'

Many papers picked up on the earlier racial criticisms. In a surprising volte-face, the *Guardian* said the show was 'rapturously received. Recently there arose a complaint that the show was in some way a slur on coloured people which would be like saying that *Madam Butterfly* offended the Japanese or that the Japanese were themselves guilty of impropriety by aping the routines of Broadway. This cant is exposed for what it is by the show which if anything is animated by affection, not contempt, for the old Southern bones and tambourine routines. With *John Brown's Body*, Dai Francis brought down the house, and John Boulter wrung every last ounce out of *If You Were The Only Girl*. Immensely professional.' The *Evening News* picked up the same thread: 'Don't read on if you expect one syllable from me about the Minstrels being a racial insult. Negroes can be proud that, however remotely, they have given the world such robust entertainment. It is a show pulsating with zest and showbiz razzle-dazzle. For sheer theatrical effrontery, I challenge you to equal black-faced Tyrolean peasants belting out *Roll Out the Barrel*. This is a triumph of slickness over vulgarity, exuberance over bad taste. In one word it is ENTERTAINMENT.'

The speciality acts were also well-received, with only Peter Kaye being criticised. He later admitted that his start with the show was disastrous. Critic Felix Barker wrote that he was the worst thing in the show, which hurt Peter deeply, though he admitted years later that Barker was right. The *Evening News* thought, 'Only Peter Kaye lets things down with the professionally-degrading trick of blaming the audience for not responding to bad jokes.' The *Daily Telegraph* agreed, saying he provided 'the biggest flat spot who blamed the audience rather too often for not laughing at his attempts to be funny.'

Advance bookings looked like outshining all previous records, and the show was set to run and run.

CHAPTER 27

After four years without a live Minstrel show, Australia again became host to yet another touring company. Kenn Brodziak from Aztec Productions had visited London early in 1969 to finalise the details for the tour, discussions for which had been going on since the previous year. The Tivoli theatres, which had reaped such benefits financially from the previous tour, had closed down in 1966, hit by the rise of television audiences. So this time, the show toured throughout the JC Williamson Group of theatres, who had been the presenting company for the first tour. Again they opened in Melbourne and covered many of the same cities as the earlier tour, but this time going as far west as Perth.

George had kept tried and trusted principals Don Cleaver and Peter Darren out of this year's summer season at Scarborough as he wanted both of them, along with third soloist Howard Davies, to headline the new Australian tour. The agreement with the Australian unions was that, once again, the three soloists, plus the choreographer, director, comedian and speciality acts could be signed up in Britain. The rest of the cast had to be Australian, though several dancers were married to other cast members, and so escaped this ruling. In a move with far-reaching consequences for George, he also asked Dorothy (Dot) Ogden, who had joined the show as a Topper in Morecambe in 1964 and was now a Mitchell Maid at the Victoria Palace, to go as the female lead: 'I had auditioned for George a while beforehand, and he said I could understudy Margaret Savage at the Victoria Palace, and asked if I would consider going to Australia for him.'

The tour had generated much publicity in Britain before the cast had even left. Typical was a feature on Don in the *Middlesex County Times*, which said, 'Going to Australia makes him a triple-Crown Minstrel – no one else has scored such a hat-trick by soloing in all three productions – Victoria Palace, touring and Oz. Don said, "All our shows serve up happiness, laughter and gaiety. And unless the formula for completely anonymous men and a row of gorgeous girls changes, we are in for a long run with the kind of show that's been filling the Victoria Palace for at least six years." '

From the start, this company had a family feel. Realising the mistake he had made in 1962 by not sending out the families with the British participants, George this time made sure wives and children went too. Minstrel Garry Hayes had been with the 1962 tour, before joining the London show and marrying Jill, who was now expecting their first child. Peter Darren took his wife, Elizabeth Milligan, who became a Minstrelette, and their five-month-old daughter Jennifer. Jennifer spent every night on tour, asleep in the dressing room, except in Brisbane where she slept beneath the stage in a collapsible canvas cot. Tenor soloist, Howard Davies' wife, was dancer Marjorie Dauncey. Another Minstrelette Helen Stewart and her husband Colin, part of the speciality act Warren, Devine and Sparks, also joined the tour. This act had been with the show since 1964 and was delighted to be joining the new Australian tour, as both Warren and Sparks were Australian. Ventriloquist Ken Wood married Keren the day before they left for Australia. The other speciality acts were comedians Denny Willis and Johnnie Mack, from the British touring show, plus all-rounder Joan Laurie who travelled with her husband and mother, Gladys Morgan, the famous Welsh comedienne. Musical director Hugh Akehurst had been with the London show for six years, as well as conducting the orchestra with the touring version; he travelled with his wife Kitty, and son Paul, 16, who worked as a dresser on the show. This family approach to the cast was vindicated when bachelor Don Cleaver made what turned out to be a disastrous marriage to one of the girl singers in the show.

Dot, Don, Peter and Howard flew out to Australia, via Singapore and Hong Kong, in early August, tasked with the job of finding the right people for the Minstrels and Minstrelettes, as the dancers were to be known. They also needed to find four Mitchell Maids. As usual, the show's publicist used the audition process to generate advance publicity. The youngest taken on was sixteen-year-old Rosalie Sowerby who was still in school by day when the show opened; she sat her leaving exams in November and only then joined the show properly. When Robert Gencey, an actor and singer, was stabbed three times in early August, JC Williamson Theatres asked him to audition for the show, though he wasn't hired. Some of the Minstrels, such as Pero Matulic, had been in the 1962 company and so were welcome experienced additions to the cast. Every part of the process was covered by an eager local press. As always, the girls had to have their hair cut short to accommodate the necessary hairpieces and wigs. Dot, who had extremely long blonde hair, dreaded having hers cut, according to many Australia papers. To let her get used to having it shorter, it was done in two stages at Edward's in Melbourne's South Yarra, which generated much publicity.

On September 22, George flew from London to Honolulu, then on to Fiji for a few days at the Fijian, Yanuca Island Resort, before arriving in Melbourne at 4am on September 29. The return journey was more straightforward. George left Sydney at 7pm on October 21, the day after the Melbourne opening, flying straight back via Honolulu, reaching London at 9.40am on October 24 - all rather quicker than seven years earlier.

Many of the items needed in Australia were flown in from Britain, particularly the lighting as the Australia theatres still didn't have sufficiently good lighting for the new show. The wardrobe, most of which was white, red and silver, was in the capable hands of Michael Angione, who worked twelve hours a day washing, ironing, repairing and polishing. The cast, though not the soloists, were weighed each week, partly to ensure that they were eating properly and also to ensure that the costumes still fitted properly.

The show opened with a grand Gala Premiere at Her Majesty's, Melbourne on Saturday, October 12. As before, the gala included a best-dressed competition, with a lot of press coverage of the audience, most of whom wore evening dress or at the very least black and white. The show was of course far better known in Australia this time round, thanks not only to the previous tour but also to the television series, the most recent of which was being screened by ADS7. Maybe this led to greater expectations among critics, but initial coverage was certainly lukewarm compared with the ecstatic reception in 1962. Critics often used phrases such as 'curiously old-fashioned' and 'why the makeup?', though they all thought it great entertainment and should 'last and last'. Aztec brought pressure to bear to persuade critics to make swift return visits, and certainly, the revues generated second time around were vastly more enthusiastic.

The cast continued the British tradition of company events and fund-raising, all of which generated publicity. They organised cast picnics and film afternoons, gave one another gifts on birthdays and held a raffle on Fridays to raise money for club funds, as well as designing the company's own Christmas cards. Twenty cast members in full costume sold buttons in December in aid of the Carry On appeal, which helped ex-service men and women. Celebrities visited the show in droves, such as the visit by Lionel Rose, who, named Fighter of the Year in January, spent the evening at the show and was feted backstage by the girls.

After four months in Melbourne, the show moved to Adelaide, where it remained for a month. Don Cleaver arrived earlier than most to do some pre-show publicity. Seven dogs, two cats and a canary, all acquired in Australia, travelled to Adelaide as pets, along with the cast members. Dot had got her fox terrier, Dixie, from a Melbourne lost dogs' home - 'I went and looked and lost my head.' Minstrel Brian Earl recalls that 'it used to roll on its back with its four legs in the air whenever we passed near it. When we took friends backstage, we used to say to Dixie, "Hey Dixie, what do the bad girls in Kings Cross do?" [Kings Cross was a notorious red-light district in Sydney.] Dixie would promptly roll on its back with legs in the air and tongue hanging out. People thought it was trained to do this.'

On February 20, opening night in Adelaide, 5AD broadcast live at 10am from rehearsals at the theatre, interviewing major players in the show. The theatre was a lot smaller than the Melbourne venue but much more modern, which made life better for the cast. The gala premiere itself was attended by Governor Sir James Harrison, who met the cast afterwards. The theatre featured black and white paper roses on the bannisters, the foyer showed off models in black and white gowns with black and white poodles, and TV and radio personalities chose the best black and white gown from the audience.

Press reaction was very enthusiastic in Adelaide, which resulted in full houses and $250,000 (£3 million) in revenue. *The News* wrote, 'top marks for a well-produced show, full of fun and laughs – so much so that one matron laughed her false eyelashes right off her face.' Because the demand for tickets was so great, two more shows were added each week which gave the cast a mere 30 minutes between shows, the same as the stage shows in Britain had every night.

Publicity followed them everywhere they went. Ventriloquist Ken Wood took his dummy, monkey Jim, to meet the real chimps at Adelaide Zoo. Channel 9 and 10, plus *The News*, filmed the company when they went horse-riding one overcast but very humid day at a riding school out along the South Road. As one Minstrel remembers, 'Tilli, [a Minstrel] just for the cameras, rode side-saddle with a ball of knitting under his arm but they didn't show that on TV as it was a bit too camp. He's knitted himself a long black and white scarf for New Zealand.' Tilli was to try for more outrageous publicity when the cast went to the Stirling Oval to play cricket against the Motion Picture Industry Social Club. He turned up in a tennis frock which he wanted to wear but Ted Hutchinson, the stage manager and captain for the day, wouldn't let him. Tilli replied that he had just shaved his legs anyway which were now a bit cold and sore!

At the end of March, the cast began the logistical nightmare of moving the show across Australia from Adelaide to Perth, which they hadn't visited in the first tour. They left Adelaide at lunchtime, getting to Port Pirie at 10 that night. There they had to change onto the Trans Continental train which arrived at Kalgoorlie twenty-six hours later. There they stopped for an hour to change trains, getting to Perth at midday on Wednesday. Friday saw a technical rehearsal in the afternoon and a full dress rehearsal in the evening, before yet another gala opening on Saturday evening.

Sadly the theatre wasn't very well designed. Built in 1904 and untouched since, the theatre's design meant that some seats couldn't see the stage at all, so the management was unable to claim full houses. Backstage was little better, with cramped dressing rooms and no showers, forcing the cast to wash off in plastic buckets in the basement. The only good thing about the theatre was that it was in the same building as a hotel, where many of the company stayed and which became the site of many parties. One such party was a fancy dress party organised by dancer Natalie Raye. Minstrels Brendan Tobin, Ted Schoon, Bernard Cashman and Lou Jacobs all went in drag. Minstrel Don Hirst remembers that 'Lou had brought some of his frocks from Adelaide and the other three borrowed gear from some of the girls. They all looked really beautiful. Ted Schoon was the best; he was so feminine it was unbelievable.'

Opening night was a huge success with seven encores, and the company quickly found themselves the focus of Perth's social life. One party which took place at their hotel was a formal social evening 'in the Banquet Hall, an old room filled with junk', according to Don Hirst. 'We spent two days cleaning it out, and it looks quite respectable now. About seventy people came, including "Tom the Cheap Grocer", who's Lord Mayor of Perth, and the Edgleys, the owners of the theatre.' A guy called Ian, who worked at the Holden showroom near the theatre, invited twenty of the cast out for the day. He took them in his cabin cruiser for a cruise down the Swan River to Fremantle and then out into the Indian Ocean. Ian also had a speedboat which he used to take some of them water-skiing. The BP refinery at Kwinana invited them as guests for the day, giving them a tour and reception before the company performed a concert for the workers. Don recalls the occasion: 'A few people sang and danced and I performed with the trio which I put together for the Red Cross concert in Melbourne last Christmas. This time Don Cleaver joined us, and our sound was very professional and polished. The workers loved us, especially when we finished off with *Green, Green*, which is in the Top Ten at the moment. The TV cameras were there and filmed our segment. After lunch, they took us on a tugboat ride. We all had great fun, and we played with the hoses, which look like anti-aircraft guns.' Perth's Lord Mayor held a reception for them, though Don remembers it as 'a rather boring event actually, we just stood around and talked to Councillors over a glass of beer'.

The cast had a ten-day break between closing in Perth and opening in Brisbane. Despite disapproval from management, Joan Laurie grabbed the opportunity to fly from Perth to London to see her Welsh corgi dog, Pluto, intending to bring him back to Brisbane with her. Pluto had been in quarantine in Britain after spending seven months with Joan's family show in S Africa. Now he was free to travel again. The journey took her nine days, she travelled 26,000 miles and paid £1,200 (£18,000) in air fares. Sadly all was in vain, as Pluto turned out to have severe chest congestion and was unable to return to Australia with her.

The company opened in Brisbane on May 21, intending to be there until June 28. The theatre was a distinct improvement on Perth's, being much more like Adelaide's inside. They enjoyed a packed house on opening night and a good season lay ahead. Ticket sales were so high that they packed in an extra show at 5.15 on Fridays, plus an extra one at 5.15 on Monday, June 16, the Queen's birthday holiday in Australia. Soloist Howard Davies recalls that the reception in Brisbane exceeded elsewhere, both on stage and in hospitality off stage. Brisbane English Club gave them an open invitation to the club's Saturday night dances, which turned out to be so good that they went back every week, with the three soloists all singing at the club during their stay. The Minstrel travelling concert party entertained at the TPI clubrooms, which everyone seems to have enjoyed. As Don recalls, 'it was very funny, as they had other people there to entertain also. One middle-aged woman gave an alto sax recital which didn't go over too well until Hugh Akehurst [the Minstrels' Musical Director] and myself, joined in to give her some accompaniment.' The cast appeared in the first edition of QTQ-9's breakfast show and visited a special corroboree [greeting ceremony] at Kangaroo Point. In true Australian fashion, people travelled from far and wide to see the show; 29-year-old Brian Clark travelled from Kajabba, 250 miles north of Mount Isa, to see the show, travelling 1500 miles, though his trip was easily beaten by one fan who amazed them all. She flew from Hawaii to Auckland, then travelled to Hamilton to see the show and reversed this trip to fly home next day, all in all travelling nearly 9000 miles and spending a fortune!

Because of a dispute on the Brisbane waterfront involving the ship on which the show's scenery and effects were to be loaded for transportation to Auckland for the next stage of the tour, the season in Brisbane was extended to July. The cast eventually flew to Auckland on July 8, having enjoyed a last supper at Big John's restaurant between the matinée and evening performances on their last evening. The flight over was uneventful - some of the cast had watched Mick Jagger arrive in Brisbane as they were leaving - though the weather in Auckland was far from inviting, making the last fifteen minutes of the flight very rough indeed. Many of the company immediately felt at home as, according to Don Hirst, 'the countryside is very English with each green field bordered by either a stone fence or a hedge. Don [Cleaver] said it was very much like the farming areas down Devon and Cornwall way.' The theatre sent two buses to transport the company into Auckland, where a nasty surprise awaited them. Don wrote to his mother, 'What a joke! The theatre's not even on Queen St proper but at the end of an arcade. The theatre inside is very old and dark. Backstage is dark and dirty but spacious for us chorus boys.' The opening on July 12 received the usual rapturous response from both audience and critics, and with $40,000 in advance party bookings alone, a successful six-week Auckland season was guaranteed. The cast attended an after-show party at a restaurant opposite the theatre, with, according to Don, 'the Who's Who of Auckland Society in attendance, not that I met any of them'. During their stay in Auckland, the company branched out into extra-curricular activities, which, given the experience of Jeff, Harry and Eric during the previous tour, one can only assume George was aware of, as there were no repercussions. They developed a cabaret performance, which became a huge success, frequently performing at what Don called 'the most lavishly equipped ballroom I have yet seen (in Auckland Town Hall)'. One such performance was at the Air New Zealand Ball, for which they were paid $300, enough to pay for a bus to take them to visit the famous mud pools at Rotorua, during their week's stay in Hamilton.

But it wasn't to be all fun in Auckland. The show suffered a major accident one Wednesday matinée, just at the end of the early *Soft Shoe Shuffle* routine, when a big fly bar, which wasn't being used in the show, was untied by mistake by a temporary unskilled flyman. It hurtled down about 35' and landed on the row of brunette dancers. The men were first alerted by the shrieks and groans from the girls. Don recollects, 'Looking round, I saw five or six bodies lying across the treads or crawling off stage. Isobel was lying with her eyes open, so I thought she was dead.' Fortunately, she was only stunned. Three of the girls were taken to hospital, though altogether, six girls were either too injured or too shocked to continue, which made the rest of the show chaos. Don explains, 'There was no time to organise anything, so we had to busk our way through the whole show. Boys ran, found no partner, so ran off again or waltzed by themselves.' The evening performance wasn't much better; everyone's positions had to be altered so much that Don thought 'it was about the same as starting a new show and going on unrehearsed. Nerves were strained all round.' Needless to say, the press coverage was exaggerated. New Zealand radio reported that a crane had crashed onto the theatre with scores being injured and rushed to hospital which resulted in the theatre being swamped with calls from frantic parents, trying to find their sons and daughters. The news went worldwide, with cables arriving for the company from the Victoria Palace cast and the *Hello Dolly* company in New York.

After closing in Auckland on August 23, the company travelled by bus south to Hamilton, where another surprise lay in wait. Don recalls, 'The funniest thing about the town is its theatre. We imagined to be performing in a Mechanics Institute Hall or a tent, but as it turned out, they have the most modern, beautiful theatre any trouper could wish for. It seats 1263, has a revolving stage, wide wings, elevator style orchestra pit, large and numerous dressing rooms and all centrally heated!' The show was already sold out for the week – at $3.80 per seat - before it opened with no time for a dress rehearsal. In response to demand, they added an extra performance on the Thursday at 5.30. The opening night was once again a triumph in front of a capacity house, with the company being entertained later by the Hamilton Operatic Society.

After a week in Palmerston, the show moved to New Zealand's capital Wellington, where Don thought the theatre 'very beautiful inside. It looks like a vaudeville theatre as the seats are red and the walls maroon. Chandeliers hang everywhere, giving it much atmosphere.' As was becoming the norm, many of the cast did a half hour TV special; the set was a coffee lounge, and the cast sat there clapping and dancing as the mood took them. They were also invited to an exhibition of Maori songs and dances by the Ngati Poneke Maori Culture Group. Don remembers them as a 'very entertaining ensemble, with a lovely style of singing. Their poi tricks were very cleverly executed, making an entertaining evening all round.'

Everyone left Wellington on SS *Maori* one Monday evening and after an overnight crossing, docked at Lyttleton Harbour at 6am on Tuesday morning. After boarding the connecting train to Christchurch, the company settled in, with everyone hiring bikes to travel around the very flat city. In another regular excursion, many cast members went by chartered bus to Mount Cook. Don explains what happened: 'It was a joy for all who went. We were picked up at 11.30 after the show, and the bus took us on a five-hour journey to the Mount. We arrived at the Glencoe Motor Inn at 4.30am to find no rooms awaiting us as they thought we weren't arriving till 9am. As compensation, the manager of the Glencoe took us up to the Hermitage for coffee and toast.' The Hermitage was built in 1884 and became an iconic destination for New Zealand travellers. Sadly some of the cast who had stayed in Christchurch were injured in a serious car accident. Natalie Reardon was the worst injured, with severe abrasions and badly twisted ligaments in her legs, which put her out of the show for good and ended her dancing career.

From Christchurch, the show travelled to Dunedin, then Invercargill, before returning to Australia and opening in Sydney in late November, where they were to stay until the following spring. To round off a successful tour, the management decided to present a brief return season throughout the entire JC Williamson Theatres circuit, starting at the Comedy Theatre in Melbourne, where the show opened on Friday, March 13, 1970 'for forty-four joyous days only'. Maybe the date was inauspicious, but the show wasn't well received, partly because the venue was obviously wrong for the show, and also because the show was beginning to wilt, though some press coverage reported it 'as bright and lively - and predictable - as ever'. The previous year, the show had been voted the second best musical production of 1969, just being beaten by *Canterbury Tales*, also British, but it had obviously begun to suffer from nearly two years of constant touring. The 'forty-four joyous days' were to prove the last of the tour.

CHAPTER 28

A triumphant return to the London stage, another company constantly touring Britain, a sell-out tour of Australia and New Zealand, and a regular television series - George could have been forgiven for thinking everything was more than rosy as the 1970s dawned. But the golden years were about to come crashing down to earth. From leading a seemingly charmed life, George faced major trauma over the next few years.

The new television series had an increased budget which was used for bigger and better scenery and up-to-the-minute costumes. But the curse of the Television Centre remained. The BBC's Bill Cotton thought that the shows now seemed a little manufactured, compared with the *Good Old Days,* performed in a theatre. He had already once again suggested moving it back to the Television Theatre where it could benefit from having a large audience, but as in previous years, this suggestion was never acted upon. Nevertheless, viewers still loved the show, even if the press was once again beginning to lose faith.

But these problems faded into nothing when almost unbelievable tragedy hit the show in July when George Inns died suddenly on holiday aged 58. Everyone went into shock. George said, 'I am shattered. He wrote to me at the weekend arranging a meeting to discuss the coming series. He was more than a business partner. I have lost the best friend I ever had. He was simply one of the good ones.' Bob Luff recalled, 'He was the greatest producer of television spectaculars this country has known. He achieved results using kindness and understanding. He never shouted and charmed the best out of his artistes. A loveable man.' The BBC's Bill Cotton said, 'The show stands to his credit as a TV producer. He created it, he nursed it, he made it an international success. We are fortunate to have the example of his work to remember.' Huw Weldon, BBC Director of Television, reported that 'the achievements of the Minstrel show, which has remained fresh, inventive and vigorous, show after show for over twelve years, are a fitting memorial to a man who was a complete television producer.' At the memorial service, held at St Martin-in-the-Fields on August 19, the Mitchell Singers sang the anthem, then ended the service by leading the singing of *The Battle Hymn of the Republic*, one of George Inns' favourites. Dai Francis opened this, then George changed the key to let John take over, then the full 29-strong choir joined in, backed by the brass section of the Minstrel orchestra. Dai said, 'Imagine my feelings when George asked me if I would sing the opening verses. It's the number I sing on stage to round off my solo spot. At first, I was reluctant because I know how these occasions affect me. However, I agreed eventually. It was, I am told, a most marvellous sound but I don't mind admitting it was a very tense moment for me as I stood there facing a packed congregation, and waiting for the George Mitchell flick of the fingers to strike up the first notes. Hours later at the theatre, we were still mourning our late producer when the same anthem came up in the show, and as far as we were concerned, we were still in church.' To add to the sombre mood, Minstrel Les Want swore he could see George Inns standing at the back of the theatre.

Once the dust had settled a little, inevitably the question on everyone's mind was whether the show should or indeed could continue at all. The BBC thought long and hard about the situation, and George must have agonised over its future. But George's widow made it easy for everyone by deciding that it would have been his wish for the show to continue. So continue it did, though something deep had gone out of the show.

Eventually, the BBC, working with George, found the perfect producer in Ernest Maxin, who had first worked with George in 1953. Like Charles Chilton and Dennis Main Wilson, he had used the singers whenever he could. From starting life as a choreographer, he soon moved to producing and directing shows. In the course of his outstanding career, he produced all the greats, including Jack Benny, Marlene Dietrich, Dave Allen, Dick Emery, Les Dawson and Des O'Connor. While producing Morecambe and Wise, Ernest was responsible for choreographing legendary production numbers such as *Preparing Breakfast, Singing in the Rain* and *the Singing Newsreaders*. He'd just won a BAFTA, but he had to finish producing a series of ice spectaculars on BBC2 before he could turn his attention to the Minstrels.

A fan of the show and of George Mitchell, Ernest Maxin wanted to do little to change the show, promising only to make it slicker and more Hollywood. He said, 'I'm very nervous - it's not easy to follow a man like George Inns. The secret of this show is to make it as glamorous as possible. In these times of inflation, strikes and wars, people want to escape into the glitter and gaiety of a fantasy world from time to time. I'm glamorising this glamorous show even more. The girls will have four times the number of costumes they've had in the past. They will be even more modern. The men will also have a more modern look. George is to be built up as a television personality.' Like George, he was a fan of the huge Hollywood spectaculars and intended to make the Minstrels as similar as he could. This involved bigger production numbers and more spectacular effects but the successful formula - singers, soloists, perhaps above all the choir spot - remained basically unchanged. Beautiful girls in wondrous costumes - costumes for the next series were to cost £4,000 (£41,000) per show - still danced through sequences on the arms of handsome men and the country breathed a sigh of relief. Ernest was to say that 'with comedy, you are either damn good or embarrassingly awful. With a musical show, pressure is as heavy, but the fatality rate is less. Our problem is squeezing into four days what in films would take six months - seven major scene changes and about ten costume changes in every show.'

Ernest was as much of a perfectionist as the two Georges. If he didn't feel the floors were clean enough before recording, he would sweep them himself. As Roy remembers, 'The floor people didn't like it, as it was crossing lines, but it helped him relax, and as he was such a perfectionist, it gave him the confidence that the floor was swept really clean.' The Prop boys made him feel right at home by giving him a wide broom covered in glitter dust and labelled *Ernest Maxin's Broom*. Clem Vickery, who joined the show later with his banjo act, recalls that 'if I played one wrong note in a chord, he'd spot it, but that's the only way to be.' No wonder George and Ernest got on so well.

Fans didn't have to wait too much longer to see what a Minstrel show under the Maxin eye would look like. A one-off show, the first produced by Ernest, was broadcast on Boxing Day 1970 and was shown as a tribute to George Inns. The show also welcomed back soloist Penny Jewkes, who had been touring South Africa. The BBC welcomed the show, saying 'There was very good handling of the Minstrels by Ernest Maxin.' However, the Board regretted a 'smuttiness about Jimmy Jewell's humour and that of Leslie Crowther who no longer seems able to play comedy cleanly'.

It was another six months before the first Minstrel series under Ernest's control started at last. Going out weekly on BBC1 in colour, it boasted a full complement of soloists - John, Dai and Andy, plus Margaret, Penny Jewkes and Elspeth Hands. Delia Wicks was back with the show following her honeymoon, and Les Rawlings completed the line-up. Guests in the first show were Neville King and the Monarchs, all currently with the stage shows. The production team remained the same, with choreography back in the hands of Roy Gunson.

George was inundated with letters after the first show. His greater involvement on screen was greatly welcomed by many, including Margot Ellis who said, 'For some time I have wanted you to come up closely to the television screen. Your shoulders are much admired.' She went on to explain that she had recently been involved in a severe plane accident while on holiday and had had to return to the UK for an operation: 'I've tried to be cheerful but tonight felt very sad, and the doctor said he did wish something could do me good and you came right up and faced the screen!'

Ernest was also delighted with the way the series had gone. Years later, he said that the Minstrels 'were the most professional group I ever worked with and were so brilliant at getting us out of problems when things went wrong.' He also introduced them to a new recording field. Ernest was a Leyton Orient fan and persuaded George to let the choir record an Orient supporters' song.

But people were furious as to the timing of these shows. Originally going out at a late 10pm, the later shows in the series were moved even later to 10.15pm. The fans' anger was vividly expressed by 'Infuriated' who wrote, 'Words cannot express my anger, as to the time the show has been put back to. The working class could watch this show when in the pub. Now it is later it is annoying to see only twenty minutes. I complained but to date, no acknowledgement. That crummy show *Coronation Street* should be put back to 10.40 after closing time, then Annie Walker would be fined for drinking after time.' Ironically this is exactly what happened in July in Ireland where a publican was summonsed and fined for having people on the premises after 11pm. He said he had invited them there to see the first *Black and White Minstrel Show* in colour. No drink was served, but he was fined £5, and those found with him were fined £3 each.

Minstrel Magic

The BBC may have been delighted and viewer research appreciative, but press reaction was very critical, both of the show itself and of its new producer. *She* recalled George Inns: 'One wonders if it has enough of its own momentum (without him) to survive. I met him once. His enthusiasm was infectious, and it wasn't until we parted that I remembered how mechanical I found those walking/singing numbers, how dreary the pounding rhythms, the sameness imposed on all the songs, how artificial and unacceptable the blacked-up men and pure white ladies. Super-successful, it seems to me a strange reflection of mass audience taste.' The *Yorkshire Post* also sadly missed George Inns: 'Time and time again, the viewers are confronted with acts of repetition, the same songs, the same jokes, the same faces. The blame for this recent failure must be laid at the door of the production team. Individual performances were as always outstanding. But the guiding hand of the late George Inns was sadly missed.' The *Birmingham Mail* queried the whole concept: 'When the BBC experimented with an all-white show a year or two ago, did the audiences diminish? If they did not, why go back to blacking-up? If they did diminish on this account, then indeed we have a puzzling and wholly irrational peculiarity of viewers.'

More tragedy was to strike George on a personal front. Although she'd been ill with cancer for months, the death of George's wife Irene in January 1972 must have been devastating. She'd been in and out of the Royal Marsden Hospital for eighteen months, and spent the last three months of her life there, where George visited her as often as he could. She had never been very physically involved with any show, probably because she had a house and two young children to look after, and most choir members rarely if ever saw her, but nevertheless the impact on George and his family was immense. A few years earlier, George had been devastated by the death of his father, Robert. The shrapnel wounds he had suffered during the war 'got him eventually', recalled George, 'when he just polished the valves of his latest car. He tried to get the sump off, and the shrapnel got him.' George adored both his parents and always remained very close. Some time earlier, George had paid for his parents to go around the world on a cruise. His father was emotionally upset when George presented them with the tickets, saying, 'I'm not taking money off my son.' George was very clear: 'You can't do anything about it, I've bought the tickets, and I can't take them back, I'll lose all my money.' So they were forced to go. They stopped off in New Zealand to see relatives they hadn't seen for thirty years. After Robert's death, George's mother Barbara moved in with George and Irene, where she remained until her own death ten years later. George's circle of loved ones was slowly diminishing.

As always, work proved a saviour and George threw himself into the new television series and the touring shows. Christmas Day this year marked their return to television after an absence of eighteen months, but unusually the show was moved to the 2pm slot before the Queen's Speech. On a cutting, leading up to this show, George wrote, 'We were shifted from our usual 8pm slot to 2-3pm to hopefully get her some viewers.'

The London and television shows had survived the loss of Tony Mercer. But could it survive the loss of another one of its original major stars? George was about to find out. At the end of 1971, John decided to leave the show. As early as June, he was saying, 'I never seem to get a chance to pull all the stops out. Everything sometimes seems too bland, and lacking in musical colour. I suppose the reason I've stayed a Minstrel so long is largely economic. When you've four children to support and whacking school fees to pay, you can't be all that fussy.' He admitted it got boring at times but 'the saving grace is that they are all such marvellous friendly funny people.' He also found the regulations against them doing other television work occasionally frustrating. Certainly, by the autumn, he had made the decision to leave the television show, though he stayed with the stage show until the following January. He explained his decision: 'The show has been marvellous to me. It will be hard to leave, but after so long being part of a team, I began to wonder whether I could stand on my own feet in show business. I've just reached forty and life is supposed to begin there, so I've decided to make a change. I've had the seven-year-itch twice while with the show. Obviously, it's a gamble giving up a regular income, but I believe I can earn more free-lancing.' Not everyone was willing to take this risk. As Les Rawlings said, 'The big frustration is when you know you have sung really well, and people say to you "Which one was it sang that song?" and you have to say "It was me." But I've seen what happens to people who leave the Minstrels. You might get fed up at times, but the show provides a lot of work and the real fans still recognise you behind the makeup. Basically, we are the last high-class singing show left on stage, and because of the format, you never have to worry about the loneliness of touring by yourself.'

The loss must have shocked George, even if it wasn't totally unexpected. However, once again, as with Tony's departure, he had another star tenor in waiting. As Ted Darling remembers, 'We all knew eventually that John was going to leave. We were doing a broadcast at the Camden Theatre; in a break, George and I were on our way to the loo. On our way through the door, George said, "Ted, it's all yours if you want it." I didn't have to think about it for too long. I made George smile when I said, "I know why you chose me, I fit John's costumes without altering." '

January 29, 1972 was the last Victoria Palace show for both John and Margaret. John was moving on to pastures new, with a three-month contract with the New Zealand Ballet and Opera Trust to appear in *Orpheus in the Underworld* during a tour of Australia and New Zealand. He also had concerts lined up throughout the UK on his return in May, as well as a possible summer season, so his optimism looked well-founded. Margaret was leaving the show as she was expecting a baby in July. She said, 'At times I've been bored, tired and fed up but I wouldn't have missed it for the world. I'll miss the show, of course. After ten years, there's bound to be a gap, but it'll be nice to put my feet up for a while and be able to cook a meal for my husband. They've told me I can come back and I probably will. Everything depends on the baby and how I feel.' In the last show, they staged a special routine together. As John remembers, 'Margaret came on with some giant green knitting and sang *This is a Lovely Way to Spend an Evening,* and I wore a placard saying *Going for a Song.*' By the time he left, John reckoned he'd blacked up 9812 times during his fifteen years with the show.

Although Ted had years of experience both with the Mitchell Singers and as a solo artiste in shows such as *Melodies For You* and *The White Heather Club,* he had some apprehension about his new role: 'Taking over from John is quite a responsibility and a challenge. It's going to be a tough test following an established star. He has become a great favourite with lots of viewers. I am very lucky to be going into a show that is so well established.' Keith Leggett said at the time that 'Ted was terrific - an instant hit. I guarantee that by Boxing Day all Britain will be asking about him.' Dai reported that 'I am delighted to welcome him to our front line.

I have worked with him for nearly ten years and have always rated him highly.' John too was supportive of his replacement: 'Ted has a fine voice, and I wish him all the luck in the world.' John and Ted were already a mutual admiration society. As Ted explains, 'John and I got on well, he was a year in front of me from our Royal Academy days. I followed him into *Music For You*. I shall never forget John singing in *Falstaff* - the best I'd ever heard. He had enormous breath control, lovely words. I always wondered how he did it.' John was equally full of praise for Ted's voice.

Ted settled in well. As he recalls, 'My early shows were live. Occasionally we stopped recordings to get something right but not often, so it was just like doing it for real. We used to have a final rehearsal for the television show on Saturday night, a dinner break around 6.30-7.30. I gradually realised that some were not going for dinner, including George. "We get together and have a few drinks in the dressing room," I was told. I joined them and got a taste for whisky. The rehearsal afterwards was the happiest ever as no one really cared. Sunday, it was eyes down and for real. I did solos for George where I could more or less choose what I sang. He and I admired each other. Apart from Dai, I probably got the lion's share of the solos. The show was always well rehearsed with no silly props.'

Ted's first television appearance with the Minstrels, at Christmas 1971, was well received. The *Stage* thought the show 'beautifully staged and retaining all its former zest and sparkle'. Ted was happy with how it had gone: 'I've got everyone to thank for making my big TV start this week so comfortable.' The fan mail started coming in immediately. Ted remembers, 'I had one from a chap saying, "My mother-in-law has already been converted to you after John." I was knocked out by anyone who took the time and trouble to put pen to paper and send a letter.' Not everyone was quite so supportive. The mother-in-law conversion was mentioned by several newspapers; one reader wrote very indignantly, 'Why is it necessary to publish such a remark? Surely the BBC Publicity Department can write Ted up without bringing in slighting references like that to John? He doesn't have to be built up at John's expense. Surely you don't think someone is just going to "replace" John - just like that! If you do, you have no realisation at all of just what place John holds in our hearts. It's going to be unbearable when the first shows without him reach us.' Evelyn Taylor rather damned with faint praise when she wrote, 'I'm sad at the loss of John, but Ted will do.' However, John Street, who hoped to become a singer himself, wrote, 'One of my greatest delights was the recent introduction of Ted Darling to the show. What a magnificent voice this young man has - and this, together with a charming personality, has ensured that he is a very worthy successor to John.'

On January 31, Ted took over on the Victoria Palace stage. He remembers this first day very clearly indeed: 'The first day was shattering. We rehearsed the television show during the day and then went straight to do two shows at the Victoria Palace in the evening. It was all very confusing. I don't remember half of it, but I survived. There was a family atmosphere backstage. I felt sorry for the chorus as they were in every routine, but they were treated well and regarded as the mainstay of the show, which they were. When I joined, their pay rose from £18 (£230) to £25 (£320) each week. The boys had two dressing rooms, one for the straight guys and one for the gays. The three original soloists shared a dressing room which was the size of a small kitchen. It got on everyone's nerves after ten years. There was hardly room for them to turn round. By the time I got to the Victoria Palace, I had my own room which was much better.'

A staunch defender of the show to this day, Ted enthused about the show in a feature at the time: 'The music I sing with the Minstrels does not expand you like opera of course, but I try to bring to it all that I have. It isn't something you can do by halves. As long as everyone gets something from the show, whether it is just pleasant memories or a nostalgic sentimentality, as long as they enjoy themselves, I'm happy. I was once asked if, as a former student of the Royal Academy of Music, I wasn't debasing my art by appearing with the Minstrels. What rubbish! It's all entertainment whatever you sing, and with this show the audience reaction is fantastic.' He also enjoyed the anonymity that John had begun to find so frustrating. As Ted said, 'It means that when I go into a pub or out for a meal, I can enjoy privacy like everyone else.' As the months went on, he realised that belonging was so satisfying that he no longer thought of a future apart from them: 'What other show gets such a wonderful reaction from the audience? Everyone knows the songs we are playing.'

But further tragedy was in store. Margaret Savage gave birth eleven weeks prematurely to very small twin girls. One little girl, Maria, lived only a few hours, and they struggled to keep the other

Minstrel Magic

one, Anne, alive. As Maggie remembers, 'The birth of premature twin girls was a great shock as it had not been diagnosed that I was having two babies. Anne was kept in hospital for a few months, slowly gaining weight.' Unfortunately, she contracted meningitis while still in the hospital premature baby unit and was rushed to Great Ormond Street Hospital for several operations.

Maggie felt able to return to the television show the following year. She remembers, 'Little Anne had gained strength, and George asked me if I could perhaps manage to do a few shows. He was very good, and I was glad to be able to manage part of the series. In fact, it helped me a lot to get over the trauma and gave me a great lift. With a very understanding husband and some good babysitters, I managed to do some shows and the radio series.' However, on the day of Anne's first birthday, Maggie announced that she was expecting another baby at Christmas. She said, 'We are thrilled, particularly after the upset last year. I don't mind if it's twins because this time I'll be prepared.' Thankfully this time baby Michael arrived safely, much to Maggie and husband Peter's relief. As Maggie recalls, 'Over the next few years, the family increased and all the time I would have to tell my lovely boss, "Eh, George, I don't think I will be able to do all of the next series." George would reply, "Oh, naw Haggis, no another yin! Well, hen, when you're ready, gee us a call." He was very understanding.'

George found a replacement for Maggie in Penny Jewkes, a long-time Mitchell singer, and also introduced Dot Ogden, back from the Australian tour, as a new soloist. Penny's return pleased many fans, as did Dot's introduction. L Seymour wrote, 'How about those two tall terrific dollies, Penny Jewkes and Dorothy Ogden. Wow! More! More!' Dot recalls feeling 'very scared doing solos at first as the others were choir singers. I was shaking like a leaf. They were also older, and you knew that they know you started as a dancer. Elspeth, who started singing solos at the same time, and I thought we'd only stay a few weeks. Once we'd stayed a few months, the others took us on board. We actually weren't very good at the beginning. No one had wanted to let me go as a dancer, and I'd also understudied some of the acts in the stage show. I was torn too - should I sing or dance? I carried on doing both until the television offer came on board when I stuck with the singing.'

But George's plans seemed to be jinxed when on Boxing Day Penny was killed in a double car accident near Peterborough. She had been playing principal boy in *Cinderella* in Leicester and had spent Christmas at her parents' house in Norfolk. She left there on Boxing Day to return to the theatre, when the accident happened on the A47 at Wansford, shortly after 10.30am. Her boyfriend, Malcolm Young, had lent her his Mercedes for the journey and she wasn't used to such a powerful car. Penny and the other car hit head on, and both caught fire. The passenger in the other car died too, though the other driver was pulled clear as the cars caught fire. The Leicester pantomime went on with an understudy, within hours of the cast learning the news. Keith Leggett remembers 'getting the news about Penny during our Christmas break. It had a devastating effect on the company as she was such a vibrant person and very very popular.'

Death still hadn't finished with the company. George was devastated to learn that Tony Mercer, for so long a vital cog in the show, had died in July 1973 at the Royal Masonic Hospital, London. After he'd left the show, he played British clubs, then went on a world tour to Australia, New Zealand, South Africa, Trinidad and Nassau. He had two heart attacks while appearing in Malta in May 1972; although they were said not to be serious, he had been in hospital for three weeks after the first one when he had the second one. He then had a third attack and was fighting for his life. In March 1973, he collapsed in the dressing room of the Pavilion, Hemel Hempstead, half an hour before he was due to go on stage in a gala celebrity concert in aid of Make Children Happy. He had a second attack shortly afterwards. He recovered enough to travel with wife Angela by car back to London where he was admitted to the Royal Masonic Hospital. Again, his condition wasn't thought to be serious but was likely to keep him out of action for four weeks. He was back in hospital in June, though press coverage said it was purely precautionary as he had slight breathing problems and was expected to be out in a few weeks. However on July 14, while he was still in hospital, he had another heart attack. His wife Angela was by his side when he died, aged 51. Roy Winbow remembers that 'the show was very flat the night he died' and George described his death as 'another shattering blow in the long history of the Minstrels'. Leslie Crowther, as president of the 300-strong Wandering Minstrels Club of past and present Minstrels, suggested a Tony Mercer Memorial Trust to commemorate a man who was a devoted supporter of all kinds of charities, particularly the Grand Order of Water Rats.

Minstrel Magic

The autumn was to turn even worse. Larry Gordon, their original choreographer, died aged 53 in September, and Laurie Bloom, their longstanding production manager, died aged 51 in October. The following month saw the death of 33-year-old Mel Cornish, who designed the television shows. George must have wondered what else was around the corner.

Even the shows seemed cursed. The press was once again in retreat. The *Caernarvon and Denbigh Herald* wrote, 'Light entertainment par excellence. It will be a sad day when the George Mitchell team disintegrates.' But most press coverage saw the show as outdated. The *Birmingham Post* critic said, 'At the risk of sounding trite, can I say what a pain the Minstrels gave me and how glad I am that I don't watch more frequently? Someone will now write and point out to me how many millions of people watch it, but I can't for the life of me imagine why. It is dull, dreary and so stereotyped.' The *East Anglian Times* thought, 'A reappraisal is also necessary in the rigidly traditional, now anachronistic Minstrels. This makeup should be firmly buried with the clichés. What a pity to spoil the fine music, the superb singing, the rhythmic movement, by daubing the men's faces with black paint broken by grotesquely-grinning white mouths. How does one believe a romantic line sung to a beautiful girl by that circus mask? Of course, it's difficult to make fundamental changes to a winner. The Minstrels are deservedly popular. But nothing would be lost by a bleach-out and what a time-saver that would be. It might even forestall complaints to the Race Relations Board.' The *Express and Star* thought along the same lines: 'There is something odd about black-faced minstrels singing coster songs. Now that the show is no longer primarily what the title suggests, what is the point of black face? It should be possible to use traditional minstrel makeup for whatever plantation melodies are introduced. There is nothing racial in this. It's just a matter of making the musical idiom fit the sequence.' One paper said, 'The programme was a pale shadow of its former self. Sadly missing were the versatility of Margaret Savage, the charming diffidence of George Mitchell and the wonderful tenor voice of John Boulter. Why did they drop the negro spiritual type of concerted singing conducted by George Mitchell? Why didn't the whole company so casually wander onto the stage for the finale in the delightful way they used to? Please, Mr Mitchell, use your influence to save the show before it goes right down the drain.'

Minstrel Magic

Reviews didn't improve as the decade progressed. The industry newspaper *Stage* asked, 'How can the BBC keep this show going, particularly at its present standard of monotonous musical arrangements, mostly unimaginative performance, and weak presentation? The audience for that is surely only the over sixties and insomniac under twos?' The *Lancashire Evening Telegraph* wrote, 'I thought the whole show was sluggish. The dancers looked a bit overweight and danced like it, and the set pieces seemed to lack zip. Perhaps the show will speed up a bit - I hope so.'

Nevertheless, newspapers were still very keen to do lengthy features on the show. To publicise one new television series, the *Daily Mail* asked, 'Has that Old Black Magic gone and lost its spell? How much longer can it go on? That sequinned-suited anonymous chorus are a *Guinness Book of Records* proof of longevity. It has become a National Institution, a kind of monument to British durability and a comforting reassurance that all is not yet up with the world. Not just old-fashioned but archaic. The public, however, have remained remarkably loyal. Most of the fan letters come from the over-70s and the under-16s. But that a lot of the generation in between still look in is demonstrated by the resilience of its viewing figures. It was getting sixteen million in the heyday, last season it was still topping twelve million – and that is 50% more than *Top of the Pops* can claim.'

The *Guardian* went on a breathtakingly patronising rampage, managing to insult the show, its fans and amazingly the black community as well, in its arrogance and assumptions: 'The Minstrels have gone beyond such pedestrian judgements as good and bad. They've scaled some wild dizzy heights where they sit safe and snug and smugly free from the normal run of abuse. A true grotesque. I am pretty sure that if I ever get the DTs, I shall see the Minstrels. And hear them too. We mustn't forget the singing of the songs for that is a very important part of this inscrutable torture. A few flat notes, a verse or two of strangled lyrics.....we all can forgive that. But who can stand this? Did you go on the voyage down Latin American way with the merry minstrels and their ladies the other week, and are you recovered yet? I'm not. But all this is simply a matter of taste. There are thousands upon thousands of people who like bad singing because they cannot hear good singing when it is sung and just do not know the difference. Fortunately, they have the Minstrels ever ready to supply their eccentric needs. There are also those who have no natural sense of rhythm and cannot really tell if anyone else is dancing well or badly. For them, there is also the Minstrel show. Still, this is all only a matter of taste.' But fans still loved it, and audience figures remained consistently high.

Sometime in the summer of 1972, Bob and George took the decision to close the London *Magic of the Minstrels* in November after only three years. The show was still playing to packed houses, selling out second house seats completely in 1970 and 1972, but George and Bob felt that three years was long enough for the show. Bob said, 'It was not an easy decision to make, especially in view of the show's phenomenal success, but I think we must consider the millions of fans who have been continually asking when we are to present a new production. There have been only two Minstrel shows in the West End since 1962 but more than a hundred television shows.'

By the time it finished, the show had run for 1833 performances, and been seen by nearly 1.9m people, making an aggregate length, with the first show, of 6187 performances with a total attendance of 7,466,509. It remained the longest running musical show ever performed in Britain until it was overtaken by *Les Miserables*. In the three years that the show had been open, each girl had worn out thirty pairs of gold shoes, fifteen pairs of silver shoes, and twelve pairs of coloured shoes. They had one new pair of long white evening gloves a week, plus one pair of short gloves per week, though they managed to make a pair of tights last two weeks! The men had a white shirt, two collars, a pair of white gloves and two pairs of white socks clean every night. They also had two pairs of shoes every six months, and every man also had eight hats.

A factor which may have played a part in the decision was that the next television series was due to go into production in late November. Bob said, 'The closing date is appropriate because it will allow us to go into our winter series without having to call upon the cast to also appear twice nightly on stage.' Of course it wasn't necessarily the same Minstrels on television as on stage, but nevertheless, the critical reviews of the last 'tired' series might well have influenced Bob and George. They might also have been affected by press coverage such as that in the magazine *Plays and Players*, which ran a Top Ten monthly guide for London shows. In August they showed *Magic* lying 4th with 1624 performances, but by September and October, it had been dropped. Reader JAG Cawdry queried this, saying they should be in, but the magazine answered that 'we do not consider *Magic* a "live" show any more than Madame Tussauds. Both may be good entertainments, but both are merely copies and not really relevant to this magazine.'

Bob's office was inundated with mail from all over the world following the closure announcement, much of it wanting the show to travel to other countries. But he had already announced that the show would be back in London at the New Victoria Theatre, opposite the Victoria Palace, in May of 1973. Bob planned to run the show from May to September each year, so this new show would be called the *Black and White Minstrel Show of 1973*. It was to have a £100,000 (£2m) budget, playing to 2574 customers per show, instead of the fifteen hundred the Victoria Palace could hold. Still running twice nightly, it would almost double the number of people who could see the show each week. Bob said he was worried about the effect that VAT would have on ticket prices, so to keep prices as low as possible, he was moving to a bigger theatre. Top ticket prices would now be £1.50 (£18).

The final show at the Victoria Palace was a real rollercoaster for everyone - sadness that the show was closing, yet anticipation of new challenges ahead. As usual, the cast managed to dream up some fun during the show. Ted Darling remembers, 'We had fun on last nights, though some of the gay boys went overboard with costumes.' For instance, Dot was meant to partner Ted but Howard Neil, dressed as a mermaid, came on in her place. As Howard recalls, 'George did not, nor did any of the cast, know what I was going to do. The only two people who knew were Marie and Ethel in wardrobe. I made the outfit myself at home and got helped into it by wardrobe and shuffled down the stage to replace Dot who was to accompany Ted for *On Mother Kelly's Doorstep*. Ted smiled and carried on as usual, the audience went wild, and Bob Luff and George apparently went white - until they heard the audience.'

The fans were devastated. Regulars Lawrence Grassi, John Ransted, Christine Vick and Eileen Morris were still seeing the show week in and week out. On the night of the last show, November 4, John, Christine and Eileen met for a farewell-to-the-show drink at a pub across the road from the theatre, before watching the final show and attending the off-stage party afterwards.

Minstrel Magic

In a further blow, Dai Francis decided he was going to leave the show when *Magic* closed. John's leaving had unsettled him, and in January he said he too was thinking of going solo: 'Millions of people all over the world know my name and my voice, but no one knows my face. It's a bit frustrating, but it gives me the incentive to get known in my own field. It isn't very satisfying to know that you play a big part in the huge success that is the Minstrels and yet walk around without people recognising you.' He already had a forty-minute solo act, during which he sang a few songs, then blacked up on stage so people could see what was involved: 'It's always a hit, and I get a tremendous ovation. Even people who didn't recognise me when I was white recognise me with the makeup. You can hear them saying "Good God, it's him." It's rather strange being in the show without John and Tony and in some ways rather sad. I felt a little on my own.'

By November, he calculated he had sung *Mammy* 5000 times, though actually, it must have been more. He said, 'I now want to prove myself as an artiste in my own right, and this seems an appropriate time. I hope to appear with the Minstrels in future television shows, if not on stage.' There seemed to be no hard feelings as Bob responded, 'I wish Dai success and look forward to his working with us again. Good old Minstrels are always welcome back in the company.' Clem Vickery, however, recalls that one of his Stompers was told a different version of Dai's departure: 'He thought the show revolved around him and asked for so much money that they decided to get rid of him. He was always the hardest to work with, a prima donna twenty-four hours a day. I toured with him later in *The Jolson Review*, and he was very temperamental. One day backstage he came across me doing an Al Jolson impersonation and took great offence, stamping his foot, because he assumed I was ridiculing him.'

As Bob had promised and despite the loss of Dai, the big event of 1973 was the opening of the new *Black and White Minstrel Show of 1973* in July at the New Victoria Theatre, London's largest theatre, seating 3000 against the Victoria Palace's 1500. Although George undoubtedly wrote the arrangements for this show, in a nice twist his son Robert directed the music, while George was committed elsewhere. To get a blend of experienced and new Minstrels in both the London and the touring companies, George mixed up the cast from the previous year's three shows. Soloists at the New Victoria were to be Ted Darling, Karl Scott, Les Want and Les Rawlings. Howard Neil remembers that 'some of the new boys from the touring show joined us. One, Gerry Cassidy, (mother to us all) had a beautiful crop of hair. We didn't realise that it was ear to ear Axminster until we were in the dressing room and it came off. He would make his face up, leaving a friar's spot on top.' Another new cast member, Mitchell Maid Helen Stewart, remembers joining the show: 'I will always have wonderful memories of my time with the show, in particular, company manager Sandy McFarlane who was my protector. I was away from home for the first time at the tender age of 18!! And he ensured that I was safe. Lovely times.'

Don Maclean was introduced as the new comic act, supporting Hope and Keen, who had left the touring company to move to London. Clem Vickery's Vellum Stompers were also signed up, plus juggler Nino Frediani and acrobats the Randels. George and Bob had had their eyes on Don Maclean for a long time. As Don recalls, 'George and Bob came to see me in a summer show I was in at Clacton in 1967. Eventually, my agent said they were interested in putting me into the Victoria Palace but thought I wasn't quite good enough then. They saw me again in 1972 when I was appearing at the Opera House Blackpool with Cilla Black, and thought I was great.'

The show had some less than welcome advance publicity in June. An advert which Bob had placed in the *Baptist Times* produced a huge outcry in its letters pages. Eva Butcher wrote, 'I am amazed and distressed to find this advertisement, complete with grinning negro characters and tights-clad females. It seems incredible that this kind of subject matter should find propaganda space in the religious journal of a Christian denomination. It is my habit to forward my copies to a Danish pastor, but I am removing this page as I should be ashamed for him to see it.' Jean Walters asked, 'What is this magazine coming to when it opens its pages to advertising secular shows whose aims are purely to make money and not to glorify God? What hypocrisy to, a couple of weeks ago, report on a greater understanding of and love for our coloured brethren and then this week to advertise a show which has caused offence to the same.' The magazine rushed to its own and the show's defence: 'The New Victoria Theatre wished to bring the attention of the people in our churches to the *Black and White Minstrel Show*. This is widely regarded as one of the few family shows which do not give offence, both on television and stage; it was for this reason that the advertisement was accepted.'

The gala opening took place on July 5, in front of a capacity audience which included John Boulter and Margaret Savage. The show did well throughout its run, with crowds pouring in, though perhaps not to the extent that they had at the Victoria Palace, a fall exacerbated by the increased size of the auditorium. Nevertheless, in a move which must have pleased George and Bob and helped refute the 'racist' slurs, Clem Vickery recalls 'standing on stage and looking out at row and row and row of black people, dressed in colourful clothes, and really enjoying themselves. I never heard anybody in the show say anything even vaguely racist. The makeup was like being a clown.'

Press reaction was extremely polarised. Those who praised it, like the *Daily Express*, called it 'a feast of colour and music', 'light-hearted undemanding entertainment' or 'extremely bright, lively and tastefully colourful'. The *Daily Telegraph* called it 'a riot of orange and lemon, tinsel and stardust - a real bobby dazzler of a show. Speedy and bright.' The *Stage* reported, 'They were greeted by a reception which rivalled the one they obtained back in the early Sixties. How well it has stood the test of time.' Even when a paper was faintly critical, it was followed by praise, such as the *Chatham News* who wrote, 'People are willing to concede the canned voices; it is little to lose in exchange for a two-hour fast-moving tour down memory lane. The stage is alive with colour from start to finish, and the pace set is breath-taking.'

But many were highly critical. The *Evening Standard* called it, 'Little more than a mausoleum of dated entertainment ideas. No doubt sociologists will one day strive to analyse the continuing appeal of this unchanging show. It is perhaps the English Dunkirk spirit which makes them cherish something that in other lands would probably be a sure loser.' An obviously false statement when one considers the success of the show all over the world! The *Eastern Daily Press* said, 'Sitting through last night's performance was to suffer slow torture. Whatever merits it had in the first place have not survived the years. The format is decidedly geriatric. Yet the crowds pour in. We would consider walking a million miles to get away from it all.'

But one traditional enemy of the show performed a U-turn. The *Guardian* wrote, 'We all gasped like kids at a circus at the sheer effrontery and garishness of the sets and costumes which overcame any piddling quibbles about bad taste. Nor could one fairly grumble about the black faces, not when they wore them as Venetian boatmen, cowboys, circus clowns, Uncle Sams and Viennese courtiers. The show is a kind of British equivalent of Las Vegas. It seems to strike some primaeval chord. Its popularity is beyond explanation, its success beyond dispute. Perhaps it is simple professionalism, perhaps superb timing and a subtle diagnosis of what the British see as spectacle, but its sense of pace, colour and momentum made it an exciting evening, at least when the singers were on. For the rest, we had abysmal comics.'

One bizarre criticism appeared in the always vitriolic *Crescendo*: 'They are back in town and probably for a long run, our peasantry being fond of their sentimental sing-alongs and always quaintly amused by the guying of imagined inferiors. The show as ever is a touching tribute to the emancipated peoples of Africa, wherein the male performers indulge in much boot blacking and adopt blubbery lips and grotesque eyes. Coloured tourists in London will be captivated; not often does a country wear its uglier aspects on its sleeves. As I've said before, the show is known in the trade as "Abe Lincoln, where are you now?" and proves that the echoes of Rastus and Bones, putting on a show for Massa under the good old Southern moon after a worthy day's work on the plantation, have not yet died away in the green and pleasant land that was once proud of having pioneered tolerance and understanding.' Such comment shows breath-taking ignorance of the history of Minstrel shows, as well as turning a convenient blind eye to Britain's role in pioneering the slave trade.

However, whatever their views of the show, most agreed with the *Evening News* who wrote, 'The Minstrels should have no difficulty keeping the legend alive for the next five months.' The *Barnet Press* agreed: 'The real magic of the show is in the Minstrels and their music. This is a show which can be heartily recommended, and it seems certain to be packing them in just as successfully as in the past.'

The change of theatre proved less successful. Audiences and the media felt the show lacked the intimacy of the Victoria Palace. Three thousand seats per show is a lot to fill, and it was now rare for the theatre to be sold out, though the touring show had no problems filling and breaking records at Blackpool Opera House, the largest theatre in Europe. Perhaps Londoners were beginning to get tired of the show? But records of a certain sort were set.

Ernest Maxin thought greater numbers of younger people were coming to see the show, attributing this to the pretty songs and ballads of popular singers like Jack Jones and Andy Williams, so that youngsters didn't think the Minstrels at all old-fashioned. One other unexpected statistic was that more patrons hired opera glasses at the Minstrel show that at any other London theatre!

The layout certainly didn't help the fast changes. Minstrels and Toppers had to race up and down five flights of stairs, which, with the energetic routines, caused problems for the Toppers - and some fun for the backstage crew. As Minstrel Howard Neil recalls, 'The girls were fitted for their beautiful lilac chiffon dresses, which were halter-necked and heavy. After we'd been onstage for about two months, the girls all lost weight. The medley was Viennese with lots of lunges over the boys' arms. With every lunge, the breasts of the now-thinner girls would fall out. You could hear the backstage boys counting how many boobs came out on one side of the stage and then there was a mad rush to the other side of the stage to count how many came out that side.'

That wasn't the only problem caused by the elaborate costumes. Howard again: 'The medley that ended the first half was *Around The World In Song*, and the last number was a Russian Troika. The girls' headdresses were covered in wire balls which, over time, came off, leaving the wire exposed. Gerry Cassidy and Nanette Tunnacliffe, after a very quick change, were directly in front of me. On they went, and Gerry turned his head to the audience. Off came the black wig on one of the exposed wires. 'Oh f...,' said Gerry very loudly, and a set of false teeth went flying off to the other side of the stage, and so did Gerry and Nanette. The lifts we were supposed to do that night just didn't happen as we and the audience were in gales of laughter.'

Other cast members had problems too. Don Maclean was also filming a series of short silent films for *Crackerjack*, in which he did all his own stunts, one of the most dangerous of which was to whiz down a garden path and down some steps, all on a bike. Instead, the wheels of the bike jammed in the garden gate and he ended up flat on his face in the road. He was taken to hospital to get five stitches above his left eye and then on to the theatre. As he walked through the stage door - eye black, and blood still streaming down his face - he heard there was a bomb scare. 'Get on quick,' they said, 'and calm down the audience.' Which is what he did. As he recalls, 'What else could I say in my condition but "I found the bomb".'

This was the height of the IRA problems in Northern Ireland, and the Provisional IRA's bombing campaign had extended to the mainland. Bomb scares were a constant feature of life, particularly in London and other big cities, where bomb scares became a nightly feature. Clem Vickery remembers another bomb scare towards the end of the run: 'It was during the clown sequence and we were wearing long striped socks, plimsolls, baggy trousers with braces. When the alert went, we ran into the street in costume, where it was freezing cold. Too cold to stay outside, we went to the nearest pub, where we got lots of funny looks. We got many of these alerts, but we always finished the show after the all clear.'

The London show closed on December 8, after five highly successful months. London wasn't to see another Minstrel show. Between them, the three London shows had produced 6464 performances and been seen by 7.8 million people.

CHAPTER 29

George was lucky to have Karl Scott in this show as, since 1972, both George and Bob's offices had been heavily involved in an argument with the Home Office over Karl's employment and residency status. George had offered a solo spot in the summer season at Paignton in 1972 to Canadian Charles Walkinshaw, whose stage name was Karl Scott. However, his working holiday permit had expired. Although he had been in Britain for four and a half years and was married to a Scottish girl, the Home Office refused to let him stay. They said he had to have a work voucher to stay but that he had to be out of the country to apply for it. He appealed against the ruling, saying, 'The Minstrel tour is a tremendous opportunity.' His hope was to stay until the following May as then he would be eligible to apply for British citizenship. The Home Office's views were that Karl had entered Britain on a student visa and had already broken the law by working, to which Karl responded by saying that as he had married a British girl, he thought he was exempt from having to notify the Home Office if he worked.

He was allowed to stay until the appeal had been heard and so he joined the show in Paignton. Equity was also supporting his right to stay. However, by the beginning of September, his appeal had been turned down. Karl was told to leave by the end of the month, as he 'had no legitimate case to remain here', despite the fact that his wife was expecting a baby on Christmas Day and had been hoping to resume her career as an opera singer with Sadler's Wells after the birth. Karl was appalled: 'My appeal on the grounds of hardship has been turned down. There are double standards. Women are expected to follow their husbands around. But if I were a Spaniard I would be allowed to stay because of the hardship to my wife if she did not speak the language. The only thing we can do now is get the law changed. My wife has a promising career in this country.' At the end of September, Karl wrote to the Home Secretary Robert Carr in a last-ditch attempt to stay in Britain, and a Labour peer arranged for Karl to meet the Home Secretary. By early October he had appealed to the Prime Minister Ted Heath. As he said, 'We still have a fight on our hands to stay, but now I am more hopeful.'

The Mitchell organisation was equally devastated, saying, 'This is a severe blow to our plans for Karl. George thinks highly of him and desperately wants to keep him.' In an effort to strengthen Karl's case, the ever-loyal George offered him, in November, the plum role of soloist on stage and television after only one season with the show. The following day, Karl again met officials in a further attempt to get a work permit, saying, 'This is the chance of a lifetime, something I could never hope for in Canada.' Bob Luff promised that, even if Karl had to leave the country, he would do all he could to help him get a work permit so he could return for the 1973 spring television series and the new London show. Bob argued that Karl had a 'unique singing voice' which was essential for the stage and television versions of the show.

It became something of a cause célèbre. Letters to national papers raged, 'What are the authorities thinking about? He has entertained millions of people so why must he go?' and 'It's a disgrace that artistes like Karl should be shunted out of this country when so many less-desirable people are permitted to stay.' A Paignton woman Dorothy Austin contacted Torbay MP Sir Frederic Bennett who took up Karl's case. She later enlisted the support of Russell Kerr, MP for Feltham and himself an Australian, also subject to the tightening laws. Mrs Austin said, 'I feel strongly about this sort of thing. Mr Scott's is by no means an isolated case. Must we throw out all those who, to me at any rate, have a right to stay in this country?'

By mid-November, Karl had lost the fight. However, a few days later, he was told that Ted Heath was personally looking into it. Press coverage suggested that Sir Frederic Bennett and 'several other sources' had been in touch again with the Home Secretary's Private Office which had resulted in the whole case being reviewed. Life picked up for Karl when a telegram arrived on Christmas Eve which said that the Prime Minister's intervention had gained Karl a reprieve of one year, because of the contract with George. Baby Karl arrived safely in mid-January.

One press cutting reveals a lot about the behind-the-scenes relationship between George and Bob. It mentions that one of the 'other sources' which had managed to get the Home Office decision reversed was Bob Luff himself. On the back of this cutting, George wrote, 'Actually I wrote to the Prime Minister - Ted Heath - and he fixed it for me.' George was the one who worked quietly behind the scenes while Bob took every possible opportunity to gain more publicity.

Karl stayed with the Mitchell organisation for several years, as principal on television and stage. But death was once again to visit the show. A few days after the show closed at Coventry in March 1976, Karl was found dead in his parked Jaguar, with a blood alcohol level of three and a half times the legal driving limit. The cast was devastated. The core singers were all in the studio, waiting to record the music for the new television series. Ann Mann, a Mitchell Singer in the Sixties and now part of the Minstrel production team, recalls it clearly: 'We got a call from Daphne Bell to say he hadn't turned up at the recording. I rang his home, and his wife said, "He's dead." I dropped the phone. What do I do now? I rang Bill Cotton [Head of BBC Television] and told him what had happened and asked what I should do. He said you have to tell them, just let Ernest know. Elspeth Hands fainted. I was crying so much I couldn't time the recording properly. I sat in the control room, tears pouring down my face. Everybody was just stunned. It was a real nightmare, one of my worst times in television.' Margaret Savage remembers it as well: 'Karl's death was so devastating. We were in rehearsal. One of the Leslies came in and broke the news. It was awful.'

Apart from the personal impact, on himself and the singers, George was faced with an immediate and urgent problem. The recording had to go ahead that day if what was a very tight time schedule was to be met. He made the instant decision to hand Karl's solo spots to long-time core Mitchell singer Bob Hunter, not only for the sound but also for the vision recordings. Karl's death also put the final nail in a proposed North American tour. As a Canadian himself, his presence on the tour had been a major selling point, though there were problems agreeing on the financial side of the proposed American part of the tour. The entire cast attended the funeral, and the Blackpool Opera House Minstrel company spent the summer fundraising for Karl's widow. Bob was so impressed with the amount raised that he doubled the final tally.

The inquest was left mystified by Karl's death. A post-mortem showed traces of a mild sleeping drug which could have added to the effect of the drink. He had recently moved to Dunstable, and his wife Mary was expecting their second child. He had arranged to go to a theatrical costumiers in London that morning and the recording session in the afternoon. He didn't drink heavily or regularly, the inquest heard, but once or twice a year he would drink a lot. The coroner found no evidence that what he did in his final hours was in any way a deliberate attempt to do himself harm. It was decided he died through misadventure, not realising the level of alcohol could be lethal.

Roy Winbow knew Karl better than many: 'He was an undemonstrative quiet guy and a gentleman in every way. We were lucky to get him. What he lacked in movement ability he more than made up for with his singing voice. Not long before his death he suffered a double tragedy in his family and had to return to Canada for a short time during the run of the show. When he returned, there was a sadness about him, some of his spirit had gone, and I felt that it wouldn't be long before he returned permanently to Canada. There was a lot of speculation about his death. Karl was not a drinker. I can say without a doubt that I knew Karl well and although he had a lot on his mind, due to his sad family losses, his death was a tragic accident and nothing more.'

Fellow soloist Ted Darling adds another perspective: 'Karl was desperate to be allowed to sing live. When we were in Bournemouth, most of us went home for the weekends. Karl didn't and agreed to do live stuff one Sunday. People came up to him and persuaded him he sounded better live. He'd been disappointed at auditions, getting down to the last three and not being selected so he became obsessed and determined to sing live in the show. I said the show had been very successful as it was for years, you can't expect people to agree the soloists should sing live. Maybe I could have fought his corner more, but I didn't want to change the way the show was - it was so successful. Why mess up something that had been so successful for such a long time? Why try something different?'

But not everything during these years was bad news. In 1971 George undertook a major new project when he co-operated with friend and composer Philip Green to write and direct a new Mass. Philip, a prestigious composer within the film industry, who had worked on many of the same programmes and films as George, wrote it as a thank you for the spiritual experience of his conversion from Judaism to Catholicism. The Mitchell Singers, renamed the Trinity Chorale for the occasion, recorded the *St Patrick's Mass* at EMI's Abbey Road Studios. The singers on this occasion included John Boulter, Dai Francis, Glyn Dawson, Bob Hunter and Ted Darling, as well as Mary Moss, Maryetta Midgley, Penny Jewkes, Daphne Bell and Jackie Stilwell. The soloist was world-famous tenor Father Sydney MacEwan whom John remembers, 'refused to sing with me'. Mitchell Singers had backed Father MacEwan, the popular tenor, years before on *The First Noel* and *Good King Wenceslas*. Phil Green had provided the orchestra on that occasion too. Reviews had called it 'sincere and seasonal'. Father MacEwan was a hugely successful international Scottish singer, who had initially abandoned his singing career in the early 1940s to follow his vocation as a priest. However, he was soon lured back to touring and recording, raising money for the building of several Scottish churches including Oban Cathedral.

Cardinal Heenan, Archbishop of Westminster, 'doubtless worried', according to George, attended the recording, intending to stay for half an hour but staying for six. He was impressed enough to invite George to perform the Mass at Westminster Cathedral and also wrote a ringing endorsement on the record sleeve, calling it 'a reverent and serious work of music containing a throbbing dynamic quality which cannot be described. It is an experimental piece of music which will not only give enjoyment but at the same time is both modern and beautiful.'

Although it had been intended to première the Mass coast-to-coast on ABC TV in the States in March 1972, it was decided to show it first at the Cork Film Festival in 1971. Philip had by now moved to Ireland to develop his interest in religious music. Philip and George chose the St Francis Chorale to join the Mitchell Singers in premièring the Mass and retained the name the Trinity Chorale, which was under the direction of George himself, with Philip conducting the whole occasion. George recalled, 'President Eamonn de Valera and the entire government turned up. The reception at the end was beyond my wildest dreams. Everyone was standing up and cheering like mad - more like a pop concert than a Mass. Happy days.'

Issued in May, the recording of the *St Patrick's Mass* received mixed reviews. The *Scotland* magazine called it 'an exciting modern score. A thrilling, beautiful and often moving new work. The singing is superb throughout.' However, Dublin's *Evening*

Press reviewer said, 'I didn't know whether to laugh or cry. This hotchpotch takes its ideas from such unlikely sources as *Danny Boy, The Scottish Soldier* and various TV jingles. Cardinal Heenan has given his approval to this record and has written an introduction for the sleeve. Of this, I can only say that the Cardinal is well known to be a kindly man and he did what he could with very unpromising material and without hurting anybody's feelings.'

One of the brightest spots of the 1970s for George personally was the award of an OBE in the 1975 New Year's Honours list. George was typically understated about the whole event: 'It probably sounds silly, but I suppose to get a show to run for so long on television and stage, it's quite an honour to get the OBE for entertaining people or services to music, whatever they called it, it's very flattering. It seems pretty worthwhile.' Congratulations poured into his office. Many came from company members, such as Delia Wicks, Keith and Nikki Leggett, and Maryetta Midgley and her brother Vernon who wrote, 'You have given great pleasure to millions of people. Long may you continue to do so.' Ted Darling wrote, 'We are all very thrilled at the news and proud to be a wee cog in your organisation. I'm sure you found the various telegrams amusing. You would have laughed even more had you heard some of the comments regarding the supposed reaction of Bob Luff to the news, but I won't go into that now. I just think 'SHE' must have enjoyed the last record you sent her best of all!' The Monarchs joked, 'Congratulations George OBE you will be known as Old Blue Eyes.' He wrote back, 'Old Blue Eyes thanks you for your kind telegram. I promise that this won't change me a bit - I still won't talk to you.' The two Leslies asked, 'What happened to home rule for Scotland?' to which George replied, 'Actually this couldn't have happened to a more surprised fellow. Home rule is still on - this is all part of a clever infiltration plan to get me into the Palace.' Past singers also congratulated him. Dai Francis said, 'You beat me to it, well deserved', and Ann Mann, now producing for the BBC, said, 'Congratulations, I've ordered a gold-edged roller caption.' Minstrel orchestral leader Freddie Clayton wrote, 'Congratulations! Schumann would have been proud of you', to which George ironically responded 'I deserved it - a) Schumann didn't really like brass, 2) he didn't have to put up with Ernie Short, 3) he never joined the Musicians Union. Sincere thanks for your letter all the same.'

Bill Cotton, Head of Light Entertainment at the BBC, called it a 'well deserved honour', and Charles Beardsall, assistant head of Radio 2, said it was 'an honour so richly deserved'. Jos van der Valk wrote from Holland, and Equity sent a telegram, as did the Chairman of the Royal Eye Hospital League of Friends of which George was still president. Sister Sheila Duneen wrote, 'It couldn't happen to a more deserving person. I noted your humility and compassion as you visited my precious patients last June at the Royal Eye.' Colonel ED Higgs, General Manager of the New Victoria Hospital in Kingston, where George was a member of the Development Committee, took the opportunity to ask for more favours: 'During the next year, we want to advertise the hospital in many ways, and if you feel you could help us from the show business point of view, we would be most grateful. I know you appreciate the problems which exist in private enterprises such as ours and we are trying to rally our forces together to produce a really major effort.'

Many who had not seen George for years took the opportunity to get back in touch. AW Dewdney wrote, 'It's always nice to see awards going to people in entertainment, especially when one knows that behind the achievement lies very many years of hard work. If the *RAPC Journal* is still around, I can almost see the headlines "From a basement in Finsbury Circus to the top of the Honours List in thirty-five easy years!" You must tell Daphne to keep trying for who knows, she may finish up a Dame yet.' Commander Glover reminded George, 'You may not remember me, it was a chance acquaintance many many years ago with Jimmy Logan when you came to a party held at my apartments at the House of Lords.' George wrote back thanking him and adding, 'I remember my visit to the House of Lords very well.' Mary Turner also reminded George of an earlier friendship: 'You very possibly will not remember me but our family used to live opposite yours in Palmers Green. Many years ago when we first used to hear your name in connection with the Minstrels, we wondered if it was the George Mitchell we had known, because we used to recall the Bookers' musical evenings too. Even on television, we were still kept guessing as only your back view was shown. However, when eventually a "full frontal" was shown, we recognised you because of your strong family resemblance to your

Minstrel Magic

father.' He answered Mary, saying, 'Of course I remember Palmers Green very well - especially those evenings with old Mr Booker and his beloved violin.' Styler Williams waited until mid-January before writing: 'I have waited until today which makes it thirty years all but one month since broadcasting-wise it all began. THE *Variety Bandbox* was on February 13, 1945, and although we all knew then that what was transmitted by that Sergeant and his Pay Corps colleagues was highly promising, none of us could envisage its fantastic development which now gets such elevated recognition.' Neb Wolters, there at the start, also wrote to congratulate George: 'What splendid news! So much has happened since those early rehearsals in the basement.'

The Songwriters Guild of Great Britain said, 'The award is richly deserved and makes all of us very happy indeed', and went so far as to place a congratulatory mention in the Guild News. The General Manager of the Performing Rights Society also added their congratulations.

The Mitchell Singers' sense of humour certainly didn't desert them over this. Bob Hunter remembers, 'We were rehearsing the music in the General Smuts pub in Bloemfontein Road. George played for rehearsals and occasionally got frustrated. If he got a wrong chord, he got quite cross with himself, and no one liked to see George cross, even with himself. Paddy said, "Don't worry, we know you didn't get your OBE for piano playing." George laughed so hard he nearly fell off his seat.'

Despite shocks such as Karl's death, the second company was still happily touring, spending long Christmas and summer seasons at loyal resorts and cities around Britain. As usual, records fell to them wherever they appeared. Huge expectations were placed by resorts on the pull of the company. For instance, in 1974 in Paignton, the Minstrels managed only 90% attendance for second houses, which led to a lot of questions being raised as to whether they were losing their appeal, as previously they had always been total sell outs. No one seemed to notice that most summer companies would have been ecstatic with such a figure. Indeed the *Terry Scott Show* managed only 74%, but no one queried this. Summer season entertainments were certainly losing their grip on holidaymakers' imaginations as by now, 10% of the population was holidaying abroad, with the number growing every year. Many people couldn't afford a holiday at all, as the 1970s were a time of dire economic gloom and people were afraid to spend unnecessary money.

Electricians' strikes, often unexpected ones, plagued the whole country in the early 1970s. To lessen the risks of the shows being plunged into darkness, Bob Luff arranged for a specially-hired generator to be parked outside the Victoria Palace stage-door, which pumped reserves of power into the footlights and the show in London went on, though not always as expected. Ted Darling remembers the problems: 'It was pretty hairy. One generator supplied one light in each room. It was so difficult to do our makeup, we'd go on with white necks and missing bits. If the power was off, the sound just wound down. We tried to sing, but if it was really bad, we called the comics in. It was just as bad when the power came back on because the sound would speed up.'

Leeds was less lucky. In February 1972, the miners' strike caused lengthy power cuts all over Britain. Electricity was rationed and a three-day week introduced. Theatres continued to manage but the touring company, currently in Leeds, were forced to put on their makeup in their lodgings to avoid using electricity at the theatre, then travel to the theatre in full makeup. But matters got even worse one night. Glyn Dawson recalled very well what happened: 'We had emergency generators in place because of the threat of power cuts. One night, the generators also stopped - they'd run out of fuel! Everything stopped, the sound and the lights. I was in the dressing room with Minstrel Nicky Shorn who immediately ran down to the stage, passing the theatre manager who was running down the corridor. 'We need five gallons of petrol,' he said to me. I was in costume and full makeup, but I offered to take my car to the garage down the road to get the petrol. One of the stage hands came too and took me to the garage where the theatre was meant to have an account. There were about half a dozen cars queuing for petrol, so I went round the outside and parked opposite facing down the hill. I was freezing as there was deep snow on the ground. The stagehand went in to ask for a five-gallon drum but was soon back saying, "Glyn, they won't let me have the fuel. The manager isn't here, only a relief manager." "Tell them I'll leave the spare wheel and come tomorrow with the money," I said. This worked, and we put the drum into the boot. Someone in the queuing cars called out, "We're on *Candid Camera!*" I said, "This is the real thing." While they were waiting for us to get back with the petrol, Neville King and Norman Collier got into the little stage car used in one of the speciality acts. It had headlights which they switched on and told yarns and jokes to the audience for twenty minutes before we returned. The next day I was told the garage manager had actually been in the audience at the theatre.'

Illness dogged both the touring and London companies but rarely did it interfere with the shows. In a mirror of the Australian accident, a scenic drop fell down during a touring show performance, and although most of the girls were whisked away in time, the heavy prop hit two of the Toppers, ending the dancing career of one of them. The London show also suffered from illness; one week they were six Minstrels short because of illness. Although Keith Leggett, as Head Minstrel, sorted it out as best he could, they were rushing up and down stairs even more than usual, and no one got their 'swing' number, the one number they got off every show. In 1970, about halfway through its second week in Hull, the company was hit by a mystery outbreak of gastroenteritis. It hit some of them so fast that they were taken ill during the show itself, which necessitated changing things instantly. Soloist Peter Pennington recalls, 'I just flopped, sapped of strength in the middle of the show.' A second principal Peter Kingston also caught gastroenteritis, causing Douggie Pearson, who understudied both of them, to be on and off stage all the time. Seven cast members had to be admitted to the isolation unit of Castle Hill Hospital, where they were kept for a few days. Les Want said the illness seemed to have affected those who occupied dressing rooms under the stage: 'Even if it is not directly concerned with conditions under the stage, any germs like flu would soon breed in the temperature there.'

But true to form, the show kept going. Not even broken bones got in the way. 'The show must go on' was never truer than with this show. Leslie Crowther backed this up: 'Sometimes you felt like the kiss of death if you had flu but the one thing that papers over those cracks is a thing called Dr Footlights, and if Dr Footlights is in the *Black and White Minstrel Show*, then you've got a double-edged weapon for recovery.' Perhaps the best example of this was Don Cleaver who suffered badly from asthma and chest-related problems and frequently needed his inhalers before and during shows.

Douggie Pearson needed more than backstage magic when he suffered several cracked ribs in a fall before one show opened. No one in the company knew of his injuries, as he carried on in spite of doctor's orders. It came to light when he had to go to hospital for treatment following one particularly agonising performance. The hospital gave him a note, saying he had to rest for eight weeks; he tore it up, saying, 'The show must go on.' Morecambe's Winter Gardens manager Robin Read said, 'I admire his courage, he has shown the real spirit of the Minstrels.'

This 'real spirit' also showed itself in the fact that Glyn Dawson spent the entire time at Newcastle in pain. He had damaged his neck months earlier but had ignored it until a game of golf aggravated the injury. He faced almost daily trips to Newcastle's Royal Victoria Infirmary to have it treated and had to wear a stiff surgical collar throughout the day. Each evening he took it off, then wrapped his neck with a black crepe bandage which was invisible to the audience. He said, 'As long as I don't turn my head by itself and remember to move from the shoulders instead, then it's all right.'

Glyn's stoicism in Newcastle was echoed by that of Lisa Hardiman who cracked a bone in her leg just before the show reached Norwich. She should have had her leg in plaster and been out of the show, but she loved it so much that she refused, had the leg strapped up and carried on, going to hospital for regular checks instead. But even Dr Footlights couldn't help ventriloquist Neville King one summer in Scarborough when he suffered such dreadful throat trouble that it began to look as if the dummies would go dumb.

Such determination didn't always work sadly. The London and television shows received shocking news when resident comic and compère Don Arrol died. Aged only 38 and with a six-month-old baby daughter, he had been hospitalised for a check-up and was away from the show for several weeks, during which time Leslie Crowther stepped into the breach. Against medical advice, he returned to the Victoria Palace after a month; the cast had decorated his dressing room and collected for flowers and a bottle of brandy to welcome him back. But he had to leave the show again after four weeks and missed recording the television show that was actually broadcast the day he died; the story was that he had food poisoning, but he died of a heart attack on May 13. Sally Barnes stepped into his place for the next two television shows, then Dai Francis took over the links. At the Victoria Palace, several comics, such as Stan Stennett, Ray Fell and Bob Andrews who had been with the show in Australia, stood in for two-week stretches before Frank Berry took over as resident. In memory of Don, the entire London cast sold flags to raise money for the British Heart Foundation.

Of even greater impact on the company was a nasty incident that happened while the show was in Norwich. Sadly the show's time there was badly tainted by the rape of one of the Toppers. During two hours of terror at the house she was staying in, the dancer was raped twice by a masked gunman, who turned out to be village policeman Robert Buttolph. She thought he was going to kill her, so she did everything he asked. Typical of media coverage at the time, some sections of the press made great play of this, as well as the scant clothing she wore on stage, to suggest it wasn't actually rape. After the attack, she drove to Peter Clare's boat - he was to give evidence of her distress at the later trial, after which Buttolph was found guilty and sentenced to seven years' imprisonment. Bob Luff altered the show rules after this, to ensure that none of the girls lived alone on tour.

Props occasionally caused all sorts of unexpected problems. Principals Peter Pennington and Les Want dragged the cannon for Derek Dene's act onto the stage one night, only for it to blow apart and into the audience, where bits of it hit a lady in the stalls and became embedded in her seat. The Mistins' xylophone came loose from its clasps and also shot off into the audience during one performance. The theatre and Robert Luff Enterprises were lucky to avoid lawsuits. Backstage equipment also turned difficult one night when most of the men came charging off stage, straight into the lift to take them to the top floor for a quick change, overloading the lift, causing it to stick. Greg Oxnard recalls, 'It was a cage of black faces, going nowhere and the seconds ticking by before we were due back on stage for the next number. They released us in time, but it was a scary moment.' Costumes also caused issues. The men wore red velvet trousers in one sequence and as Roy Winbow remembers, 'They were made with red velvet upholstery material. From the front seam around the crotch to the back, they were only held together with a facing, so they all broke within two weeks.' One show broke with tradition in that they used a sequence which started with them wearing brown bowlers and Edwardian costumes, then after thirty-two bars of music, there was a frantic change into ski pants, Afro wig, striped top and straight into Beatles numbers. However, it was out of character and didn't work.

Even the weather conspired against them. The summer of 1976 proved to be a strange one for all resorts, probably because of a lengthy heatwave, which made the summer the hottest in the UK since records began. A severe drought only made matters worse, though the Minstrels were doing better business than any other seaside show in Britain, playing to capacity business. But the heatwave caused unforeseen problems. A joke did the rounds backstage that they wouldn't need their makeup if the heatwave continued much longer, but there were other problems, as Ted recalls: 'Wearing the costumes was bad enough in the heat, but we dreaded sunburn. If we got burned by the sun, it was hell doing the fast costume changes, so we had to be very careful.' Minstrel Andrew Sketchley had enormous problems keeping his makeup on as he sweated so heavily under the stage lights. John Wallace also remembers the problems caused by the sun: 'The high temperatures under lights, together with the elaborate costumes, meant that people fainted on stage. There was so much movement and action that the audience usually didn't notice that anything had happened. Understudies stood in the wings to take over if anything went wrong.' The company were offered salt tablets to counteract the extra drain on their bodies, caused by the heat, made worse backstage by the fact that the hot water pipes ran through the dressing rooms.

Money problems surfaced this season, compounded by the heat. Head Minstrel Roy Winbow recalls, 'I had a huge argument with Bob Luff when I asked for another £5 (£40) per week for the singers. Some of them were existing on baked beans.' One of the speciality acts had boasted that they'd had an increase of £500 (£3,800) per week, which wasn't true but served to increase tensions within the company. Bob told Roy that it was none of his business, to which Roy retorted, 'Yes, it is if they can't perform properly. They were falling like flies because of the heat and lack of nourishment. He told me to go away, which I did but I got the increase. Ossie told me later that Bob liked me because I stood up to him.'

But the touring companies always enjoyed lots of fun despite the trials and tribulations. Cricket and parties, as well as football, often with celebrities like soccer legend Laurie McMemeny and England and Yorkshire cricketer Don Wilson, all involved the

Minstrel Magic

locals and integrated the company with the resort. George enjoyed supporting these events and often turned up to the Sunday games if they were close enough to London. In 1971 the two Minstrel companies played against each other in a cricket match for charity. The London company, including John, Dai and Andy Cole, travelled to Eastbourne, where the touring company was settled for the summer season, in special coaches chartered by Bob Luff. The Eastbourne players included Neville King, Glyn Dawson, Les Want, Frank Berry and Peter Pennington. They used the occasion to have the first ever summer reunion, inviting lots of ex-Minstrels and Toppers. Over a thousand spectators attended the match which ended in a tie. That evening, Bob hosted a private party for nearly two hundred guests at the Winter Gardens Pavilion, which John and Dai attended. Despite Bob's hope that it would become an annual event, only one more match was played two years later.

The towns where the show played always supported the company, particularly during long seasons such as those at Christmas and in the summer. Invitations to social events flooded into the theatre, many of which were accepted by the whole company, occasionally with unfortunate results. In 1971 in Bristol Les Want remembered that 'I'd been to Bristol before and met the people from the Harvey's Sherry distillery, so I organised a tour. There was a bar at the end of the tour – every conceivable drink. Pros being pros, we sampled everything in sight and left at 3pm. We certainly needed black coffees to sober up. That night it was very hard to do the "hats and canes" routine.'

The same year, White Funnel invited the company out for the day on the ferry from Southampton to the Isle of Wight which was a success, though a similar visit in 1974 when the show was in Paignton nearly proved disastrous. The Royal Navy invited them onto HMS *Whitby* which was travelling around the coast of the UK on a recruitment drive. As Head Minstrel, Roy recalls it well, because of the problems it later created: 'They took us out on liberty boats from Torquay Harbour, thirty miles out into the Channel, where we spent most of the time in the wardroom. A lot of drink was consumed. We had two shows to do that night, of course, which inevitably turned out to be awful, though we kept pumping black coffee into people. Jim Lavelle's bowler fell off, and instead of leaving it, he decided to go after it across the stage. But he just kept kicking it further and further. Off stage, after the first house finale, choreographer Roy Gunson, who was present that

[377]

night, told me to get everyone into the dressing rooms. I'd never seen a face on him like that. I was terrified he'd be furious. But he said, "I hope you're all pleased with yourselves. I can truthfully say, without a shadow of a doubt, that that was the funniest show I'd ever seen. It was hysterical."'

Animals always made for great publicity. In 1971 five Toppers went on a publicity trip to Windsor Safari Park where three of them played with the lions, but the other two wisely stayed in the car! A couple of years earlier, while the London show was in Scarborough for the summer, John and Dai, plus some Minstrels and Toppers, visited Flamingo Park Zoo to 'audition' their black and white killer whale Cuddles. Cuddles was fed fish by Topper Brenda Lloyd, and then did his show to *Twist and Shout*. Dai said, 'It may not be the normal type of song we sing, but I think he passed the audition.'

CHAPTER 30

George was by now wealthy, telling *Reveille*, 'Mine is not a rags-to-riches story. I have always been comfortably off. Now I am very comfortably off. Rich. I suppose I could retire tomorrow and have enough money to live on well for the rest of my life. But I do not want to retire. I love my work too much. I know it sounds corny, but my girls and boys really are one big happy family. I know them all by their first names, and they call me George.' But sadly George wasn't able to enjoy the luxurious lifestyle his hard work and wealth should have brought him. He had invested most of his wealth in property, but in the mid-1970s, George ran into serious financial trouble, suffering badly in the economic crunch and losing £500,000 (£5million), according to one newspaper.

The 1970s were a time of economic upheaval. The country lurched from bust to boom and back to bust as the Chancellor sought to steady the rocking economy. But frequent changes in policy only made matters worse, and the economy slid into chaos, becoming over-stimulated. The banks started throwing money at anyone, but instead of it going into industry as the government hoped, it went into property which provided unprecedented money-making opportunities with the redevelopment of the urban landscape. Industry stagnated, and the government found itself powerless against the unions. Strike followed strike, budget followed budget, but the yo-yo economy just swung more and more wildly out of control. In November 1973, the Bank of England at last acted, calling in some of the banks' liabilities to be held on special deposit but it was too late. The City was in trouble and property prices plunged. The country found itself subjected to the biggest credit squeeze in living memory.

For the next couple of years, it was the comfortably off who suffered. High inflation, a low pound, coupled with a property crash and a stock market slump, meant the richer you were, the less disposable income you had. House prices went through the floor, and land values halved within a year. It was the worst economic storm of post-war times. Chancellor Denis Healey cut and taxed as much as he dared, but wage settlements continued to rise, and so inflation rose fast too, and living standards declined for the rest of the decade. By 1976 it was obvious nothing had worked, so Chancellor Healey was forced into drastic public spending cuts. The government was forced to bail out several banks and put severe restrictions in place on what they could back with their money. This time it worked and the economy stabilised. But it was too late for George's fortune.

George recalled this dark period in his life: 'I was in a terrible mess. With Barclays Bank, I started to rebuild Kings Road from the Chelsea Pensioners' Home up to Sloane Square - a certain winner. Suddenly Callaghan and his new Labour government stopped investments of that kind and I was suddenly bankrupt.' He wasn't without assets, though; as Dot remembers, 'By now, all his assets were in bricks and mortar, but he was cash-poor.' He still owned a house in Tolworth which he had bought for his sister, a flat in Worthing, provided for a disabled relative, and a block of offices in Sevenoaks which, as he said, 'were a potential source for a bit of cash'. He also, of course, retained the large house in Traps Lane where he was living, together with his mother, Barbara.

But George now had a more fundamental problem. By the mid-1970s, the show was nearly twenty years old. This in itself wasn't an issue - audiences still flocked to the live shows, and the television series were still eagerly anticipated, drawing millions of viewers. But something was changing in the Minstrels themselves. Head Minstrel Roy Winbow recalls that new cast members didn't have the same dedication to the show that earlier minstrels had done, seeing it merely as a job for the season and a stepping stone to the next engagement: 'It used to be seen as the peak of your career if you could say you'd been a Black and White Minstrel, people would walk up to us and ask for autographs. Being a Minstrel was seen as a big thing, you were enormously respected and loved, but by now, some new cast members just did as little as they could to get by. They didn't stay long, especially as they didn't fit in with the more experienced cast members who saw the show differently.' With personnel changing far more often than previously, the family spirit that had been the bedrock of the show's success started to seep away.

Indicative of the new attitude that was creeping into the company, Roy remembers problems in Bournemouth in 1973. As was usual, the resort wanted to involve them in the brochure for the following year's season: 'It was normal for brochures to be done the previous year and to feature the current year's shows. However, this year, when we were asked to have photos taken specifically for the 1974 brochures, some cast members objected, demanding to be paid. On the relevant day, I asked those who wanted to be involved, to stay behind on stage and the rest could leave. Previously everyone would have stayed, but now, about half left. We just rearranged ourselves, and the photos looked great.'

The following year the Paignton summer season took many from the 1973 London show. Roy recalls that 'we had problems with the members of the London company as they thought they were superior to those of us from the touring show, yet the London lot were actually very inexperienced and already showing signs of a different attitude to the show.' Although there had always been a friendly rivalry between the two companies, there had never been any feelings of superiority in either one, so it came as an unpleasant shock to longstanding Minstrels such as Roy.

This summer season was to end on a sour note, initiated by the London imports. When someone suggested that the Minstrels should 'wash off' for the closing show finale, both Roy and company manager Martyn French told them very firmly they were not to – 'After all, the show was still continuing, and there were huge fans in the audience,' says Roy. 'It's one thing to play around on the last night of a show which is finally closing, but we were still touring' - but some of the cast did 'white-up'. There were more problems too. Roy recalls, 'Ted was singing a romantic number, and two stagehands came onto the treads at the back of the stage, and stood with their backs to the audience, making out they were weeing. There were lots of bits and pieces like that. A lot of them tried to change the choreography too.'

The same cast was involved in even worse ructions when the stage show closed in Manchester in mid-March after a Christmas season, with what became a memorable last night. Despite the fall-out from the 'whiting-up' on the final night at Paignton the previous summer, similar problems were to emerge in Manchester. The same group who had played up in Paignton had already been in trouble earlier in the Manchester season when they gate-crashed a reception to which only the principals had been invited. One Minstrel got so drunk that he stripped off. Much to Roy's annoyance, Bob's office failed to give him and company manager Martyn French any support over this issue, which probably only served to encourage the last-night shenanigans. There had been a huge party on Friday night, the day before the closing shows, and this group started drinking halfway through the first house on Saturday. As Roy recalls, 'When they threatened to run on stage and disrupt one of the comedy acts, Martyn and I tried to hold the door shut to keep them in the quick-change room, but failed. They were well gone by the start of the second house, and it collapsed into total anarchy. By the second half of the second house, Martyn and I thought of locking them in a dressing room - some of the Toppers were involved too, but we could have managed with the reduced numbers on stage - but we felt they'd break the door down. They were doing the routines, but adding bits as they felt like it, and then they all washed off for the finale.' The theatre's stage carpenter wrote to Bob Luff in disgust at the number of bottles he found in the dressing rooms after the show. The Touring Managers' Association took the culprits to a tribunal, where Roy and Martyn had to give evidence. Roy remembers it well: 'They started accusing me of lacking discipline and of things in my private life, which I told them had nothing to do with the accusations.' The drunken Minstrel had his Equity card removed for two years, two cast members lost their cards for one year, and two more were suspended. After the hearing, Roy remembers being threatened by the now ex-Minstrels. Both Martyn and Roy were called to Bob Luff's office and reprimanded for allowing it to happen at all, though one wonders what more they could have done, in the face of determined rebellion. Roy recalls that 'George wasn't present in Bob's office for this - he sat back and let it go.'

These problems spilt over into the following years too. Tensions surfaced backstage when one principal, keen to be Head Minstrel himself as well as a principal, clashed with experienced Head Minstrel Roy Winbow. The power struggle spilt over onto the stage when Roy had to go on for another principal whom he understudied. As Roy recalls, 'For the first time ever, there was no understudy tape, so I had to sing to someone else's voice, and that's difficult. Also because of the tensions, I often felt sidelined on stage. The office wasn't impressed.' The clash resulted in Roy being forced out of the show the following year when he had to leave temporarily as he needed a cartilage operation, caused by years of dancing on hard stages and studio floors. George was, however, told a different story by the rival principal and Roy was effectively barred from returning to the show.

And this changed attitude wasn't confined to the singers and dancers. When the show opened in Bristol for the Christmas season in 1976, it was the speciality acts who came in for a barrage of criticism. Both the theatre and the local *Evening Post* received letters and phone calls, complaining that some of the jokes told by lead comic Roy Hudd and the Monarchs during the show were too blue for a Christmas entertainment. Ray Dade took a family party including grandparents and children and said, 'Perhaps the show should be renamed the *Black, White and Blue Show*. It seems a great pity that in a show such as this, hardly a joke was cracked without mention of sex, lavatories and similar subjects.' Edna Honeywell wrote, 'The show was spoilt for me by the lavatorial humour of the Monarchs, not forgetting the occasional tasteless joke from Roy Hudd. After all, this is supposed to be a family show, and it would be nice just for a change to have a clean, unsuggestive night's entertainment.' Gladys Garner wrote to the *Western Daily Press* to say, 'The show was utterly spoilt by some of the supporting acts whose filth was unbelievable in what was supposed to be family entertainment.' Roy was very upset that people found his act objectionable, 'but I just cannot see it. I have been using this act for two years, and we get just as many children in the first house in the summer as at Christmas, without any complaints. Anyone who thinks this is objectionable can't have been watching television over Christmas.' He believed audiences realised that the show was a fast-moving spectacular revue, not a pantomime, and he tailored his material accordingly. The theatre was equally astounded: 'We're getting something like 12000 people a week, and we get one person who is offended by whatever they find disgusting. They can find far worse on television every night. It is not blue humour, it's just modern humour. The majority love the show, and business has been so phenomenal that we're going to run out of seats soon.' The controversy actually encouraged some to see the show. Malcolm Rowley wrote that 'having read the recent articles and letter, I went along with some reserve - and enjoyed the whole show without reservation. Everyone on stage obviously worked very hard but equally appeared to enjoy their work. I strongly recommend all Bristolians to support this production.'

CHAPTER 31

Throughout its life, the *Black and White Minstrel Show* was subjected to ever-present racist accusations, mostly led by the press, but apart from the protests of 1967 and 1968, no one took much notice. Even in the early 1970s, a protest in Bradford hardly troubled the smooth onward flow of the show. Roy Winbow remembers that 'there was a protest by students from the University, but it had little impact, and the demo didn't contain any coloured people of any race.' At this time, Bob Luff wrote that 'it's been proved that our show has improved relations with coloured people. We often have the Commonwealth Office and other organisations requesting tickets for visiting VIPs. Recently we had parties of Pakistanis and Jamaicans in, and they have written to us to say how much they enjoyed themselves. They are not offended. Gone are those days when coloured people were portrayed as gormless idiots. How anyone can think that our show is racial or offensive is truly beyond me. It certainly isn't coloured people who complain.' George would have been heartened when, along with many earlier similar sales, the show was sold in 1977 to the independent black state of Swaziland.

The *Manchester Evening News* perhaps got to the heart of the conundrum when it reported that 'the socially conscious can spend a sleepless night worrying about the show. Why is it that the men are black and the girls white? Why aren't some of the men really black? And why do they have those funny white mouths and eyelids? It is comic to hear black (well, light tan shoe polish) men singing *Scotland the Brave*, but distinctly eerie when they break into a ditty in praise of Texas, one of the most racialist states. But worrying about it gets one nowhere - it is like trying to unravel the sexual complications of principal boy girls and male dames in panto.'

Some sections of the British press were, however, consistently outspoken against the show. The *Guardian* and the *Daily Mail* rarely had a good word to say about it. The *Guardian* regularly published articles such as this one: 'There is an area where the

Minstrels offend and cannot be forgiven. This is, of course, the racialism implied in the men blacked up and wearing 'negro' woolly wigs. Some years ago, black actors protested against the show by going along to the auditions and offering themselves as the real thing. But this entertaining and original protest fell upon deaf ears and uncaring hearts. Perhaps even funnier was the BBC's attempt to sell the show to America. They just couldn't fathom their attitude. It would be against the law to show it on American television. For a season the men behind the show pondered. Then they came up with something new. So you remember the masqued [sic] minstrels? What a bizarre sight was that! The show was a failure. Perhaps they should have worn gags as well. And leg irons. So they returned to the burnt cork, and the show went on. It is a success, and nothing succeeds like success. But where are the protests from the black community? With the single exception of those auditions, there have apparently been no protests from the blacks even though we know that they find it offensive. Often when I am watching the show, I find myself laughing at the sheer awfulness of it, and then I catch myself and try to imagine what it would be like if I were black and my children were watching their race being held up to ridicule in this peculiar way. Then I wonder what it is doing to my own children seeing blacks portrayed in this comic fashion. Of course, they mean no harm. They see themselves as purveyors of wholesome family entertainment, and the black-faced singers are not meant to cast a slur upon the black race any more than the steely-eyed woodenly smiling ladies are meant to libel the female sex. But they do both, and it is time it was stopped. If the blacks – and the ladies – won't do it, perhaps the music lovers should.'

In an equally patronising inaccurate article, *Crescendo* also attacked the show savagely: 'It survives and thrives for just one reason. It has a gimmick. The males effect black skins, blubbery lips and grotesque eyes. Echoes of the Deep South, where the coons would put on a show for dear old massa - except of course that any coon dancing with a white girl would have been likely to lose a leg, if nothing else. This blatant denial of emancipation, with its intentional or unintentional sniggering and cowardly racialism, panders to the basest instincts. It perpetuates the comforting myth (to some) of white supremacy by guying the black man. It is a peculiarly British thing, with its mixture of hypocritical morality ("We are such a clean show") and outrageous insensitivity. And it surprises me not at all that it is highly successful. As a nation, we are unfortunately remarkably thick-skinned where the feelings of others are concerned. White Americans tell me it couldn't be staged in the States, being offensive to black citizens. Naturally, they flock to see it here. It doesn't offend them; on the contrary. Some become quite ecstatic. They'd be less ecstatic of course if these were real black men dancing with all those Southern-belle types. And so would a lot of other people. In fact, there are two ways this show could end up dead. One way would be for the males to be white and the other would be for the males to be genuinely black. Which is all very very nasty and what the BBC can be thinking about, when continually featuring this pandering unpleasantness, I really don't know. Would a little moral leadership be too much to expect? Naturally, at the faintest breath of criticism, sanctimonious hands are raised heavenwards. Oh, the calumny! Why, some blacks love the show! These pained expressions of innocence should impress no right-minded person. Great rewards, however gained, are always vociferously defended.'

As the 1970s progressed, criticism became stronger, though British television and film were remarkably indifferent to racial sensibilities. Perhaps the funniest sitcom of all time, *Fawlty Towers*, produced its mere twelve episodes in 1975 and 1979. It created the wonderful character of Manuel, who, despite being played for sympathy by Andrew Sachs, nevertheless poked fun at the stock character of the dumb foreign waiter, let alone what it did to those who lived in Barcelona. The Bond film *Live and Let Die* used black actors, but that didn't stop it caricaturing and ridiculing the black communities, with its digs at voodoo, corrupt post-Colonial black politicians and black gangsters. *Till Death Us Do Part* ran from 1974 until 1981. True, Alf Garnett's character was meant to be the one who was being made fun of, but not everyone got the joke, and the language remained problematic. In *It Ain't Half Hot Mum*, Michael Bates blacked up until 1978 when he died, though the series ran till 1981 and wasn't banned until 2012 and only then after consideration had been given to reshowing it. Even then, the BBC only said that it had an 'undertone of racism' even though his character was a true caricature. None of these shows was attacked during the 1970s, vitriol seemingly reserved solely for the Minstrels.

In 1975 they once again came under attack on racial grounds, when a leading immigration association told MPs that 'the show is grossly insulting to coloured people, and encourages ideas of superiority by whites' though they provided no evidence to support this. The attack came in evidence given to the House of Commons Committee on Race Relations. A report from the committee, headed by Labour MP Fred Willey, spotlighted criticism of television programmes by the Association of West Indian and Afro-Asian Minorities, which said the show damaged harmonious race relations. In rather a patronising manner, it told the committee, 'The British can laugh at themselves, but the coloured people have not yet learned to do so. They are sensitive - and what may be traditional to the West can be interpreted as grossly insulting to them. Television programmes can do a lot of good in furthering the ideas of a multi-racial society, but they are as much capable of harm.'

One reporter, agreeing with a Larry Adler review of a book *Blacking Up*, wrote, 'The headmaster of a junior school in this area, emboldened by the lead the BBC has taken [in televising Minstrel shows] is seriously thinking of putting on a Minstrel show in his school. This is a bad look-out for the self-image and self-respect of the black kids in his care, not to mention the work he's doing to reinforce in the minds of all the whites in the audience the image of the black man as a capering simpleton.'

Letters the following week questioned why the reporter didn't also castigate other musicals with white dancers and singers as showing white men as 'capering simpletons'. Readers wanted to know just why the reporter thought the makeup made such a difference. Many respondents pointed out that this was theatre, not real life. Many also reasoned that racism should work both ways and not just in relation to colour. Amanda Gaines enthused, 'Of course the show is racially offensive. I for one am incensed by the implication that I spend my whole time prancing around in gingham flounces with matching frilly knickers, fishnet tights and sparkly shoes. Also by the idea that, upon meeting a young man in a park, I will immediately burst into song and twirl my parasol at him. We blonde pink-cheeked Caucasians have had a lot to put up with over the years - dancing about with that silly Andy Pandy, appearing on packets of Dolly Mixtures and - the final insult - having effigies of ourselves entwined in tinsel and stuck up on top of the Christmas tree!' GL Pearson asked, 'Do not the people who protest about the show on racial grounds realise that they are doing more harm to race relations than the show they are beefing about?' T Whittington pointed out an anomaly: 'In a recent episode of *Rising Damp*, few lines were funnier that those the insulting and unspeakable Rigsby put to his black lodger about his "jungle" background. Yet to my knowledge, there has never been any hint that this programme might contribute to the incitement of race riots, any more than the sight of say a Scotsman being insulted over his traditional stinginess by an Englishman might lead to mobs of frenzied dirk-waving Scotsmen setting on the nearest Sassenach. So let's have no more nonsense about the pleasant and inoffensive minstrels being insulting to black residents. The only insult is the implied suggestion that these people do indeed have an IQ sufficiently low for them to be offended. Let's face it, compared with the highly amusing and quite outrageous *Rising Damp*, the Minstrels are about as controversial as the local horticultural society's annual fete.' Repeats of *Rising Damp* continue to be shown on mainstream television to this day.

A further national outpouring of support was generated later in the decade, following a syndicated review by TV critic Grant Lockhart, who wrote, 'I sincerely hope the BBC is preserving some of the latest series in the archives. It will be interesting to see what the average citizen thinks of it around the year 2000. Of course, there is always the possibility that the show will still be running on the telly even then.' People bombarded newspapers with letters of protest at Grant's attitude. Marjorie Skirrow wrote, 'His article made me see red! It may appear old hat to him, but millions of people like and enjoy the show. The question of race relations doesn't enter into it. We are talking about a musical show which is colourful and light entertainment. Surely no different from pantomime which kids of all ages love and look forward to. Long live the Minstrels!' John Morris called Lockhart 'extremely biased. He talks of monsters being created, dinosaurs that won't lie down, and grotesque golliwogs. When I buy a jar of marmalade, I pay no attention to the golliwog on the label. The great majority who watch the show are entirely unconcerned about the colour of the faces. I enjoy it because of the scenery, the music, the singers, costumes, movement, girls, skilful production and last but not least the old songs. I sincerely hope that the show will continue to "assault our screens" for a very long time.' An unnamed correspondent asked, 'Do we ban Guy Fawkes because it is no longer relevant, is Santa Claus an anachronism to be banished?

Come, Mr Lockhart, use your intelligence which you claim the show insults. If the show is a firm favourite with the middle-aged and elderly, then what is wrong with that? Why not indulge them for a change instead of pandering constantly to younger viewers?' Grant Lockhart even managed to offend someone who didn't like the show. The *Derby Evening Telegraph* printed an anonymous letter which said, 'Though holding no brief for the show, I feel I must write to defend them from his attack, if only to counter some of the misconceptions he appears to have - his naïve belief in the ultimate good taste of the great British public, which has not prevented us from being subjected to the continually boring soap operas, so called comedy shows and quiz programmes. And what of those perennials, the *Eurovision Song Contest, Miss Britain, Miss World*? He objects vehemently to the grotesque golliwogs of the show but does he object to opera or ballet, both of which rely heavily on the world of make-believe to reach their public?' Many other reviewers agreed with the *Bristol Evening Post* who wrote, 'Seeing this programme made me wonder how anyone could have possibly taken offence at them on racial grounds. The makeup is so obviously a convention of no more than end-of-the-pier significance.'

Even the addition of the young black comedian Lenny Henry to the line-up didn't stop the protests. After he'd left the show in 1979, he occasionally made guest appearances as the show toured the country, one of which was in 1982 at the Fairfield Hall, Croydon. The local council tried to ban it but howls of outrage forced them to back down, and the show went ahead. In 1985 the show returned for three days to Croydon, as Bob and George decided to ignore the possibility of this happening again. But true to form, Croydon once again provoked outrage, but only after the show had long left town. In September, the Labour group on Croydon Council, led by Bob Brooks, called for the show to be banned from the Fairfield Halls, on the grounds that the 'patronising racism' could upset the black community in Tory-run Croydon. The *Croydon Midweek Post* was inundated with letters supporting the show and the story quickly hit the national press. Their editor's *Comment* column said, 'The fuss seems to be a classic case of the Labour Party getting its priorities totally wrong. Labour Councillor Bob Brooks describes the show as utterly banal. It's a personal criticism, and that's fair enough. But with the support of a number of colleagues he goes on to attack the show for its "complete disregard for the feelings and sensitivity of a large section of the community in Croydon". The show may be old-fashioned and may not appeal to all tastes, but it is a fact that it appeals to thousands of people. More than 3000 people turned up to see the show in Croydon. They no doubt went along to see what they felt was good, honest and clean light entertainment. I am sure that they were not politically motivated. I am also certain that the Fairfield bosses were right to host the show. Labour would be right to kick up a fuss if the Fairfield was not providing what local people wanted. But in this case, they were.' The paper gave over its entire *Letters* page to the issue. NH Leonard sarcastically wrote, 'Bob Brooks is quite right to attack racism in entertainment. There really is too much of it - particularly in the titles of popular songs. Just consider the following: *White Christmas* - surely an outmoded colonial type sentiment. It should now be retitled *Multi-racial Christmas*. *A Brown Bird Singing* - derogatory. Should be changed to *A Young Lady of the Different Pigmentation Singing*. *Black Bottom* - nasty, insensitive song and dance of the nineteen twenties. Title should be changed to *Multi-coloured Bottom*. *Yellow Dog Blues* - unpleasant slur on our Far Eastern cousins. Change to *Honourable Gentleman Most Unhappy*. *Tutu Tootsie Goodbye* - celebrates Afrikaner desire to be rid of worthy archbishop. Song should be banned and all recordings destroyed. As for the theatre, is it not high time that *Ten Little Niggers* was altered to *Ten Little Persons of Afro-Caribbean Origin*.' D Jacques wrote, 'It's not often that newspaper reports give one much to laugh about but this report really amused me, it really was so funny. There are so few really good comedians about today that these councillors could be hired to perform. Who knows? They might attract an audience of 3000. Black and white, or maybe just black?'

Support for the Labour group came from H Taylor who said, 'The Fairfield Halls Chairman is to be condemned for insensitivity in supporting the revival of black minstrelsy. One is disappointed that no knowledge of international or even local history appears to inform the judgement of so senior a Tory when he speaks of traditional entertainment. Councillor Mead believes the Minstrels have been performing for about twenty-six years. Obviously, the learned councillor is ignorant of the origin of our Great British Tradition. Black Minstrelsy originates in the slave plantations. The white 'Masters' contrived such entertainments to caricature blacks as simple creatures and hence legitimise their claims of superiority over their slaves. It was intended to be a highly racist entertainment. This show is a direct descendant. Please note that over seventy years ago Croydon's greatest composer (himself a black man) Samuel Coleridge-Taylor was disgusted by such distasteful spectacles. Black people resident in Croydon today are still offended. Let no one be surprised at that.'

The show was playing in Hull when this controversy broke. David Atkinson, vice-chairman of the Hull Commission on Racial Equality, who had obviously had no problem with the show until now, decided to jump on the bandwagon, branding the show 'racist and offensive'. In a completely illogical statement, he said the show presented blacks as 'rather simple, happy-go-lucky' people and 'lesser human beings, not taken seriously because they were black: 'I don't think most white people would understand that in Hull, it is one of those things that doesn't actually register unless you happen to be black. I would have hoped the theatre management might have had more sense than to encourage it.' A spokesman for the theatre said he was surprised by the criticism: 'The show is the best in good, clean family entertainment and part of a distinguished theatrical tradition.' Three nights of its week in Hull sold out before opening.

CHAPTER 32

George and Bob had collaborated in many ground-breaking moves over the years. They were always keen to try out new things and were ever on the lookout for new challenges. The autumn of 1974 produced perhaps the greatest challenge for the Minstrels since opening on stage in 1960. When the two summer shows closed in September, and with no London show running for the first time in over twenty years, half of George's minstrels and Toppers were now to find themselves out of work. These included Glyn Dawson who had been with George for nearly twenty years, and long-time soloists Andy Cole and Peter Kingston. But those whom George retained found themselves doing a very different type of autumn tour, a seven-week tour of some of Britain's top clubs.

This was the greatest era of club land. Bob said, 'Our shows have always created a big demand in theatres and will hopefully continue to do so, but the club circuit has grown so rapidly and become such an important part of the show business scene that we have decided to mount this special production. Our extensive research has shown that there is a market for a show of this kind, and clubs all over the country have been quick to show their enthusiasm for a package that offers a complete evening of entertainment.'

This club tour was an entirely new experience for the show, the first time it was performed without the usual proscenium arch on stage. This necessitated rechoreographing the show because they were used to an audience conventionally in front of them, but in the clubs, the audience was to the side as well. Room was much more limited too, so the variety acts were cut down to two, though George still managed to get twelve Minstrels and twelve Toppers onto the stage.

One of the variety acts nearly didn't make it at all. Between closing in Paignton and opening at Wakefield, the first club venue, Don Maclean fell 16' during filming for a *Crackerjack* stunt and injured his spine and neck. He was being winched up by a crane to simulate being shot high by a jet of water and was wearing a

Minstrel Magic

fireman's helmet. His head hit a windowsill, and the cable snapped, dropping him downwards. The helmet saved him from further injury. A few seconds earlier, he had been 75' above the ground. Although he was wearing a surgical collar, he hoped to be fit enough to open in Wakefield - and he was. Don recalls that 'George and Ernest had dreamed up the idea of me coming on, in the television show, in a big dustbin on wheels with a door, a star and my name. The door would open, and I'd come out and do my act. I'd do gags about George - he liked it if he was made fun of. He had a green Rolls Royce which I called the gherkin on wheels. Anyway, we took the dustbin on the club tour, though we had to scale it down.'

The logistics of a club show were very different, as Roy Winbow explains: 'When it came to the logistics of sound and lighting, this was headed up by George Wetherall, [Bob Luff's long-standing Chief Electrical and Sound Engineer] who had at his fingertips two guys who had the technical know-how to be able to take down and set up the miles of cabling required to operate the masses of lights and the sound systems. And who were willing to tour. Apart from anything else, they needed to be total screwballs to be able to work under the restricted conditions and cope with the long hours required to ensure the show went along smoothly, and yet they still found time to mix socially with us. The motivation behind these guys was staggering; whatever time you went to the club, these guys were there, beavering away at the equipment to make sure it worked. I felt certain sometimes that they lived and slept with the system. George always went on ahead, to pre-empt problems. We must never forget the technicians because they were never seen, rarely heard, they were the phantoms behind the scenes who provided the expertise that made the shows and the performers look and sound good.'

And look good they did. The show opened at Wakefield Theatre Club, Britain's No 1 cabaret nightspot, where the *Derby Evening Telegraph* called it 'a marvellous extravaganza, colourful, noisy and superbly well organised'. They played to full houses every night and could have sold out twice over. Ted Darling recalls, 'It was a gamble whether we would succeed in clubland since we had only played theatres before, but our run in Wakefield opened up a new avenue.' Les Want said that 'I have been amazed by our response here. The people are so friendly, and the audiences have been very appreciative.'

Minstrel Magic

After two weeks, they closed in Wakefield on Saturday and travelled to the famous Double Diamond Club in Caerphilly, where they were due to open on Sunday. However, their initial reception here was to be very different. Head Minstrel Roy Winbow remembers, 'In Wakefield, they really looked after us. Then we travelled overnight to Caerphilly, where we were due to arrive at 9am the following morning for the promised breakfast. The coach and trucks could only just manoeuvre into the car park, which was otherwise empty, with no one there to meet us. We went into the club which absolutely reeked of beer and cigarettes. I eventually found two cleaners who knew nothing about us, not even that we were performing there that evening. Eventually, George, Ossie and Roy Gunson arrived. "Everyone happy?" asked George, to be met by a resounding "No!" Breakfast was quickly rustled up, and the show went on as planned that night. After an initially quiet first night, the rest of the two weeks quickly sold out, as in Wakefield, with a staggeringly good reaction.' Roy recalls, 'The club had a huge dance floor, which we used to its fullest extent, which made such an impressive show, right in the audience.' The last night was to be memorable. Roy again, 'In one routine, a member of the audience joined in, doing backflips and other acrobatic routines. It was totally amazing. At the end of the show, the club manager thanked us for a fantastic two weeks. Then the entire audience got to its feet and sang *We'll Keep a Welcome in the Hillsides*. We were completely overcome.'

The tour travelled on to the Talk of the Midland in Derby, where they performed in a small converted cinema with a roll-out stage. After Derby, they travelled to the Lakeside Country Club, Camberley, and ended at the New Crewta Club Solihull, which was above an ice rink. Roy recalls, 'This was the first time we had ever experienced a roll-out stage. It had a big spring on it so it could move back and fore. One night, the bolts came adrift, and the stage started to go backwards!' Security was extra-tight in Solihull - the Provisional IRA had sensationally bombed two Birmingham pubs three days earlier, killing twenty-one people and injuring 182 - and Roy recalls, 'Everyone who came into the club had to be checked by security guards. Gerry Cassidy and Peter Sutherland enjoyed it so much that they went round and round the club, going in and out as often as they could!'

Minstrel Magic

The club tour of 1974 had been so successful that Bob repeated it in 1975 but with a startling new addition. In what was seen as a major coup, the young black comedian Lenny Henry joined the show. The sixteen-year-old, inaccurately but perhaps inevitably, was heavily promoted as the first black artiste to appear in the show, conveniently forgetting the tap-dancing Clarke Brothers, as well as the several black artistes who had appeared in the very first show.

Henry later explained how he joined the show and also signed to Bob Luff as his manager: 'My [then] manager took me to meet Bob Luff at London's Portman Hotel. Bob was a powerful, articulate businessman, bald-headed and very smart. I was 16, and there was a sweets trolley. While I was eating, Bob and my manager decided I would do the Minstrel show. I was so impressed by the food I forgot to say, "Hang on a minute, isn't that a bit stupid? Why would you put a real black guy in the Minstrels?" Suddenly I was signed up as second spot comic. It was a weird thing because at first, I thought it was really funny, but the warning bells went off when I saw the publicity posters for it. It was me with one of the Minstrels, and I'm wiping the black off his face, and he's pretending to wipe the black off mine. It hurts thinking about it now.' In 1985 in the *Black and White Media Show*, Lenny said, 'Because I was young and impressionable I sort of had to give in. I was doing jokes about the colour of my skin, and now I look back and think, oh no, that was awful, but I had to go through it, and I've learned.'

Some of this seems to have benefited from hindsight. Certainly, contemporary quotes show a contented Henry. He said, 'I'm delighted to be joining the Minstrels show. Joining them is a great step forward. At least I won't need any extra makeup.' He scoffed at suggestions he was joining a show that presented a patronising 'Uncle Tom' image of blacks: 'I don't think that comes into it at all. Doing the show will be a great experience for me, and I'm very grateful to them for signing me up.' He also said he had not received any critical comments from fellow blacks. 'They're very excited for me and wish me the best of luck.' He also said that blacks and Asians in the audience were there to see him. But paradoxically he felt they were critical of him for being in the show, even though they were enjoying the show. He later said his manager and Bob forced him to make these remarks, which sits strangely with the fact that Bob immediately became his first professional manager and managed his career for many years. Later still, there is evidence Lenny once again changed his mind, fondly remembering his time with the show. Dancer Penny Rigden remembered a party at Lenny Henry's years later where George was also present, so Lenny obviously harboured no great resentment against George at least. Singer Helen Stewart recalls, 'I saw Lenny Henry on stage and sent him a note backstage asking if I could meet him for a chat, though I would understand if not. He jumped at the chance, and we had a really good natter, with him introducing me to people as "from the Black and White Minstrels". He's now intimating he was under pressure to make derogatory remarks, but then he said how grateful he was to the show for getting his career up and running.' Maryetta Midgley recalls, 'Lenny fitted in really well, a lovely guy. Unfortunately, it got political, and he kept pushing for the men to be black.' Don Maclean also remembers, 'Lenny was truly delighted to join what was the top variety show of its generation. His mother Winnie and all his brothers and sisters came to see him and were equally pleased.' In the later BBC4 *Timeshift* programme, Jim Pines, black author of *Black and White in Colour,* supported the choice Lenny had made: 'The truth is the avenues of opportunities for people like that were so incredibly narrow that on this hand, go into a show that is notionally humiliating you, this hand, don't go into a show at all. Which would you choose?' The Minstrels provided an unbeatable education in cabaret and pantomime, so it's understandable why he joined. In later years his programmes featured portraits of friends and relatives, then satirical sketches of black British characters so it could be argued that he was poking fun at these characters, even if affectionately, whereas nothing in the Minstrels poked fun at anyone.

Whatever his real feelings, Lenny made the most of the five years he spent with the show: 'I learned a lot about working a big audience. I watched Don Maclean like a hawk. He stormed the audience every night, was always there for me and gave me loads of advice. When the tour was over, I thought that was it - but oh no, I did the Christmas show at Coventry, further summer seasons at Great Yarmouth, Bournemouth and Blackpool.' Minstrel Peter Dee spent a lot of time with Lenny during these years, 'teaching him to do Rigsby from *Rising Damp*'. He also attended the cast parties and turned out for the football team. But by 1979, Lenny felt he'd had enough: 'It was kind of soul-destroying because none of my friends came to see it. The jokes were boring – "And now the only one who doesn't need makeup", "When Lenny cries, he gets little white lines crawling down his face" - I took part in these jokes because I didn't really know any better.' However, it's certain his mother and many of his family watched the show, and nobody ever mentioned blacking up. They always spoke about the lovely songs, great sets, wonderful costumes. He also complained that no one came to see him as a comedian, failing to realise that no one ever came to see the Minstrels for the comedians - they were an added bonus.

The 1975 club tour started off at Jollees at Stoke-on-Trent, where Roy Winbow recalls, 'We had to change costumes and then come on from the opposite side of the stage, so we had to rush through the kitchens in full costume, where they were cooking chicken in the basket.' From Stoke, the show moved to Britain's major club venue, Caesar's Palace at Luton, managed by the redoubtable and hugely successful resident director George Savva. Caesar's Palace was possibly the most successful club in the South, and probably the most consistently profitable club in the UK. Roy Winbow recalls that 'Caesar's Palace was probably better than most venues. Other clubs you had to fight against the noise of diners and clinking glasses, but at Caesar's Palace there was a different style of audience, used to popping into London to see shows, and so there certainly was far less noise.' In this club, a single curtain opened round the edge of the stage, but at one performance, Ray Lavender and Julie Morgan got caught in the curtain and couldn't get out until it closed again. After Luton, the show moved to the Showboat in Cardiff, then the Golden Garter in Manchester. The *Cheshire Observer* had booked a coach to take readers to see the Manchester show, which proved so popular that they had to book a second coach. The *Altrincham Guardian* had to book three coaches to fulfil its readers offer! The tour finished with two weeks at Batley Variety Club.

Audiences still loved them but the press, as well as the BBC, was turning against the television show, though the media continued to rave about the stage shows. The press consistently ran out of superlatives when reviewing the stage show but were never so keen again on the TV shows, as the theatre shows consistently outperformed their nominally superior TV cousin, proving the show's deep firm roots in music hall history. Reviews always used terms like 'the best of the best, the acme of light entertainment from rainbow land'. Even the *Stage*, which now hated the television shows, thought 'the production numbers have the audience gasping with the sheer beauty of the sets and the talents of the artistes'.

Audiences flooded in year after year, breaking theatre, resort and even national records for the percentage of seats filled. There were queues at theatres day after day with people trying to book tickets and an almost non-stop demand for tickets during the hours the box office was open. Often the queues stretched out of the theatre and along the pavement. Bucking a trend that was catching on fast, the Minstrels were still providing two shows a night - most resorts and theatres were moving to one show per night - but demand was so great that two shows a night easily sold out.

George and Bob were still adamant that their touring shows would continue in Britain, even though the financial outlay was very considerable. As George said, 'To stage a show costs a fortune compared with ten years ago. It's a big gamble to stake out a show of this size. Our touring shows cost as much as one in the West End. As they are family shows usually booked in twos, threes or fours, they represent fantastic value since we try to keep down our prices. Closures of theatres have reduced the choice of places where summer shows can be staged, apart from Paignton, Scarborough, Eastbourne and Bournemouth.' Bob Luff was to say, 'We are all extremely proud of the fact that our touring shows are now in their fourteenth consecutive year. I think it is true to say, though a sad reflection on the British theatre, that up until very recently ours was the only company continually on tour in Britain.'

But despite George and Bob's promise to keep the touring shows touring, even these shows were feeling the financial pinch. Probably because of his parlous financial position, George ran a record three summer shows in 1976. More shows hopefully meant more profit but also the initial outlay was greater. Great Yarmouth opened first, with only nine Minstrels in the company, apart from the soloists. Bookings flooded in and broke records as usual, but budgets were tight on this show. Certainly having only nine Minstrels meant none of them had the usual one routine off, and there were no spare costumes because the costs had spiralled. Bad enough that the men's velvet sombreros trimmed with gold brocade for the finale cost £25 (£180) each, but the girls' costumes, sequinned outfits in gold brocade and red velvet, cost £500 (£3,800) each.

At least running so many companies allowed George to re-employ some singers he had had to let go, including Glyn Dawson. As work with George was dying away for everyone except the main principals, Glyn had done a cruise in early 1976, having done over seven thousand stage performances for George and forty six television shows. After this summer season, George tried to persuade him to go with the show when a version joined the SS *Navarino* for a lengthy cruise the following year. But Glyn refused, 'I couldn't do it as I was already booked for panto, but wouldn't have done it anyway because I'd just done the earlier cruise around Africa and didn't want to be away from home that long again.'

The Paignton show gave comedian Roy Hudd a chance to join a show which had 'always been one of my favourite shows, both on stage and television. The productions, always beautifully staged, have a vitality and exuberance about them which make the shows sheer entertainment from start to finish - which to me is what show business is all about.'

The principal company was based in Blackpool for the summer and broke records all season. Produced by Ernest Maxin, it featured Ted, Bob and both Leslies. The Opera House was the largest theatre in Britain, seating nearly three thousand, and produced one of the Minstrels' biggest ever stage presentations. Seats quickly became unavailable for any second house and difficult to find for first houses, in what was an incredibly successful season. Groups came for weekends from as far away as Ipswich on the opposite side of the country, with the *Ipswich Evening Star* having to organise repeat visits. Heartened by such success, George resolved even more to continue the touring version.

The financial blows of these years were softened, for George at least, by a transformation in his personal life. Much to his surprise, he and soloist Dot Ogden were now in a relationship, even though there were exactly thirty years to the day between them. She had been part of the Minstrels for thirteen years, moving from role to role. In late 1963 she had auditioned as a singer, but as there were no vacancies, she joined the Toppers instead. She remembers, 'You had to sing in the dancing auditions, just to check you weren't completely out of tune.' George had kept her in mind since the auditions and sent her to the Minstrel show in Morecambe in 1964 as her first job. She gradually moved through the ranks and in 1969 had gone out with the second Australian tour as the principal female lead. She returned when the tour ended and rejoined the show, both on television and stage.

It was this tour of Australia which brought them closer initially. Dot recalls, 'We'd always been very good friends, ever since he came out to Australia to open the second tour in 1969. I acted as hostess at many of the parties, so we spent a lot of time together, though he was a difficult man to get close to.' The friendship blossomed into romance after George's wife died but George soon hit the financial rocks and for a while, worried that this would threaten his relationship with Dot. George remembered, 'I asked Dot if she would consider marrying me even though I was flat broke. She said I was a silly old twit and she'd thought I'd never ask.' There was a certain level of surprise among his singers when the wedding was announced as many of them had assumed he and Daphne Bell might well get together, now that George was a widower. Glyn Dawson recalled, 'We all thought Daphne Bell was the favourite if he remarried but it was no great surprise to me when he and Dot married, I knew they were close.'

The wedding itself, in August 1977, was relatively small, as the tiny church of St John the Baptist on Robin Hood Lane, Richmond, could only hold thirty people. Dot was working at a local hairdresser's at the time 'because the TV series had finished and I needed to work'. The night before, George's son Rob and housekeeper Mary organised a party at George's house in Traps Lane, while Dot stayed with a friend in Richmond. As she recalls, 'I was supposed to be meeting my Auntie Alice, Auntie Ethel, Auntie Lois and my mum. Alice had picked them all up in her Morris Minor in Suffolk, and they drove through East London with great difficulty and were already two hours late. By the time they'd driven round and round Richmond Park, looking for Richmond Gate in the pouring rain, they were even later. We'd arranged to meet at 7, and they turned up at 9.' Dot was furious because it left no time for a meal and a bath and to do her hair.

The following day, it was still pouring, and when Dot and her brother arrived at the church, all she could see was a sea of umbrellas, covering all the little old ladies from Dot's hair salon, who had come to watch the wedding. These umbrellas kept her dry all the way to the tiny church. She entered to the *Arrival of the Queen of Sheba* 'which George chose, as he chose all the music. He thought it appropriate with tongue in cheek.' Dot had her little niece Helen, aged 6, as a bridesmaid and George's grandsons Kieron 2½ and Callum, aged 18 months, as pages, wearing specially made kilts. When they went into the vestry to sign the register, Dot recalls that 'Alison [George's daughter] and the boys came too and the boys said, "Welcome to the family, Grandma." ' The weather relented as they left the church, with the sun shining for twenty minutes which allowed them to have some photos taken, then it thundered and poured all the way to the Richmond Hill Hotel. There were one hundred and twenty people at the reception, including quite a few choir members, though people like Ted Darling and Les Rawlings, who had been with George for very many years, weren't able to leave the show in Scarborough. George's Rolls was doctored with tin cans and kippers for their departure, but their suitcases were filled with rubbish to fool people into believing they were going away that night. Instead, they went straight back to Traps Lane and drank champagne while they opened their presents. They flew to Malta later and were looking forward to an anonymous time there. But it wasn't to be. At the airport, they bumped into an old choir member who was working on check-in, and by the time they got to Malta, the press had been tipped off, and the airport was full of photographers. Dot recalls, 'Probably the guy at check-in tipped off the press. We hadn't realised that the show had been on Maltese TV a couple of months earlier, and the wedding was in the British papers which reached Malta before we did. We had a great time in Malta and made lots of friends, including Oscar Lucas, the band leader. When we returned to Britain, many newspapers asked for interviews. Bruce Forsyth and Anthea Turner had been married a few months earlier, and they'd been slated by the press because of the age difference, and we were terrified it would happen to us too, but it didn't, none of the papers mentioned it.'

Malta made such an impression on George that two Maltese tours were arranged in 1980 and 1981, yet another new venture for the Minstrels. After the show closed at Scarborough in September 1980, the show flew directly to Malta by special invitation. A week before opening night, all twenty performances at the Valletta Conference Centre had been sold out, and a further eight lined up. A special Gala show was attended by the Governor of Malta and the British High Commissioner. Production Manager Sandy McFarlane recalls that they 'received a tremendous ovation'. The *Sunday Times* reported, 'What a spectacle of colour we're missing on our black-and-white TVs...Non-stop tuneful entertainment, and the virtuosity of resident singers, Les Want, Les Rawlings and Adrian Lee, together with the other front liners in the company offer a spectacle of rhythm. George Mitchell's vocal arrangements constantly mix evergreens into one compact medley and does this to perfection, brought to a crescendo with the rendering of *When the Saints* with which the Minstrels go marching behind the Conference Centre's curtain, leaving the audience enthralled and eager for more.'

Social activities were as usual much to the fore in Malta. They were invited onto a 23-metre motor yacht *Dorado* by owner George Cassar, who placed the yacht at their disposal for his birthday party. Enjoying a sumptuous birthday, the cast were able to take a well-earned rest from their performances, embarking at the Customs House for a leisurely boat trip to Comino where they swam. Someone soon started a sing-song, accompanied by an onboard violin and guitar duo. Later that evening - there were no shows on Mondays - the group was entertained by Paddy Stubbs and his wife to drinks at their villa. A few days later, they visited the inmates of the St Vincent de Paul Hospital, after which they visited the Karin Grech Hospital.

The company was back in 1981, immediately after the Bournemouth show closed and was welcomed back with open arms. A popular local discotheque Dewdrops hosted a champagne party for the cast in their downstairs wine cellar, where, according to the *Sunday Times*, 'they enjoyed themselves tremendously and commented favourably on the hospitality bestowed upon them by many Maltese.'

CHAPTER 33

The touring shows were obviously on a high and here to stay but the television shows, where it had all started in 1957, ended with a 21st anniversary series in 1978. The BBC's lengthy retreat from the show started in 1972 when their General Advisory Council, made up of sixty laymen from various walks of life, attacked the show as being bad for race relations. 'There was some division of views about the value and acceptability of both *Till Death Us Do Part* and the *Black and White Minstrel Show*,' said a statement later. Their concern was about the blacking up, not the show's content. The Board welcomed its return in 1973, praising its pace, colour and entertainment, though some wondered if the central idea had not somehow run into the ground so that it now looked a shade old-fashioned. There were occasional mutterings from panel viewers that it was stale and dated, that it had 'lost its zip' and that the new leading artistes were not as good as the old, but clearly it continued to delight the vast majority of viewers, who called it 'tuneful, lively, fast-moving, colourful, spectacular and beautifully dressed, forty-five minutes of sheer delight'.

A year later, the Minstrels' grip on the Christmas television schedules was fading, with no Christmas show at all, though the BBC had second thoughts and brought it back in 1975 but not on Christmas Day itself. Both Lenny Henry and Don Maclean appeared in this show, along with the cast of the touring show, for many of whom this was to be their first appearance on television. The BBC seemed once again to be firmly behind the show, publicising it widely, saying, 'The whole company glitters, huge snowflakes shine in the silver sets, and Christmas cheer is spread with a lavish hand. It should really be called the *Red and Green and Silver and Gold Minstrel Show*.' George was still changing the basic format in an attempt to keep the show vibrant. He began to use four male and four female soloists which left little room for the choir who almost reverted to the background act they had been in the very first shows. The show was seen in 7.15 million homes and did well in the ratings, but the *Stage* was highly critical: 'It needs three major contributions to put some life into the proceedings: a good director with some flair for staging, a choreographer to be given some more rehearsal time, and a musical director with some verve and attack in his arrangements. The show should have sired a new popular light musical show for the Seventies but it has not, and now the black faces look like an out-of-date entertainment gimmick and silly into the bargain when the singers are also in additional colourful costumes. The whole show is still coasting along from the last series on the audience's goodwill. Professionals in light entertainment must cringe at the lackadaisical-looking, downbeat presentation and so many close-in shots of people obviously miming.'

But the BBC was certainly still backing the show as they were still attracting guest stars of high calibre, such as *It Ain't Half Hot, Mum* stars Windsor Davies and Don Estelle, with their hit single *Whispering Grass*. The third show in the 1975 series saw actor Arthur Lowe recreating his role as Captain Mainwaring from *Dad's Army*, when he appeared in uniform, singing and dancing with the Minstrels through a medley of wartime songs, with one critic saying 'He was a revelation as a song and dance man'.

And George was still enjoying it all, saying, 'We have such marvellous audiences that I enjoy doing all I can to give them the musical pleasure they deserve. The challenge of new shows makes it hard to keep up the standard to which people have become accustomed. There are critics who declare that we present nothing but a load of old corn. It isn't so. Everything is carefully chosen and getting the music written and rehearsed keeps me busy enough without taking on anything else. My work is purely my hobby, and I enjoy doing it. I'd still be doing it if it wasn't my bread and butter. I have a lot of good friends and have worked together with them for a long time in the most pleasant of circumstances. When you work with the same people for so long, and you work so well together, it comes through as you perform that you are enjoying yourselves, even though you may be working your heads off. It's just like having a good football team.'

But the writing was on the wall. As the *Daily Mail* put it, 'Though the Minstrels have survived rock 'n' roll and the Beatles, punk rock and even the Race Relations Board, they may finally succumb to BBC indifference. Once it was the pride of the Beeb's glittering showcase, rarely was a production made without one of the top brass sitting on the wings. The top men don't look in anymore, nor has it retained its traditional peak hour slot at the weekend.'

The BBC was by now determined to get rid of the show, on television at least. The weekly Programme Review Board saw some straight talking between the Controller of BBC1 Bill Cotton and senior executives. Comments ranged from 'the Controller of BBC1 wondered if this format had now had its day' and 'the head of TV Drama serials considered the show an anachronism in the modern world' to 'the general manager of Enterprises said that the show still sold well'. These comments were first made in earlier years, though were certainly indicative of their views by 1976 as well. With social attitudes changing rapidly, the BBC felt it had to address the problem, as they saw it, of the show. Bill Cotton was later to say, 'I think it had come to the end of its natural life on television. I also felt that there was this racist implication in it and it's all very well people who are not black saying, "I didn't think about it that way", it's about the people who are black.' He may have thought this in later years, but he said nothing to this effect in any of the contemporary BBC's Board minutes.

George was now much more involved on-screen. Although viewers approved wholeheartedly, Bill Cotton disapproved, reporting to the Board of Management that he knew 'George wants to be involved more in the presentation but this aim will have to be contained'. Richard Afton, who had founded, named and run the Toppers during the early years with the BBC, agreed: 'I do think it's time his appearances were eliminated. He adds nothing to the programme. In fact, because he wears a dinner jacket while the rest of the cast are in costume, he detracts from it.'

Initially, the decision seems to have been made to end it in 1976. The stage company was used in the Christmas special which also featured ventriloquist Keith Harris, as well as Pam Ayres and comedian Les Brian. In yet another first, this show included its first known black Minstrel when Floyd Pearce, known as Clyde, joined the company, becoming probably the first black man to reach the incredibly high Mitchell standards. He joked, 'I just had to put some white around my eyes and lips' but in fact, he had to put on full makeup for the cameras. As Dot remembers, 'George always wanted a mixed choir but had never found anyone with the necessary voice and sight reading skills. Clyde, however, was good enough - we'd have had more if we could have, George would have loved them.' Sadly not everyone approved and George must have been disheartened by a letter in the *Evening News* from R Callingwood who wrote, 'I spotted the black man. What is the matter with George Mitchell to spoil another good English tradition that has been ours for years?'

In yet another first, at the end of the final show, all the men washed off their makeup, and the series closed with the men and girls walking out of the studio arm in arm to celebrate the end of yet another successful series. This proved highly popular with viewers, with remarks such as 'nice to see the Minstrels without their blackening' though the show itself was thought to be 'not quite as good as its predecessors.' The last shot showed a lonely hat on the treads.

But no matter what the BBC intended, George was determined to get the television show to its 21st anniversary in 1978. One highly significant clipping in George's collection was from the *SE London Mercury* in 1976. Its significance lies, not in what it actually says - 'the hopelessly out of date Minstrels, who still have legions of fans, give you dare ol' tyme religion on Saturday evening' - but in what George has written on it: 'I have decided to stop in two years' time whilst I'm still winning.'

Budget cuts and downgrading the show to Tuesdays may have been the price that George had to pay to get even the twentieth series agreed in 1977. Ann Mann remembers, 'Those last series were a bit sad. The budgets were lower, and Bill Cotton wanted to ditch them. Figures were dwindling, and it wasn't as it had been, not as good as in the Golden Rose days. Towards the end, they couldn't afford new costumes, and it was beginning to look tatty. They did a lot of '20s and '30s numbers so they could use the same costumes.'

These budget reductions had more ramifications all round. The grumblings over the low pay for the Minstrels and Toppers reached such a pitch that the company made Roy Winbow and Chris Connah go to Equity to find out why their pay was so low. Roy recalls, 'The guy at Equity confirmed that, because of the reduced size of the show, it had been downgraded and everyone was paid at B class rates, instead of A class, though the technicians were paid at full rate. We were told that this had been agreed between Equity and the BBC, with George's eventual reluctant agreement. Chris and I took this information back to the company who weren't happy, but of course, there was nothing they could do about it.' Sadly this episode had severe consequences for Roy who had been Head Minstrel for much of his seven years with the show on stage and television. As he recalls, 'George got to hear about this and said he felt I'd gone behind his back, though I was only doing what the company had asked me to do. He didn't want to know me after that.'

But the BBC wasn't going to give in to another series without exacting even more revenge, other than financial. Producer Ernest Maxin was by now the major BBC producer, and as such, in a shock move, the Corporation transferred him to the *Morecambe and Wise Show*. This really was a slap in the face for George and the Minstrels as it took the BBC's top producer away from what had been for years the BBC's flagship programme and so deserving of the BBC's top producer. Now it was relegated to the second ranks. George fought hard against this, but this was one battle the BBC was determined to win.

The Minstrels' new producer, Brian Whitehouse, took a very different view of the show from Ernest Maxin. He was determined to change everything he could - even the virtually sacrosanct conducted segment. The only previous change to this sequence had been to allow the girl singers in occasionally, though it remained a male preserve for many series. The heart of the sequence was the singers' static nature, providing a quiet contrast in the midst of a constantly moving show. Now Brian wanted to introduce movement and special effects. George was very dubious and again fought hard, but once again was over-ruled. The first show horrified George, singers and audience alike. While singing *Chloe*, the singers were to start on their backs, come up through smoke, then lift and sway with the girls, while clouds of smoke wafted all around them. But the props, nearly always well-behaved in the Minstrel shows, sided with George. The smoke billowed and curled so much that the singers were virtually invisible.

Brian learned his lesson and appeared to give up all hope of introducing any changes to the show, saying, 'There is always the temptation for a new producer to make changes. But you can't change the Minstrels. They provide something you never find elsewhere on TV. They are glamorous, extravagant, different.' But he managed to get his own back by implementing two more fundamental changes to the show. From the start, the Minstrels were 'singers who could move', rather than dancers. The men who sang on the soundtrack were not always - or indeed not often by now - the men who appeared on screen, but they were still all

Mitchell Singers. Brian was keen to give both men and girls more complicated dance routines, but the men, as singers, weren't capable of this. Consequently, a production decision was taken to draft in professional dancers to front the routines, so at least it appeared as if the men were managing these new routines. This, of course, meant that there was even less correlation between the men on the soundtrack and those on screen. George hated this decision and fought it hard, but was again overruled, and some Young Generation dancers were brought in. Roy Winbow remembers how aghast these dancers were at the amount and speed of work produced by the Minstrel company: 'They told me that they were used to doing a couple of routines a fortnight, with far more practice time, and getting paid a lot more for less work. They couldn't believe the amount of work we were doing or the level of pay we were getting. It also caused rumbles among our own company as the Young Generation dancers were being paid twice what we were and did far less work in rehearsals.'

The singers were now forced to use idiom in their songs. From the start, both Georges had insisted on the correct pronunciation of words like 'them' and 'that' rather than the patois accent of the West Indies. Now Brian insisted that native accents were used, as had always been the case with Scottish and Irish songs. George was furious but helpless in the face of orders from above.

At least giving in to these compromises meant George got his wish and the show returned in 1978 in a series of six programmes in the BBC's *Prize Winners* season. In an unexpected move, George managed to persuade Dai Francis to return for this anniversary series, which celebrated twenty-one years of the show on television. Dai explained, 'When George called me, I thought it would be great to return to the show. Not that I needed to get my voice in tune. I've been singing around the country in the between years.' He was joined by Ted, Les Rawlings and Bob, as well as Dot Ogden and Gaye Collins. Unable to appear in the first four shows as she had just given birth to another child, Margaret Savage returned for the final two shows in the series. She said she had to rush to get her weight down for the show, but the temptation to work with Dai again gave her the incentive: 'I heard Dai was appearing and I thought it would be fun as he is one of the originals - and there are not many of us left. It was a bit of a marathon - each show takes a week of rehearsals - but it was very enjoyable, and the baby thrived too.' Roy Winbow, now ex-Head

Minstrel Magic

Minstrel of the stage shows, had to fight hard to get into this series, after having appeared in most of the series throughout the '70s. Having been forced out of the stage show the previous summer, he waited in vain for a call for this television series. Eventually, after being told by the office that he wasn't wanted 'because of what you did', he phoned producer Brian Whitehouse, who arranged for Roy to appear in the series. Ventriloquist Keith Harris was also kept on board, as was Pam Ayres, with Ann Mann's husband, Brooks Aehron appearing in most of the shows.

The show's return was welcomed by the majority of viewers who reported to the BBC, and the first edition didn't disappoint. A few thought the format had changed slightly for the worse, and also regretted the lack of a female soloist in the first show, but for most, the colourful costumes and sets and the high standard of performance made this a 'most entertaining forty-five minutes'. Dai's return was welcomed by most, as was Margaret's return later in the series. For example, FC Johnson wrote, 'Here is one of the most underrated artistes in show business, with a wonderful voice, capable of dealing with songs of all types, a great sense of comedy and such verve and personality. Why this girl was not given her own TV spot long ago, I cannot imagine.'

At the end of the final show, in a move that surprised George, he was presented with his second gold disc for sales in the UK of more than £300,000 worth of *Thirty Golden Greats with the Joe Loss Orchestra*. George recalled, 'This was hard to take as I knew the album hadn't sold a million. I reckoned about half a million. I rang them after the show to ask what the hell was going on and they told me the goalposts had been moved, the crash bang wallop pop groups had to get a gold single for the kids to buy them, and they were being dished out for a single, never mind an album.'

Although the accepted wisdom seems to be that no one knew this was to be the last series, there is much also to show that George may have planned it this way. Not only had he written, two years earlier, that he would stop in 1978, but he was later to record in his taped memories that 'I decided to retire when Dot and I got married - she was 30 and I was 60 - and this was our last TV show. It only came off when I refused to have the show's budget cut. I knew everyone at the BBC by their first names, from the car park attendants to the cleaners - they all called me George, and it was sad to have to say goodbye after all those years.' George also never tried to get a further series. However, others have portrayed the events differently since. Ex-producer Ernest Maxin recalls, 'Suddenly it all came to a stop, a standstill. I used to meet with other producers and writers in the canteen at the BBC and the corridors and offices, and I never heard anybody ask, 'What's happening with the Minstrels?' It was a bit heart-breaking actually.' Principal Les Want repeatedly said in later TV shows on the Minstrels, that they just stood around after the series ended: 'When we did the last TV show, you sit around and wait for the contracts to come through for the next series, but they never came through this time. George made enquiries, and the BBC said, "Well, we don't think we can put it on again because it would be offensive to the ethnic minority of the country." And it was left at that. We still have never had a notice to say it's officially ended.' But Les was not in the last series, whereas Roy Winbow, who was, is adamant the entire cast knew: 'We all knew it was to be the last series. The BBC had tried desperately hard to get it off after twenty years, but some executives and George himself fought hard to get the twenty-first series, an important anniversary.'

In a further blow to the show, Ossie Whitaker died in October 1978. Ossie, who had originally worked for George, had moved to the Robert Luff Organisation, specifically to handle all the Minstrel stage shows, and his death was a severe blow to both George and Bob. But in true show business tradition, the show went on, and not just the Minstrel shows. Glyn Dawson recalled, 'Ossie died the day before Phyllis, Pauline [Ossie's wife and daughter] and I were due to do a show as we did around the hotels - we did operatic duets and such like - but we still did the show.' Roy Winbow thinks that 'After Ossie died, Bob and George lost interest in the show. Bob was staging other shows, and George was busy with Dot as well as being in financial trouble.'

The last two shows were devoted to viewers' requests. Even more telling, was the dedication, to George Inns, of the final sequence of the final show on July 21. This included many of his favourite songs from the very first show in 1957, some of which had not been used in shows again until now, such as *Carry me back to Green Pastures, Gentle Annie, Ring Ring de Banjo, Kim Kum Ki-me oh, Nellie Blyth, Golden Slippers, Campdown Ladies* and inevitably *When the Saints Go Marching In*, though oddly the conducted sequence was *Born Free*, rather than the more obvious *Michael*.

CHAPTER 34

The BBC hadn't quite finished with the Minstrels, though. Bombarded with letters to bring back the show, they compromised and returned it to Radio 2 in January 1981, in the capable hands of Ann Mann. She said at the time, 'I was steeped in the repertoire obviously, and people don't want change, so the first programme will be strictly Minstrel songs.' Later she recalls, 'It was so strange, we used a lot of the same songs, and it still produced the audiences.'

The BBC was to televise one more Minstrel show when *Halls of Fame* was transmitted in December 1984 on BBC1. This first of a new series, with Roy Hudd, looked at famous British theatres and started with the Victoria Palace. The show featured George and the Minstrels heavily and effectively marks their last new television show. The audience was ecstatic to see them, and the Victoria Palace once again rang to Minstrel songs. Both Dai Francis and Ted Darling appeared on stage with some of the cast from the show which had toured Butlins camps that summer.

Discontent at the show's absence from television continued to rumble on. In 1985 the *Belfast Telegraph* wrote, 'Sadly they have disappeared from the entertainment scene', while the *Yorkshire Evening Post* printed a letter from George Garnett asking, 'Why does the BBC not ever show the Minstrels these days? I am certain this delightful entertainment was enjoyed by millions of viewers. There must be dozens of recordings they could show instead of all this Yankee rubbish they continue to inflict upon us!'

R McCallam from Cumbria was ahead of the game when he wrote to the *Daily Mail* in early October to ask, 'Is the BBC proud of the fact, that, as well as the show being included in the *Guinness Book of Records* as the world's longest-running song-and-dance show and the world's most popular stage show, this year marks their Silver Jubilee? It would be fitting to have this historic occasion marked with at least one spectacular. We can have sex and violence, four-letter words, and repeats in black-and-white of Al Jolson and Eddie Cantor films. Yet an all-British TV hit, suitable for the whole family, is dropped from our screens because of the "black" issue.' Surprisingly the BBC had already decided to mark the occasion, though ironically only on radio, by broadcasting an hour-long special *Magic of the Minstrels* in October.

Listeners were overjoyed to hear the show again. The *Radio Times* published a letter from P and W Tolley who wrote, 'How we enjoyed this show and oh, how much we miss the show on television. To remove such entertainment on the grounds of offending black people is incomprehensible. Bring them back minus their greasepaint and call it just *The Minstrel Show*; who cares what colour they are, it's the great entertainment value that counts.' Kenneth Bindoff agreed, writing, 'Tut, tut, BBC! Surely you should have bowed to the loony lobby and called them the *Multiracial Minstrels*?' The *Manchester Evening News* used a letter from Harry Hughes who thought, 'Of all the persons paying the BBC bigwigs' salary, there must be at least a million wishing to enjoy repeat showings of the tuneful Minstrels.'

All to no avail, of course. Despite the countless letters, both to the BBC and in the press, calling for the show's return, and despite the far more offensive offerings being continually televised, which provoked outrage from large sections of Britain, the BBC was not going to be moved from its ban on the show. Ironically, five years after the BBC had effectively banned the show, ITV was to screen the very last appearance of the Minstrels during a *This Is Your Life* programme on Stan Stennett, in which George, Dot and a group of Minstrels plus Dai Francis, appeared. Producer Malcolm Morris wrote to thank them for helping: 'Stan was obviously delighted to see you, and so were we.'

More controversy was to be generated in October 1986, this time by the BBC itself. 1986 marked BBC TV's 50th anniversary, and special programmes ran throughout one week in November to mark the occasion, culminating in *That's TV Entertainment*.

The news broke in October that the BBC was intending to obliterate the Minstrels from its memory by refusing to show a *Black and White Minstrel Show* as one of the forty-two golden oldies that were screened in anniversary week. The closest they came was allowing a fifty-second clip in the anniversary show itself and this for a show that had brought untold millions of pounds to the BBC in foreign sales as well as worldwide prestige and was the acknowledged award-winning world leader in light entertainment. The shock was all the greater in comparison with 1961 when the Minstrels had been at the forefront of the BBC Silver Anniversary celebrations. Dot recalls that 'George was desperately hurt by the way the BBC just wiped the show from their memory. They always see the Minstrels and the makeup, but that's only one little bit of the show. They forget the content of the rest of the show. If it had been contrary to what people wanted, they wouldn't have been successful. It wouldn't have lasted at all. People would have complained. It was public demand.'

Headlines ran in all the press – 'Black and White Minstrels banned' - with most papers reporting that the decision had been taken 'for fear of upsetting immigrant viewers'. The editor of the *Sunday Independent* summed up the opposition to the BBC succinctly: 'Sometimes I can hardly believe what I read in newspapers. BBC TV deciding not to show a Minstrel programme in case it offends. Offends who? With all those black-faced men and pretty white girls, was it not the greatest image of racial integration the entertainment industry has ever seen? Al Jolson blacked his face as a tribute to the musical talents of American Negroes. But with black coffee and blackmail becoming "racist" words, what next? "Coloured Magic" chocolates? "Monochrome" whisky? Very-dark-brown widow spiders?' The *Sunday Sun* nearly exploded: 'The BBC seems to be kowtowing to extremists once again. Can eighteen million people really have been so misguided for twenty years when they enjoyed this show? Deemed "unacceptable", the feeling is it would insult immigrants. That is surely an insult to the immigrants' intelligence, as well as the millions who enjoyed the show. Daft notions like that and the baa baa green instead of black sheep suggestion do more to provoke racial resentment than harmony, among sane-minded people of any colour. I see they're leaving *Fawlty Towers* and *Colditz* in the schedule. What about upsetting Spanish waiters or reviving memories of Hitler?'

The *Wigan Evening Post* asked, 'Don't you think the Beeb has boobed in banning this show? Did you see Bill Cotton saying they had tried to film sequences from the show using white-faced minstrels? Honestly, did you ever hear such clap-trap? So it is neither black nor white faces for the BBC....no, it's red instead. Does it also mean that Al Jolson will never appear on BBC TV again?' [The BBC was to repeat *The Jolson Story* and *Jolson Sings*

Again on more than one occasion]. The *News of the World* said, 'No one took the mickey out of anyone. All this is getting ridiculous. Today the famous Al Jolson would be accused of racism, though he was Jewish.' BBC TV Managing Director Bill Cotton retorted, 'The show was one of the most popular entertainment programmes of all times. It ran for twenty years and won international awards - but it's absolutely out of the question now.'

People flocked to support the show. Ex-principal Roger Green, in a report carried by all major papers, said the BBC ruling was unfair: 'This is a purely political decision, and there's not a lot we can do about it. I'm not a racist. I am not colour-prejudiced in any way, and the Minstrel show does not in any way set out to mimic black people or put them down.' Mr K Wilson wrote to *Today*, 'It may well be a bit old-fashioned, but the show still brings enjoyment to many older people. Your correspondent should remember that this show is a descendant of the old American minstrel shows that did so much to spread jazz and blues music at the start of this century.' Claudette Rees, in the *Daily Mail*, said, 'Every time I see an article about colour and how certain advertisements, children's nursery rhymes, or poor old Golly on the Robertson jam pot affects, upsets or corrupts, I cringe. And now they've picked on the Minstrels. I came here from South America in 1961, and my family is dark. Sometimes I call my little one very affectionately "golliwog". Why should the BBC have feared the old favourite would now be viewed as "racist and patronising"? There is no way I would expect my five daughters to come to me and tell me that they have not made it because of their colour. The question of colour offending is pure nonsense. And to continue putting a stop to things that are enjoyable and part of our children's birthright is totally unacceptable.' One fan wrote repeatedly to the BBC asking for an explanation of the omission. When a bland reply landed on his mat, from someone in the Correspondence section, he wrote again and again, demanding a reply from the Director General to whom he had written his first letter. Sadly, the BBC continued to ignore the correspondence.

The shows might no longer have been seen, but that didn't mean they weren't heard. Certainly, the BBC still played their records. In March 1988 *Good Morning Britain* said that the majority of requests in their postbag were for the Minstrels. And fans were still doing their utmost to get it back on television. George Simpson wrote to the *Aberdeen Evening Express*, 'I'm sure many viewers would be glad to see the Minstrels back on TV. I for one would welcome the return of this fast-moving music programme.' Mr Simpson seems to have been on a national campaign as he also wrote to the *Star*: 'This was the best ever show on TV. Today we see so many repeats, but unfortunately, the enjoyable Minstrels who everyone loved so much are not among them.' And he wasn't alone. The *Birmingham Evening Mail*, calling for a revival of old classic TV shows, was inundated with letters nominating the Minstrels. Every single letter they published mentioned the show. HJ Blandford said, 'I would not hesitate to recommend those wonderful shows. The singing and dancing were nothing short of superb so that if folks were not so much interested in dancing, you could join in singing the lovely songs that were a great part of the show.' Ernie Lewis wrote, 'I too would like to see a re-run of these shows, but perhaps I am fortunate in that I have all the records they made.' The *Aberdeen Evening Express* printed a letter from V Bryden: 'I wish we could have the show back. Their singing and music were a treat - they were so talented.' The correspondence went on for weeks, obviously touching a deep well of desire for the show's return.

In November 1988, retired gamekeeper Leslie Stone, 64, of Devon, formed an official pressure group to get the show back on TV. Papers far and wide printed his letter about the pressure group. He received masses of support from around the country from older and younger people, but to no avail. The BBC said, 'The show has run its course.' He was still running the group the following April and had written to the Queen asking for her support, which of course she was unable to give. By now, he had written five letters to the BBC including one to Director General Michael Checkland and one to BBC Chairman Marmaduke Hussey, plus a letter to his MP. They had, however, refused to reply to Leslie who thought that 'very bad mannered'.

Later, in the 1990s, when the *Sunday Post's* TV critic, Colin Cameron, bemoaned the lack of good family entertainment on TV, dozens of readers backed him, among them Bob Douglas from Glasgow who wrote that he had bombarded the BBC with requests for the shows to be repeated but with no success. At least he got a reply, as the BBC wrote back saying, 'The show would cause deep and considerable offence to many black people in Britain.' Their opinion was that it was a caricature of negroes living in slavery and could be seen as reducing their suffering to the level of popular entertainment. Bob conducted a straw poll which showed both white and black viewers disagreed with the BBC, saying it would not only be acceptable but welcomed. But the BBC stood by their decision. So Bob changed tack and suggested that they showed *Around The World In Song*, *Masquerade* and *Music Music Music*, but the BBC said they couldn't give an answer at the moment but would give it their 'deepest consideration'. Of course, nothing ever came of this - the BBC was determined to sideline George and everything he had been associated with, not merely the Minstrels, which rather weakened their racist argument.

Bob received much support from readers, among them S Henderson who highlighted the BBC's double standards: 'I don't accept the BBC's excuse that offence would be caused to many blacks. My wife and I have often complained to the BBC about foul language, gratuitous violence and overt sex which offends us. Nothing is ever done to correct this situation. It must also be borne in mind that Al Jolson films are occasionally screened on different channels – to the delight of many.'

In a neat turnaround, the television show which had been the first to take TV back into the theatre now returned completely to its historical theatrical roots in music hall. Television might have shunned the show but the public still loved it and the touring show, now very definitely the No 1 company, toured Britain until 1988.

George, aged 61 when the last television series was broadcast, might have been forgiven if he was contemplating retirement. But not a bit of it. Never one to sit around doing nothing, he was still finding new ways to drive the show forward, even after twenty-one years. In March 1978, in yet another first for the show, a Minstrel company set sail on the SS *Navarino*. The largest Greek ship sailing the Mediterranean, this 23,000-ton luxury cruise liner carried only one hundred and forty passengers, all in staterooms, and one hundred and twenty stewards. On March 18, it set sail from Villefranche for a lengthy timetable of fortnightly cruises to the Greek Islands, Yugoslavia, Venice, Jordan, Egypt and Tunisia. Bob Luff said, 'It's an exciting challenge for us. Nothing like this has been done before; in fact, it's the only medium we haven't tackled.'

Minstrel Magic

Rehearsals for the specially adapted performance began in London on February 20, and the company flew out in the middle of March. Initially, George had trouble finding singers who were prepared to join this show. None of his experienced singers seemed willing to go - Glyn Dawson had turned down the offer, and the other principals were with the stage show in Britain or had families they weren't willing to leave. According to ex-Head Boy Roy Winbow, people were increasingly reluctant to commit to the work and high standards demanded by George, in any case. But find them he did, many of them having been with the show in earlier years.

During a fortnight's cruise, they did four different shows, each consisting of three routines, always done on the nights they were at sea. The principals did their own cabaret spots on other nights, while the chorus did a cabaret in one of the smaller lounges called *From Bach to Barbershop*, a potpourri of everything. The first three of the four shows were done white-faced, the final show in full Minstrel makeup and used all the traditional songs. There were two performances of each show as there were two dinner sittings for passengers. Every time they sang the name of a place such as *Carolina Moon* or *Alabama*, they would get applause from different parts of the audience, depending on where they came from - most passengers were from the US. They also managed to do some songs in other languages to compliment the French, German and Italian passengers.

As there were only four Minstrels and two principals on the ship, it made it difficult to do the show if, for any reason, someone was off. One memorable day when the ship was docked in Israel, the two principals, Andrew Sketchley and Michael Tuckey, were delayed returning from a visit to Tel Aviv. They were passengers on a train which had been hit by a grenade and machine-gun bullets, fired by terrorists during the never-ending conflicts in the area. Although they were looking forward to going on as the understudies, Frank McFadden and Peter Mitchley were also worried about how the show would look with only two men left in the chorus. They were very glad indeed to see Andrew and Michael racing down the quayside, just as the ship was about to set sail.

The weather inevitably produced some nasty moments for the cast. One particularly bad storm sent them falling on top of the passengers at their tables, sending glasses flying. During another storm, they gradually slipped down the stage while they were down on one knee singing *Kumbayah* in the conducted sequence. 'It was like trying to dance on a slippery slope,' recalled Frank. The show ended with a *Bahia* sequence, done white-faced, though Frank recalled that, during one tempest, his face matched his green costume.

Despite George's reluctance to send the show abroad again, a third Australian tour started in 1978 and ran well into 1979 so once again, he and Bob were running three companies. George's finances probably contributed to this move, but people were still flocking to the shows, so he was happy to provide them with the entertainment they craved. And they were certainly still drawing the crowds. In 1979 the summer season show in Bournemouth was the most successful in Britain, having attracted a bigger percentage of patrons in relation to the size of the theatre than any other venue in the country.

Gradually the theatres and the companies got smaller and smaller, though George and Bob made the most of every anniversary. In 1980, the twentieth anniversary year of the stage show, the summer show returned to its first summer season base, the Futurist Theatre in Scarborough. On June 25, the anniversary of the day they opened in Scarborough (though not of course the real anniversary of the stage show which had opened in Bristol on April 18), they held a lunch party at the Futurist where a cake in the shape of a Minstrel's hat was cut by Mayoress Mrs Bob Bedford. The mayor said he and his wife had seen the first show twenty years earlier and most since, and the links with Scarborough had been a success story. Roland Curtis [there is no evidence as to who he was] thanked the mayor and said they were very proud of their association with Scarborough where their first show had been the forerunner of the phenomenal success, the like of which was never likely to be repeated. Sandy McFarlane, the show's production manager, proposed a toast to absent friends and recalled that there had been something like six hundred Minstrels over the years: 'They are scattered all over the world. They will be thinking of us today just as we are thinking of them.'

The 1981 summer tour was publicised as the 'twenty-first anniversary on stage'. In something of a major coup, Bob persuaded Dai Francis to return to lead the company, and he also returned the following year in Eastbourne. This season was a hit from start to finish, helped by Bob's policy of low ticket prices. The

Minstrel Magic

Daily Star ran a feature which reported the English Tourist Board as saying stars in summer shows were making too much money. Therefore ticket prices had to rise, and holidaymakers were being ripped off. The paper did a survey, which showed that in Eastbourne people were particularly impressed with the Minstrels. Prices ranged from £2.25 (£8) to £3.25 (£11), and for that people got 2¼ hours of entertainment that would have cost at least £8 (£27) in London.

The *Eastbourne Gazette* said, 'When it comes to doing the impossible, the sensational Minstrels are in a class of their own.' The *Eastbourne Herald* reported, 'Yes, they are wonderful. Yes, they are the nicest summer show company the Congress ever had. Yes, they are a kind and generous bunch of artistes who are a credit to themselves and do their profession proud. But there's more of course. I was struck by the fact that it really is the Minstrels, Maids and Toppers who command, direct and present the enormous impact which every Minstrel show has made since the legend was launched 20 years ago. Tonight means goodbye to a grand company, the wonderful, magnificent Minstrels.' The same paper printed a letter from Peter Bedford, Director of Tourism and Leisure, who wrote, 'I'd like to express our sincere thanks to Bob Luff and the show for presenting what has been a most happy and most successful summer season. They have all worked like Trojans to present a superb, talented and colourful show which has been seen by over 120,000 people. It has been a most difficult year for resort show business, but the Minstrels have done a truly magnificent job, not only on stage in a marvellous production but in their spare time in attending and opening numerous functions in and around Eastbourne from which local charities have benefited considerably. The entire company have endeared themselves to the people of Eastbourne.' Bob responded a week later: 'I'd like to express our very sincere thanks to all the local residents and visitors whose wonderful support and appreciation have made possible one of the happiest and most successful seasons the Minstrels, and I believe the Congress, have ever enjoyed.'

The Minstrels were still setting theatrical records. One summer season in Eastbourne saw the show set new business records at the Congress when box office receipts were the highest for any week in the theatre's history. That week also saw the highest attendance figures ever for the theatre, and they were expected to break even these records in the following week, the last of their summer season. By the end of the season, the total financial returns created a new summer show record for a thirteen-week run.

But as ever, controversy followed them. Mr Tokely, president of the Bournemouth Hotels and Restaurant Association, provoked outrage when he said in July, 'It's time to get away from a diet of *Black and White Minstrel Shows* and give residents and visitors a change.' A Holliman wrote to the press, saying, 'He is wrong. The "diet" of which he speaks has been enjoyed by between 800,000 and 900,000 people during the past four seasons of the show in Bournemouth. At 5.30 each evening, coachloads of people from all over the New Forest and further afield, together with hundreds of local fans can be seen alighting at the Pavilion. It is a show performed by a very talented company who put everything they've got into every performance and the applause at the close of each show is absolutely rapturous. I would also like to praise those cast members who carry out many extra-curricular duties before their evening shows.' An unnamed person wrote, 'How dare he make such uncalled-for remarks. Does he realise the members probably do more to support this town by their attendance at various charitable activities than any other entertainers? How would he like to keep stage makeup and costumes on all day while attending fetes and other events, then, after little or no rest, make straight for the theatre for two energetic shows? We are thrilled they have brought their sunshine and warmth to Bournemouth.'

But trouble lay ahead. Bob had booked the show for a week at the Liverpool Empire in February 1983. Sadly the previous year's Toxteth riots had dominated the headlines when disturbances, following the arrest of Leroy Cooper, rapidly turned into full-blown riots with pitched battles between police and youths. The initial mayhem had lasted for nine days and spread throughout the city, leaving a thousand police injured, five hundred people arrested and nearly one hundred and fifty buildings destroyed. Six months later, feelings were still running high, resulting in the minstrels being threatened with pickets. Controversy raged the week before the show was due to open when Merseyside's Community Relations Officer Paul Summerfield, supported by Rashid Mufti, spokesman for the Liverpool Eight Defence Committee, called for the show to be banned by the local council: 'My concern is that a show like this shows black people in caricature. There is still tension on the streets and this show will certainly do nothing to improve the atmosphere.' The press was inundated with letters, like the one from Herbert Holder who wrote, 'Here we go again with the "Race Industry" peddling inane remarks about the show. His sanctimonious remarks about bad taste are offensive and is the sort of talk that feeds the supposed friction in the first place. I recently saw a travel poster proclaiming "Aussies Go Home" and wonder what he would make of that. No doubt if a similar tongue-in-cheek poster had used the words "Indians" or "Jamaicans", there would be uproar. Let's have an end to this mindless tripe. The rest of us will think for ourselves and enjoy our minstrel records in peace.' In the *Northern Echo*, DH Midgley wrote, 'For how much longer is the indigenous population to put up with being told how to run the country and what we should be allowed to see? THEY may not like the show, but I do. Perhaps they should be told there are some things they do of which we don't approve.' W Jones thought, 'How silly for black people to get angry about this famous show. I've seen many minstrel shows over the years. None of them belittled, ridiculed or insulted blacks. Why stop an old tradition for such ill-informed sensitivity?'

Support for the show came from three knowledgeable quarters. Glyn Dawson wrote to the *Daily Express*, saying, 'As an artiste associated with the show I can state categorically that there is no hint of racialism in it and never has been. Apart from providing work for dedicated performers in a highly professional field, the show brings light relief to thousands from the normal everyday stress which affects us all. The friendly approach of the show cuts through any barriers which may be felt for any reason by members of the audience.' Dai Francis publicly said, 'What a shame some people feel like that. Minstrel shows are innocent entertainment. We must be the most successful show in the world and have given pleasure to countless millions everywhere.' The criticism was described as a 'load of rubbish' by Barrie Stead, general manager and artistic director of the Theatre Royal, Nottingham, where the Minstrels had often appeared: 'They attract massive audiences and do not present a caricature of blacks. It's a mix of both colours. As far as I'm concerned it's a piece of well-tested family entertainment.' Despite the controversy, the show went ahead with its Liverpool booking, proving as usual very popular with audiences.

And success continued to mount. The baking hot summer of 1983 saw a return to the format of earlier years when demand for seats was so great that George and Bob staged two summer shows. One show returned to Eastbourne for the second year running, while the other opened at another favourite venue, Paignton. In another coup, George persuaded both Dai Francis and John Boulter to return to lead the shows. Both seemed glad to be back, but it's obvious they were still unable to shed their links with George and were still living in the shadow of their connections with the show. The Eastbourne show was once again well-received. The ever-supportive *Eastbourne Herald* called it 'sheer 100% entertainment. A nightly crowd-puller. A first class cavalcade of colour which moves along fast and faultlessly. I left feeling I had just witnessed one of the most excellent shows ever staged at that theatre.' As previously the paper reviewed the show throughout the season, later reporting, 'On a warm night they had four encores of their best numbers...and THAT is Minstrel Magic.' The *Eastbourne Gazette* thought it 'a stunning extravaganza, with all the ingredients to make it one of the biggest crowd pullers the theatre has ever known. The show of the summer.'

Press praise was just as enthusiastic for the Paignton show. The *Western Evening Herald* reported, 'There are very few stage shows today which have such a strong cast and such precision, and with its fast moving items and the glittering costumes, the routines make it an ideal summer show for the dullest of days.' The *Torbay News* enthused, 'It takes about five seconds to realise the show is a hit. Colourful, energetic, foot-tapping and heart-warming - the show is a delight.'

In yet another departure for the show, the company spent the whole summer of 1984 travelling as they appeared at Butlins in Bognor Regis on Monday and Tuesday nights, using the other nights to appear at Butlins in Barry and Minehead. In 1985, their Silver Anniversary year, the Minstrels toured twenty towns throughout England. The specially adapted show was very much smaller than in its heyday, using only eight Minstrels and six Toppers, with six people involved in the speciality acts. At one time the show had used sixteen Minstrels alone! The show, staged by Sandy McFarlane, used sequences from previous summer shows, such as *A New Orleans Medley, Bonjour Paris, A Tribute to Uncle Sam, Cockney Knees Up* and *A Sentimental Journey*, with soloists Les Want and Frank McFadden. The tour was produced by Brian Shaw Management and the Robert Luff Organisation, the first time Bob had allowed another collaborator. This tour involved even more travelling for the company. It opened for three days at Harrogate, where it broke all box office records, then moved for another three days to Southport and Dartford, where it spent a week. The *Kent Evening Post* posed the question, 'Could it be that British blacks might object to the show? Not a bit, says Sandy McFarlane, "It's only the white do-gooders who do the objecting." They were in spectacularly colourful form.' The *Dartford Chronicle* reported 'pure magic. They were encored so often I lost count, and every pair of hands in the packed audience must have been raw with clapping.' After Northampton, Clacton, Lowestoft and various other South England venues, the company landed for a week in Weston-Super-Mare, where the *Bristol Evening Post* said 'familiarity breeds content'. A note of discontent was sounded while they were in Worthing when the *Worthing Gazette* printed a letter from KB Kersey, who sadly had misremembered the original shows: 'The singing was as good as anything we recall from the original company. We were, however, expecting the show as we remembered it from ten or twenty years ago. Unfortunately, the actual singing and dancing comprised only about 50% of the show. Two comedians had quite a long stint each in both halves of the show, and there was also a xylophonist. I would have preferred to have seen the traditional comedy interludes, with the entire company on stage and the cross-talk taking place in the forefront.' He seems to think he is talking about the original *Black and White Minstrel Show*, but of course, they never did this traditional minstrel show routine.

The following year, George again sent the show on a fourteen-week summer tour of Britain, which started at Nottingham in July. They also spent every weekend this summer at the Embassy Theatre in Skegness. This show featured Ted Darling, Les Want, Frank McFadden and Adele Stephenson, with now only six Minstrels and six Toppers. The show was reducing with each season. Once again, it stayed in venues anything from two days to a week; the logistics of moving the show and cast so often must have been overwhelming, so presumably everything was much simpler for these tours.

But the end of a thirty-year era was now in sight. Sadly when the 1988 tour came to an end in the autumn, George decided that enough was enough, and the companies which ran the shows ceased to operate. Dot was to say years later, 'It had run its course. It had been on for so many years and don't forget, by that time George was way into his seventies. He'd lost the spirit of it, and he really didn't want to go back to it - I think the climate was right for it to stop. It stopped at its height, and that's what he wanted. He didn't want it to dwindle down to end-of-the-pier type shows.' Daphne Bell, who was still working with George on the shows, recalls, 'What an amazing and wonderful time we had. It wasn't a job of work, it was a very enjoyable life. I look upon all old friends as family. I sang all the time, all TV, recordings, radio. I didn't finish until George packed it in himself. It just petered out.'

CHAPTER 35

From the beginning, the enormous success of the stage show had inevitably spawned copycat shows which made George and the BBC furious but which everyone seemed powerless to halt. While Bob was doubtless thinking of all the money he wasn't getting, what bothered George, of course, was that there was no control over the quality of these copycat shows, which to such a perfectionist would have been torment. He was also afraid that the fans would be misled about what they were going to see. According to Dot, he was always 'very unhappy with splinter shows, shows that tried to mimic the Minstrels. He always said that some had real talent so why not go off and do something with their voices? Some of these shows got very close with their posters. But he eventually said they're going to do it anyway, we can't keep suing them.' Ironically it was now to be the copycat shows which helped to keep the memory alive.

From the start in 1960, there had been shades of things to come. Back then, Bob had sent the BBC a newspaper cutting about an amateur show using the same title, The *Black and White Minstrel Show*, which deeply concerned him. In a telling comment, they admitted there was little they could do as 'titles are always tricky things'. One of the main reasons that Bob had been able to run rings around the BBC when he was trying to put the show on the stage was because they knew they couldn't stop him just using the title in a slightly different way.

Despite these earlier doubts about their rights to the show's title, the BBC quickly became fiercely protective but never consistent in protecting their rights to the show and the name. One year, a Methodist church asked the BBC for permission to use the title for their proposed minstrel show. The BBC refused, saying that Bob had exclusive rights. However, the following year, when Bob told the BBC he'd heard of a Guernsey show with the same name, the BBC took action, writing to the hotel concerned, who countered saying theirs was not a stage show but cabaret called *Black Bottoms*. However, one fan who clearly remembers this show is adamant it was a stage Minstrel show. Nevertheless, the BBC accepted the hotel's explanation at face value and backed off from threatening any further action.

Yet later, after weeks of negotiations, they told a York youth club to change the name of its forthcoming show from the *Black and White Minstrel Show*. York's producer said, 'It's probably just a shot across our bows. This summer the show's at Scarborough. I suppose it's near York and the BBC wanted to clear the point.' In any event, they changed it to *Rowntree's Youth Club Minstrel Show*. However, no action was taken by the BBC or George against a group called *The Manchester Black and White Minstrels* who entertained disabled people. Equally Buxton Amateur Dramatic and Operatic Society produced their own version of the *Black and White Minstrel Show* which George obviously knew about, but no action at all was taken to stop it.

In 1965, the London company at the Victoria Palace learned that a Southsea minstrel show was planning a summer season, during which the singers would be miming to pre-recorded voices which were not even their own. Soon advertising appeared asking for singers, dancers and 'soloists, one of whom should be a Bing Crosby type, another Al Jolson and another a lyrical English tenor type'. It became clear that the show was actually using a pirated copy of the Victoria Palace tape. Head Minstrel Arthur Lewis took his concerns to Equity, saying, 'We want this show stopped unless the people actually appearing make their own pre-recording. I want to protect the livelihood of the Minstrel singers in particular and entertainers in general. If it's not stopped, it's quite conceivable one choir in London could do every recording for every show, and singers and dancers such as us would be out of work. It's conceivable you could hear Maria Callas' voice singing in strip shows in Soho.' But Equity remained powerless to stop such theft because, ironically, 'Nothing was laid down in black and white'.

The Musicians' Union proved equally helpless - or hopeless - a few years later when George and Bob turned their attention to a proposed new tour of Japan, Hong Kong and Singapore. Although, by now, George was less keen to send shows abroad - 'We have enough to do here, doing even fewer shows to keep the standard right. There is always plenty of time to conquer other fields if that becomes necessary' - Bob was keen to negotiate a third overseas tour to include Australia and New Zealand as well. However, in a serious threat to the show, events in Australia doomed this project, at least for a few years. George and Bob became aware that the entire musical content of the current stage show had been taped and duplicated, when Keith Leggett, George's ex-right-hand man now living in New Zealand, sent him newspaper cuttings and a tape recording of the show, taken while it was in Auckland. George's orchestrator Alan Bristow confirmed the duplication, as did EMI's Walter Ridley who made a technical comparison for George. The pirated production, presented by Prestige Productions in conjunction with the New Zealand Broadcasting Corporation, had already toured Australia and was now in New Zealand, due next to appear at the Grand Opera House, Wellington. George wrote to John Norton, General Secretary of the Musicians Union, saying, 'Their programmes even detail the same musical scenes in the same sequence as ours. Not only are my vocal arrangement and original music duplicated exactly but also, where possible with their orchestral combinations, parts of Alan Bristow's backings. Even hand claps, tap dance routines and other non-vocal effects are identical.' Because of this pirated production, Bob was told by Australian impresarios that it would be pointless to attempt any third tour by the Mitchell Minstrels. George and Bob asked to meet the Musicians Union and the New Zealand High Commissioner to resolve the issue, but nothing was done. George wrote on his copy of the letter to John Norton, 'Chat - LOTS, Action - NIX as expected.'

Even before the stage shows finished, tribute spin-off shows of a different sort were playing summer seasons throughout the country, and even in Australia and New Zealand. These shows profiled past Minstrels and so were more 'genuine' but George and Bob still fretted that they had no control. The publicity for shows which included past Minstrels inevitably always mentioned the fact that the participants had appeared in the *Black and White Minstrel Show*. The New Minstrel Show with ventriloquist Ken Wood, who had been with the second Australian tour, put out pre-publicity which rode on the back of the show: 'The *Black and White Minstrel Show* has kept the tradition alive. This show is designed to bring this high standard of entertainment to theatres in the provinces, many of which have not seen a Minstrel show.' Scarborough went into Minstrel overload one summer, rather hypocritically driven by Bob himself, when Glyn Dawson starred in *Minstrel Melodies* at the newly revamped Minstrel Lounge at the Futurist complex, now owned by Bob. This ran in direct competition to Dai Francis in *The Jolson Revue* at the Floral Hall, which local press called 'the Minstrels by any other name'. A successful show called *The Minstrel Stars*, starring John Boulter, Andy Cole, Margaret Savage and Peter Kaye, did Sunday concerts along the South coast for several years. Dai Francis also managed to get away with it when he starred in *The Minstrel Stars* at the Royal Hippodrome Eastbourne one summer where they played to packed houses. Presumably, people objected more to the lack of actual star Minstrels in the show, than to the quality of the show itself.

Some of these productions went to great lengths to imitate the show as closely as possible. Michael Wooldridge, a long-time fan, ran versions for years, shows like *Memories of the Minstrels* and *Magic of the Minstrels*, which used past Minstrel singers, such as Les Want, Bob Hunter and Margaret Savage. He even tracked down original costumes. The shows travelled Britain, spending summers in places such as Blackpool, Eastbourne and Worthing. Producer Tony Peers added *Magic of the Minstrels* to the attractions on offer, with a show that toured throughout Britain, though George, and later Dot, refused to let such shows use George's arrangements. Inevitably the shows used far fewer personnel so the original sound couldn't be recreated. Nevertheless, audiences flocked to see them, to enjoy once again a faint taster of the past days of glory.

George was also seriously worried by shows which had nothing at all to do with the original productions and casts. Girling Productions' summer show, the *Spectacular Minstrel Show*, at the Margate Winter Gardens, ran for sixteen weeks in the summer of 1991. In its seventh year at this venue, it broke all advance bookings records and promised to be 'as close to the original show as possible', breaking all theatrical records for the venue. A show toured New Zealand, frequently mistaken, at least in advance, as the genuine article. In 1992, *That Old Minstrel Magic* played to capacity audiences throughout the provinces but, following protests from the Commission for Racial Equality, no members of the cast appeared in black-face. An attempt by one of the lead singers to do so was rapidly quashed.

George's fears about such shows were borne out time and time again. He couldn't stop ex-Minstrels appearing on stage claiming to have been with the show; this was nothing but the truth, but there was, and still is, a fine line between claiming past links with the show and maybe suggesting to the public that this was a version of the official show. People and press continually misunderstood that this wasn't the real show. Local press always used headlines such as 'Minstrel coming'. When *Stars from the Black and White Minstrel Show* appeared at Hastings, starring Margo Henderson, George Chisholm and Sally Barnes, all of whom had, of course, appeared in the show, one local paper gleefully announced, 'The Black and White Minstrels are at Hastings with characteristic charm at the forefront.' The resort was fortunate that customers didn't demand their money back as had happened several years previously! When the *Yorkshire Observer* ran a feature that two local girls were appearing in the *Black and White Minstrel Show* in Southport, George was forced to write to the paper explaining that it was not a genuine show and no one could use the title because of copyright issues. George constantly issued statements saying, 'The title is owned by the BBC and the only shows that can be presented legally are those by companies with impresario Bob Luff in association with me. The highly acclaimed new production which appeared at Eastbourne last summer is now making a successful tour of Australia and New Zealand with an Australian cast. A specially devised version featuring our principal British soloists is appearing at Butlins' theatres throughout the summer. Neither Bob Luff nor I have any connection whatsoever with any other Minstrel-type show this summer. I am worried that fans of the show may go to see the tributes expecting the real thing. Hundreds of singers, dancers and guest artistes have appeared in our shows, and we accept that they all have the right to be billed as "from the *Black and White Minstrel Show*" although they may not have appeared with us for six, or even twenty-six, years.'

And he was proved right in 1972 when trouble flared in Bournemouth in late September. A Sunday show at the Pavilion Theatre was billed as *Stars of the Black and White Minstrels*, starred George Chisholm, Margo Henderson and Jack Beckett. Trouble started during the show, with angry shouts and people walking out. Afterwards, a crowd gathered demanding their money back. One man said the show offended against the Trade Descriptions Act: 'We were led to believe we would be seeing the genuine Black and White Minstrels but there was not a black face among them.' Someone else said, 'The show was nothing like value for money.' The following day the entertainments manager refunded everyone's money, while Bournemouth Entertainments Committee said that the posters had been misleading. Bob was swift to dissociate himself from the show, saying, 'We are not in any way responsible for or associated with this show.' Similarly, *The Minstrel Stars,* with Bob Hunter and Tom Conway ran into trouble with audiences and George alike. Complaints to the theatre's management led to a hastily-issued denial that there was any attempt to con the public. The statement said they had always gone to great pains to explain that the show was not the official one, that they had stuck to the legal billing at all times and that it did not claim to be the *Black and White Minstrel Show* but did have stars who had appeared in it. In yet another spin-off show, a Bournemouth show, starring Glyn Dawson, also caused complaints. Resident Les Saxon complained to Bournemouth Council that the show was a 'backwards step', but the council refused to take it off. Les had appeared in *Cats* and *Hair* in London in the 1960s and had been part of the group from *Hair* that had picketed the show at the Victoria Palace. Glyn recalled, 'He blocked me going onto the pier, saying, "You're not going to work tonight, I'm stopping you." I said, "You tell me I'm not going into the theatre, I'm telling you you're going into the sea." He tried to stop everyone, but the show went on.'

These episodes vindicated the BBC's decision to work with Bob Luff in staging the first Minstrel shows in 1960. They had realised he would be able to stage a show using people from the television programmes and call it *Stars from the Minstrels* without infringing any copyrights. By working with Bob, they and George had guaranteed the quality of the stage shows; now, without that quality, these shows were not being well received.

But George was occasionally supportive, particularly if the show was for charity. The best-known venture was probably the *Angus Black and White Minstrels* who were given permission to use the title, as long as they were a charity though George added, tongue in cheek, 'I think you ought to call yourselves the *Arbroath Smokies!*' He also sent them some musical scores so they could be as authentic as possible, and a case of the proper stage makeup so they could look just right. The very happy Angus Minstrels sold out all 7,000 tickets in three and a half hours that year and continued to perform sell-out shows until 2005 when the makeup was removed, and the name changed to *The Arbroath Minstrels!*

Minstrel Magic

George also came to the rescue of the Cuxton Minstrels Christmas variety show. When they couldn't find silver lamé knickers anywhere for their dancers to wear, Wardrobe Mistress Marie Worth invited them to rummage through their costume warehouse, where they were given twelve silver lamé leotards which they adapted.

The extent to which the show was still embedded in the national consciousness, twelve years after the last television show and three years after the stage show had stopped, was proved when seed manufacturers Thompsons and Morgan created a new carnation, called the Black and White Minstrels. This was their major seed production for 1990 and deemed the flower of the year. In bud the flowers were silver; as they unfolded and assumed carnation-like form, their rich dark centres appeared with each fringed petal tip highlighted in pure white. Publicity said, 'There are no bright colours, yet there is impact as they glitter and sparkle like sunshine on icicles.' No one complained.

The race-relations industry was by now in full swing but so stupendous had been the Minstrels' success for thirty-one years, that they remained a deep part of the national consciousness, even though they were no longer seen on television or stage. They were as fundamental to British culture as the Beatles or Shakespeare and still provoking comment. One ponderous newspaper article bizarrely wrote, 'This show clearly struck a chord with the sexually rabid and latently racist in our society,' which prompted a Chinese nurse who had come to Britain in the 1960s to relate her happy memories of the show. A high proportion of her fellow trainee nurses were from West Africa and the Caribbean, and the Minstrel show was their favourite programme. She ironically added, 'The sexual rabidity and latent racism rather escaped us. But then at that time, the race relations industry had not yet got fully into its stride.'

Every time the 'colour issue' came up, no matter what the context, the Minstrels were mentioned, until it seemed as though the makeup had been the entire nature of the show. It became a knee-jerk reaction, with everything else about the show and the Mitchell choirs entirely forgotten.

Liverpool Council provoked uproar when it demanded that Robertson remove the popular Golly from their jam jars. Black workers at the Robertson factory told agitators to 'pipe down' but to no avail. As the *Malton Gazette and Herald* wrote, 'Nothing racial about him at all, he was loved by all, as were the Minstrels, and now we see the end of an era, brought about by narrow-mindedness.' The *Kettering Evening Telegraph* printed a letter from Paul Crofts, criticising a Minstrel show, which provoked a response from Heather Edwards who wrote, 'His letter shows he has no knowledge of the tradition behind the Minstrels. A minstrel was a singer and entertainer in medieval days. A hundred years ago and more in the States there were minstrel shows performed by negroes which were immensely popular. They were so popular in fact that white entertainers copied them, blacking their faces to show they were pretending to be negroes (to keep up the continuity). When the BBC brought out their up to date version, they added white entertainers to a "blacked up" cast, simply as a contrast. Far from denigrating negroes, the BBC was paying tribute to them for creating a form of entertainment which has stood the test of time. The show ran for a long time which proves it must have been popular.'

The *Liverpool Echo* reported, 'Wirral councillors are considering whether to ban a [Minstrel] show at the Floral Pavilion New Brighton on the grounds that it is racist. The argument is that the shows are reminiscent of slavery. I believe most people - and that includes black people - accept such shows for what they have always been, simply a form of entertainment. Or perhaps I should say that was the case until it became fashionable to criticise them as having a deeper and insidious message. Censorship in any form is dangerous. Where do you draw the line? Is the musical *Oliver!* to be banned because it reflects the exploitation and degradation of the poor in the workhouse days of Dickens? The would-be do-gooders who thrust this sort of simplistic approach to racial problems down people's throats do enormous damage. By treating side issues - golliwogs on jam jars is another favourite - as matters of importance, they cause irritation and resentment among the majority population. Far from removing intolerance, they feed it. But the greatest damage they do is draw attention away from the real issues.'

Councils were running scared of the 'colour issue' everywhere. One Left-wing councillor tried to have *Land of Hope and Glory* banned at a Remembrance Festival, saying 'I wouldn't want to hear this racist song in our multi-cultural community.'

Controversy surrounded Southampton Council's banning of *Showboat* as being racist, which led to press outcry. The *Worcester Journal* widened the debate by writing, 'I would like to thank Channel 4 for showing *Mammy* and *Wonder Bar* and point out the reason why the BBC doesn't show any Al Jolson films. It is because it thinks them racist. Not only Al Jolson but the Minstrels and Eddie Cantor have suffered. But isn't this two-faced when the BBC allows programmes on Hitler, Mussolini and sitcoms such as *In Sickness and In Health*?' Makeup remain the issue for political lobbies, to the point of ludicrousness. In 2009, in Britain, a touring play about Al Jolson decided to play his Minstrel scenes without makeup, even though it was obviously an integral part of the story. This was despite Equity giving permission to use the makeup. Equity said it was normally opposed to actors blacking up, but spokesman Paul Brown said a production about Al Jolson could be 'one of the very limited times when we might not actively object because it is about a white artiste who blacked up'.

They even got embroiled in the gun debate. After the Hungerford Massacre in 1987, Mary Kenny, noted *Daily Telegraph* columnist, wrote, 'I have sympathy for the freedom argument. For the world is also too full of bossy-boots who would curb our freedoms; trade unionists coercing frightened young typists into joining unions; feminists objecting to Miss World or indeed the portrayal of any pretty girl anywhere; dogmatists at the BBC who refuse to screen the Minstrels.' Freddie Clayton, who led the orchestra for most of its run, wrote to support her: 'I can assure one and all that neither musicians nor cast would have taken part in a show that denigrated anyone, ethnic or otherwise. Most of us were weaned on such greats as Armstrong, Holliday, Fitzgerald, Basie and Ellington, and to suggest that the Minstrels in some way demeaned these marvellous artistes or their people is a nonsense. If the *Jolson Story* and Alf Garnett can come into our homes via TV, and rightly so, then the arguments against showing the Minstrels are, to say the least, spurious. It does seem a shame that a minority of a minority should wield influence to such a degree that the BBC - against the wishes of many of their top producers - should show such a pusillanimous attitude towards a show that brought such pleasure to millions over so many years. So take a deep breath, Michael Grade, and re-run the series; the series of which it can truly be said, "They don't make them like that anymore."'

CHAPTER 36

George and Dot were still living in Traps Lane in New Malden, where life was very sociable. George was very proud of this house: 'I had a nice house with three floors and a full-size snooker room, and all mod cons. It had an old Tudor wall which was National Heritage. I wasn't allowed to touch it because the walled entrance to my garage was a hunting lodge of Queen Elizabeth 1. The tree behind my garden was the one described by John Galsworthy, who lived nearby at one time, at the end of his famous *Forsyte Saga*. During the war, Eisenhower lived up the road, having a good relationship with the lady who drove his car.' Dot recalls, 'We'd give dinner parties two or three times a week for business and pleasure. Mary was still our full-time housekeeper, but she didn't live in. George was now suffering from emphysema because of the smoking, which he never tried to give up. He wouldn't be George if you took drink and cigarettes away.' And he still enjoyed his food, much as he had during the restaurant outings in Amsterdam years earlier. 'He adored fish, prawns - but no other shellfish - fillet steak, roast beef, haggis, vegetables, puddings,' recalls Dot. 'Plus the occasional brandy and wine. He liked Stilton, port and Shropshire blue but hated offal and scavenger fish.'

But things were about to change. George's sight, never strong, deteriorated to the point where he needed a cataract operation. Although the operation itself went well, one day when George decided to cut the grass, he looked down to see where he was going and everything went wrong. He was blind for the next eighteen months before they were able to operate again and restore his sight.

His general health was also deteriorating. He was now in his mid-seventies, and the emphysema wasn't improving. Dot recalls, 'He'd pick up everything. If he got a cold, it would knock him for six for weeks.' Everything changed when they went to Florida for a holiday. 'We loved it so much,' remembers Dot. 'George had been through five or six years of bad health by now, and Wansbeck [in Traps Lane] was becoming too big, so we had to move. We wanted a small base in England and one in Florida, so we bought a plot of land in Kissimmee in Florida and built a house there. While we were doing that, we tried to get American residence but George failed because of his age and health, so we stayed there for six months of the year and spent the other half of the year in England.'

When the Traps Lane house was sold, George and Dot discussed where they would base themselves for their six months in Britain. George wanted to go back to Scotland, but Dot recalls, 'I said, "No way, it's too cut off and far away, and it won't be as you remembered." We used to go up every year at Christmas to see the grandchildren. The last time we went, we just caught the last train home because of the snow, there wasn't another for four weeks. George said, "I'm being silly, aren't I?" So we took the middle course and decided to live in the Midlands - we had family near, and it had good communications and airports. So we sold Wansbeck and came to Albrighton at the same time as we built the house in Florida. My sister Margaret lived in one bungalow, and we lived in her other bungalow for about five years - we did it up and lived in it for the summer months, spending the winters in Florida.'

George and Dot enjoyed life in Florida. They had a wide circle of friends and frequently entertained visitors from Britain. Margaret Savage remembers this period very fondly: 'George and Dot were very kind and invited us (and now four children!) over to their fabulous house in Kissimmee, picking us up at the airport and treating us like royalty. The children had the best time ever with Disney visits all arranged, they couldn't have spoilt us more. The next time we went was at Christmas, and on New Year's Eve, they had a party for all their friends. We had a great Hogmanay party. I tell you the Glenfiddich was flowing that night and between Dot and myself, the Highland Fling and the Gay Gordons were given a fair belting. We won't forget those holidays or their kindness.'

In February 1997, George was celebrating his 80th birthday and Dot her 50th. By now, they were beginning to think that perhaps they needed a more permanent home in the UK. As George recalled in Florida a few days before their joint birthday, 'We now need a home in the UK, so that's our major worry at the moment. We'd like to stay in Florida but six months a year is all we're allowed. 'Tis a strange web we mortals weave. OK but it's never been dull or boring from my point of view. In a few days, Dot hits the dreaded 50, and on the same day, I shall be 80. It will be very interesting to see what happens next. I have a weird idea that a few people, still in the business, will arrive the night before the party and leave the day after - a very expensive way to get a glass of plonk and a chicken leg. Dot says that's rubbish, C'est la vie, mes amis, - or it's been a funny old life. No complaints. Best asset is Dot who really should be made a saintess by the Pope, but I don't think he's into women.'

Needless to say, a party did happen! Son Robert turned up, as did John and Anna Boulter. George, thrust into his hated limelight, made a speech: 'Here comes the moment I've been dreading, talking into one of these contraptions [a mike]. I'm blessed by having very many friends, many of them have gone to a lot of trouble and expense to be here. I must mention my son, Rob, he's a pretty good pianist and a first class conductor. You will notice he looks like Rasputin. I don't see any resemblance at all to me, but Dot can.' Dot thanked John and Anna for travelling from New Zealand where they now lived, and joked, 'Thanks for coming over and entertaining us so well tonight; you didn't have to sing for your supper, I'd have fed you anyway.' The main speech was made by son Rob who said, 'Time for me to get my own back! He only ever gave me two bits of advice. First bit was never to go into show business and the second bit which he still told me today was "get your hair cut". So you can see I've always followed his advice.' [By now, Rob had long hair and was a respected musical director.] 'I was in here last night playing that pianoey thing and it was obvious he was thinking about the land where he was born, because he likes these little mementos of Scotland around him, and last night it was an old Scottish cordial, this one made by a certain Mr Johnny Walker, and it reminded him of home. I think that's why he came over here because it's so like Scotland over here, and it reminded him of bonny Falkirk, all the coal mines and iron foundries, and of course, the climate is exactly the same, this time of year. I was playing *Tea for Two*, which was the first thing I ever learnt to play when I was about three, and he taught it to me, and I've always wondered why he taught me that tune. It's taken me fifty years to find out, and he told me last night. I said, "Do you remember, why that song?" and he said, "Because it's the only bloody tune I could play." I remember when I was a kid. We could all play better than him, and yet this man created so much wonderful music, and I'm not just saying that, all you need are two ears and a heart and a soul. You've only got to hear two or three notes, and you're going to be moved. Beautiful, beautiful, beautiful. It's my gorgeous step-mother's birthday too. Now, this is not a step-mother you get in Disneyland. Dot has looked after my dad for twenty years, and I would like to say thank you because if she hadn't been with him for twenty years, he'd have been up there now and he'd have been teaching some poor bloody angel how to play *Tea for Two* on a harp!'

But sadly, although the Florida sunshine helped his emphysema, George started having transient ischemic attacks (TIAs). At first, they occurred about once a month but then got to be a couple of times a day, affecting the Menière's disease which still plagued him. Just after his eightieth birthday, he had a major stroke, which left him in a wheelchair and meant that flights and insurance became increasingly difficult. They sold the Florida house and bought a house in Albrighton. Dot remembers, 'This house, which was wheelchair-friendly, had been empty for quite a while. Everything else we'd seen had had corridors which are a nightmare for wheelchairs, but this house had already been converted because the lady and her husband were both in wheelchairs, but it needed a lot doing to it.' When George's health allowed, they spent the time travelling in Europe, Scotland, Spain and Malta.

In what must be seen as the most astounding tribute to George as well as the show, there was one more surprise in store for George. Ventriloquist Neville King, a long-time speciality act with the show, and who had married Topper Joan Lambert and become a very close friend of George and Dot's, realised that 1997 marked the fortieth anniversary of the very first television show, as well as George's 80th birthday. He now suggested to Dot that they arrange a reunion for everyone they could manage to contact. Dot was enthusiastic, and it was agreed to keep it secret from George. In May or June, a couple of months before the planned reunion, George was still in hospital following his stroke, which made it easier for Dot and Neville to keep the arrangements secret. Dot wrote to Joan and Neville to say, 'George seems to be doing better these last two days although his right leg is still not doing anything. He's having physio to try to make it useable, let's keep our fingers crossed. Daph (Bell) has been staying with me this last week, but today she must go home, so I'm off to put her on the train at Wolverhampton. George will be in hospital for at least five more days.'

The first reunion was planned for Sunday, August 3 at the Patshull Park Golf and Country Club in Shropshire, chosen because its proximity to Albrighton meant that George wouldn't suspect anything until he arrived at the reunion. Neville and Joan had spent months tracking down as many people as possible, constantly impressing on everyone the need to keep it all very secret, so that George would have the greatest possible surprise. Every phone call to someone tended to produce yet more names, and gradually nearly two hundred people were able to attend, with many more sending apologies, a testimony to everyone's fond memories of both the show and George. Pat Heigham, the sound technician who had filmed the show in the early '60s after they had won the Golden Rose of Montreux, recalls, 'Although it was thirty years since I had left the Corporation, just two phone calls started a tracing route for the original Crew 3, and enough people were tracked down to fill our own table at the event.' People travelled from far and wide. Ernest Maxin, working in Berlin that weekend, took time off to fly to Britain, travel to the reunion for two hours, and fly back to Germany the same day. John and Anna Boulter travelled from New Zealand, and Danae Marsh travelled from Norway.

The room, filled with round tables, was festooned with black and white balloons everywhere. Neville had produced display boards filled with photos and record sleeves, and Pat Heigham's thirty-five-year-old film ran on a monitor. Joan King had placed a book on the piano and asked people to write messages to George in it. Many people had brought their own scrapbooks and mementoes, and the room buzzed with laughter and chat. Over it all, the soundtrack of *When the Saints Go Marching In* played constantly.

Suddenly through the big glass sliding doors, people could see George and Dot approaching. George, still in a wheelchair, believed he, Dot and Daphne, who had been staying with them for a few days, were about to have lunch with Neville and Joan in a belated celebration of his 80th birthday. As they entered the room, everyone spontaneously started clapping as well as joining in with *When the Saints*. Maggi Lawlor recalled, 'It was just the most moving thing when George came in, and we all broke into *When*

Minstrel Magic

the Saints - we were all in tears.' Carl Ewer remembers it as being 'so emotional with the singing'.

A startled George suddenly realised what was happening and joined in with the singing and clapping, before wiping away tears. Turning to Dot, he asked, 'Did you know about this?' Neville said, 'George, this is your day. We want you to make the best of it, mate. We want to thank you for the best years of our lives. There's not going to be a dry seat in the house. I know you want to talk, so it's only fair we have a who's who, so Joan and I are going to conduct one. When we sent these letters out, the strange thing is the first man to send a cheque back was Landed.' Glyn Dawson bounded to the front to be duly presented with his name tag and the microphone, after which he reiterated his famous audition story. More and more people were called forward - Margaret Savage, Delia Wicks, Mary Moss, Mary Oakley, Peter and Jenny Dakin, Peter Clare. People from the really early days attended, such as Jose Cooper, who had been one of the twins in the wartime shows and had married Alan Cooper. Production staff were there, including Charles Chilton who had used the choir in so many radio shows, and his daughter Mary who had danced in many Minstrel shows. Technicians such as cameraman Ian Gibb from Crew 3, Eddie Stewart, senior cameraman, and Dave Sydenham, Technical Operations Manager, all joined Pat Heigham's table. Bob Woolman from the BBC said, 'I first worked with George in 1957 in Studio G, that was the *George Mitchell Glee Club*, then we went into the theatre with the Black and Whites, and it was a most enjoyable time.' Elspeth Hands was there with her two daughters who wrote in the book, 'We won't forget great moments in your Florida swimming pool, love you loads, Lucy. I had a lovely time, won't forget it, Love, Suzie.'

Many people brought messages from absentees. Minstrel Ray Lavender told the gathering, 'One very special friend of mine sends her best love to George. This lady gave me my chance, and she gave lots of you the chance too, and she's not here at the moment - Shelagh Delaney.' John Boulter remembered absentees too. It was his birthday, so he was treated to a rousing chorus of *Happy Birthday* before he said, 'Such a lovely thing, today, a once-off in anybody's life. A great many of us owe our complete stage career to this man over here, for which we thank you very much. I nearly had a heart attack earlier because there was someone coming down and it looked just like Tony. So I'd just like to say Dai's not here, Tony can't be obviously, so why not give a welcome if they're still up there, to absent friends.'

So many people had stories to tell and thanks to give to George. In a moving tribute, producer Ernest Maxin said, 'Of all the shows I have produced and directed, and that's nearly three hundred of them, the show that gave me the greatest pleasure, the greatest thrill that came from inside here, was the Black and White Minstrels, because that is the greatest show that ever got to the heart of the people in this country. George himself is a genius, there'll never be the likes of this man again. How he could write arrangements for years and years and years and every time it was fresh, an inspiration, absolutely wonderful. I want to thank you for giving me the golden years in TV.'

Principal Les Want became quite emotional: 'I'm known as a joker, but I really want to be serious. To follow up on what Ernest Maxin said, my son is a paramedic in Los Angeles, and I went over there for the very first time last year, and I went to see Jolson's tomb. It was like Admiralty Arch and Jolson's voice singing, and right at the bottom there's an epitaph, "You ain't heard nothing since" and I want to say this - as far as British show business is concerned, as far as our show is concerned, they ain't heard nothing since. If you look in the *Penguin Encyclopaedia of Music*, we are the last and most famous minstrel show in all of show business history, and I'm sure we're all very proud of that.'

Pauline Whitaker, who had been a principal in *Music Music Music*, as well as the daughter of Ossie and Phyllis Whitaker, both of whom had lengthy associations with George, recalled, 'I was brought up on a diet of George which put a lot of rhythm in my life. Ossie and Laurie Bloom will be looking down on us today and girls, he'd be so proud of you - he was such a stickler for dress and looking right, not just on stage but off as well. My mother is nearly 88 now and would love to have been here today - they could have run around in their wheelchairs outside here and had a race. She still remembers the lovely days of Daphne and the auditions for the Black and Whites, and she remembers when Glyn came in and sang so beautifully.'

Stan Stennett told a few stories of his time in the show, ending with 'a quick story about Glyn. Last year we were doing a show, dare I say it, called *The Minstrels 1996* with John Boulter too, and we had a great time, bringing back wonderful memories of what used to be, and we're driving from Folkestone, Glyn and I, and I'm going to drop him home. He said, "Want a biscuit, lovely?" "Aye, I'm a bit hungry." So he gives me the biscuit, and they were quite nice. I said, "These are nice, whose are these?" Glyn said, "They're mine." If nothing ever happens to me again, I'll always look back on my time with the show and the great people like George Mitchell and George Inns.' As everyone was introduced and received their name tag, they went to speak to George. Maryetta Midgley was sitting very close and remembers, 'I loved the first reunion. George said "I'd know you anywhere," to everyone.'

After everyone had been introduced, Neville called on Ruth Madoc. Ruth had been a Mitchell Maid in the Victoria Palace for eighteen months, before moving on to become most famous perhaps as Gladys in *Hi! Di! Hi!*. She had her own stories to tell: 'Mr Mitchell, as you will always be to me, dear friends, from a wonderful show and a wonderful era. I have to say that I came into light entertainment almost by default because, before I went into the VP [Victoria Palace], I was trained as an a-a-a-actress, and all I ever wanted to be was an a-a-a-actress. Well, I saw the usual cattle market audition, and of course, I was out of work, so I thought I'll have a go. I shall never forget my audition because Glyn must be the only Welsh person who can actually sing on key. We either sing just below the note or above it and I was told in no uncertain terms that I was very sharp. It was due to the show that I met people like Leslie Crowther, George Chisholm and Margo Henderson, and also thanks to George and to Ossie that we youngsters got a discipline. We were able to do wonderful work, sing those wonderful songs, all arranged by George who's a past master at his art, and we also had great expertise in the production, albeit whenever the tape used to go waa waa or stop, and we used to rush down from whatever change we were doing, but they were great days and innovative days as well because the show was one of the very first shows to be taken lock stock and barrel off the TV into the theatre. So my career is thanks to George, to Bob Luff who would never let me out of my contract, 'cos I was always dying to get out, being an a-a-a-actress, but I must admit that, had I not had my eighteen months with you all, then I would probably be in the bowels of the Barbican carrying a spear in some Shakespeare. I feel it a great honour to have been asked to present this lovely present to George, I do owe so much to the show.'

Neville and John carried in a large parcel which they presented to George. Once he'd torn the covering off, it turned out to be a large gilded mirror, on which were engraved the names of all who had contributed to the present, men on one side, girls on the other. One line of names was longer than the other and George, quite overwhelmed by everything, joked, 'It's obviously all wrong, the unbalance, but apart from that, it's all right. I didn't expect anything except lunch today. It's been wonderful, carried me back so many years. Without you all it wouldn't have happened,' to which Neville retorted, 'Without you, it wouldn't have happened as well, so it's 50-50.'

There was a second presentation. As Neville said, 'Hundreds wrote in to support this,' as he handed over an album stuffed full of letters from ex-members of the show. Joan said, 'This book contains them all. If we started to read them, we'd all be in tears. This is just one: "Dear George, this is just to say thank you for your wonderful contribution to British show business. The Black and Whites were magnificent. Have a nice night and make sure Les Want buys a drink. Jimmy Tarbuck."' Everyone burst into *For He's a Jolly Good Fellow*, after which George said, 'I've never been so overwhelmed in my life. It's very very difficult.'

The letters in this album came from far and wide, many from people who were also present at the reunion. Person after person thanked George for the wonderful chances the show had given them - 'happiest memories', 'a fabulous first job', 'very close to my heart'. Mary Moss wrote 'so many happy years - my whole singing career started the day I joined the Mitchell Singers.' Angie Astell said, 'Thank you, thank you, thank you for helping to make my days with the Minstrels the happiest of my life.' Enid Allison recalled, 'I have a host of lovely memories of the shows I did as a George Mitchell Singer and the many friends I made over the years. I remember Dot as one of our dancers who did a great cha cha cha at parties! Little did we know then that she would become Mrs George Mitchell. I remember George as a very genuine unassuming, gentle man who gave so much pleasure to so many with his shows.' Bunny Losh wrote, 'Many many thanks for a wonderful memory of music and fun. Schumann was very clever to allow you to use his transposition methods! You helped me buy my house!' Early choir members weren't forgotten. Don Clark stated, '1941 doesn't really seem all that long ago. All good wishes.' The letters came not only from singers. Charles Chilton wrote, 'It's a

Minstrel Magic

long way from *Cabin in the Cotton* - it was a privilege to be associated with you.' Long-time company manager Martyn French added, 'I often think of the Minstrel days, one still remembers the company as they were, young and full of life.' Joyce Mortlock, BBC costume designer, thought, 'He brought music, humour and glamour to the stage and screen. There is nothing to compare in entertainment today. Congratulations to George for such a glamorous musical extravaganza that was enjoyed by millions of theatre, television viewers and (never to be forgotten) radio listeners.' Even previous opponents sent letters, such as 'Congratulations and best wishes, King George and all his minstrels, from the Cliff Adams Singers and all of us at *Sing Something Simple*.'

The memories continued to roll out. Ted Darling said, 'I hope someone reminds you of the George Mitchell Singers. How I remember sweating blood for dear Charles Chilton - dozens of *Variety Bandbox* programmes with Vic Oliver. Remember us trying to cope with the double chorus *Sanctus* from the Verdi *Requiem*? Hardly Dai or Tony's cup of tea. Thank goodness for John and Patrick Halstead on the tenor line. I will always hold fond memories of our numerous trips to Holland and those wonderful evening meals together.' Caroline Woodhams wrote, 'I was a wild and woolly Mitchell Maid and full of mischief. However, I learnt so much from that year (not least how to put on my makeup and look immaculate in ten minutes flat) and being part of that team in that situation finally smoothed off some of those rough edges and gave me a self-confidence and feeling of ease with people that has never left me. It was a year of enormous fun.' Maggi Lawlor said, 'We would be singing away all harmonising and then - in you would walk! One look from you and we couldn't sing a note! What a teacher you were.'

Everyone was overwhelmed with the reunion itself. Les Want added to the book, 'What a wonderful day. I wouldn't have missed it for the world. What I said in my speech - unrehearsed. Thank you for the most wonderful years of my life. So sorry for the upsets along the way.' Margaret Savage wrote, 'So many thanks for the great years. Today was just pure dead brilliant.' Her first-born daughter, Anne, who had survived meningitis as a baby after her twin sister had died, came with Margaret and her husband and she too added to the book: 'Thank you for a really wonderful day, and I will see you in Kissimmee.' Peter and Jenny Dakin, both of whom had been with the Minstrels, thought, 'What a wonderful day, so wonderful to see everyone. What a knockout day this has been.' Pat Heigham, the BBC technician, remembers the occasion well: 'How wonderful it was to be there. I was so pleased there was a good turn-out of the camera crew with whom I was involved. I had not seen them for about thirty years, and I believe it is a wonderful example of the respect in which George is held, that they wanted to be there. The moment George entered the room, we were all singing along with the tape (not miming!!!) since we knew the routines almost as well as the Minstrels themselves!! I caught Eddie Stewart, No 1 cameraman, wiping away a tear, as I was myself. It was a highly emotional moment. It was such a pleasure to see familiar faces again. John Boulter, Stan Stennett and Maryetta all remembered me, which was a wonderful thing for a young twenty-year-old technician, who in those days was really rather star-struck by the show-biz aspect of an award-winning light entertainment show. A really really happy time in my career, and I was pleased to hear that George was a stickler for perfection at each performance, as I have subsequently tried to base my own approach to a production to be the very best that can be done at the time to create the best result.'

Other technicians were keen to add their memories. Adrian Stocks, BBC TV Sound Supervisor, who mixed the sound for many of the television shows, recalled, 'I have so many happy memories of working with George and the Singers in their various forms. The most enduring memory of all, of course, is of the undefinable magical effect which the two Georges had on all who worked on the show. It was not just that we felt very privileged to be working on it, but because they were so great to work with, we were desperately anxious not to let them down. Some say "Never look back". Nonsense. We did adventurous things on a small budget in those days, and I am very grateful to have played a small part in them. I thank George for all the pleasure he had brought to so many.' Dave Sydenham was the show's technical manager with George Inns, and he recalled, 'It was a very happy team with the two Georges leading the way.'

Neville and Joan King were delighted with the reunion's success, adding their own tribute to the book: 'For Joanie and me to put on this great day together was a joy....you be very proud, both of you, that so many people love you. The day will live in my memory forever. I have never seen so much affection given in one day!' Joan added her own tribute: 'They say you have to give to receive, well, you gave us all such a lot. Let's hope that today we have returned just a little of what you so rightly deserve. We shall be forever in your debt for giving us all such wonderful memories. So many have thanked us for organising this day, I can only say it gave me such a thrill, there were many times when I could hardly read letters through my laughter and tears, everybody has such fond memories of you. You were given a special gift and in return have given something so special to so many, you have touched the lives of all who have come into contact with you.'

Despite being overwhelmed, George thoroughly enjoyed the day, being quite rejuvenated, according to Dot. Demand for more reunions grew and have now taken place every year since, with new people still being traced. George and Dot looked forward to every one, but George's health was still declining. As Dot recalls, 'He spent his time doing crosswords, reading newspapers, listening to music and watching TV. He'd read four or five books a week - he liked Frederick Forsyth, John le Carré, all spy thrillers, murder mysteries. He'd read biographies of people he knew. He also enjoyed having people to the house for coffee or drinks and to sit for a few hours with him.'

Dot eventually persuaded him to start recording his memories, as a start towards writing his autobiography, but as he was extremely reluctant, it was always a bit of a 'stop-start' effort. He littered the tapes with self-deprecating comments such as 'It's possible many of these memories are rubbish as I am aware that my brain is not what it was and nor is my memory' and 'I can't really remember what I did yesterday, but strangely enough I can remember quite clearly lots of things that happened before I could even speak.' Dictating his memories wasn't something he enjoyed, so he took every opportunity to stop for a break: 'This seems to be a pretty good place to stop at the moment and have a wee drop. I'm babbling on here, and I've just realised everything's out of order, and I don't know where I am. Having just listened to that lot back, I have a funny feeling it would have sounded better if I'd put on a slightly more refined Scottish accent rather than that awful Cockney one I've got. I don't like the sound of that at all [he adopted a Scottish accent here] it's much easier for me as I spent most of my life down there. Where did I get to? I've no idea.' Later he'd say, 'I can't top that so I'll stop to take a drop of the hard stuff. One more - mum used to make Welsh Rarebit for afternoon tea -

once she said, 'Afore you eat that, George, halve it into quarters.' His last tape mentions, 'Kindly note that I haven't plugged the *Black and White Minstrel Show*, probably the most successful show. I didn't let success go to my head - because it had got there years before. A long way from Carron Ironworks and my old grandfather who told me exactly what would happen - full circle.'

Towards the end, he couldn't be bothered even with these pastimes. The strokes got worse, and eventually, he died peacefully in his sleep on August 27, 2002.

The funeral became a true Mitchell affair. Many choir members and Minstrels turned up at the little village church in Albrighton, though it wasn't a large funeral. Glyn Dawson remembered, 'Stan Stennett and I went to the funeral together. About eight of us sang *Kumbayah* in the church. It just happened on the day - John, Margaret, me. It should have been difficult, but it was no problem because it was all part of the business. His son Rob played the accompaniment.'

Despite the huge successes of his life, Dot recognises that there was a fundamental sadness in George towards the end of his life: 'Prior to the Black and Whites, the world was his oyster, and he could turn his hand to anything, but once they were on, he felt no one could get beyond that and consider him for anything else. That upset him quite a lot. He'd have liked to have done other stuff, particularly religious stuff which in those days was so dismal. He'd have liked to have done a programme about spirituals. He was so busy with the Black and Whites that nobody came from the other end of the BBC to ask him to do anything else. He was not a musical snob, he'd turn his hand to anything and wanted to spread his wings more.' So the show which produced such happiness for so many millions of people worldwide and such tremendous worldwide success and wealth for George became a straitjacket from which he could not escape to produce the wider musical items he wanted to. Even so, in perhaps the greatest tribute to George, Dot recollects that 'he always said he was so lucky to be doing what he loved, something he'd have done even if no one had paid him to do it.' As George himself said, in a typically modest way, 'I always say I don't believe in luck. I've never allowed a margin for luck in my work - never taken a chance on things turning out all right on the night. But of course, I was lucky. Lucky to get the chance to make my living at something that was my delight in life.'

AFTERWORD

The BBC thought they'd killed off the show from the public consciousness by taking it off the screens, but they were wildly mistaken. It just refused to die. Seventy-three years after George's first broadcast, sixty years after the first Minstrel show at Earls Court, thirty-nine years after the last television show and thirty years after the stage show closed, George's legacy is as vibrant as ever, still deeply embedded into people's consciousness. The music keeps going, as do imitation stage shows. The only thing missing these days is the makeup.

References to the Minstrels have always popped up in a wide variety of television shows. In the Sixties, *That Was The Week That Was* ran a skit on the show, Margot in *The Good Life* made passing reference to the show in one episode, and more recently, Bo Selecta included comments in one show. In 1973 The Two Ronnies based one of their famous musical skits on the show, calling it *The Short and Fat Minstrel Show*, though The Goodies, who did a crueller skit in 1977, were rather cruel to George, making him look entirely unable to keep time with the music. However, the episode was done affectionately, and what's more, in full makeup! It was also reshown on ITV3 a few years ago, with no outcry whatsoever. Incidentally, the singers were from the Fred Tomlinson Singers, run by the man who had been George's rehearsal guru for so long. The award-winning *Spitting Image* and *Little Britain* both had Minstrel skits, which were perhaps less kindly that the Two Ronnies. Nevertheless, it shows how deeply embedded the show remains, sixty years after its first broadcast, with modern programmes such as *Call The Midwife* using it in several episodes. A few years ago, the National Media Museum in Bradford showed one of the original television programmes, followed by a talk, both well attended.

And it's not only in Britain that the show's memory is warmly held in people's hearts. In 2008, Paul Henry, the presenter on *Breakfast*, the leading morning television show in New Zealand, commented in passing that a cricketer with sun protection face stripes looked like a Black and White Minstrel. The station's switchboards lit up instantly with masses of all hugely supportive responses. Not one person phoned to complain, with everyone calling for its return or recalling warm memories of the stage and television programmes. In response, the programme dug out a clip of the show. Coincidentally, the weather man, who roved around New Zealand in a different place every morning, was in Russel in the Bay of Islands that day. Someone among the crowd told him that John Boulter now lived 'just down the road'. The studio presenter suggested that, if John were listening, he should get down to where the weather man was. Following the next item, they had tracked John down by phone and spent five minutes chatting to him live on air about his memories of the show. The presenter also knew that Keith Leggett also now lived in New Zealand. The item ran over into the following day when the presenter told viewers that a huge amount of feedback had poured in throughout the day, 'all saying how entertaining the show was and not at all offensive, especially when compared with the sort of stuff on television today.'

For decades after its TV demise, its name cropped up in any and all discussions on racism and the media, and gradually the history of the show was rewritten. Such discussions focused solely on what was seen as the 'caricature' of the makeup but how this was then deemed 'racist' was beyond many commentators, who rarely stopped to place it in context or think about what the makeup actually meant. It became the defining element of the show, and the rest was forgotten - it broke George's heart. The show represented all that was best in the world of light entertainment. It was magical and full of colour, entertainment at its best, family fun and friendly. Yet gradually its memory became contorted and warped. The repeated focus on the 'racist' element of the show gradually became adopted as the truth, simply because it was repeated so often, slowly turning the show and all it stood for into something racist and hateful, forever associating George and his singers with something they were all vehemently against.

BBC2 screened a *Politically Incorrect Evening* in 1998 which examined programmes such as the Minstrels, *Miss World* and a whole range of comedy programmes from *Till Death Us Do Part* to Benny Hill. In it, singers Les Want and Pam Rhodes were interviewed, though neither they nor any other participants, including black Kenny Lynch, condemned the show. BBC4, in its

Minstrel Magic

TimeShift slot, featured an entire programme on the Minstrels, slanted mainly towards the 'racist' aspect. Once again, ex-members were interviewed, such as Les Want and Bob Hunter. But when Granada Television, for Channel 4, tried to produce a programme dealing entirely with the racist aspect of the show, they failed to find anyone who would give them anything worth using for their slanted view, even with the BBC4 example of clever editing!

The show continues to feature in all sorts of high profile 'lists'. Recently voted among *The One Hundred Worst Television Shows Ever*, an anachronistic placing due entirely to political correctness, rather than artistic merit, it consistently fares worse than arguably far more racist shows, such as *Love Thy Neighbour*, *Fawlty Towers* and *Till Death Us Do Part*. The Minstrels rose higher and fell further. Never mentioned in such contexts are *It Ain't Half Hot, Mum* or *Rising Damp*, which remain popular and repeated on satellite channels. Mimicking other races by means other than makeup is presumably acceptable, though why this should be remains a mystery, one never addressed by the politically-correct lobby.

The wider world also retains a strong interest in the Minstrels, certainly in the music at least. Visit eBay or Amazon and reference after reference pops up. At the time of writing, eBay is listing over four hundred items for sale, ranging from albums to books, programmes to biscuit tins. Type in 'black, white, minstrels' into Google, and you'll get about three million hits, everything ranging from George himself to sales of CDs, vinyl albums, features on the main performers, and newspaper reviews of past shows and tribute shows. And this music still sells. Most of the albums have been reissued on compilation CDs, *The Best of the Minstrels* and *The Very Best of the Minstrels*. Such releases can't use the title The *Black and White Minstrel Show*, as the BBC consistently refuses permission for anyone to use their copyrighted title. Nevertheless, customers know they are buying the original albums, with original photos used on the CD covers.

You'll also be directed to discussion sites, ranging from Britmovies to tvheaven. Even today, chat rooms buzz with discussions about the pros and cons of the show, with the vast majority supporting the show. Comments tend to follow the same trends as any of the controversies throughout the show's history. One typical discussion took place on the IMDB website in 2006.

Minstrel Magic

Started in February by fablock, (s)he posted the comment, 'The Minstrels may well have been hated and considered racist by the "liberal thinking elite" but there were fifty-five million people in this country during its near thirty years run and the vast majority of those that had TVs enjoyed it immensely. It was always entertaining. It neither set out to be, nor was, racist. Don't forget, Al Jolson was white and loved equally by both blacks and whites. Similarly the BBC's *Black and White Minstrel Show* had singers with good voices.' A few days later, welshnick asked, 'Who actually takes offence at this and why? This was not racist – it merely showed people dressed as Kentucky Minstrels singing and dancing. The fact that most of them were white is neither here nor there. If this is being described as racist, then anything containing drag acts must be called sexist, and any show that has a gay actor playing a straight guy must be called homophobic because the gay actor is not portraying his true self.' Laurence01 agreed: 'Hear ear [sic], I couldn't agree more.' Sthom-1 wrote, 'The Minstrel show....was only offensive to those who wanted to be offended. It was by and large harmless family entertainment. *Big Brother*, on the other hand, features perfectly disgusting behaviour by publicity-seeking idiots, and everyone thinks it's great.' More agreement came from an anonymous chatroom member: 'When I was a child we had black dolls and the minstrels, and we loved each other and had no racism. The ones who stop these shows are the ones with the problems. Whatever next? Blackboards taken out of schools? Blackberries removed from our diet? Black cars outlawed? Leave us people who enjoy the shows and love our neighbours alone.'

Past Minstrel stars also keep the memory alive in other ways. A few years ago, Brian Earl, who appeared as a Minstrel in the second Australian tour, had a thought in an idle moment: 'I wonder where the rest of that company are these days?' A few phone calls later, he had tracked down several. In an effort to find more, he started a website, aimed at those still in Australasia. Suddenly, as with the reunion, it took off. And as with the reunion, someone knew someone who had kept in touch with two or three more. The website expanded to include anyone who had ever had anything to do with the show – singers, dancers, technicians, speciality acts – and ended up including over a thousand names, covering everywhere in the world. Sadly some were no longer alive, but more people were traced, every month of its existence.

Sadly Brian died in early 2009, and the website foundered. However, several pages on Facebook reunite past performers or fans, even seventy years later.

Clem Vickery still regularly performs his one-man show, talking about his time with the show, and recreating the Minstrel songs and routines. Ray Budd reports he is still 'still going strong, still singing solos. I travel some distances giving talks and demonstrations entitled *Reminiscences of a Black and White Minstrel* to remind people of the days when the show was without a doubt the finest TV light entertainment in the world. Perhaps if more viewers would write to the BBC, we could even have some of the old shows repeated. Don't bring up that old one about racial discrimination – they still show the old Jolson movies, don't they?' In 2007 the West End staged a play called *Black Slap and Sequins*, written by Paul Haley, himself a past Minstrel. The well-received show was set in the boys' Victoria Palace dressing room, with Black and White Minstrel music playing in the background throughout. The Minstrel reunions are still an annual event, now held around the country to accommodate far-flung cast members. Minstrels and Toppers, technicians and production staff still attend, eager to catch up on the latest gossip.

It is totally fitting that George's headstone reads 'The song is ended but the melody lingers on'.

ABOUT THE AUTHOR

Eleanor Pritchard has been a freelance writer most of her working life, producing features and articles on everything from tourist attractions to health, real life stories to celebrity profiles. She also edits two specialist magazines. This is her first book, though there are plenty more in the offing. She lives in rural Wales with her husband and loves spending time in Australia with her daughters, sons-in-law and grand-daughters - plus their dogs.

ABOUT THE PUBLISHERS

Saron Publishers has been in existence for about ten years, producing niche magazines. Our first venture into books took place last year when we published *The Meanderings of Bing* by Tim Harnden-Taylor. A further volume is due out in time for Christmas 2017. Further publications planned for 2017 include *Seven Monmouthshire Writers*, a collection of short stories and poems from Penthusiasts, a writing group based in the beautiful town of Usk, and *Frank*, a novel by Julie Hamill.

Join our mailing list by emailing info@saronpublishers.co.uk. We promise no spam ever.

Visit our website saronpublishers.co.uk to keep up to date and to read reviews of what we've been reading and enjoying. You can also enjoy the occasional offer of a free Bing chapter.

Follow us on Facebook @saronpublishing.

Follow us on Twitter @saronpublishers.

www.ingramcontent.com/pod-product-compliance
Lightning Source LLC
Chambersburg PA
CBHW021114300426
44113CB00006B/139